THE ARCTIC FRONTIER

THE ARCTIC FRONTIER

◀ ◆ ▶

edited by
R. St. J. MACDONALD

Published in association with the
Canadian Institute of International Affairs
and the Arctic Institute of North America by
UNIVERSITY OF TORONTO PRESS

© *University of Toronto Press 1966*
Reprinted 1970
Printed in the United States of America
for University of Toronto Press,
Toronto and Buffalo

ISBN 0-8020-5169-3

Foreword

THE IDEA of the Arctic Ocean as a mediterranean sea is a shock to those of us—and that includes about all of us—who cannot shake ourselves free of the Mercatorean vision. Yet this theme is repeated by many eminent contributors to this volume. "It is difficult to impress upon the public and industry at large," says Mr. Michael Marsden, "that the most essential quality of the Arctic is not cold, or gold, or polar bears, but a central position in the world community." This is essentially the theme of this study. It is not a book about the Canadian North; it is about our North as a frontier and our relations with the world beyond that frontier. It is about the Arctic community of which we are one of the major members, along with the Soviet Union, the United States (Alaska), Denmark (Greenland), Iceland, and Norway. If the Arctic community is not bound together by the common philosophy of the Atlantic community, it is at least bound together by common interest and perhaps common fear. The technological revolution is bringing our community to more vigorous life.

This book is an exercise in perspective. As Mr. Rowley points out, ". . . the terms east and west lose their normal significance at the North Pole." Canadians have always looked eastward across their Atlantic frontier and thought much of the implications of this orientation on their foreign relations. Increasingly they have recognized the significance of the Pacific frontier linking them with Japan and the Far East. As for the Southern frontier, their preoccupation is obsessive. It is time, however, that we recognized fully that we are not a three-sided country. Both the hot and cold wars of the past quarter century have roused our consciousness of the strategic importance of the northern frontier, and it has become a commonplace to describe Canada as a kind of Belgium between the Soviet Union and the United States. However, the substitution of intercontinental ballistic missiles for aircraft may diminish the strategic significance of our North—although it is unlikely ever to revert in our minds to the position of an impenetrable barrier we can comfortably ignore. This book by no means neglects the military importance of the Arctic, but it endeavours to widen the scope of our interest.

Finally, this volume is not just another one of those tiresome arguments about the surpassing importance of the Arctic—the Stefansson syndrome. It deflates as well as inflates. Its purpose is to assess as precisely as possible the implications of the Arctic frontier, not to induce either visions or nightmares. It is intended not only for Canadians but also for others interested in the polar regions or in the shape of the world at large.

The appearance of this volume marks the conclusion of three happy years' collaboration between the Arctic Institute of North America and the Canadian Institute of International Affairs, made possible by a generous grant from the Ford Foundation. The Foundation's grant to the CIIA was designed to stimulate research and policy studies on, among other things, strategic questions and Atlantic relations. Our interest in contributing a unique perspective to international issues, a view from the Northwest on the Atlantic, led us to explore this joint project with the eminently authoritative Arctic Institute. Without their knowledge of the field and its experts, a work of scholarship would not have been possible. Under the joint sponsorship of the two institutes a number of distinguished individuals were invited to a planning session in Montreal in February, 1963, under the chairmanship of Mr. C. M. Drury, at that time Chairman of the Montreal Branch of the CIIA and a former Governor of the AINA, now Minister of Industry in Ottawa. Others who took part were: Mr. George V. Ferguson, Editor-in-Chief, *Montreal Star*; Mr. W. M. Gilchrist, President, Eldorado Mining & Refining Limited; Mr. John W. Holmes, Director General, CIIA; Dr. Trevor Lloyd, Chairman, Department of Geography, McGill University; Mr. M. Marsden, Director, Montreal Office, AINA (now Assistant Professor, Department of Geography, Sir George Williams University); Mr. G. R. Parkin, Assistant to the Executive Director, AINA (now Co-ordinator, Development and Extension, AINA); Dr. John C. Reed, Executive Director, AINA; Mr. Gordon Robertson, Deputy Minister, Department of Northern Affairs and National Resources (now Secretary to the Cabinet); Commodore O. C. S. Robertson, Governor, AINA (now Head, Theme Exhibits Co-ordination, Canadian Corporation for the 1967 World Exhibition); Gordon Smith, formerly Professor of History, College Militaire Royal de St. Jean, P.Q. (now Lecturer in History, University of the West Indies, Trinidad); Dr. O. M. Solandt, Vice President, Research and Development, Canadian National Railways (Governor, AINA, now Vice President, Research and Development, de Havilland Aircraft of Canada); and Professor Dale Thomson, Department of Political Science, Université de Montreal.

Both institutes are deeply indebted to the busy men who gave us the benefit of their wide and varied experience in defining our intentions and working out the pattern of the study. We should particularly like to thank the Department of Northern Affairs, its Deputy Ministers, Mr. Gordon Robertson and subsequently Mr. Ernest Côté, for their guidance and encouragement and for the indispensable collaboration of their staff. Needless to say, neither the Department nor the government of Canada is responsible for any of the many and varied opinions expressed by the authors. None of those who attended the planning session is responsible either. It was our policy to select as authors the best authorities we could find and not to impose on them any pattern of thought whatsoever.

We were extraordinarily fortunate in persuading Professor Ronald St. John Macdonald of the Faculty of Law of the University of Toronto to assume the responsibilities of editor. His qualities of scholarship, his editorial experience, his capacity for swift and thorough work, and above all, perhaps, his tact and good nature have made him an admirable moulder of a project which it was never easy to keep disciplined. Working with him has been a great pleasure.

To write the book we have had the services of the most respected authorities in their fields and we are grateful to them for their willingness to contribute. We sought not only a compendium of information but also a spectrum of opinion. Inevitably there have been some overlapping of subject matter and some contradiction of opinion. We have made no effort to eliminate them. This is an experimental study, intended to open up an important subject for discussion rather than say the final word on it.

On behalf of the CIIA I should like to thank the Executive Director and staff of the Arctic Institute of North America for their unstinted co-operation, and in particular I wish to thank Mr. G. R. Parkin. If it had not been for Mr. Parkin's enthusiasm and imagination and his lifelong interest in the work of both institutes, the project would never have been conceived.

JOHN W. HOLMES

December, 1965 Canadian Institute of International Affairs

Contents

THE ARCTIC FRONTIER

The Arctic Setting

◄ MOIRA DUNBAR* ►

VILHJALMUR STEFANSSON said in one of his many books that if the average American or European university graduate had ten ideas about the Arctic, nine of them were wrong. That was in 1922, when the Arctic was much more remote than it is now, and furthermore Stefansson was not above a little exaggeration in order to drive home a point, but the point was nevertheless valid. Things have changed since then. The aeroplane has opened up the North and Eskimo prints and carvings have made it fashionable, while a spate of books and articles in popular magazines have, or should have, brought enlightenment to many. In spite of all this, however, the average Canadian still has only a very vague idea of what the northern part of his country is really like, and even less appreciation of Canada's position on the globe and her spatial relationship with her various neighbours.

There are a variety of reasons for this, two of which stand out, one historical and political, and the other cartographic. The first is the strongly east-west development of settlement in Canada along the transcontinental railway lines, and the second the standard Mercator map, which treats the world as an unrolled cylinder centred on the equator, with the top and bottom stretched out of all proportion and leading nowhere. Only a polar projection gives a true idea of Canada's position in world geography, but most of us are so unaccustomed to seeing such a map that it looks strange and unreal to us, and either North America or Eurasia appears to be upside-down, depending on which way you look at it.

Nevertheless that is the shape the top of the world is, and a few figures may serve to emphasize where Canada is placed in it. The

*Directorate of Physical Research, Defence Research Board, Ottawa.

northernmost tip of Canada, Cape Columbia in Ellesmere Island, is only a little more than 1,000 miles directly across the pole from Severnaya Zemlya, and less from Franz Josef Land, the northern extreme of the Soviet Union, but it is 1,750 miles from Churchill and 2,600 from Ottawa. Resolute Bay, in the centre of the Canadian Arctic Archipelago, is only 600 miles farther from Leningrad than it is from Ottawa. The relationships within Canada itself can be pointed up by two facts. First, of the nearly 4,000,000 square miles that make up the area of the country, over 1,500,000 are in the North-West Territories and Yukon. Less than a quarter of the total area can be said to lie within the southern belt of continuous settlement, whereas more than a quarter is north of the treeline. Secondly, the geographical centre of Canada lies in the district of Keewatin some 250 miles north-northwest of Churchill.

Canada, then, is unquestionably an Arctic country, and must consider the implications of her position. These implications were not very great as little as twenty or thirty years ago, because the difficulties of polar travel made the fiction of the Mercator map a virtual reality. The 4,000 miles of trackless bush, tundra, and ice-encumbered sea that separate southern Canada from Eurasia by the polar route formed so complete a barrier that the two continents might as well have been on different planets. But with the development of aircraft and nuclear submarines the distances have shrunk to their true proportions, and the implications of Canada's position have become considerable. It is the purpose of this book to examine these implications, and of this chapter to outline the physical environment against which they are set.

ARCTIC AND SUB-ARCTIC

Many different criteria have been used to delineate the limits of the Arctic. The Arctic Circle, a purely astronomical concept, is meaningless from any other point of view. Various climatic lines have been used, of which the most popular is the 50° F. isotherm for the warmest month. All these are arbitrary and only partially satisfactory. Much more meaningful from the point of view of human activity is the northern limit of trees. This line, which the proponents of the 50° F. isotherm claim coincides with the latter (it does, more or less, in most of Eurasia, but not in Canada), forms a real division of vegetation, climate, and habitat. This is expressed in the range of most of the native mammals, including *Homo sapiens*, as it marks the boundary in North America between the Eskimo and Indian cultures. It is shown on Map 1.

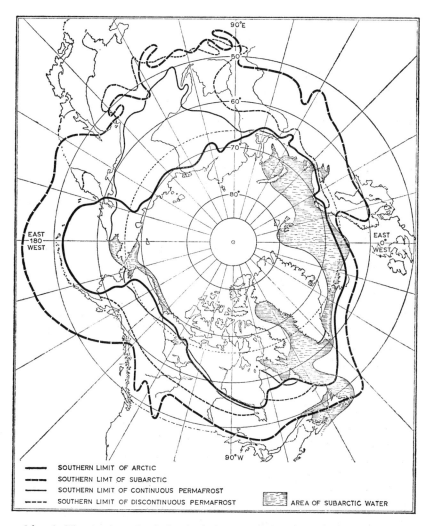

MAP 1. The Arctic and sub-Arctic limits are continued across the sea areas to show what zones the islands fall in. They have no significance for the waters.

Even more difficult to define is the sub-Arctic. In fact no completely satisfactory definition has ever been put forward, and it is necessary to compromise on some arbitrary climatic boundary. The definition used here is those lands where the mean temperature exceeds 50° F. for not more than four months of the year, and where the mean temperature of the coldest month is not more than 32° F.

THE LAND MASSES

The Arctic is made up of a central sea surrounded by land masses. Starting from Norway and reading eastward, these are the continents of Eurasia and North America and the large island of Greenland. North of the two continents there are islands, those of Canada forming as it were an interrupted continuation of the mainland and presenting a fairly straight outer coastline to the Arctic Ocean, and those of Eurasia being made up of separate groups, some quite close to the mainland but two of them, Spitsbergen and Franz Josef Land, entirely separated from it. Between Greenland and Norway is a large channel, which is divided in two by Spitsbergen at the north end and Iceland at the south. The states facing on to the Arctic Ocean are thus Norway, with her dependency Svalbard (made up of Spitsbergen and a number of smaller islands), the Soviet Union, the United States (Alaska), Canada, Denmark (Greenland), and Iceland. By far the greatest length of arctic coastline belongs to the Soviet Union (about 4,000 miles), the second greatest to Canada, which with 1,500 miles is well ahead of Alaska with 900. Greenland has a north coast about 500 miles long, and Norway about 100. Sweden and Finland, also Arctic countries, have no Arctic coast.

Topography

The physical features and landforms of the Arctic and sub-Arctic are largely northward extensions of those farther south. Nevertheless the landscapes that surround the Arctic Ocean have much in common with each other and may be treated as one region.

The outstanding structural feature of the northlands is the existence of three shields or platforms of very old, hard, and stable rock, the Canadian Shield, the Scandinavian Shield, and the Central Siberian Platform. These ancient land surfaces have been worn down over many millions of years and scraped by ice sheets to form the sort of rocky terrain familiar to all who have seen the shores of Georgian Bay or the Laurentian country. Around the edges of these shields have been laid down later sedimentary rocks, limestones and sandstones, which form flat plains and plateaus. Beyond the submerged edges of the shields are regions of mountain ranges. This very much simplified picture of the northern land masses is shown on Map 2.

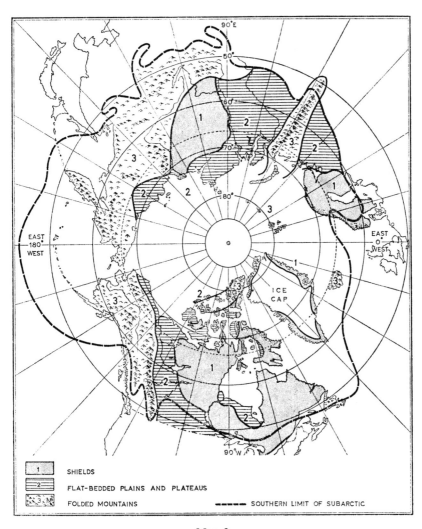

MAP 2

The shields

Largest of the shields is the Canadian Shield, which stretches from
Labrador to Great Bear Lake and is shaped rather like a saucer, highest
round the edges with a depression containing Hudson Bay in the middle.
The highest points are on the eastern edge, where it has been uplifted
to form glacier-topped mountains up to 7,000 feet high, extending from
southern Ellesmere Island through Baffin Island to the coast of Labrador.

Inland it slopes downwards to form areas of rocky plateaus, hills, and lowlands. Glaciation has removed the soil from some areas, deposited quantities of loose gravel, sand, and clays in others, and so disturbed the pre-glacial drainage systems that there is left an apparently endless number of lakes, through which the rivers wander with seeming aimlessness. Topography varies from fairly high hills, as in the Laurentians, to quite flat plains, but always with the same outcrops of rugged rock, scarcity of soil, and high incidence of lakes.

The Scandinavian Shield covers most of the Scandinavian Peninsula, the whole of Finland, and adjacent parts of Russia, and its surface features are very like the Canadian Shield. As in Baffin Island a high uplifted edge faces the sea, forming mountains which in Norway reach heights of 7,000 and 8,000 feet. Eastward the terrain slopes down to the low lake-studded plains of Finland.

The Central Siberian Platform differs from the other two in that its ancient hard rocks outcrop in only a relatively small area in the northern part. The rest is overlain by a thin layer of flat-lying sedimentary and volcanic rocks forming plateaus which do not differ essentially from those of the second physiographic region except in heights, which in some areas reach 3,000 to 5,000 feet. In some places the wearing away of the high plateau and the cutting of deep river valleys has created mountains, but for the most part the Siberian Platform consists of tablelands divided by rivers. Another significant difference between this and the other shields is that it was largely undisturbed by the glaciers of the Pleistocene glaciation, and therefore neither suffered the removal of soil nor the deposition of clay and boulders that are the legacy of the glaciers, nor is there the profusion of lakes typical of the other shields.

The flat-bedded plains and plateaus

Surrounding and overlying the edges of the shields are areas of generally flat-bedded rock strata which have been protected from crustal upheavals by the stability of the shields and which form essentially flat lowlands or plateaus up to 1,000 and 2,000 feet. In North America these include the Hudson Bay Lowland, a flat and largely boggy area on the west coast of Hudson Bay which was below sea level at the end of the glacial epoch and has therefore a covering of marine sediments; the Mackenzie Lowland, which is a northward extension of the prairies; a number of plains and plateaus which cover the greater part of the southern half of the Canadian Arctic Archipelago; and a coastal plain along the north coast of Alaska. In Eurasia two enormous plains, the Russian and West Siberian lowlands, lie between the Scandinavian and Central Siberian shields, separated from each other by the Ural Mountains. The West Siberian Lowland is so flat that the low-water mark of the River Ob 1,850 miles from its mouth is only 300 feet above sea level. North of the Central Siberian Platform is the broad North Siberian Lowland, 150 to 250 feet high, which includes the island group of Severnaya Zemlya. In the Taymyr Peninsula the Byrranga Range interrupts the plain, rising to about 3,000 feet. To the east again is another area of coastal lowland, which includes the New Siberian Islands, and which like the Alaskan coastal plain separates the mountains from the sea.

Although all these areas are far from alike, they fall into a number of patterns all or almost all of which are represented on both sides of the Arctic Ocean. Some have the confused lake-strewn surface left by the Pleistocene ice sheet, some have a boggy or dry stony surface, some are drained by large rivers like the Ob, Yenisey, and Mackenzie, others by short insignificant streams. All have a generally flat surface, though cut in the case of the plateaus by deep river valleys and sheer coastal cliffs which form a barrier to surface travel, and all share the same types of tundra or northern forest vegetation.

The folded mountains

The third main structural province is made up mainly of ranges of mountains thrust up by movements in the earth's crust beyond the edges of the stable shields. Highest and most striking is the group that includes the Alaska and Yukon mountains (the northern part of the Rocky Mountain system or North American Cordillera) and that continues across Bering Strait and down into the Kamchatka Peninsula. The rest of northeast Siberia is made up of a more complex collection of ranges and blocks of mountains, but the resulting topography is sufficiently similar to group them together here. These mountains reach heights of 20,300 feet (Mount McKinley) in Alaska and 15,675 feet (Klyuchevskaya Mountain) in Kamchatka. The greater part, however, is below 10,000 feet. In Kamchatka and the Aleutian Islands there are active volcanoes, the only ones in the Soviet Union and the United States respectively.

The Ural Mountains, which form the traditional boundary between Europe and Asia, run north and south, continuing northward into the island chain of Novaya Zemlya. These mountains are older and more worn down than those of eastern Siberia, but they nevertheless formed a barrier to expansion, just as the Appalachians did in North America. They reach a maximum height of 6,180 feet and have many peaks over 3,000 feet.

A third area of folded mountains runs across the northwestern part of the Canadian Arctic Archipelago and northern Greenland to Spitsbergen, with maximum elevations in the order of 7,000 to 8,000 feet. Included in this region for convenience rather than by conviction is Iceland, which is made up almost entirely of volcanic rocks and consists mainly of a fairly high plateau (2,000–3,500 feet), large parts of which have been broken up by faults and upthrusting to form more varied and hilly topography.

Glaciers

All the mountain areas contain some glaciers. Outstanding of course is the Greenland Ice Cap, which is about 700,000 square miles in area and covers by far the greater part of the island (or group of islands, as it now appears to be). It reaches heights of 10,000 feet, and is large enough to form a separate climatic subregion. There is no other ice cap of comparable size or thickness in the Arctic, but there are many areas, for example east Baffin Island, north Ellesmere Island, and Spitsbergen, where only the peaks rise above the ice, and the archipelago of Franz Josef Land is almost completely ice-covered. Of the mountain areas probably the Urals have the fewest glaciers, but there are some in the northern part of the range, and the north island of Novaya Zemlya is largely covered by glaciers. Even Iceland has several small ice caps, from which no doubt it got its name, and there are a few on the plateau areas of the Canadian Arctic Archipelago.

Permafrost

Throughout most of the Arctic and sub-Arctic all or part of the ground contains a layer which is perennially frozen. This is called permafrost and is a source of many problems to the engineer engaged in building or road-making. The southern boundaries of continuous and discontinuous permafrost are shown on Map 1.

The permafrost layer may be of varying thickness up to 1,500 feet and more, and may start a few inches or several feet below the surface. Above it is the so-called active layer, which thaws out in summer. The disturbance or removal of the active layer leads to thawing of the permafrost below, and it is this that causes engineering problems such as displacement of foundations, slumping of airstrips and roads, and so on. Methods to deal with the problem have been developed and usually work satisfactorily. Repeated working of the soil for agriculture also tends to lower the permafrost level, and in areas of low precipitation, which includes most of the Arctic and sub-Arctic, this may do more harm than good, allowing the water to escape and the surface to dry out.

THE ARCTIC SEAS

The Arctic is essentially a basin, the centre of which is occupied by a large mediterranean sea into which drain all the surrounding land masses. The Arctic Ocean is 5 million square miles in area and 4 million cubic miles in volume, and is divided into two main basins by the submarine Lomonosov Ridge, which runs from the north coast of Greenland across the Pole to the New Siberian Islands. Each basin has depths of over 4,000 metres. The continental shelf which borders the land masses is narrow on the North American side (20–50 nautical miles) but on the Eurasian side it extends to 450 miles and more, and is usually under 100 metres in depth. Peninsulas and island groups divide this wide shelf into four marginal seas. These are, from Alaska westward, the Chukchi, East Siberian, Laptev, and Kara seas. A fifth sea, the Barents, with rather deeper waters, leads out of the Arctic Ocean into the Norwegian Sea. On the Canadian side are many relatively narrow channels, which separate the islands of the Canadian Arctic Archipelago and which form a minor outlet from the Arctic Ocean into the North Atlantic by way of Baffin Bay, while west of Alaska the narrow Bering Strait, only 46 miles wide and 50 metres deep, connects the Arctic Ocean with the Pacific. The main avenue for both intake and outlet of Arctic Ocean water is, however, the wide channel between Greenland and Norway.

The waters that occupy this basin consist of a cold surface layer about 200 metres thick, a warmer layer of Atlantic water down to about 900 metres, and a cold bottom layer. The productivity of the true Arctic waters is rather low. Plankton, the tiny plant and animal organisms that form the basis of all marine life because they are the food of the larger life forms, are present, but not in very large quantities. Fish fauna is therefore poor both in species and in numbers. Seal and walrus, and the polar bear which preys on the seals, are found throughout the area in varying numbers.

Round the edges of the Arctic Ocean is a zone in which the Arctic water mixes with Atlantic and Pacific water and which to the oceanographer constitutes the sub-Arctic (the marine sub-Arctic does not coincide with the land sub-Arctic). In this zone (Map 1) the production of plankton is the highest in the world, and it is not surprising that it includes some of the major fishing grounds, such as the Newfoundland waters and the Norwegian Sea.

Sea Ice

The main body of the Arctic Ocean is covered the year round with pack ice. This is an agglomeration of pieces of ice from a few feet to many miles across and from a few hours to several years in age. It is continually in motion, pieces separating or splitting to open up leads, or being squeezed together to form ridges of broken ice that may be 10 to 20 feet high (in extreme cases near a coastline much higher) and which extend for a corresponding and greater depth below the surface, down to about 120 feet. The result is a very rough surface, over 70 per cent of which is ice over a year old. Where the pressure has not thickened the ice, it is 6 to 12 feet. In summer about 14 to 16 inches are lost by surface melting.

Even in winter the ice cover is not complete, but is reduced by movement to around 90 per cent. In summer it decreases to about 70–80 per cent and in some areas even less, while the fringing seas become either ice-free or greatly reduced in concentration. An exception is the north-west part of the Canadian Arctic Archipelago, where the ice usually remains fast from coast to coast.

The main feature of ice drift in the Arctic Ocean, and also of the surface water circulation, is a general movement from the area north of Bering Strait to the Greenland Sea, which is called the Trans-polar Drift. In the area between north Alaska, the Canadian islands, and the Pole there is a separate clockwise circulation known as the Pacific Gyral. Almost all the ice carried by the Trans-polar Drift leaves the Arctic Ocean between Greenland and Spitsbergen. This represents a tremendous amount of ice loss per year, which is replaced by ice formed in the cold and shallow Siberian fringing seas and by Pacific Gyral ice as well as by growth in the area of the Trans-polar Drift itself. Ice in the Pacific Gyral, on the other hand, may remain in the gyral for years before escaping across the Pole, and so the oldest and heaviest ice in the Arctic Ocean is to be found in this area.

Surface vessels operating under their own power are not, up to the present time, able to operate in the Arctic Ocean proper, but nuclear submarines have proved well suited to the environment. In the surrounding seas there are navigation seasons ranging from about four weeks to three months and more.

Some publicity has been given in recent years to the scheme of a Russian engineer to clear the ice from the Arctic Ocean by building a dam across Bering Strait and pumping the cold surface water out into the Pacific. The technical problems involved are of course tremendous, but assuming that they could be overcome, there remain many doubts expressed by scientists in the Soviet Union and elsewhere as to whether the operation would in fact result in the melting of the ice, and if so whether the effect on the climate of the northlands would be beneficial.

CLIMATE

Two things everybody knows about the Arctic: it is perpetually and unbearably cold, and there is a lot of snow. Neither of these is completely true, and indeed the second may be said to be completely untrue, as shall presently be explained.

Temperature

That the Arctic climate is cold is unquestionable. Mean annual temperatures are mostly below 20° F., and a mean as low as —9° F. has been estimated for the centre of the Arctic Ocean. However, these figures are not based on extremes of winter cold. The Arctic is for the most part essentially a maritime area, and the moderating maritime influence on temperature is quite noticeable in spite of the ice that covers the water surface for much or all of the year. Thus minimum temperatures are not on the whole extreme. The notable exception is the Greenland Ice Cap, on the inland heights of which the lowest temperatures in the Arctic (but not the sub-Arctic) have been recorded, in the order of —85° to —90° F. Over most of the Arctic, however, extremes are around —50° to —55° F., which is comparable to Regina or Winnipeg. In the region of the North Pole the maritime effect exerts such a modifying influence that even here extremes are only around —55° F. The coldest temperatures in our hemisphere are not found in the Arctic but in the sub-Arctic, as we shall see.

The factors that nevertheless combine to give the Arctic the lowest yearly means of the Northern Hemisphere are the persistence of low temperatures over long periods, and the shortness and coolness of the summer, which varies from about ten weeks in the south to about four weeks or less in the north, with average temperatures below 50° F. Extremes as high as 72° F. have been experienced even in the northern Canadian islands, but these are so rare and of such short duration as to have little significance. In the Arctic Ocean the summer maxima barely exceed 35° F. The thaw line, however, extends all the way to the Pole, and all the winter snow, with the exception of a few drifts, melts every summer, along with a considerable quantity of sea ice.

In the sub-Arctic, conditions are somewhat different. Here, in contrast to the Arctic, there are several large areas of strongly continental type, and it is in the mountainous areas of sub-Arctic eastern Siberia that the coldest temperatures in the Northern Hemisphere have been recorded— —96° F. at Oymyakon, —93.7° F. at Verkhoyansk, where the January mean is —58 F°. A low of —81.4° recorded at Snag in the Yukon Territory is still the lowest recorded temperature in North America excluding Greenland. Summer temperatures in these areas are high, almost comparable to those of southern Canada. Means are over 60° F. for July, and temperatures of over 90° F. are not uncommon. Thus the mean annual range of temperature is enormous, 81° F. at Dawson City and a staggering 117° F. at Verkhoyansk.

In coastal areas of the sub-Arctic, such as Labrador, the winter temperatures are much milder (January means from 0° to 10° F.) and summer temperatures lower (July means of 50° F. to 60° F.). Iceland, although most of it qualifies as Arctic by virtue of a July mean below 50° F. and absence of trees, has essentially a sub-Arctic climate of an extreme maritime nature, with mean temperatures for the coldest month as high as 28° and 30° F. in coastal areas.

Windchill

Temperature is not the only factor affecting the sensation of cold. Windspeed is also important, and the concept of windchill, introduced as recently as 1945, is now fairly well known. Thus a temperature of 10° F. with a wind speed of 20 m.p.h. is equivalent for human comfort to —30° F. with no wind. On the open tundra complete calms are relatively rare and windchill factors tend to be high. In the sub-Arctic forest, on the other hand, although in many cases the temperatures may be lower, windchill tends to be less owing to the shelter provided by the trees.

Precipitation

Total precipitation in the Arctic is low, and becomes lower as you go North. In general it ranges from about 15 to less than 5 inches per year. At Eureka on northern Ellesmere Island the mean annual precipitation is only 1.74 inches, which is comparable to the desert areas of the world. This comes as a surprise to most people, especially as over much of the Arctic the so-called land areas seem to consist largely of lakes, and the land in between is frequently wet and boggy. This apparent anomaly is due to the permafrost, which prevents the water from escaping into the ground, and to a low evaporation rate in summer.

Most of the precipitation in the Arctic falls in summer and about half of it in the form of rain, so snow-cover in winter is generally light. Winds however keep it continually moving, frequently creating blizzard conditions when no snow is falling, and forming deep drifts in the lee of buildings and other obstructions. Exposed surfaces tend to be blown clear and the snow becomes hard-packed by the wind.

In the sub-Arctic precipitation is higher, 15 to 20 inches in most places and much higher in maritime areas such as Labrador, the southern tip of Greenland, and the Scandinavian Peninsula. The snow in the forests is not subject to blowing as on the tundra, and lies soft and deep. Thus the Indian was forced by his environment to invent the snowshoe, which is unknown and unnecessary to the Eskimo.

VEGETATION

The vegetation of the northlands falls into two main divisions, Arctic and sub-Arctic, or tundra and forest. Although the individual plant species involved may vary considerably from one area to another, the type and form of the vegetation is remarkably uniform, and it is, in fact, the vegetation, along with the climate, that forms the chief unifying factor and makes it possible to speak of the Arctic as one region in spite of all the variety of topography.

The chief characteristic of the tundra is the absence of trees, the vegetation consisting of creeping shrubs, grass-like plants, lichens, and mosses. Several zones are recognized within this region, graduating, more or less from north to south, from almost barren ground with a sparse covering of small alpine plants, to a fairly dense growth with small shrubs several feet high.

The forest is the coniferous boreal forest or taiga, with larch (tamarack) and spruce as dominant species, the latter replaced in some parts of Eurasia by pine. North of the true taiga there is a broad zone of open forest, where the trees become smaller and more widely spaced, with low shrubs and abundant mosses and lichens, and this graduates into the forest–tundra, where clumps of open forest are interspersed with tundra vegetation. Deciduous species are also found in the forest zone, notably poplar and birch, but in relatively small numbers. On the south the taiga graduates into the zones of mixed and deciduous forest, but these are generally outside the area defined as sub-Arctic.

RESOURCES

Natural resources may be divided into renewable and non-renewable resources. The former are mainly animal and vegetable, the latter mineral.

Renewable Resources

The renewable resources of the Arctic and sub-Arctic include fisheries, fur-bearing and other animals, forests, potential grazing and arable land, and hydro-electric power. In all of these the sub-Arctic is much richer than the Arctic. The contrast in productivity between Arctic and sub-Arctic waters has already been referred to. It should be noted, however, that as the division between Arctic and sub-Arctic differs on land and sea, most of the highly productive sub-Arctic waters fringe on Arctic lands and therefore provide a fisheries resource for what must be looked on as an Arctic area (see Map 1).

The only commercial fur-bearer of the true Arctic is the Arctic fox.[1] In the sub-Arctic there are mink, sable, marten, fox, muskrat, beaver, squirrel, fur seal, and others. The most important animal other than fur-bearers is the reindeer, which is domesticated in Lapland and Siberia. Herds have been successfully introduced into Alaska and the Mackenzie Delta region, and it would undoubtedly be possible to extend this industry greatly should a demand arise. Another animal that may be potentially domesticable is the musk-ox, which produces wool as well as meat, but so far no conclusive experiments have been made.

Forest resources are by definition limited to the sub-Arctic, where, in Canada, and even more so in the USSR, they are enormous. Transportation is at present a limiting factor in their exploitation. Alaska and Sweden also have large sub-Arctic forest resources.

[1] Just recently in Canada there has arisen a demand for ringed seal skins, but this may be short-lived.

Grazing and agriculture both present considerable untapped possibilities in the sub-Arctic, and the former even in parts of the Arctic. In Eurasia, and more especially in Europe, the sub-Arctic boundary includes considerable areas of cultivated land. Farther north the Russians have established limited agriculture in many areas to provide local food supplies, and in Alaska successful mixed farming has been established in the Tanana Valley ever since the gold rush, and in the Matanuska Valley since 1935. In Canada the Peace River district and the Clay Belt of Northern Ontario and Quebec are both within our definition of the sub-Arctic, but beyond these only small-scale and experimental farms have been established, notably up the Alaska Highway and at Fort Simpson in the Mackenzie Valley. With the exception of the Peace River district, all these developments supply local needs only, and in general this is the only kind of farming likely to be developed. It will come as a result of, rather than as a reason for, settlement, and its success will depend on the ability of scientists to develop new crops and methods, and possibly to domesticate new animals, and of the potential farmer to adapt himself to their use.

Hydro-electric power resources are very considerable and await only the demand for their development. On the southern fringes of the sub-Arctic some large developments have already taken place. Farther north, in the USSR, construction is in progress on several hydro-electric stations, and also on a geothermal station in Kamchatka and a tidal station near Murmansk. Plans are also believed to be well advanced on an ambitious scheme that will reverse the headwaters of the Pechora and Vichegda rivers into the Volga system. In Canada there are a number of power developments to supply mining areas in the Yukon and Mackenzie districts and the northern provinces, and a large development is planned on the Hamilton River in Labrador. Here again the sub-Arctic has the edge over the arid Arctic, not only because of greater precipitation but because in general the rivers are longer. However, in Arctic Canada there are considerable possibilities in the northern mainland, and the extremely high tides of the Hudson Strait area (up to 54 feet in Ungava Bay) are another potential source of power.

Non-renewable Resources

These include all the mineral resources, and it is on them that most northern development has been based in the past and probably will be in the future. A map of known mineral resources in the northlands would show the same marked advantage of sub-Arctic over Arctic that we have noted in renewable resources. In this case, however, it would be misleading, reflecting a lack of exploration rather than a scarcity of minerals. The deposition of minerals is not affected by the differences of climate and vegetation that separate Arctic from sub-Arctic, and there is no reason to suppose that the northern parts of, for instance, the Canadian Shield, are any less rich in metallic ores than the southern parts. They have just not been explored in detail.

The shield and mountain areas of both North America and Eurasia are among the important ore-bearing regions of the world, containing large deposits of iron ore, gold, silver, copper, nickel, lead, zinc, and uranium, to name only some of the most important. Canada and the USSR are both large producers of these metals, Canada producing more than half of the world's nickel and large proportions of the lead, zinc, gold, silver, platinum, and uranium. By far the largest producing area for most of these is the mining district of Northern Ontario, only part of which lies within the sub-Arctic; but significant quantities of most come from more northern areas, such as the Yukon Territory, Great Slave Lake, Athabasca Lake, and northern Manitoba. The most northerly mine in Canada is the uranium mine at Port Radium on Great Bear Lake, now closed, and the largest producer of iron ore in the country is the Schefferville (Knob Lake) area on the Quebec-Labrador border. The USSR leads the world in iron ore production and is second in gold (Canada is third), and a large proportion of the first and most of the second are mined in the sub-Arctic. A major new discovery of copper and nickel has been made near the mouth of the Yenisey, and recently the only diamond-mining operation in the northern regions was opened at Mirnyy in the Lena Basin. Northern Sweden is a large producer of high-grade iron ore.

Coal is known to exist in the North in considerable quantities, but much of it is remote from existing markets and has never been worked. The chief producing areas are in the USSR: the Kuznetsk Basin in southwest Siberia, which is just within our sub-Arctic boundary, the Urals, and the Pechora Basin. Spitsbergen, a minor producer, has the most northerly mines in the world.

Potential oil reserves in the North are very considerable, conditions favourable to its formation existing in most of the sedimentary rock areas of the Arctic and sub-Arctic. Present producing areas include the northern Alberta oilfield, which extends into the sub-Arctic, Norman Wells in the Mackenzie Valley, southern Alaska, and a large area on the west side of the Urals. Other proved deposits in Alaska and the

USSR await future development, while active exploration is in progress in many areas. In Canada parts of the Arctic Archipelago show great promise, but so far test drilling has been unsuccessful. A well-known but hitherto unuseable source is the Athabasca tar sands, an enormous stretch of bituminous sand along the valley of the Athabasca River. Recently an economically feasible extraction process has been developed and several companies have obtained operating permits.

POPULATION

It is difficult to obtain population figures for the exact area of this study because it cuts across administrative boundaries. An idea of the relative densities may be got from the following figures. The USSR had an estimated population for the whole Arctic and sub-Arctic region in 1951 of 29.5 million, of whom more than half were in the European north, and about 300,000 in the Arctic. Native peoples accounted for rather less than 2 million. More recent estimates give a total of just over 5 million north of 60° N, of whom 3.5 million are in Europe and about 800,000 are natives. Comparable estimates for Canada give a little over 1.5 million for the whole region, of whom about 61,000 are native peoples. North of 60° N there were, in 1961, 38,000 inhabitants, of whom 18,200 were natives (11,500 Eskimo, 6,700 Indian). Comparison by latitude does not mean very much, however, as Canada north of 60° N is predominantly an Arctic area whereas the USSR in this region is more than half sub-Arctic. The population of Alaska in 1960 was 226,000,[2] of which about 44,000 were natives, while Greenland in 1960 had a total of 33,113, most of them natives.

The native population of Arctic and sub-Arctic Canada consists of 11,500 Eskimos and roughly 50,000 Indians. Alaska has about 20,000 Eskimos (this figure includes one or two thousand Aleuts, natives of the Aleutian Islands) and 14,000 Indians, and Greenland approximately 30,000 natives of Eskimo and Eskimo-European race, making a total native population of about 125,000 for northern North America. The native peoples of Eurasia are more varied, ranging from the reindeer-herding Lapps in the west to the coastal-dwelling Chukchis and Eskimos (very few of the latter) in the far northeast. Most of them are forest-dwellers, and most of the Arctic areas are very sparsely populated. Some of the islands have no native population. In Canada the Eskimos extend

---

[2]This includes the Panhandle, which is outside our region.

north through the islands to the Parry Channel, and there are now two groups north of this, though both were established by the Department of Northern Affairs rather than the Eskimos themselves.

COMPARISON OF THE AMERICAN AND EURASIAN ARCTIC

From the foregoing we may conclude that the Arctic and sub-Arctic are separated from the Temperate Zone not by physiographic features, which in fact tend to run north and south rather than east and west, but by criteria of climate and vegetation; that the dividing line between temperate and sub-Arctic is vague and hard to define and therefore of little real significance in human activities, whereas the line dividing the forested sub-Arctic from the treeless Arctic is one that imposes a real change of habitat on primitive man and is not without significance for civilized man; and that there are great similarities between the corresponding zones of North America and Eurasia. Nevertheless there must clearly be differences between the two continents. Let us now take a look at some of them, and more especially at the differences between the northern regions of Canada and the USSR.

A glance at Map 1 will show that there is a considerable difference in distribution of Arctic and sub-Arctic in the two continents. In Eurasia the Arctic line, or treeline, dips below the Arctic Circle only in the Urals and the extreme east, and for much of its length lies around or even north of the 70th parallel. In North America it nowhere reaches 70° N and dips down 55° N on the coasts of James Bay and Labrador. The sub-Arctic line on the other hand, with one notable exception to be discussed later, is fairly constant, fluctuating back and forth across the 50th parallel. This, combined with the fact that the land areas of North America extend considerably farther north than those of Eurasia, results in a much higher proportion of Arctic to sub-Arctic lands in North America than in the USSR. If we exclude Greenland with its large ice cap we find that the actual area of ice-free land north of the treeline is very much the same for North America and Eurasia, while including Greenland the Arctic area of North America is almost double that of Eurasia. The area of boreal forest in Eurasia, however, is more than double that of North America. Another way of expressing this is to say that in North America 38 per cent of the northland is true Arctic; in Eurasia, only 13 per cent.

Thus when we talk of the vast northern territories of the USSR we should remember that they in fact significantly exceed our own not in the true Arctic but in the sub-Arctic, which as we have seen is in many ways more productive. This is an advantage that is apt to go unnoticed. There is in fact a tendency to use the term "Soviet Arctic" rather loosely to include a great deal of the sub-Arctic, and to equate this with the Canadian Arctic in a more exact sense. Even such an authority as Terence Armstrong makes the statement that ". . . whereas Arctic America and Greenland have only one indigenous racial group—the Eskimo—the north of Eurasia counts a number of distinct peoples." (*The Russians in the Arctic*, p. 108.) Both halves of this statement are true but they are wrongly related. The peoples that he goes on to describe are as we have seen mostly sub-Arctic forest-dwellers, and a true comparison with North America would have to include the northern forest Indians as well as the Eskimos. And, in fact, most of the developments that the Russians speak of with justifiable pride—though sometimes a touch of exaggeration—and which are often described as "Arctic," refer actually to sub-Arctic areas.

The second feature that strikes us in Map 1 is the northward retreat of the Arctic and sub-Arctic limits on the east side of the North Atlantic. This is of course due to the influence of the Gulf Stream. What is remarkable is that this influence, and that of the atmospheric circulation associated with it, extends all the way to the Urals. This is shown clearly by the position of the sub-Arctic line and even more strikingly in the permafrost limits; there is practically no continuous permafrost west of the Urals and only a rather narrow zone of discontinuous. However, this advantage is to some extent offset by the far southward extension of the permafrost line in central and eastern Siberia, where it is considerably farther south than in Canada.

Other advantages of the Soviet North are that the much less extensive glaciation experienced has left them with more and better soils over much of their sub-Arctic; that their large north-flowing rivers are navigable to the heart of the country; and that there is a larger native population to help in developing the area. On the other hand the vast size of the continent leads to more extreme climatic conditions in eastern Siberia; nowhere in Canada can we match the 117° F. mean annual temperature range of Verkhoyansk.

PRESENT STAGE OF DEVELOPMENT

The development of the Eurasian and North American northlands has followed similar lines, but with Siberia usually a step or two ahead of

North America and the European north way out in front. Thus for instance Archangel has been a port since the Middle Ages, and Russian traders had penetrated to the Pacific by the end of the seventeenth century, at a time when in North America the eastern seaboard was still at the pioneer stage. The reason is not far to seek. Conditions in northern Europe, as we have seen, are less severe than in comparable latitudes elsewhere, while the proximity of populated Europe naturally led to an earlier exploration of Siberia than of remote North America, which for all practical purposes was not even discovered until the end of the fifteenth century. It is therefore not surprising that the Russians penetrated first to the Pacific, or even that they were the first to reach the Alaskan coast. To them after all this was no longer a journey east-bound than it was for the British westbound.

On both sides of the Arctic Ocean a hunting economy predominated among the native peoples. With the coming of the white man the fur trade became the basis of the economy, along with whaling and fishing in some areas, and on the southern fringes of the sub-Arctic, lumbering. Development beyond this stage was very gradual, but accelerated sharply after the revolution in Russia and somewhat less sharply in North America after the Second World War.

The Soviet Union began to develop its northlands in the 1920's, thus re-establishing and increasing the lead which had to some extent levelled off in the nineteenth century. There were a number of reasons for this, the chief one being that they were surrounded by unfriendly neighbours and were obliged to be self-supporting, so that exploration for essential minerals was important and use of the Northern Sea Route highly desirable for economic as well as strategic reasons. Furthermore, in spite of the vaunted internationalism of the Communist movement, a new national feeling was generated, and enthusiasm for the development of their own great north gave an outlet for this feeling and helped to distract the attention of the masses from the lack of improvement in conditions closer to home. The result is an impressive record of achievement, of establishment of industries and improvement of transportation in the north, so that now there are five cities north of 60° N with populations over 100,000, of which two, Murmansk and Noril'sk, are on the edge of the Arctic. The Northern Sea Route now has a season of about three months and carries freight to the order of 1.8 million tons a year.

This it will be clearly seen is a considerable contrast with Canada, where there is only one city north of 60° N with more than 1,000 inhabitants (Whitehorse with 5,000). Alaska has two over 10,000

(Anchorage with 44,000 and Fairbanks with 13,000). As has already been suggested, it is not always valid to make comparisons by latitude, but with such an extreme contrast the inference is clear, and there is in fact no North American city in the entire region with over 100,000 inhabitants. One must take into account, however, the size of the developing country, and it should be borne in mind that there are only sixteen cities of over 100,000 in the whole of Canada—small wonder that there are none in the far North. Another factor that must be allowed for is that many development projects in the USSR have in fact been uneconomic, and have been undertaken for political, social, or other reasons. This could not be done except under a totalitarian system. Development in Canada is bound to be slower and will depend on such things as ore bodies and oil resources that are economically worth extracting.

Considerable mining activity has already taken place in the Canadian Arctic. Nickel has been mined on the west side of Hudson Bay north of the treeline, though the mine is now closed, having exhausted the ore of sufficiently high grade to be worth the transportation. Iron ore exploration has been going on in a number of Arctic areas, and the latest discovery, in northern Baffin Island, is very promising. Lead-zinc deposits are being explored in the same area, and an asbestos mine on the south shore of Hudson Strait is due to go into production soon. Oil exploration is also going on in the Arctic islands; it remains to be seen how much will be found and whether it will be worth extracting.

The Arctic, in fact, is opening up. Defence installations have played an important part in this, providing base facilities and sometimes transportation for scientific parties in what would otherwise have been for many a prohibitively expensive enterprise. Weather stations in remote areas have fulfilled a similar function, besides providing essential weather data. Commercial airlines now use the polar routes as a matter of course, something incidentally foreseen by Stefansson in the early 1920's when most people thought he was dreaming; his only mistake was that it has come far sooner than he predicted. Scheduled air services are also operating to such remote points as Resolute Bay in the centre of the Canadian Arctic Archipelago.

CONCLUSION

What then are the implications to Canada of the physical facts of geography? Primarily it must be left to the other writers in this series to supply the answer; but it may be worth noting here a few considerations that strike a geographer. Stefansson in "The Northward Course of Empire" propounded a thesis that may be summarized as follows. Man started off as a tropical animal. Throughout the course of history he has expanded his habitat northwards, and in every stage of this expansion he has regarded the zone immediately to the north as being uninhabitable. There is, Stefansson argues, no reason why this process should stop before the entire globe is included. The argument that the Arctic is unsuitable for year-round habitation does not stand up according to this theory in the face of similar statements made in the past about places now regarded as home by large numbers of people. Stefansson quotes a learned commission which pronounced Manitoba unfit for settlement by Europeans, and statements in the Canadian House of Commons to the effect that the Canadian Pacific Railway, if built, could not possibly be operated in winter.

This is an intriguing theory with the force of history behind it, and who is to say to what extent it will or will not be projected into the future. There is no longer any doubt that man is capable of living quite comfortably in the Arctic. This has been amply proved. Settlement, however, is not based on the ability to survive but on the ability to make a living, and permanent settlement in the North will depend in the long run on demand for the resources of the North. At the moment the only resources likely to be required are minerals. Should such a demand arise, it would combine with pressure of population to make Stefansson's prediction come true, because the North is about the only area remaining for population to spread into. Settlement will probably proceed gradually from the South, as indeed it has never stopped doing, pushing occasional long tentacles ahead to more remote areas here and there.

The fact that development is problematical does not mean that we can afford to neglect and ignore our northland. The Arctic is part of our country and we should therefore make it our business to know about it. Secondly, it is one of the few relatively untouched areas in the world in which to carry out environmental studies which may be of great importance to both pure and applied science. Third, it is to our advantage both strategically and economically to know what the resources of our northland are. The iron ore deposits of Labrador were reported by A. P. Low in the 1890's, but were not developed until over fifty years later. I have heard this quoted as an argument to prove that Low was wasting his time and the taxpayer's money. But if he or somebody else had not discovered the ore, how could it have been developed when the time was ripe? If the ores and oil reserves now being explored in the Arctic islands have to wait fifty years to be exploited it does not mean that the work now being done on them will have been wasted. And at the rate that technology is advancing it seems unlikely that the wait will be that long. Canada cannot afford to sit back and wait for the North to become important. It is important now and must be studied in all its aspects, defended against possible attack, whether by air or submarine, and developed as the need arises.

REFERENCES

ARMSTRONG, TERENCE. *The Russians in the Arctic*. London: Methuen and Co., Ltd. (1958).

BERG, L. S. *Natural regions of the USSR*. New York: The Macmillan Co. (1950).

DUNBAR, MOIRA, and GREENAWAY, K. R. *Arctic Canada from the Air*. Ottawa: Queen's Printer (1956).

GORDIENKO, P. A., and LAKTIONOV, A. F. *Principal Results of the Latest Oceanographic research in the Arctic Basin*. Izvestiya Akad. Nauk SSSR, Seriya Geograficheskaya, 5 (1960). Translated by E. R. Hope, Def. Res. Bd. Can., Feb. 1961, T350R.

KIMBLE, G. H. T., and GOOD, DOROTHY (ed.). *Geography of the Northlands*. Am. Geog. Soc. Spec. Pub. No. 32 (1955).

METEOROLOGICAL DIVISION, DEPT. OF TRANSPORT, CANADA. *Climatic Summaries for Selected Meteorological Stations in the Dominion of Canada*. Toronto (no date).

SATER, JOHN E. (co-ordinator). *The Arctic Basin*. Washington, D.C.: Arc. Inst. of North America (1963).

STEFANSSON, V. *The Northward Course of Empire*. New York: Harcourt, Brace and Co. (1922).

Resources and Communications in the Arctic

◄ MICHAEL MARSDEN* ►

PART I: RESOURCES

Introduction

THE PROBLEMS of the Canadian Arctic may be said to be as old as Canadian history, since the first attempt to colonize Canada was made not along the St. Lawrence, but in Baffin Island at Frobisher Bay. Colonization was attempted because of an accidental discovery of "gold" made while trying to use the Arctic's most valuable resource: its location. Frobisher was trying to find the short route to Cathay when he became entangled in the illusions and difficulties of Arctic settlement. If it is true that he failed for logistic reasons and because he had misjudged a resource, there is cause for wondering if things have improved greatly in Canada's North since 1578.

It is still difficult to impress upon the public and industry at large that the most essential quality of the Arctic is not cold, or gold, or polar bears, but a central position in the world community. The world's land masses are grouped mainly in the northern hemisphere; and the most densely populated centres are also in the north, even north of the Tropic of Cancer. The notion of the Arctic Ocean as a new "Mediterranean" has become a truism without being fully understood. The construction of the DEW Line did a great deal to impress the public with the fact that there is a way over the roof of the world, but unfortunately the political separation of east and west and the presence of transportation

*Department of Geography, Sir George Williams University, Montreal. Acknowledgement is gratefully made for the assistance of Commodore O. C. S. Robertson, Arctic Institute of North America, Montreal, in the preparation of Part II.

systems oriented east-west across the Atlantic and Pacific has eliminated any practical utilization of this knowledge.

Canada's record wheat sale to the Soviet Union in 1963 travelled 8,500 miles, in some cases, when it was grown within 5,700 miles of the final consumer. This is not to suggest that it would be more practical to ship over the Pole given the existing networks, but it is an indication that in a world in which free trade is being increasingly advocated it might be worth reviewing our attitude to the Polar Basin as a practical Mediterranean. The USSR wants the atomic-powered icebreaker "Lenin" to operate in the High North, not for prestige reasons, but because the shortest marine route linking the extremes of the USSR passes to 80° N. The great industrial complexes of the modern world—Europe, North America, and Japan—lie grouped about this basin some 6,000 miles apart, and China will be similarly close.

Hence even if the Arctic were a wasteland it would need to be understood in terms of transportation and communication, because of the wealth about its perimeter and the possibility that distribution costs can be reduced by using shorter routes through the polar basin. In a world of free trading the ability to use the Arctic areas freely for transportation could represent enormous wealth.

The question of resources within Arctic regions is another matter. There are extreme points of view about the resources of the North, particularly in Canada. Yet the fact is that there is a considerable body of information about potential resources in Alaska, Canada, Greenland, northern Scandinavia, and Arctic USSR. What does not exist is a clear understanding of the means of exploitation in terms of transportation networks and potential markets. Problems of capital investment and long-term markets require vital decisions. In the last forty years Soviet geographers have done considerable work on the problems of regionalism and inter-regional transport systems, yet according to Slavin (Director of the Section of Natural Resources and Economics of the North, Soviet Council for Studies of Productive Forces) the old and clearly defined plans for regional transport systems have been abandoned in recent years. For example, in the Yakut Republic and the Magadan area, plans to provide rail links to the Trans-Siberian railway have been abandoned in favour of less expensive road links, and Slavin talks of railroads for some future time "not in ten or even twenty years." This attitude was no doubt fostered by the new attitude of the Soviet government to economic developments in the north, the basic approach now being determined by the need to justify operations in "economic" terms. Although it is difficult to recognize a basis for their assessment of values it is quite clear that the old attitude of regional development for prestige and as a matter of political principle is being reviewed and changed. There are doubts and uncertainties, then, in the USSR as well as in Canada.

A review of resources is complicated by the fact that in the Soviet Union the Arctic proper, that is, the area north of the treeline, is not distinguished for economic purposes from the Boreal Forest (taiga) so that generalized figures are given for the "Extreme North"[1] rather than for the Arctic itself. It is also difficult to compare cash values directly and sometimes misleading to quote quantity. Although it is possible to identify true Arctic communities and Arctic resources, there are practical reasons for accepting the Russian notion of an "Extreme North." This notion coincides very roughly with everything north of 60° east of the Urals and includes the true tundra west of these mountains, but "rayony" or regions of the Far North may have extensions well south of that line. The Extreme North concept also has the advantage of emphasizing practical differentiation and utilization. In Canada there is an administrative cut-off along the 60th parallel, the Federal Government being responsible for the Yukon and the North-West Territories. The regions can thus be compared reasonably with the Russian North although developments in the northern areas of Canadian provinces should not be ignored, and figures pertaining thereto must be considered in the total context. Alaska and Greenland are generally treated as units and will be so regarded here, although not defined in the same terms as the northlands of Russia and Canada.

Renewable Resources

A fact to be faced by the Arctic enthusiast is that the renewable resources of the Arctic area proper, that is, the tundra zone, are pathetically poor. Intensive work by such units as the Wildlife Service of Canada and the Arctic Unit of the Fisheries Research Board has shown that the take which could be harvested safely is almost incredibly low. It is a matter for debate whether all such Canadian resources, exploited to 100 per cent efficiency, would feed the 40,000 residents of the Yukon and the North-West Territories.

Outside the Arctic proper there are potential forest resources in the Yukon and North-West Territories. Southern Yukon Territory could

[1]For problems in definition of the northern lands of the USSR, see T. E. Armstrong, "Soviet Terms for the North of the USSR," *Polar Record*, vol. 10, no. 69 (1961).

produce 100,000,000 board feet per year. There are also half a million acres of potential agricultural land, and it is an interesting sidelight that forest clearance during the Klondike days produced most of the present farmlands. In fact only four and a half million board feet are now produced, with another million feet of round lumber used in crude construction work. Major development is, moreover, unlikely because of the larger and more accessible resources in northern British Columbia. Perhaps this "resource" should be regarded only as a potential reduction in the cost of colonization. It is obvious that in order to provide a larger group with a high standard of living, food and other biological resources will have to be taken into the Arctic rather than taken out. This does not mean that exploitation of the existing resources cannot form a significant part of the economy of the North-West Territories during future development, but it does mean that they cannot be considered to be a major productive sector of the economy.

In the Soviet Arctic the Russians have been working for more than twenty years at the systematic exploitation of renewable resources, and institutions such as the Reindeer Research Institute at Noril'sk have done constructive and detailed studies in order to assess the exploitable components of the animal populations. Regulation of the take has been strict for more than thirty years, and the marketing of such things as fox furs and seal fur has been under national control so that there is a relatively precise understanding of the animal resources.

Fox fur has been an export of the Soviet Union since 1950, and the sale has had a seriously depressing effect on the price of Arctic fox for Canadian suppliers. The fact remains, however, that the money which can be described in these terms is relatively small. For example squirrel furs in Canada earn almost as much revenue in a year as the Arctic fox. Arctic furs do not compete in value with the ranch-raised furs—chinchilla, fox, and mink—whose total value is twice that of the entire wildlife take of any one year, and sixteen or seventeen times the value of the Arctic take. Eleven million dollars, the value of wild fur take for the whole of Canada during 1960, is hardly significant in terms of maintaining a population, while the actual return from the Arctic was in the region of $1,000,000, or less than $100 per head of the native population and something like $25 a head for the total resident population of the North-West Territories and the Yukon. There is no reason to presume that the USSR, Greenland, and Alaska are relatively any better off.

It is very difficult to assess the combined value of all the natural resources being exploited in the Russian North. Fishing has been a principal activity in Russian Arctic waters since the 1920's, but most of the fish caught are consumed locally.

In Alaska the fur trade, which made the wealth of so many Russian Alaskans, has declined to an annual total of around $6,000,000, but the fisheries catch, particularly salmon, can exceed $100,000,000 per annum after processing and forms a most significant part of the state's export. Rogers (1962, pp. 33–34) claims that fish and wildlife resources net $118,000,000 a year and have become Alaska's greatest true resource. This still represents less than $500 per capita.

When renewable resources rank so low it becomes reasonable to consider tourism as a relatively important factor. The USSR runs domestic tourist cruises in boats well north on the Yenisey. Tourism has never accounted for more than $450,000 in one year in the North-West Territories, but there was a peak of $4,000,000 during 1962, the "Festival year," in the Yukon. There are some 27,000,000 North American hunters and fishermen and many of them could be attracted to an area which is endowed with large and varied quantities of game and fish. The Batelle Report for the Alaska and U.S. Highway Commission estimates 800,000 tourists in Alaska during 1980 and 500,000 in adjacent sectors of Canada. The Tourist Development office of Canada's Department of Northern Affairs forecasts a more conservative 50,000 to the Mackenzie in 1980—a potential revenue by present figures of $15,000,000, which is highly significant when contrasted with the total annual value of the existing fishing and fur industries of less than $2,000,000. It does not need to be emphasized that tourism will depend very largely upon adequate and cheap transportation systems, together with adequate and pleasant accommodation. The problems of providing transportation for such a facility are, however, more easily overcome since northern points may be adequately served by aircraft, Hovercraft, and other vehicles with relatively small payload capacities. These in turn are the high revenue types of operation which could be integrated easily into southern systems.

It would seem fair, then, to dismiss the renewable resources if we are talking only about developing and exploiting new land for wealth or power and to see them only as a supplement to the future reduction of costs of occupation. It is significant however that in a number of cases Russian planners have turned to the notion of "rape" of resources. This implies the utilization of a renewable resource at a rate which destroys the producer; in other words, treating it as a non-renewable resource and trying to realize a great deal of money in a short time. For example, one species of seal was effectively exterminated because its fur would bring a high price and there were sufficient numbers of seal available to make the hunting out of the species a source of capital for other developments. There is possibly some argument for adopting this attitude toward the seals of the Canadian Arctic, where they are the largest single renewable resource in the area, and when seal fur is now at a premium on the international market, being used in high-style clothing and ski wear, etc., in Europe. In 1963 a sealskin in good condition commanded a better price than an Arctic fox. It might be economically wise to exploit this resource to the point of near exter-mination of the species if it was guaranteed that the proceeds would be invested in a permanent capitalization of future industry in the Canadian Arctic areas. Conservation in this case might even be unwise since the potential market for fur seal will certainly decline relatively, and may decline permanently, so that what is now regarded as a resource for conservation may become a worthless possession.

With that emotionally debatable exception there is not much point in discussing biological resources of the Arctic regions, and certainly there are no untold riches. It is the non-renewable resources that must provide any incentive to occupation of the Arctic lands.

Non-renewable Resources

USSR

Gakkel' of the Arctic and Antarctic Institute in Leningrad says that "the purpose of exploration in the Arctic has been the search for, and subsequent utilization of, the very rich natural resources of the remote northern margins of the country, as well as the raising of the material welfare and culture of the poorly developed small nationalities of the North." He adds, "but the first task was the solution of the transporta-tion problem of Arctic navigation." (Gakkel', Ya. Ya. 1962, p. 265.)

Terence Armstrong of the Scott Polar Research Institute in Britain has made a good short summary of mining in the Soviet Arctic.[2] He points out that the exploitation of mineral resources is the major economic benefit to the USSR of its Arctic territory and that while detailed information about production was withheld for a long time, enough generalized information has become available since 1956 to make review possible.

According to Armstrong, the mines of Noril'sk have been providing copper and nickel together with small quantities of platinum and cobalt since 1940. Nickel and copper have been among the resource deficiencies

[2]T. E. Armstrong, "Mining in the Soviet Arctic," *Polar Record*, vol. 10, no. 64.

of the USSR, and in fact during the war of 1941–45 lend-lease accounted for 70 per cent of the country's needs, so it is clear that these metals have a premium value to the Soviet Union. Since the development of Noril'sk (which has been producing one-fifth of the country's total supplies of those metals) alternative supplies have become available in the southern Urals, and from the mines at Petsamo (acquired from Finland and now called Nikel') which provide a very high proportion of the nickel needs of Russia. The Russians built a railroad from Noril'sk to Dudinka on the river as early as 1937. The city has grown; it now numbers more than 100,000 people, has train, road, river, and air connections, and is becoming a centre of considerable importance in the development of the surrounding region. In terms of strategic value it is possible that only the platinum is now of high priority in a rarity sense, and that the relative importance of nickel has declined.

Gold production is another interesting matter discussed by Armstrong. Gold has been mined in the Russian Arctic since the 1840's in the Lena Basin and at true Arctic mines on the Vitim and Aldan Rivers. Yakutskya now produces 20 per cent of the nation's gold, and most of this is in Arctic or sub-Arctic areas. The Arctic sector of the Indigarka-Kolyma area to the east (Kamchatskaya oblast') produces even more, possibly as much as 60 per cent of a national total which may reach 15,000,000 troy ounces and is second to South Africa by only a small margin. The interesting peculiarity is that, because of their difficult locations and local conditions, the cost of exploitation is extraordinarily high, and Kowalewsky, writing in *The Times* is quoted as saying that the cost of mining is something like five times the actual selling price of gold in the west. Considering the large sales of gold to the West in the past three or four years, it is obvious that the metal is being used at a severe premium to finance vital imports and aid the Soviet Union's foreign aid programmes. (Armstrong, 1960, p. 17.)

Slavin (1960) claims that the Aldan area of Yakutia, already mentioned, is a principal and important sector of the Soviet economy. In addition to the gold deposits, there is an extremely large diamond province discovered since 1945 along the Vilyui River. The total quantity of diamonds mined in this sector is sufficient to meet all the industrial needs of the Soviet Union for a number of years to come. This particular find has been a boon to the Soviet Union in view of the fact that diamonds are on the United States' list of prohibited strategic exports and there are problems with other suppliers. No precise figure is given, but previous demands for diamonds had been as high as 10,000 carats per annum. Significantly, perhaps, in view of our later comments on transportation, the diamond-mining sector is being linked to the more settled areas by a 150-mile road to Muktuya on the Lena rather than by railway, in contradiction to the previously announced plans for territorial development.

The region is also the principal and vital supplier of mica (about 11,000 tons per annum). Natural gas found locally has been piped into the regional centre of Yakutsk. Tin is being exploited near the River Yana and exported by road from Ege-Khya to Kuiga, a small village on the river itself, for transportation. There are also significant tin and tungsten resources being utilized in Iultin and Omsukshan, the latter shipping its ores via the new Arctic port of Pevek.

In the Magadan region a new mining and processing mill was built at Iultin in 1959 in order to utilize the large deposits of tungsten and tin. A modern workers' town was built, associated with the mill, and it was linked to the sea at Egvekinot by a highway over 125 miles in length. As part of a deliberate policy the Soviets have encouraged the metallurgical research institute in Magadan to centralize work in the area rather than import equipment, and parts of the mining and processing equipment were not only designed in Magadan, but manufactured in small towns adjacent to the city.

Coal has been the most widespread and best exploited resource of the Russian Arctic since pre-Soviet times. The Russians are not above using coal as a fuel on a very large scale, and resource maps up to the '50's even catalogue peat deposits. Most Arctic settlements are heated and fueled with coal, and coal has been used on some Polar expeditions for heating, melting ice, and so on. The remoteness of the settlements and the high cost of transport have made exploitation worthwhile on a local scale, and the availability of this resource has reduced the cost of settlement in the North. There are, however, two northern coal fields which could be called nationally significant. The most famous is the Pechora coal field which was first opened up immediately before World War II. Production is now in excess of 16,000,000 metric tons per annum, and the chief city, Vorkuta, with some 55,000 inhabitants, is linked by railroad to the Leningrad urban network. There are also large reserves of rock salt and potash being worked nearby. The railroad has been a key factor in developing this western part of the Soviet Arctic and there are plans for branch lines. Vityazeva (1961, p. 51) estimates the reserves of Pechora to be in excess of 260 billion tons, with one-quarter of those reserves in extremely high-grade coking coal, ideal for use in blast furnaces. He sees a potential production of 30 to 35 million tons a year in the area, with 23 to 25 million tons of coking coal. He thinks that the consumers of the coal will be the new steel plants of the Urals; but he also envisages a possibility of exporting (presumably to Eastern Europe). A number of Soviet geographers have pointed out that there is considerable wastage at present in the burning of extremely high-grade coals for prosaic tasks, and it is undoubtedly an objective of Soviet economy to utilize these high-grade materials more efficiently.

A more recent discovery with perhaps even greater long-term significance is that of the iron ore field and the South Yakut coking coal field, located less than 70 miles apart in the Chulman sector of the Aldan River, previously mentioned for its gold resources. It is proposed that these deposits be exploited in order to provide a steel complex in the far eastern provinces of the Soviet Union. It should be noted that other sources of coal and iron are well known in much more accessible parts of the Soviet Far East, but that economic calculations suggest that production in an area where the two materials lie adjacent to one another would be cheaper—again emphasizing the dominant role of transport in the economy.

Arctic oil, while economically important, only accounts for some 2 per cent of the Soviet total. Natural gas production is, however, a significant resource, and Armstrong quotes a figure of 10 per cent of all natural gas production of the Soviet Union in 1958; some 3,000 million cubic metres. The Soviet seven-year plan, 1959–65, included the piping of this gas to the relatively new Ural industrial region.

That the Russians have a sound grasp of general principles of Arctic economics is underlined by the tone of a December 1963 news release from the Novosti Press Agency. In describing an uncommonly powerful gas gusher discovered north of the Arctic Circle, Dr. Gurari of the Siberian Research Institute of Geology, Geophysics, and Mineral Resources, emphasized factors less obvious than the large size of the find. He said research had indicated gas would be found at shallow depths. Prospecting could be with light equipment, thus avoiding problems of transporting heavy equipment over the tundra. He stressed the advantage of using the smallest possible quantities of material in new Arctic developments, and he postulated prospecting and drilling with only helicopter support.

Clearly all the mineral products except coal and gas have a special strategic value to the USSR, which may explain why they have developed them in Arctic and remote areas. Timber is also important in the economy of Russia's Extreme North, but it is difficult to find figures. It is used as a fuel, in construction, and is "exported" to other regions of the USSR.

In concluding our description of the resources of the Russian Arctic it is worth quoting Slavin extensively (referring to the northeastern Arctic only) in his summary definition of the resource areas and the attitude of a central government to them.

The Soviet Northeast today represents a vast 'island' equal to approximately one-fifth of the entire territory of the USSR. Its situation as an island is determined by the fact that it can be reached only by seasonal waterways; from the north along the Northern Sea Route which is in operation for only slightly over three months a year, from the east via the seas of the Far East six to eight months a year (only the Petropavlovak-on-Kamchatka port is ice-free the year round); from the west along the Lena River. The Aldan mining and industrial district alone is connected the year round with the railway network by the Amur-Yakutsk highway. Further development of industry in the Northeast, will require the building of railways to connect the territory of the Yakut republic and Magadan Region, as well as the whole of the Northeast, with the country's railway network. This is not a matter of the near future, of the next ten to twenty years, but it is an economic necessity and will be realized. This will result in speeding up the rate of industrial development of the natural resources of the Northeast which is demanded by the requirements of the rapidly growing economy of the Soviet country. [Slavin in 1960, p. 554.]

And elsewhere,

The capital invested in the construction of highways (over 4,000 kilometers), sea ports, the development of aviation lines, the setting up of numerous auxiliary enterprises for industry and agriculture, the construction of Magadan, a modern city and of numerous workers' townlets—investments running into many thousands of millions of roubles—has been fully repaid . . . [Slavin in 1960, p. 552.]

The notion of value for money invested is relatively new in Russia. The notion of the Arctic "island" has significance for all Arctic lands.

Canada

In Canada the picture is not such a grand one nor does it figure so largely in the national economy. The total production of all mines in the Yukon and the Northwest Territories during 1962 was only $31,000,000, or 1.1 per cent of total Canadian production. This was a decline from $36,000,000 in 1960 and continues the decline from the peak year of 1954.

A new tungsten mine on the Flat River, between the Hyland and the Nahanni, which will actually export via Yukon Territory, has a $3,000,000 per annum potential. The Port Radium mine, which used to produce $5,000,000 worth of pitchblende during the year, was closed in 1962, and the Rankin Inlet Nickel Mine, which was a significant producer of nickel for several years, has also closed down. A large deposit of lead and zinc in North Baffin Island is being investigated, and there is much speculation about a find of very high density iron ore made in the last two years. These ores are now being prospected and evaluated and it seems probable that there is a deposit of high-grade magnetite of a quality equalled only by those at Kiruna in Sweden (68% iron) and big enough to allow shipment of 1,000,000 tons per year. Studies are being made of access to the coast and to shipping for exploitation purposes. It should be noted that the interest here is sparked by the extremely high quality of the ore concerned and, unlike most resources encountered in the Canadian Arctic areas, there may be an incentive to exploitation for the southern market regardless of high moving costs.

There has been a great deal of speculation about the lead-zinc deposits at Pine Point on Great Slave Lake. A 437-mile railroad from Grimshaw has been built to provide access at a cost of something like $85,000,000, so the resource must be one which offers a very rapid and significant return. It is thought that the mine will produce annually 215,000 tons of ore concentrates for at least twenty-five years, but it should be noted that the concentrates must be moved almost 1,400 miles either to Trail for smelting or to Fort Saskatchewan near Edmonton.

In the Yukon Territory, which has a long tradition of mining and is associated in most minds with the famous "gold rush," the actual mineral production is relatively low. In fact, for 1960, the total value of all operations, which included a major silver, lead, zinc, and cadmium mine, a significant placer gold operation, and a small coal mine, was only $12,000,000. There has been a major find of iron, this time in the form of jasper-haematite. A rough estimate suggests a reserve of 20 billion tons. However, it is unlikely to be exploited in any circumstances since its only easy access is to the Arctic Ocean, with its limited shipping season and total lack of port facilities. The apparently more sensible routing would take materials south and west across the Cordilleran mountains to the Pacific, but rough estimates indicate that the cost of transportation to the coast alone would exceed the current world price of iron ore per ton delivered to the consumer.

Oil is the largest potential resource of the Canadian North. The potentially oil-bearing sedimentary basins of the western provinces are best known in the Alberta area in the sector adjacent to the Canada-United States border. The structure, however, extends northward through the Mackenzie District and reaches the Canadian coast on a belt almost

240 miles wide fronting the Arctic Basin. Furthermore, there is to the east and north, in the Queen Elizabeth Islands, a very large extension of the same potentially oil-rich sedimentary sector. Using arbitrary but relatively conservative figures for the quantity of oil available per cubic mile in the US, it is possible to estimate the colossal potential of twenty-one billion barrels of oil and a hundred and fifty trillion cubic feet of gas. According to Mr. B. G. Sivertz of the Department of Northern Affairs, (1961, p. 566) the total represents something like seven times the present discovered resources of oil and gas in western Canada. The president of a major oil company drilling in the Canadian Arctic during 1963 publicly stated his opinion that the potential resources of the Canadian Arctic Islands alone exceed those of the entire Middle Eastern oil fields. Whatever the facts may turn out to be, at present over 117,000,000 acres are under permit for exploration, and there have been a dozen wildcat drill holes.

R. A. J. Phillips of the Department of Northern Affairs has pointed out that there is some urgency about Canada's attitude to the oil resources. While it is true that the current potential production per annum is in excess of requirements, there is a forecast for a requirement 100 per cent greater before 1980, and an equally valid forecast for a sharp falloff in oil requirements in the period immediately following 1980, owing to the introduction of nuclear power on a commercial scale. The fact is that these vast resources of the Canadian North may only be of value to mankind during the next thirty to forty years, and every year lost in tackling their exploitation is actually a direct and final loss of potential revenue to the nation.

Once the presence of oil is confirmed and a positive national attitude towards such resources developed, it may become urgent to study methods of transportation and exploitation. It is not inconceivable that oil might be the one thing Canada's North would have to exchange with the Russian North in a postulated future era of international good will and trade, since it is known that a great number of Siberian thermal-electric power stations are utilizing even wood—of all inconceivable things—to power the plants.

In considering northern Canada, it makes good sense to include certain developments in the northern sectors of the provinces, where there are active mining operations in subarctic conditions on the true frontiers of settlement. There were two uranium mines on the north shore of Lake Athabasca still functioning in 1963. The Flin Flon mine, astride the Manitoba-Saskatchewan boundary, produces significant amounts of copper, zinc, gold, silver, cadmium, selenium and tellurium. Other mines in Manitoba include Lynn Lake (nickel, copper, cobalt), Chisel Lake (zinc, lead, copper), and Thompson (nickel and copper). It is worth noting that Gould, in his famous Bowman lecture, classes INCO's Thompson development as unequivocally "polar," so extreme are the conditions encountered (Gould, 1958, p. 6 and fig. 9). Even Pickle Crow in North Ontario (gold) and the Chibougamau gold and copper workings should be considered in this context. The huge iron mines of Schefferville, Labrador City, and Gagnon are also generally considered part of the northern economy. During 1963 an asbestos corporation was reviewing the potential near Diana Bay in Northern Quebec. The mines mentioned outside Quebec produce $74,000,000 of material per year and the gross value of iron exported from Quebec is in the area of $150,000,000. These operations, which are definitely pioneering in nature, have a very significant production value.

Alaska

At first glance the Alaskan economy provides a simple, clear-cut, and favourable picture: exports from the new state regularly exceed imports by several millions of dollars; but an intimate review of internal conditions reveals the same general uncertainty of direction and a perhaps typically Arctic illusion of wealth. The import-export figures exceed $200,000,000 per annum and there is a domestic budget of $600,000,000, but the presence in the state of some 30,000 military personnel prevents realistic assessments of the economy. Military personnel accounted for 65 per cent of Alaskan population at a World War II peak, and in 1957 still constituted more than one-fifth of the citizens, while government paid more than 50 per cent of the payroll in the state. Resource harvesting employed only 10 per cent of the population, while 66 per cent of all employment arose directly or indirectly from government activities (Rogers, 1962, p. 94).

George Rogers (1962, p. 35) has pointed out that much of the American faith in Alaska's vast mineral resources is based almost solely on the fact that the state has produced three-quarters of a billion dollars worth of gold since 1880, and one-quarter of a billion dollars worth of other metals. One boast that is frequently made is that Alaska processes thirty-one of the thirty-three minerals regarded as strategic for national defence; yet it can be shown that claims to produce the metals as significant resources are in fact somewhat tenuous, although there are undoubtedly deposits waiting to be found and exploited since less than one per cent of the land mass has been adequately explored for minerals. In recent times, however, the actual current exploitation of minerals has declined steadily, and the annual total is now somewhere in the region of only $25,000,000, including a surprisingly high percentage of sand and gravel used in airfield construction, road grading, etc.

The tremendous hydro potential of the Yukon River at the proposed Rampart Dam site must be reconsidered since the 1963 Good Friday earthquake. The state and its people are reviewing the future in critical and realistic terms. In view of the existence of the producer nations on the sides of the relatively small triangle around the Polar Basin, it is natural to find the state studying possible trade links with the Japanese market. Up to the present time, imports have been predominantly from the United States in a proportion of more than two hundred to one, and even the export economy, with its furs and canned fish, is oriented to the United States in the proportion of more than sixty to one. It will be some time before the studies that are now in progress can reveal whether the state will have a viable economy if it is oriented to some other production area.

Greenland and Spitzbergen

In Greenland the economy, though vigorous for its kind, is a small one. A population of 33,000 depends for a living mainly on fishing, together with a little fur trading and some marginal sheep herding. The cryolite mine at Ivigtut, soon to close, is a unique producer of a specialized flux for the aluminum industry. Since two-thirds of the annual production of about 40,000 tons goes to the United States, the mine has served as a valuable dollar-earner for Denmark. Zinc and lead mines producing 28,000 tons of ore per annum have now closed down. The only other mining activity is performed by a very minor coal producer on the west coast. Since Greenland has undergone a relatively thorough geological survey there is little likelihood of new mining activities. Mining produce accounted for more than one-half of $9,600,000 of exports in 1962; while fish in various forms—mainly salted cod— accounted for another $3,000,000. There are no forest resources.

There is no overall transport system other than coastal shipping, though the government has initiated air services that include the operation of helicopters. Communication is by radio. Greenland's income is significant in helping to maintain the Greenlander, but there is a large annual subsidy by the Danish Government, and it seems doubtful that Greenland will ever be a significant producer except in local terms.

Spitzbergen, under Norwegian sovereignty since 1925, has no resources other than its immense coal deposits, estimated at 800 million tons. The coal is worked by Norway and Russia and exported to those countries respectively, total production being less than 1,000,000 tons per year. It is difficult to assign a cash value to the product, but it is undoubtedly a profitable operation since Spitzbergen does not maintain any significant community or facilities other than the mines. Coal is especially valuable to Norway, which has no mines of its own.

All authorities agree that transportation problems represent the principal obstacle to the development of the Arctic and the utilization of its resources. We will presently produce figures to show that transportation, although a major factor, is not a dominant factor in the high costs of northern development, as was shown by a study of the high costs of Arctic mining. It is, however, a cost factor whose reduction would reduce the costs of other penalties upon development, such as the supply of power and labour, the provision of capital at low interest rates, and the not inconsiderable items of extra heating and inventory maintenance required by remote situations.

PART II: TRANSPORTATION AND COMMUNICATION

Transportation into and through the Arctic is at present expensive and relatively difficult. The nature of the terrain, the persistence of sea ice, and the rigors of the climate are the principal limiting factors. The last decade has seen the development of new vehicles and techniques for operating successfully within an Arctic environment, but their cost in development, production, and operation are much higher than costs for vehicles and techniques employed in similar operations within temperate climates. Some of these costs are due to the relatively small size of existing demand, but there are a considerable number of variables, and it is not easy to make a generalization applicable to the entire Arctic zone.

Historically the greatest tonnages transported into or through the area have been carried by sea, but there is evidence to indicate that in recent years the trucking industry has moved more material into the North-West Territories of Canada in an attempt to shortcut the sea route around Alaska to the areas served by the Mackenzie River system. Trucking operations so far have been entirely in the west and have concentrated upon providing an adequate link between the Transcontinental railroad and the Mackenzie River system and upon supplying the Yukon Territory district.

Marine Transportation

USSR

The most efficient marine transportation route presently used in the Arctic is the Northern Sea Route. This comprises the Barents Sea, four passages around Novya Zemlya, the Kara Sea, the East Siberian Sea, the Chukchi Sea, Bering Strait, and the Bering Sea. This route has opened communication to the interior of eastern and central USSR by linking the river mouths, and has made possible the exploitation of resources of the area. The route has halved the distance between the ports of European USSR and those of the Soviet Far East. Only the Barents Sea is open all year round for conventional shipping. Generally conventional ships can only operate betwen late July and early October. However, by employing icebreakers as ice escorts and ice working ships on the route, the navigation season has been extended anywhere from a month to two months.

The USSR has paid much attention to the development of this sea route, and we might ask why, for it would appear that the North is not of particular importance to the Russian economy as a whole. The area served by the Northern Sea Route has a population of approximately five million people; two of its cities—Archangel and Murmansk—have populations of approximately a quarter of a million each, and at least another eight have populations ranging from sixty thousand to a hundred thousand. The Route is so important because of its strategic location. Not only does it provide a number of links with east and west, between northern and southern river systems which serve a cross-section of Siberia, but it also provides an east-west link between an essentially non-Arctic area (Archangel and Murmansk) and the two-Arctic regions of the north and east. The function of the Northern Sea Route in this case is to provide a direct bridge to the western European economy which parallels and strengthens the function of the central Siberian railway.

While none of the area's contributions to the Soviet economy are overwhelmingly important, they are nevertheless significant. Much of the material travelling on the Northern Sea route originates in non-Arctic areas and is delivered to non-Arctic areas by relatively cheap transportation routes using the river systems and the northern water. Apart from the considerable help provided by icebreakers and ice-strengthened ships along the Route, there are numerous fuelling stations and an excellent ice- and weather-reporting service. These services illustrate the total investment, including elements of the gross national investment, essential to northern development.

In 1960 some two hundred and seventy ships plied these waters, carrying over a million tons of cargo. Most of them were between 2,500 and 3,500 gross tons, though some were of 6,000 gross tons or better. Tonnages are restricted because of the Route's shallowness; in many places the limiting draft is somewhere between 20 and 25 feet.

The key to this operation is the use of icebreakers working in conjunction with ice observation aircraft. In 1960 two important additions were made to the Russian icebreaking fleet, the atomic-powered "Lenin" (16,000 tons displacement and 4,400 horsepower and the Finnish-built diesel electric "Moskva" (12,800 tons displacement and 22,000 horsepower). These ships operated throughout the season with eight other icebreakers of over 5,000 tons displacement. There is also a large fleet of icebreaking tugs. Many of the ships employed are ice-strengthened, i.e., capable of independent movement in all but the heaviest of ice. The best example of this type of ship is the "Lena" class, built in the Netherlands between 1954–1957, of 8,200 horsepower and with a cargo capacity of 6,500 tons. It is understood that, in addition to the six Dutch-built ships, others of the same class have been constructed in the USSR. The large pool of very experienced icebreaker officers and men, some with better than thirty years' experience in this type of ship, is one of the biggest factors in the USSR's success with icebreakers.

The ports served by the Northern Sea Route lie, in the main, at or near the mouths of the south-north flowing rivers and near the major straits. The river ports serve as trans-shipment points for cargo bound in and out of the interior. The main terminal ports are Archangel and Murmansk, in the west, and Magadan or Vladivostok, in the east. The main intermediate ports are Anderma, Dikson, Dudinka, Igarka, Kozhevnikovo, Tiksi, Ambarchik, Pevek, Provideniia, and Anadyr, most of which have alongside berthing.

North American Arctic

The shipping routes of North America are rather different, since the Northwest Passage cannot be considered a commercially sound route. Shipping operations are divided into western and eastern Arctic operations.

Ships enter the western North American Arctic via the Bering Strait, and may reach as far as Shepherd Bay. The tortuous and only partially surveyed route has a limiting draft of about 25 feet. The main ports served are Point Barrow, Barter Island, Tuktoyaktuk, and Cambridge

Bay, with many small intermediate trading posts, Royal Canadian Mounted Police posts, and missions, none of which can be classified as ports. All cargo operations are of the over-the-beach type, except at Tuktoyaktuk, where wharfage is available, and even there a bar imposes a limiting draft of about fourteen feet.

Tuktoyaktuk is the main trans-shipment point for goods coming down the Mackenzie River, the only south-north flowing river in North America which is navigable and connects with the transportation systems of the Canadian interior. Ocean shipping cannot use it because of shallow water in its delta. By sharp contrast with the Russian rivers it is used to support Northern posts rather than to export the raw resources of the hinterland.

The navigation season for this route extends from about August 1 at Point Barrow to about the third week of September.

In contrast to North America's western Arctic, the eastern half—with the exception of the ice of the Middle pack in Baffin Bay—presents less difficult conditions. The waters are deeper, the land bolder, and the hydrographic surveys, while nowhere approaching adequacy, do give some aid to the navigator. The main ports have wharfage or a reasonable lighterage system. They are: Goose Bay; Frobisher Bay; Churchill in Hudson Bay; Thule and Sonderstrom, both having good ports, in Greenland; and Resolute in the Parry Islands, with adequate lighterage and a shipping season from early August to late September. While the other ports, such as Hall Lake and Coral Harbour, do not have wharfage or established lighterage, in most cases they do have adequate beaches with hardstands and adequate road systems to clear cargo from the beach area.

It is a striking fact that, unlike the Russian Northern Sea Route ports, all the North American Arctic ports are built to receive, not export, cargo. The only exception is the grain port of Churchill, which, though a main Canadian export port, does not figure in the top twenty-two by tonnage handled. In 1959 some fifty-nine ships carried away approximately twenty-two million bushels of wheat and brought in some six thousand tons of general cargo. The port also handled some twenty-three thousand tons of ore and thirty-seven thousand gallons of petroleum oil, and lubricants. The port generally handles a coastal trade of better than fifty thousand tons.

The Canadian-American Joint Weather Stations in the Queen Elizabeth Islands are, in the main, supplied by airlift, only Eureka being supplied by large icebreaking cargo ships.

The icebreakers employed in the western North American Arctic are operated by the U.S. Navy and the U.S. Coast Guard. They are of the "Wind" class, six thousand tons and 12,000 horsepower. The Canadian Coast Guard operates one smaller icebreaker in the Canadian sector. In the eastern North American Arctic the Americans operate two or three "Wind" class icebreakers and the Canadians operate a fleet of some ten icebreakers of various classes. Some of these, like the "Sir John A. Macdonald" and the "d'Iberville," are icebreaking cargo ships possessing all the capabilities of icebreakers, and good cargo capacity besides. In this section of the Arctic the Danes, the Americans, and the Canadians operate a considerable number of ice-strengthened ships.

The greatest quantity of material in the Western Arctic is handled by tug and barge coming down the Mackenzie system from above Great Slave Lake. The traffic is handled essentially by three companies, one of them government-owned. There is a wide range in the age and capability of the equipment used. A small part of it is modern, but some of the tugs are up to forty years old. The system supplies communities along the Mackenzie, including the oil town of Norman Wells which has a small refinery and can produce in excess of 400,000 barrels per annum. On the open sea east from Mackenzie through to Spence Bay there are some tug and barge operations which supplement operations by the larger cargo ships.

Vast improvements can be made in the design of icebreakers intended for ice escort work. Similarly, greater knowledge of ice behaviour and ice working operations have shown that ice-strengthened shipping can carry out tasks formerly reserved for icebreakers. The differential in cost between an ice-strengthened ice working ship and an icebreaker is formidable.

With increased knowledge of ice behaviour comes increased capability of conventional shipping in ice-infested waters. The development of satellites which can view ice cover over the whole polar basin daily is a major advance in this field.

The nuclear submarine

While the nuclear submarine has not yet been used as a commercial cargo carrier, it might be well to take a look at its present capability. In the last six years nuclear submarines of the US and USSR navies have demonstrated that they can operate in ice-covered or ice-infested waters during any season of the year, and can transit very shallow areas, avoiding ice of prohibitive draft. Special types of sonar equipment are used to guide the submarines passing under ice obstacles, and safely bring them to the surface through the ice cover.

It is only fair to assume that the use of submarines in the Arctic will continue to improve through advanced hull design, more efficient and less costly reactors, more sophisticated sonar equipments, and increased knowledge of the Arctic Ocean. Greater knowledge of local ice conditions and bathymetry will be necessary to facilitate landing, but this knowledge is relatively easy to procure. An air-bubbler system can be used to keep a docking area free of ice where there is a sufficient influx of underlying seawater of appropriate salinity and temperature. This would allow a submarine to surface at the port all year round.

While the present cost of the nuclear submarine cargo carrier may be prohibitive except for very valuable cargoes of high density, thought might well be given to the design and operation of a nuclear submarine tug with homogeneous cargoes being carried in a simply constructed dumb submarine barge.

Advancement in methods of marine cargo carriage and terminal handling in Arctic waters waits only upon demand. Much of the needed knowledge is already at hand, and further data can easily be ascertained.

Surface Transportation

Heavy surface transportation in the Arctic has been tied historically to a network of roads. Specially configured wheeled or tracked vehicles have been found to be reasonably efficient over frozen tundra or on firm unridged sea ice or uncrevassed glaciers. In the case of frozen tundra, once the covering above the permafrost begins to thaw and provide an "active layer," the wheeled or tracked vehicle can become hopelessly mired. Sea ice, subject as it is to the stresses and strains of tides, currents, and winds, makes a relatively unsafe roadbed except for a short period in winter along the land-fast ice. In order to count on all-year use of tracked or wheeled vehicles over the tundra country, it would be necessary to extend the road network throughout the proposed operating theatre: a difficult task at best and highly uneconomical unless the terminus is at a densely populated centre (unlikely at present) or in an area of highly priced raw resources. It must be remembered too that the payload ceiling on this form of transportation is very low over long distances, in spite of the recent development of trucks with a 55-ton payload.

There are a variety of experimental vehicles such as the Rolygon, which has an extremely large cylindrical or sausage-shaped "wheel" under low-pressure inflation which can support the vehicle in water and move it over the roughest terrain. Its payload is small, however, and its handling is awkward. There are other experimental vehicles, but the principle is probably established that long-term arctic development plans should look to the technological improvement of more normal types of vehicles rather than to specialized "beasts" with exotic functions.

There is one development, however, which offers a radical departure from previous principles and which has a specific advantage for northern operators. This is the air cushion vehicle, or Hovercraft, a number of which are now in operation, and at least one of which can be bought on the open market. Although the vehicle itself will only rise inches above the terrain, the development of a flexible "skirt" has allowed one of the vehicles in operation to clear obstacles up to six feet in height. The Hovercraft is thus indifferent to the surface over which it passes and it can carry a considerable payload. The Saunders Roe SRN2 MKII is presently demonstrating a capacity to haul twelve tons of cargo, and engineers have postulated a 200-ton Hovercraft, a unit which is competitive with small boats. Such vehicles can cruise at 70 or 80 knots and would be able to operate on a river system during all seasons—summer, winter, break-up, and freeze-up.

This advantage should not be underestimated in considering the high capital costs of the vehicle. The Hovercraft could operate over the most elementary trails and roads, and over pre-existing systems of rivers, roads, and railways. It is undoubtedly a vehicle with enormous potential. Attention should be paid to its development and encouragement offered to the manufacturers. After flexibility, not the least important item in its capacity is its ability to load cargo at a warehouse, proceed overland to water or roadway, carry out its main journey, and then ascend the land surface again for direct delivery to the terminal warehouse or consumer, thus saving trans-shipment costs between systems.

In view of the high cost of road construction, the Russian development of *avtozimniki*, or snow roads, is extremely interesting. Over a period of fifty years or more the Russians of Siberia have developed a system of packing down a roadbed over snow which can be used for some five months of the year. In general these snow roads provide access to areas which have no normal roads, and therefore they are particularly valuable. Although no figures for costs are available, it is necessary that these roads be inexpensive, as they are lost with the annual spring thaw. The system is flexible and offers almost unlimited coverage at low costs. Along the rivers of Siberia, snow roads have been used to replace shipping during the period of freeze-up. Up to ten years ago the roads were laid on the river ice as it formed, but since the early 1950's, there has been a tendency to put the snow roads along the river bank since it was found that it was possible to pack a snow road before the river was completely frozen and that the road would last until well after the break-up of ice on the river.

The only parallels in Canada and Alaska have been the trails cleared to allow caterpillar tractor trains to haul heavy supplies to new locations; for example, between the Mackenzie River and Great Bear Lake, and on the Arctic Alaskan slope during oil explorations. It is almost certain that the Russian system is more sophisticated because it has a permanent function: the annual link-up of productive areas with the national transport network, as contrasted with the short-term purposes for which the North American roads were used. However, North Americans need not feel humiliated by the contrast. A Soviet publication of 1958 dealing with *avtozimniki* at length mentions methods of repairing the type of damage resulting from use by horses and carts.

Radio and Telecommunications

An important tool in developing any area is the direct communications system, which supplements transportation routes not only for social purposes but for obtaining urgently required materials at short notice and for reducing problems of inventory stockpiling. It is also a fact of modern life that personal communication is essential to even the most simple business operation. In 1962 the Trans-Canada Telephone System produced an excellent study of communications in northern Canada. The study pointed out that the Yukon Territory is served by the Canadian National Telecommunications group and that the latter are expanding facilities in the Mackenzie area of the western Arctic where work is to begin soon on a pole line to Inuvik. Teletype service is already available in such communities as Whitehorse, Dawson, and Fort Smith. There must obviously be a good communications system linking the DEW Line stations, but, generally speaking, the eastern Arctic, a larger and less coherent region, is less completely served, with the notable exceptions of Cambridge Bay, Cape Parry, Cape Dyer, Frobisher Bay, Hall Lake, and Resolution Island. The latter are connected to telephone networks by microwave or tropospheric scatter systems, and Rankin Inlet, Asbestos Hill, and Southampton Island are connected to the general network via high-frequency radios. There are small local exchanges at a large number of communities, but they are not connected to the national system.

The leasing of specialized high-frequency radio equipment to field parties and projects in the North has been a recent development. With this equipment the user can make direct radio contact with an appropriate exchange service and thus get access to the national network. Although there are some obvious limitations to the method, mainly concerned with transmission conditions, the system has been used successfully by several companies, notably Bell Telephone of Canada, in providing support for the Baffinland Iron Company at Mary's River in North Baffin Island. Bell of Canada also took over the telephone system in Resolute Bay during 1964.

The Trans-Canada Telephone System study points out that there are two basic handicaps to development of communications systems in the North, the first being the small size of the total market. Although it may seem striking at first to learn that there are 12,000 telephones north of 60°, this figure is hardly an inducement to companies to make major investments. The second handicap is that even this small market is a shifting one, as illustrated by the fact that there were, for example, only 45 gold mines in Canada in 1962 as opposed to 144 in 1940. Many of the communities to be served are in fact ephemeral.

The biggest advance in communication ability has occurred when there has been a military requirement (such as the DEW Line), and defence funds have been available. Communications systems are then used by civilian contractors involved in the defence activities. Whether or not the defence demand is ephemeral hardly matters, since the existence of the northern communication routes must inevitably benefit the majority of the citizens in the North.

It is interesting to note that there are working in the Canadian North many small and several quite substantial non-commercial systems, not linked to the public networks. These include the very widespread system of the Department of Transport, almost 100 stations of the Hudson's Bay Company, and a provincial Department of Natural Resources radio system operated by the Saskatchewan government. In addition, there are considerable numbers of small parties, and semi-permanent stations, like the Devon Island Base of the Arctic Institute of North America, that utilize high-frequency radio and address themselves only to a single centre of communication from which messages may be relayed.

In Alaska the major part of the communication system is, perhaps surprisingly, government operated. Apart from the highly sophisticated "White Alice" system, a defence network with 3,100 miles of tropospheric scatter connections, the adequacy compares with that in Canada. In Greenland, apart from town phone exchanges, communication is by high-frequency radio. Little is known of the Soviet systems but there is reason to believe they are relatively primitive outside the large communities. Most northern stations use radio, and until the late '50's, at any rate, public information and even private messages were sometimes sent over public-service broadcast stations.

Air Transportation

While the greatest bulk and the essential basis of Arctic supplies have been waterborne, the most significant new development has been the widespread use of aircraft. Aircraft have opened up interior regions and vastly increased mobility over the entire area. By means of aerial photo surveys and survey reconnaissance techniques they have also speeded acquisition of knowledge of recently unknown lands, and hence directly fostered development.

In the Soviet Union a number of northern cities have regular scheduled services and it is probable that a very large number of smaller communities have less regular but frequent contact. All services are provided by the national airline, Aeroflot, which maintains aircraft for every function, from main-line jet service to bush charters and even polar expeditions. The Russian claim to be the first to introduce aeroplanes into the Arctic with Nagurski's flights of 1914 in Novaya Zemlya is almost certainly valid.

In the years after 1924, contact was maintained by air with a number of northern settlements (using a significant number of women pilots), but the routes generally followed existing river systems and worked out of airstrips, however primitive. In the late 1930's Russia excelled in polar flying, making significant transpolar flights, and established the famous expedition North Pole I entirely by air. Soviet pilots have displayed a remarkable attitude to landing on sea-ice, as witness the rescue of survivors from the Chelyuskin in 1934 by large and ungainly four-engine bomber aircraft. It is startling for anyone familiar with Canadian bush flying to see films of twin turbo-prop tricycle under-carriaged aircraft in normal Aeroflot livery landing on floes of the polar

pack in apparently routine operations, or helicopters flying in mid-
winter darkness at drifting ice stations near the pole. A variety of aircraft on wheels, skis, and floats are used, as well as advanced-design
helicopters, but it is difficult to get descriptions of the unusual types,
and the total numbers may be quite small.

In Canada, aircraft were relatively late in reaching the Arctic, but
as soon as bush planes became numerous in Quebec and Ontario during
the late '20's there was an immediate spread into the north. The numerous lakes and waterways invited invasion by floatplanes, and by 1929
floatplanes were prospecting and surveying to the northern limits of the
mainland and probing beyond. Very soon ski-wheel aircraft were exploiting similar environments when they were frozen over in winter, and a
tradition of northern flying evolved which is different in character from
the Russian tradition. There are numerous small companies which exist
only to provide charter services, usually departing from points along
three regular scheduled northern routes operated by three rather larger
companies.

A further development has been the big-wheeled, very small aircraft
which will land almost anywhere any time, and will perform much more
cheaply tasks that had previously called for helicopters. The world's
northernmost scheduled airline runs to Resolute, NWT. Considering
Canada's large civilian helicopter fleets, it is probable that in numbers
and versatility Canada is a world leader in northern flying. Canada
also makes the only planes specifically designed and sold for northern
operation: de Havilland's Beaver, Otter, and Caribou.

In Alaska, development followed a similar pattern but in a less
favourable environment, so that the number of planes and pilots has
not been so large; in fact commercial planes were probably outnumbered
by private aircraft in the 1960's. In another sector, however, Alaska
is markedly advanced. Because of its position, Alaska provided a base
or a goal for many of the early spectacular flights such as the flights of
Hubert Wilkins, the airship transits of the polar basin, and Chukalov's
over-flight from the USSR to California. Today these large long-distance
aircraft in transit have been replaced by the USA-Oriental flights using
great circle routes with landings at Anchorage or Fairbanks. There is
also considerable military flying. Access to Alaska for passengers is
usually by plane from the US West Coast. The US Air Force, incidentally,
also operates a number of transport planes in polar environments,
together with search and rescue operations of astonishing versatility.
A real achievement has been the operation of such large planes as the
C-130 from sea-ice and snow-fields.

PART III: CONCLUSIONS

So much for an outline of the Arctic's economy and transportation networks. It is clear that a number of factors occur again and again, and that a realistic appraisal of the Arctic areas should be based on these recurring factors rather than on any one of the potential resources themselves. After all, statistically the land has an average value per square mile that approximates the value of land elsewhere. It is the exploitation that is the problem.

First and foremost among the factors to be considered is the notion that the Arctic is "another country." Slavin describes Northeast Siberia as an "island." Arctic supplies for Canada travel by ship and by air except along the new Yellowknife road. Alaska is only reached from the United States via ship, plane, or a road through another country. Greenland is remote from Denmark, as is Spitzbergen from Norway. This characteristic of the Arctic alone is enough to give pause to economists and planners. It is much easier to develop primitive land within your operational boundaries than it is to reach beyond the zone of development with its railroads, roads, and other services shared by the national community.

Second, it has become obvious that so far in most cases exploitation has been for materials of strategic importance or with a high scarcity value to the nation concerned: uranium and gold in Canada; nickel, gold, and diamonds in the USSR; coal in Norway; cryolite in Denmark. In Alaska it seems to be otherwise until we consider the military establishment—Alaska's biggest cash resource—and it then becomes clear that the (probably reluctant) activity is enforced by the unique quality of location. In all Arctic areas, resources other than those with scarcity value have been ruthlessly "hygraded," only the richest being used.

Third, emphasis has been placed on the high costs of transportation in the North. Even the Soviet literature expresses concern about "high costs," and the new wave of economic justification has caused cutbacks in Soviet long-range planning. This notion bears amplification since it probably holds the key to development.

First of all, the high costs of one particular and important northern activity, mining, are not due solely to transportation. Mr. W. K. Buck of Canada's Department of Mines and Technical Surveys has produced the following breakdown of a $4.75 penalty on every ton of ore mined in the Arctic: $1.00 for transport costs; $1.00 for power supply; $1.00

for inducement pay and associated costs of labour; $1.00 for increased capital investment; 50¢ to maintain an inventory that would support a remote operation; and 25¢ for added heating costs. It should be noted, however, that a number of these costs turn again on transport; e.g., an element in the high cost of heating is the high cost of transport for fuel. The need for a large inventory is a direct reflection of the inadequacy of the transport system, and both capital and labour premiums are indirect reflections of the remoteness. Power may or may not involve transported fuels. It would be fair to guess that about one-half of the penalty reflects transportation costs. The other half represents the cost of pioneering.

Facilities in a city cost less because they are shared among a number of consumers. A pioneer enterprise must provide its own consumers. There are no existing roads; no trucking service to rent, lease, or use; no railway express; no scheduled public air service; no food and clothing retail outlets; no dormitory township for labour. All these items demand increased capital investment by the operation to supply the deficits, and represent investment costs that do not affect new industries in, say, Hamilton or Toronto. Although it has been pointed out that these costs are in turn increased by transportation costs, they should not be confused with them. They represent true pioneering costs, the cost of an extension of the national capacity; and, depending upon the adequacy of the solution, they should be so regarded.

A single enterprise can provide the stepping-stone for a long-lived community. One could quote, as examples, Yellowknife and, not Schefferville, but its economic satellite Seven Islands, which now has a population twice that of Schefferville and has become Canada's second export port in terms of tonnage handled. This contribution to the national economic capacity should be taken into account in considering relations between such an enterprise and all levels of government. It is particularly worth noting that this whole problem is not Arctic in nature—*it is universal for undeveloped areas.* At a recent seminar on communications in Montreal, M. Chauvet of Petropar compared his new problems in Arctic Canada with his old ones in the Sahara.

As to transportation itself, there is no serious technological problem. That is not to say that there is no room for improvement in terms of technique or reductions of cost, but rather that the present scarcity of systems is an economic and not a mechanical problem. This is borne out by the communist withdrawal of plans for rail systems in the Soviet Northeast. Dr. O. M. Solandt of C.N.R. has given figures for road and rail construction. In most parts of Canada a development road can be built for $40,000 to $70,000 a mile. By contrast a branch railway costs between $100,000 and $250,000 a mile depending on its sophistication and the terrain. Once built, however, it has a clear superiority over other modes of transportation, given enough traffic. Such a line could handle more than ten million tons of traffic per year at 1¢ per ton-mile, and a train using it could haul 10,000 tons at a time with a three-man crew—the equivalent of some 300 large trucks and their drivers. Unfortunately, in order to break even, a longer railroad (say one hundred miles) would have to operate near capacity if the Royal Commission on Transportation figures of 100,000 net ton-miles of traffic per mile per year is acceptable.

To emphasize the problem of capital in the North it is worth paraphrasing Dr. Solandt once again. For a 100-mile railroad costing $17,-500,000 and hauling 200,000 tons per year, the interest alone would amount to ½¢ per ton-mile. (Solandt, 1961, p. 97.) While this might not concern a Soviet planner in the same way, it is certain that he would still inhibit investment if he regarded interest charges for what they really are—the cost of lost opportunities elsewhere.

Most writers emphasize that the transportation problem in the North demands a variety of answers. Railroads tend to serve a limited number of points and are inflexible. Trucks have limited capacity but make good distributing agents. Boats, although cheap on a per-mile basis, are restricted by the seasons. Aircraft, particularly bush-planes, have high mobility and flexibility but are restricted to small payloads and expensive mileage so that they presently handle only expensive, small loads, mainly people. The planner should look deeper than the actual vehicle technique to less romantic but more practical aspects of the transportation problem.

The biggest single operation cost of transportation in an area without facilities is handling. Accordingly, transfers from boat to truck to plane, or boat to beach to truck to warehouse, should be discouraged. When goods are perishable, the need for protection against the environment compounds the cost, and the bill for heating warehouse inventories over long periods is a major one for any Arctic concern down to the level of the housewife. Some stations may only receive one resupply per year, and problems of short-term labour, handling, storage, and bookkeeping costs are all considerable. Studies should be made similar to those which induced the U.S. Army to maintain central warehouses in the home country and resupply bases by air-express overseas at a saving of millions of dollars per annum. Some European motor manufacturers use the same technique to enable dealers in North America to operate with a minimal stock of spares, and Western Electric has gone even further by using a central computer system which can be consulted from the DEW Line by teletype and, without human intervention, suggest possible redistribution from a variety of stores along DEW Line, thus eliminating duplicating stores at every site and materially reducing the total value of spares necessary. The system depends, of course, on regular aircraft connections between sites.

The type of thinking just summarized may be more rewarding than any foreseeable technical development. An ideal system would maintain a steady annual flow and eliminate stockpiling. Service should be available weekly or even daily, and supplies should be handled as little as possible. Piggyback trailers trucked from railhead to waterway on the Mackenzie are a good start on this technique, but it should be carried further, possibly to include aircraft operations, and certainly over a wider area. Victory in the race may ultimately go to a service operating in this way rather than to any one restricted service, however cheap of itself.

The primary and generally unappreciated advantage of a Hovercraft over all other systems in the North is that it could move from warehouse to warehouse. As a tender to a ship it could come off the sea over ice (eliminating time often lost by current icebreaker-convoy techniques) and over the beach direct to its land destination, in contrast to the present situation where supplies may be transferred from ship to a tender, from the tender to the beach, from the beach to a truck, and from the truck to a warehouse. It is in these prosaic operations rather than in its glamorously radical principles that a Hovercraft offers a future. The Hovercraft is, however, incidentally and contrary to popular opinion, an efficient and economical device in pure mechanical terms.

Secondary to this idea, but still prior to actual vehicle development, should be the idea of reduction of weight in the materials of living. Canadian enterprises in the Arctic import up to 19 tons per man-year in supplies to maintain life and operations. Lauritzen boats took more freight *in* to the mine at Mestersvig than they brought out. We have mentioned Russian searches for gas that can be exposed by lightweight equipment, and the deliberate decentralization of the manufacture of heavy mine equipment to factories in, for example, the Magadan Region. Canada has exploited this notion in only one area—the oil refinery at Norman Wells, and even there only limited use is made of the oil, by-products are not used at all, and all additives are brought in from the South.

This brings us to the great paradox in Canadian Arctic operations.

In an area where the most modern and sophisticated equipment is required, many activities actually possess outdated, even old-fashioned equipment. The RCAF only recently updated the transport aircraft it uses in the North. DOT stations are not remarkable for their modern vehicles; and housing, with a very few brilliant exceptions, has been stereotyped and limited in its function. The situation is more striking in the case of civil airlines. Canada should take pride in having the northern lines now in operation, including the world's northernmost scheduled airline. But all these lines operate outdated aircraft from primitive facilities. This does not mean the aircraft are unsafe or unreliable; their record ranks with the best on that score. But in areas which demand extra efficiency they lack the refinements and cost reductions of more modern planes; and they even operate at a penalty. C-46's, C-47's and DC-4's are still to be seen in regular service in the North. This is because of their low capital cost. Because of the uncertainty about our Arctic future, and because of the ephemeral nature of demand, there are no investors willing to put out enough capital to ensure much better returns by using the modern aircraft employed on lucrative southern runs, and none willing to provide cost-reducing modern handling and storage facilities. It is safer to make a modest profit in an operation that can be wound up at short notice relatively painlessly. The same applies in general to the Mackenzie River barge operations and even the DOT marine operations equipment, in spite of the extremely good new "breakers" like the "Sir John A. Macdonald."

This "timidity" may represent pure Canadian horse-sense if events show no progress in Arctic areas as a whole. The process will have been disastrous, however, if any other northern government is successful. The real problem is the matter of inducement to capital. No Arctic area has easy access to the gross national investment of any country. Low train fares, private cars, cheap and varied food, movie shows and coffee houses, space flight, and Disneyland are only available to a population which has access to a large national investment. A Canadian in the South commands the service of a railroad network representing billions of dollars of capital for only cents a mile, and can move as little or as much as he likes whenever it suits him. Because the Arctic is "another land," the same is not true of the North. If it were true, the northlands would surely have at least equal potential with Canada's southern lands. Canadian ingenuity devoted to solving this particular problem would not only enrich the nation but provide an example that would almost certainly be applicable to underdeveloped areas anywhere in the world. Nowhere on earth does a small nation of such individual wealth have such a large virgin territory, and nowhere is there such an opportunity for an exercise in rational geography that could benefit great numbers of humanity by example.

REFERENCES

ARMSTRONG, T. E., "Mining in the Soviet Arctic," *The Polar Record*, vol. 10, no. 64 (1960).
———"Soviet Terms for the North of the USSR," *The Polar Record*, vol. 10, no. 69 (1961).
GAKKEL', Ya. Ya., "The Exploration and Development of Polard Lands," *Soviet Geography: Accomplishments and Tasks*, published in translation by American Geographical Society as Occasional Publication no. 1, New York, 1962.
GOULD, L. M., *The Polar Regions in their Relation to Human Affairs*, New York, 1958.
ROGERS, G. W., *The Future of Alaska*, Baltimore, 1962.
SIVERTZ, B. G., "The North as a Region," *Resources for Tomorrow—Background Papers*, vol. I, Ottawa, 1961.
SLAVIN, S. V., "The Soviet North," *Queen's Quarterly*, vol. LXVI. no. 4, 1960.
SOLANDT, O. M., "Railways and Trucking," *Proceedings—Second National Northern Development Conference*, Edmonton, 1961.
TARACOUZIO, T. A., *Soviets in the Arctic*, New York, 1938.
Trans-Canada Telephone System, *A Study of Communications in Northern Canada*, Montreal, 1962.
VITYAZEVA, V. A., "Questions of the Integrated Utilization of the Natural Resources of the Komi ASSR," *Soviet Geography—Review and Translation*, vol. II, no. 2 (1961).

The Administration of
Northern Peoples: The USSR

◄ TERENCE ARMSTRONG* ►

IT MUST BE SAID at once that the Soviet treatment of minority peoples
in the north is a hazardous topic for any western commentator. The
Soviet system of government is claimed by its practitioners to be the
most enlightened in the world. It is especially important that the claim
should appear to be substantiated in this particular field of administration, for two reasons: the treatment of minorities in general, and
primitive minorities in particular, is a subject on which there were
solemn pronouncements by Lenin himself, involving fundamental principles of sociology, and these pronouncements later acquired the status
of dogma; and—a more practical consideration—there are minority
peoples in many countries, and the Soviet Union would like to make a
strong appeal to them. The Soviet government thus has compelling
reasons for painting a rosy picture, and at the same time no non-Soviet
observer has been permitted to study any of the northern peoples since
certainly the 1930's, probably earlier. So Soviet publications, constituting
the main, virtually the only, source material, are not likely to present
much which is unflattering to government policy, and the outsider seeking to determine the truth has no way to check his findings. This chapter
has been written because some, at least, of the material is straightforward
matter of fact and unlikely to be disputed, and because there is little
else in English to which a serious enquirer may turn. Almost the only
thing, in fact, is the Dunns' very useful analysis, published in 1963[1];

*Scott Polar Research Institute, Cambridge, England.
[1]Stephen P. Dunn and Ethel Dunn, "The transformation of economy and culture in the Soviet North," *Arctic Anthropology*, vol. 1, no. 2 (Madison, 1963),
pp. 1–28.

but this is primarily a study of cultural change occurring in the northern peoples, and is not directly concerned with administration as such.

It is necessary to generalize on many points, because to discuss separately the experience of each people would require too much space. Corroborative detail is lost in the process of generalizing (there is some, fortunately, to be found in the Dunns' paper), but this is not the only drawback. A spurious sense of uniformity, or evenness in treatment and experience, may be imparted. So the reader is invited to be on his guard.

The sources are given in detail in the footnotes. I should mention here that I have drawn heavily, by courtesy of the publisher, on a recent work of my own.[2]

THE PEOPLES

There are a number of minority peoples in the North of the Soviet Union. How many of them should be included here is a matter of opinion, for there is no one generally accepted southern limit of "the North." A Soviet term in common administrative usage, "the small peoples of the North," includes several peoples on the lower Amur, which is rather far south, and excludes the two largest peoples, the Komi and the Yakut. It seems reasonable, therefore, to include these two, and exclude the Amur peoples, while retaining the rest of those understood by the Soviet term. On this basis, the peoples number nineteen: the Aleut, Chukchi, Dolgan, Entsy, Eskimo, Kamchadal, Ket, Khanty, Komi, Koryak, Lamut, Lapp, Mansi, Nentsy, Nganasan, Sel'kup, Tungus, Yakut and Yukagir. Some are tundra dwellers, inhabitants of the true Arctic, but most are forest dwellers in the sub-Arctic.

A word on nomenclature is necessary. In the early 1930's the Soviet authorities renamed many of these peoples, often replacing the old name with a self-designation. Some of the new names eliminate ambiguities, or permit more accurate identification, and so are useful, but others have failed to gain acceptance, even in the Soviet Union. Both names are given, but it is necessary to prefer one for ordinary use in the text (as in the preceding paragraph). The choice has been determined by common sense, and without seeking to impose consistency. Names are given in the singular, unless the plural is better known (for instance, Chukchi rather than Chukcha).

[2]T. E. Armstrong, *Russian Settlement in the North*, Scott Polar Research Institute Special Publication No. 3 (Cambridge, Eng., 1965), especially chapter 10 and appendix 1.

The population figures given are those of the 1959 census. They are summarized, with additional information, in Table I. Under the census regulations, each individual could declare and thus determine his own nationality. The location of the peoples at the same date is shown in Map 1.

Nearest the Finnish frontier are the Lapps, called in Russian Lopari, or more recently Saami. Throughout the period of Russian settlement, that is since the twelfth century, they have lived in Kol'skiy Poluostrov, the peninsula of Kola. The Lapps in Soviet territory speak the same dialect as those in northern Finland, Sweden, and Norway, but they are the smallest of the four groups, numbering 1,760 out of some 30,000. The Lappish language is one of the West Finnic group, part of the Finno-Ugrian language family. The Russian Lapps are either reindeer herders, or fishers, or both, and have tended to keep to the interior of the peninsula. In Soviet times there has been a great increase of the Russian population in the region, and little is now heard of the small Lapp community, of whom nearly 30 per cent regarded Russian as their native language in 1959.

Across the entrance to the White Sea to the east lies the Pechora basin, the national home of the Komi, formerly called Zyryans, the largest people in the North. For eight centuries or more they have lived on the northward-flowing Pechora and the southward-flowing Vychegda, and since the fourteenth century they have recognized Russian dominion over their territory. They number 283,000 (this total excludes their cousins, the Komi-Permyaki, who live further south and number 140,000). Their language is one of the Permian group, another member of the Finno-Ugrian family. Thanks to pioneer linguistic work by St. Stephen of Perm, who died in 1396, a few Komi became literate in the fifteenth century, and there is now quite a considerable literature in the language. The Komi are primarily an agricultural people, but in the North some of them are hunters and reindeer herders.

To the north and east of the Komi live the peoples who used to be called Samoyed, and whose language group still has that name (the Samoyed languages make up, together with the Finno-Ugrian family, the Uralian language stock). There are four northern peoples in this group: the Nentsy (22,800), formerly called Yurak or simply Samoyed, the Nganasan (720), formerly Tavgi Samoyed, the Entsy (350), formerly Yenisey Samoyed, and the Sel'kup (3,700), formerly Ostyak Samoyed. The correspondence between old and new terms is not always exact. The peoples hunt, fish and herd reindeer in the tundra along

TABLE I

THE NORTHERN PEOPLES OF THE SOVIET UNION, 1959*

People	Population living in or near their homelands[a]	Percentage who consider their national language as their native language	Administrative region in which most live	No. in region mentioned, and percentage the national group forms of the total population of that region	
1. Lapp	1,760	70	Murmanskaya Oblast'	1,687	0.03
2. Nentsy	22,845	85	Nenetskiy Nats. Okrug	4,957	10.9
			Yamalo-Nenetskiy Nats. Okrug	13,977	22.4
			Taymyrskiy Nats. Okrug	1,878	5.6
3. Nganasan	721		Taymyrskiy Nats. Okrug	682	2
4. Entsy	not listed[b]	97			
5. Komi	282,780	89	Komi ASSR	245,074	30.4
6. Khanty	19,246	77	Khanty-Mansiyskiy Nats. Okrug	11,435	9.2
7. Mansi	6,318	59	Khanty-Mansiyskiy Nats. Okrug	5,644	4.6
8. Sel'kup	3,704	50	scattered		
9. Ket	1,017	78	scattered		
10. Dolgan	not listed[b]				
11. Tungus	24,583	56	Evenkiyskiy Nats. Okrug	3,474	33.7
			Yakutskaya ASSR	9,505	2
12. Lamut	9,023	81	Yakutskaya ASSR	3,537	0.7
			Magadanskaya Oblast'	2,780	0.8
13. Yakut	236,125	97	Yakutskaya ASSR	226,053	46.4
14. Yukagir	440	52	scattered		
15. Chukchi	11,680	93	Chukotskiy Nats. Okrug	9,975	21.4
16. Koryak	6,168	90	Koryakskiy Nats. Okrug	5,101	18.5
17. Kamchadal	1,096	36	Koryakskiy Nats. Okrug	900	3.3
18. Eskimo	1,111	85	Chukotskiy Nats. Okrug	1,064	2.3
19. Aleut	399	22	Chukotskiy Nats. Okrug		
	629,016				

*Main source for Table I: *Itogi vsesoyuznoy perepisi naseleniya 1959 goda. RSFSR. (Results of the all-Union census of population of 1959, RSFSR.)* (Moscow, 1963), pp. 300-302, 321-37. The totals for the USSR are slightly higher. The former are given here, since they exclude at least some of the northern peoples living away from their northern homelands, and are thus the nearest possible approach to the totals "living in or near their homelands."

[a] The population figures given are the totals living within the RSFSR.

[b] Apparently errors of enumeration. The present number of Entsy is believed to be 350, and of Dolgan, 3,900. (*Trudy Instituta Etnografii im. N. N. Mikiukho-Maklaya: Novaya Seriya*, Tom 84, 1963, pp. 33, 92.)

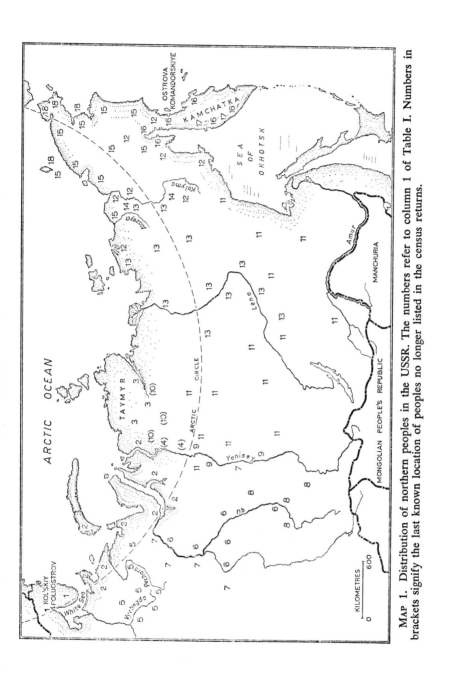

MAP 1. Distribution of northern peoples in the USSR. The numbers refer to column 1 of Table I. Numbers in brackets signify the last known location of peoples no longer listed in the census returns.

the coast from the White Sea to Taymyr. The Nganasan, living on Taymyr, hunt wild reindeer in addition to the other pursuits. They are the most northerly indigenous inhabitants of the Soviet Union. The Entsy, a very small group, are being rapidly assimilated by their neighbours, but their absence from the 1959 census returns was apparently a mistake by the enumerators. The Sel'kup, although Samoyed linguistically, are more like their neighbours the Khanty in their way of life, reindeer herding being known only among some of them, and in those cases learnt from their northern neighbours. Half the Sel'kup regarded Russian as their native language in 1959.

The Khanty, formerly Ostyak, are probably the descendants of the Ugrians of the early Russian accounts, who lived in the Pechora basin and later moved eastwards across the Ural range to the lower Ob' region, where the Khanty are found today. They number 19,250. Their language is one of the Ugrian group (which includes Magyar), part of the Finno-Ugrian family. The people were originally hunters and fishers, and they acquired an interest in reindeer herding from their northern neighbours. They were for long not distinguished from their closer neighbours, the Mansi or Vogul (6,300), to whom they are related and with whom they share many aspects of their culture. The two languages closely resemble each other.

The Ket, also known as the Yenisey Ostyak or Yeniseian, live on the middle Yenisey. They have no ethnic link with their neighbours (which made the old name of Yenisey Ostyak misleading), and their language is now classed with the Palaeosiberian complex, the other members of which live much further east (the term Palaeosiberian, or, as some scholars prefer, Palaeoasiatic, is used to designate a number of languages which belong to no other group; most have little or no relationship to each other). The Ket number 1,000. They are the only survivors of a group of peoples speaking related languages, the others—Kot, Asan, and Arin—having been assimilated by their neighbours. The ancestors of the Ket probably came from the south. They were primarily hunters and secondarily fishers. Reindeer were used for transport. Under Soviet rule fur farming has been introduced.

Continuing eastwards, the next group of peoples encountered are the Tungus. The Tungus themselves are a very wide-ranging people, found also in the Manchurian provinces of China and the Mongolian Peoples' Republic. Because they are distributed between several countries, it is convenient to retain the old name of Tungus, rather than adopt the new Soviet term Evenk, which is the self-designation of the northern branch. The word Tungus is still used in Soviet literature for the language group of the Tungus and related peoples (as in the case of the word Samoyed), a group which forms, with Manchu, one of the main subdivisions of the Altaic family. The Tungus people number 24,600 and are spread thinly over an enormous area between Taymyr on the Arctic Ocean, the Sea of Okhotsk, and the Amur river. The northern Tungus are nomadic reindeer herders and hunters, while the southern Tungus farm cattle and horses. As the map shows, a large part of the territory in which Tungus are found is also inhabited by the numerically much stronger Yakut, so that it is not surprising that in the 1959 census a third of all Tungus in the Soviet Union considered Yakut to be their native language.

The culture and language of the Lamut (new Soviet appellation Even) are closely similar to those of the Tungus, and some ethnologists have felt that the two should not be separated. The Lamut, numbering 9,000, live on the shores of the Sea of Okhotsk and the Arctic Ocean. The name itself is derived from the Tungus word for sea. The Dolgan (3,900) are another small group of Tungus origin, and are also reindeer herders and hunters. They live in the southern part of Taymyr and on the lower Yenisey. They have all adopted the Yakut language, a fact which has often caused them to be confused with the Yakut and has presumably led to their absence from the 1959 census returns.

The Yakut, 236,000 strong, are the second most numerous of the Soviet northern peoples. They speak a Turkic language. It has generally been thought that they moved northwards into their present territory of the middle Lena basin not long before the Russians arrived in the seventeenth century, but recent archaeological evidence casts some doubt on this. They have apparently for long had horses and cattle, and only a minority in the north have been reindeer herders. They have always done well as traders. The unusual fact has been noted that in mixed Yakut-Russian communities, the Yakut language often proved the dominant one, and the Russian inhabitants even in some cases forgot their own language. There is a considerable literature in Yakut, based on the important linguistic studies commenced, mainly by Russian exiles, in the second half of the nineteenth century.

To the north-east of the Yakut live the Yukagir, sometimes called in Soviet usage Odul, a people who have seen better days. When the Russians first reached their lands three centuries ago, the Yukagir occupied a wide belt of tundra between the Lena and the Anadyr'. But their numbers and territory have shrunk, and now the people no longer

have an ethnic unity. There has been much assimilation into neighbouring Lamut, Yakut, and Russian groups, and of those 440 who still
called themselves Yukagir in 1959, a third regarded Russian as their
native language. Their own language is classed with the Palaeosiberian
complex. They were chiefly hunters and fishers when the first Russians
arrived, but reindeer herding was also practised, this evidently being
an innovation borrowed from the Lamut, and it gained in importance.

The Chukchi, or, as they were for a short time called in Soviet usage,
Luorovetlan, have lived in the extreme northeast tip of Asia for as
long as there has been any contact with the Russians. Their language is
one of the Palaeosiberian complex, and is related to those of their
neighbours, the Koryak and Kamchadal. They number 11,700. Most
are reindeer herders, following their herds in the tundra as far west
as the Alazeya, but about a third of the people have always lived a
settled life on the coast, fishing and hunting sea mammals. The Chukchi
offered more resistance to the Russians than most northern peoples, and
for this reason, as well as their remoteness, they became Russian
subjects only in 1789, nearly a century and a half after the first contacts.

Living in small enclaves within the Chukchi territory are the Asiatic
Eskimo, called in Russian Eskimos, numbering 1,100. These are the
only representatives in the Soviet Union of the most widespread of all
Arctic peoples. Their language is related to those of the other Eskimo,
but most closely to those of the south Alaskan Eskimo groups. The
Asiatic Eskimo were, and remain, sea mammal hunters.

Neighbours of the Chukchi to the south are the Koryak, for a short
period called by their self-designation Nymylan in Soviet literature.
They have lived on or about the isthmus of the Kamchatka peninsula
since first contact with the Russians, but were wider spread along the
shores of the Okhotsk and Bering Seas in the seventeenth and eighteenth
centuries than they are now. They, too, resisted the Russians fiercely,
and many Russian pioneers were ambushed and killed in their territory.
They number 6,200, and their language is related to Chukchi and Kamchadal. They are reindeer herders, hunters of sea mammals, fishers, and
fur hunters. The sedentary groups, mainly in coastal settlements, have
been skilled dog drivers.

The more southerly part of Kamchatka is the home of the Kamchadal.
They are normally called Itel'men in Soviet usage, but the correspondence is not always exact, since Kamchadal is used by some ethnologists
to denote the Russian-aboriginal métis, who now greatly outnumber those
of purer native stock (1,100). Kamchadal was also sometimes used in

the eighteenth and nineteenth century to mean descendants of early Russian settlers. The aboriginals were a true fishing people, and had no domestic animal except the dog. They have now become hard to distinguish from the Russian "old settlers." In 1959 nearly two thirds of them regarded Russian as their native language.

Finally, there are the Aleut, one of the smallest peoples (400), sometimes called in Soviet usage by their self-designation Unangan. Most Aleut live outside the Soviet Union on the Aleutian Islands, which became United States territory in 1867. Some, however, were introduced to the uninhabited Komandorskiye Ostrova (Commander Islands) by the Russian-American Company in 1825 or 1826 in order to exploit fur resources, and these islands remained Russian. The descendants of the original settlers, augmented by further importations of Aleut, Eskimo, and others, are still there. The Aleut physical type predominates, but the language, which is closely related to Eskimo, does not, for in 1959 over three quarters of the Aleut regarded Russian as their native language. The Aleut were primarily sea mammal hunters, but learnt to hunt on land also. Both occupations continue today, together with some agriculture.

The combined total of these peoples in 1959 was 630,000. The administrative areas in which they lived had a total population of 2,700,-000, so that the northern peoples, taken together, were in a minority of one to three.

RELATIONS WITH THE STATE SINCE 1917

For any adequate comprehension of how these peoples are faring today, some outline of their experiences at least since the advent of Soviet power is necessary. It would be possible to go back further, to their first contact with the Russians in the twelfth to seventeenth centuries. But the purpose of this essay is not primarily historical. All that need be said here is that in the period of the tsars, while the official attitude towards these peoples was mild and humane, the administration was so ineffective that they were in practice neglected, and were taken advantage of by any unscrupulous traders who came along.

The main source for this section is the basic Soviet work on the subject, M. A. Sergeyev's *Non-Capitalist Path of Development of the*

Small Peoples of the North, published in 1955.[3] The prime object of that very full account is to demonstrate how these peoples are advancing to socialism direct from their primitive state, by-passing the capitalist stage through which more advanced societies pass. This is one of the great theoretical issues referred to at the beginning of the chapter,[4] and the conclusions that the work will reach, therefore, are never for a moment in doubt. But the author does bring a great deal of factual material into his argument, and there is no reason to suppose that much of this is not perfectly trustworthy. The Komi and the Yakut, however, are not included in this study, presumably because their more advanced culture made their problems rather different from those of the smaller peoples. Unless the contrary is stated, this work of Sergeyev's (pp. 213–409) may be taken to be the source of any statement of fact about the small peoples.

From its earliest days, the Soviet government was aware of the problems posed by the minority peoples in its territory—these peoples were both numerous and turbulent—and always had a more or less definite policy which it was trying to implement. Within two weeks of the October Revolution in 1917, the Declaration of Rights of the Peoples of Russia was issued, proclaiming the equality of all peoples and the free development of national minorities. This document is still referred to in the Soviet literature, but is not very easy to find—perhaps because it voices some sentiments no longer acceptable, such as the election of generals by their troops (Armstrong, 1965, appendix 4). The Commissar for Nationalities, responsible for putting the Declaration into effect, was Stalin.

At first the political situation was such that there was little opportunity to implement the policy anywhere in the country, and none at all in the North. For the northern peoples, the first step was taken in 1922, when a section was set up within the Commissariat to deal specifically with them, because it was already clear that their problems were rather different from those of other minorities. This section's activity had the following objectives: to organize a system of administration suitable to the cultural background of the peoples; to protect them from exploitation; to provide them with the means of production, clothes, and food; to

---

[3]M. A. Sergeyev, "Nekapitalisticheskiy put' razvitiya malykh narodov severa" ("Non-Capitalist Path of Development of the Small Peoples of the North"), *Trudy Instituta Etncgrafii imeni N. N. Miklukho-Maklaya, Novaya Seriya,* Tom 27, 1955, pp. 569.

[4]V. I. Lenin, *Polnoye Sobraniye Sochineniy,* izdaniye 5-oye (*Full Collected Works,* 5th edition), Tom 41, 1963, pp. 245–46.

regulate use of hunting and fishing grounds, and of reindeer pastures; and to initiate all-round study of these peoples, with a view to determining the best way of introducing them to socialism. Quite energetic and far-reaching action was taken in these directions, and an important part was played by the Commissariat's journal *Zhizn' Natsional'nostey* (Life of the Nationalities) in drawing attention to problems and communicating the results of field investigations.

It was at this early period that suggestions were put forward by some leading Russian ethnologists, such as V. G. Bogoraz and V. K. Arsen'yev, for creating "native reservations," to which non-natives would be denied access. This proposal was not accepted at the time, and is strongly disapproved by Sergeyev, who makes quite clear his view that any preservation of the separate entity of northern peoples achieved by such methods is much less important (if important at all) than the march to socialism, shoulder to shoulder with the Russian people.

In 1924 the Commissariat of Nationalities was abolished in connection with the new constitution, but the work of the section concerned with the northern peoples was continued on what turned out to be a larger scale by a special committee created in that year. This was the Committee of Assistance to the Peoples of the North (Komitet sodeystviya narod-nostyam severnykh okrain), to give it its full title, but it was normally known as the Committee of the North (Komitet severa). Because the Commissariat no longer existed, this Committee was made directly responsible to the Central Executive Committee, the supreme executive body, and it had executive powers. The Chairman was a leading Party figure and a Deputy Chairman of the Central Executive Committee, P. G. Smidovich, who had no previous connection with the north, but the members were highly-placed administrators and anthropologists (including V. G. Bogoraz, P. Ye. Ostrovskikh, and L. Ya. Shternberg) who had specialized in these peoples. It was an influential body, and its activities during the eleven years of its existence (1924–35) were of great importance. The main task was envisaged as trying to get the peoples of the north to help themselves. This was very difficult at first, in view of the lack of detailed information about their situation and their needs. The Committee thus always saw its function as a double one: to carry out and stimulate study of the peoples, as well as to introduce and implement measures designed to help them materially. A good idea of the Committee's scope and work may be derived from study of its journals *Severnaya Aziya* (*North Asia*), which it published jointly with a learned society from 1925 to 1929, and *Sovetskiy Sever*

(*The Soviet North*), published from 1929 to 1935. Almost all the measures to which reference will be made below resulted from the Committee's actions.

One of the first tasks requiring attention was the provision of administrative machinery of a type appropriate for conveying the principles of Soviet government to these peoples. It was first decided, in 1926, that the clan should be the basic unit, and that the local equivalent of the village soviets of the rest of the country should be clan-based "native soviets." This was put into practice, but it was discovered to be, from the regime's point of view, a mistake. The elders of the clan simply became the officials of the soviet, and the chance of such a body carrying through novel and probably unpopular measures was obviously small. There was a change-over, therefore, for purely ideological reasons, to territorial soviets. This was made during the period 1929–32 by creating "national districts," with the main object of helping to fashion a national culture for the peoples. The new idea was to have territorial administrative units, down to quite small dimensions and numbers, named after the dominant minority people of the region, and in which that people would have certain administrative rights and duties. There were three grades of such national districts—*okrug* (district), *rayon* (region), and *sovet* (soviet) in descending order of size. Their powers were greater than those of their predecessors, the clan-based native soviets. All nationalities living in the region came under their jurisdiction, and business was conducted in the language of the people for whom the district was named. By the end of 1932, there were nine *natsional'nyye okrugi,* 82 *natsional'nyye rayony* and 462 *natsional'nyye sovety* among the small peoples of the north. Membership of the Executive Committees [*Ispolkom*] at *okrug* and *rayon* level varied between 33 and 97 per cent native. This system of administration is still in force, and the numbers of national districts have been modified only comparatively slightly (see Map 2). The peoples deemed to require an *okrug* were, and are, the Khanty, Mansi, Nentsy, Dolgan, Tungus, Koryak, and Chukchi. The Komi and the Yakut, as the largest peoples, had already before this been allotted higher rungs on the nationalities "ladder." The Komi were accorded the status of an autonomous province in 1921, as the Zyryanskaya Avtonomnaya Oblast', to be up-graded in 1936 to Komi Autonomous Soviet Socialist Republic, or Komi ASSR (one rung below Union, or Constituent, or Republic, of which there are sixteen in the USSR). The Yakut meanwhile achieved in 1922 the status of Autonomous Soviet Socialist Republic—Yakutskaya ASSR—which they still possess. Under the 1936 constitution, all national districts down

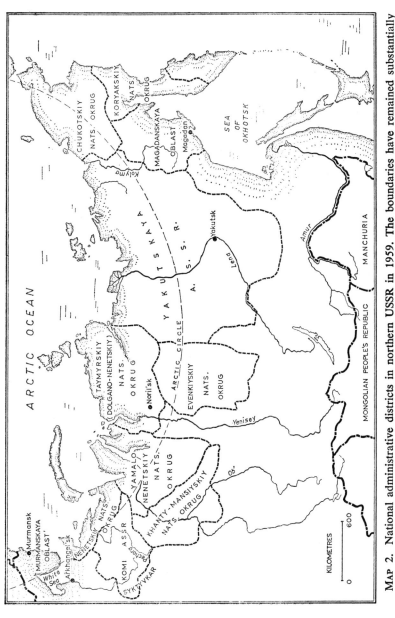

MAP 2. National administrative districts in northern USSR in 1959. The boundaries have remained substantially the same since the early 1930's.

to *okrug* send deputies to the Soviet of Nationalities: an ASSR sends eleven, and a *natsional'nyy okrug* one.

Another matter of the first importance was to determine what concessions the state could make to these peoples in recognition of their special position. Here the tone was set by the decree of the Central Executive Committee and the Council of Peoples Commissars of the USSR of September 29, 1925, which granted them exemption from certain state and local taxes. The exemptions applied also to persons other than north Siberian natives, provided they were living in the area and following the same occupations as the natives. Subsequent decrees amended, and in general enlarged, the exemptions. One of the more important is the decree of March 28, 1928, of which a translation is published by Taracouzio but the date is given incorrectly.[5] Later, exemption from military service and labour service was also granted. Again, the Komi and the Yakut were not included in these enactments.

The main impact of Soviet administration on the northern peoples was undoubtedly in the sphere of the organization of labour, with its culmination in the collective farm idea. The first step in this direction was the setting up of integral co-operatives in 1926. These were essentially co-operative stores or trading posts, through which the government channelled both its buying and its selling. "Integral" implied that all branches of the economy were dealt with together, in contrast with other parts of the country where there was normally a separate co-operative for each. They seem to have worked well. They were subsidized, being used by the government to get equipment into the hands of those who could not afford it. Similarly, the government adjusted the prices charged for consumer goods and taken for furs in such a way as to maintain a reasonable balance. Later, as the peoples and their economy became more advanced, the simple integral co-operatives were replaced by more specialized forms. This was the period during which private enterprise and the old trading methods were squeezed out. A series of edicts to this effect were issued between 1925 and 1932. Also at this time game regulations were revised in order to improve long-term hunting prospects.

The next step was the introduction of collectivization, which started in 1929. The intention was that the blueprint of collectivization as applied in more southerly agricultural regions should be substantially modified for the North, but, probably as a result of the upheavals occurring in other parts of the country, and the consequent stiffening of

[5]T. A. Taracouzio, *Soviets in the Arctic: An Historical, Economic, and Political Study of the Soviet Advance in the Arctic* (New York, 1938) pp. 457–58.

the government's determination, this was by no means always done. By 1931, only 12 per cent of households had joined collectives, and in some areas the process had not been started at all. Evidently opposition was strong and effective, for a decree of the Central Executive Committee of June 22, 1932 makes it clear that, in the official view, serious mistakes had been made, particularly through trying to go too fast. It was emphasized that the only collective unit which was then appropriate in northern conditions was the so-called "simple producers' union" (*prosteysheye proizvodstvennoye ob"yedineniye*), corresponding to the "association for communal working of the land" in other parts of the country. This apparently envisaged, at least in the earliest stages, no more than some sharing of equipment. The drive for membership was continued, and by early 1934, 36 per cent of households had joined. But these included only 10 per cent of the total number of domesticated reindeer. This sector was acknowledged to be the weakest, and opposition among the reindeer herding peoples was such that many animals were slaughtered rather than permitted to join collective herds. Between 1929 and 1933 the number of domesticated reindeer in the USSR is admitted to have fallen, for this reason, by 30 per cent, or about 450,000 animals.[6] These were violent and tragic times for the northern peoples, and it is no wonder that the process of collectivization was long drawn out. By 1940, 75 per cent of households had joined, the proportion varying locally from 55 per cent in northern Yakutskaya ASSR to 99 per cent in some southerly areas. It was only during World War II that completion is reckoned to have been achieved, and 97 per cent of households were said to have joined by 1948.

Linked to the programme of collectivization was the settling of nomads. Nomadism was seen as a primitive way of life, "unworthy in a socialist state"; it was also seen as a wasteful method of production from the economic point of view, and, although this was not publicly acknowledged, the administrators must have felt that it was politically undesirable for any group of citizens to be out of reach of authority in this way. The fact that could not be overlooked, however—although some enthusiasts tried to do so—was that large herds of reindeer cannot stay in one place the year round. Settling could never be complete, therefore, and the more sensible reformers[7] distinguished between "way-of-life nomadism," which they sought to eradicate, and "production

[6]F. Ya. Gul'chak, *Severnoye olenevodstvo* (*Reindeer Industry*) (Moscow, 1954), p. 26.

[7]Ye. D. Kantor, "Problema osedaniya malykh narodov severa" ("The Problem of Settling the Small People of the North"), *Sovetskiy Sever*, 1934, no. 5, pp. 3–10.

nomadism," which was an essential part of any system of herding reindeer. What happened during the 1930's and later was that a certain number of individuals in a reindeer herding people were encouraged— often, no doubt, obliged—to remain in one place, and with the labour force thus gained, new activities were undertaken, such as fur farming and other branches of farming suitable to the locality. The base of settlement was normally the headquarters of the collective farm. So nomadism remained, but on a reduced scale.

Provision of education was always considered a central task, particularly as it was a necessary prerequisite for effective sovietization. The first steps were taken through the Cultural Bases [Kul'tbazy] and Red Tents [Krasnyye chumy], which were set up at selected points to provide educational, medical, technical, and social facilities. The first need was to convince the natives of the desirability of education, and this was by no means easy, especially as the nomadic existence of most of them meant that it was a question of leaving their children to board. A few mobile schools were also organized to meet this difficulty. The course was at first a two-year one. Instruction was supposed to be in the native languages, but this was generally impossible initially, both because many of the languages had no written form, and because there were no teachers able to speak them. These two problems had now to be tackled. The linguistic one was attacked with great energy. With the example of Komi and Yakut before them, both languages which had long had written form, thanks to the work of Russian linguists, Soviet specialists recorded the languages of some of the smaller peoples, and in 1931 grammars and readers started to come out in Ket, Mansi, Khanty, Nentsy, Sel'kup, Tungus, Lamut, Chukchi, Koryak, and Asiatic Eskimo. In some of these cases, too, the linguists were able to build on the work of prerevolutionary pioneers (a fact not always acknowledged in Soviet accounts). The alphabet used for all these languages was a unified one based on the Roman alphabet. But in 1937, when a number of books had been published, this alphabet was replaced by another based on Cyrillic, and this second one has been in use ever since.

The problem of teacher training was assailed with no less vigour. On the initiative of the anthropologists V. G. Bogoraz and L. Ya. Shternberg, a northern group was formed within the "workers' faculty" [Rabfak] at Leningrad University in 1925, and it accepted the first nineteen students from the northern peoples. The group grew, changed its affiliation several times, and then in 1930 became the Institute of the Peoples of the North (Institut Narodov Severa), with 195 pupils from 19 peoples. On the death of P. G. Smidovich in 1935, the institute added his name to its title. Its objectives were to give secondary and higher education and teacher training to selected pupils, and thus build up cadres which would in time be able to administer their own peoples' affairs; and also to provide a centre for study of the peoples. This second objective was achieved through the institute's Research Association, staffed by members of the northern peoples as well as by Russians. Thus by the middle and late 1930's many northern natives had returned to their homelands as teachers; and also many local officials—chairmen and members of soviets, administrators, party officials—were native graduates of the institute. The number of students was by now running at about 400, a third of them women. The institute was closed at the outbreak of war in 1941, and never reopened in that form, but its work was continued by other institutions.

As a result of these measures, the teaching of the northern peoples in their own languages became a reality. The number of schools grew rapidly. In the area of the "small peoples of the north" (i.e., excluding Komi ASSR and Yakutskaya ASSR, and including the lower Amur), the number of schools grew from 6 in 1925 (there had been rather more before the Revolution) to 131 in 1930, to 338 in 1934, to 450 in 1939; and the percentage of children of school age who attended them grew from 20 per cent in 1930 to 60 per cent in 1934 to presumably about 70 to 80 per cent in 1939. At the same time efforts were made to instruct adults as well as children. In country districts most of the schools were boarding schools, and the pupils were both native and Russian, if the reported experience of two *natsional'nyye okrugi*, the Taymyrskiy and the Evenkiyskiy, is typical.[8] In the case of the Komi and the Yakut, there is also a marked record of growth, but the starting level was higher. In the territory now covered by Yakutskaya ASSR there were 173 schools in 1913 and 592 in 1950, with an increase in pupils from 4,460 to 65,000[9]; while in Komi ASSR the schools grew from 309 in 1915 to 792 in 1960, and the pupils from 14,500 to 112,000.[10] But it must be borne in mind that there was, during almost all this period of expansion, and in almost all areas, a great influx of Russians and other Slavs into the north (the last column in Table I shows that the

[8]V. N. Uvachan, *Peoples of the Soviet North* (Moscow, 1960) pp. 115–16.
[9]N. M. Kovyazin, "Kolkhoznoye stroitel'stvo v natsional'nykh okrugakh kray-nego severa SSSR" ("Collective Farm Development in the National Districts of the Far North of the USSR"). *Izvestiya Vsesoyuznogo Geograficheskogo Obshchestva*, Tom 87, Vypusk 1, 1955, pp. 11–22.
[10]P. P. Vavilov, ed., et al., *40 let Komi ASSR: Ocherki o razvitii ekonomiki i kul'tury Komi respubliki* (*Forty Years of the Komi ASSR: Outlines of the Development of the Economy and Culture of the Komi Republic*), (Syktyvkar, 1961), pp. 110–13.

northern peoples were by 1959 in a minority in all the administrative districts in which they lived); so that much of the expansion in education was not directly concerned with the northern peoples, although they no doubt benefited from it.

Medical care was another service which the state provided. Special expeditions were sent out in 1926–27 to assess needs in this respect, and they led to establishment of medical aid points, "fel'dsher" points (a "fel'dsher" is a medical assistant who has not received full doctor's training), and hospitals at certain Cultural Bases. By 1938, there were said to be 20 town hospitals, 182 country hospitals, 71 medical aid points, and 231 "fel'dsher" points in operation—altogether some 540 medical institutions—in an area which excludes Komi ASSR and Yakutskaya ASSR. Both these last, however, were equipped at least proportionately well by that date.

These, then, are the main ways in which the Soviet state sought to influence the life of the northern peoples. A final point into which it is relevant to enquire is the effect of all this upon their economy and way of life. Again it must be remembered that there was a flood of immigrants from the south all through this period, and the reason for this was the drive for industrialization, which was always accepted as a major objective for the whole Soviet state. Most of the measures affecting the northern peoples were prompted by the missionary desire to do right by them, which naturally meant bringing them the benefits of socialism. But how far were the peoples themselves implicated in the industrialization programme? The main way in which they were found to be useful was in their local knowledge, as guides, providers of reindeer transport, or assistants to geological prospecting parties. But some of them did become workers in the undertakings established by the Russians, particularly in those concerned with their traditional pursuits, such as fisheries. Others went into the timber industry, others again became mechanics, radio operators, or craftsmen of various qualifications. Thus in 1935, 2.3 per cent of the industrial labour force in the North were classified as members of the northern peoples. No doubt among the Komi and the Yakut the proportion was higher, for they had long shown themselves able to do the same things as the Russians did. But the movement does not appear ever to have been on a large scale at all. There was no rush into the mines, for instance, which were the chief manifestations of industrialization. The relative strength of the native and immigrant population in the whole of the Soviet North at this time was probably about 60 to 40 per cent, so the figure of 2.3 per cent just mentioned is extremely low; and even if there were four times as many Komi and Yakut working as industrial labourers, that would still have been low.

In the main, the northern peoples continued to do what they always had done—hunt, fish, tend reindeer, or farm. The way in which these pursuits were organized was altered by collectivization, but the pursuits themselves either remained the same, or were quite closely related to the traditional ones.

THE PRESENT POSITION

The two decades of the 1930's and 1940's were the period of greatest change for the northern peoples. I shall try to show what their position is now, when the stamp of sovietization has been imprinted upon them. The word "now" must be interpreted rather flexibly, for there is an inevitable time-lag in obtaining information, and in any case the major source, Sergeyev's book, takes the story only as far as the early 1950's. So the present must be stretched over a decade.

First, consider the benefits which Soviet rule is reported to have brought to these peoples. Most of their members have remained followers of their traditional occupations, so this is an important direction to look for effects involving the majority of the population. Collectivization was brought in with violence and suffering in many parts of the North. But once established, in what way were the natives likely to be better off? First, there were many technological introductions, and much help of this nature: for the hunters, better rifles and traps, and sensible wild life management methods; for the fishermen, better boats and tackle; for the reindeer herders, veterinary advice, help with control of predators, information on feeding, selection for breeding, and so on. In addition, there was provision of the necessary training and equipment to set up the new, but related, branches of the economy, such as fur farming, cattle raising, and crop growing.

Similarly, there was material help in housing. Russian-type wooden houses were introduced and sold at half cost price, on deferred terms, to northern natives. In many cases, though, the original designs were retained, and the Russian help took the form of providing better materials. The same was true of furniture and fittings, clothing and food. Sometimes the Russian form was accepted, sometimes the old form was retained, sometimes a new form was evolved from a blend of old and Russian.

In education and other cultural matters, much progress is also apparent. Literacy figures published in the 1959 census results show improvement from moderate levels in 1939 to remarkably high levels in 1959.

Natives are not distinguished from Russians in the published results, but figures are available for country districts of the seven *natsional'nyye okrugi* and two *avtonomnyye respubliki*—regions which contain a reasonably high proportion of natives. These show literacy levels of the 9 to 49 age group, both sexes, varying in 1939 between 46.8 per cent in Chukotskiy Natsional'nyy Okrug and 89.9 per cent in Nenetskiy Natsional'nyy Okrug, and in 1959 between 85.5 per cent in Yamalo-Nenetskiy Natsional'nyy Okrug and 98 per cent in Komi ASSR. The mean for country districts of all nine regions advanced from 72 per cent to 93.7 per cent.[11] Publication of school books in the languages recorded in the early 1930's continued; there were 80 such works published between 1945 and 1950. The predominance of boarding schools, and the free maintenance of children in them, is quoted as a special benefit accorded to the northern peoples.[12] Forty per cent of teachers in northern schools were recruited in the North in 1949[13]—not yet a majority, but a reasonable proportion.

The attracting of members of the northern peoples into positions of responsibility in the administration of their own affairs has also been effective. Among the more prominent have been the Koryak Bekerev, the Chukchi Otke, the Nentsy Gudyrev, Tesida, and Panyukov, the Khanty Pukhlenkin and Savin—all deputies of the Supreme Soviet; and the Tungus Kaynachenok, chairman of his local regional executive committee [*okrispolkom*], and Uvachan, party secretary for Evenkiyskiy Natsional'nyy Okrug. Many Yakut fill high positions in their own republic. The present President is a Yakut lady, and many members of the Council of Ministers and quite senior party officials are Yakut. This is probably true of Komi ASSR also. Some, but not all, of the eleven deputies which each ASSR sends to the Soviet of Nationalities are Komi or Yakut. One of the most prominent Komi is Professor V. Starovskiy, the head of the Central Statistical Administration in Moscow. On a broader cultural front, there have been more successes. There is a Yakut historian, Basharin, and a number of Yakut writers—Kulachikov, Mordvinov, Zolotarev, Zverev, Ivanov. Among the other peoples there are also writers and poets: the Tungus Platonov and

---

[11]*Itogi vsesoyuznoy perepisi naseleniya 1959 goda. RSFSR* (*Results of the All-Union Census of Population, 1959. RSFSR*) (Moscow, 1963), pp. 144–45.

[12]Z. P. Sokolova, "O nekotorykh etnicheskikh protsessakh, protekayushchikh u sel'kupov, khantov i evenkov Tomskoy oblasti" ("Some Ethnic Processes among the Sel'kup, Khanty, and Tungus of Tomskaya Oblast' "), *Sovetskaya Etnografiya*, 1961, no. 3, p. 50 (English translation in *Soviet Anthropology and Archaeology* [New York], vol. 1, no. 2, 1962, pp. 50–56).

[13]E. Koutaissoff, "Literacy and the Place of Russian in the Non-Slavic Republics of the USSR," *Soviet Studies*, vol. 3, no. 2 (Glasgow, 1951), p. 122.

Salatkin, the Nentsy Vylko and Istomin, the Koryak Kekketyn and Yayletkan, the Chukchi Rytkheu, the Lamut Tarabukin, the Khanty Lazarev. The Khanty Tereshkin has made learned contributions to the study of his own language, and works in the Academy of Sciences Institute of Languages at Moscow. Sergeyev lists in his bibliography (pp. 562–6) over 200 published works by representatives of the smaller northern peoples, either written in Russian or translated into Russian. Most of the successful products of the northern peoples are graduates of the Institute of the Peoples of the North or of its successors. They are primarily good Soviet citizens, their indoctrination in Marxism-Leninism has been thorough, and their views on affairs beyond their personal experience are naive. This much is clear from those of them who make their views known (writers such as Rytkheu), and those of them who have been abroad (officials such as Uvachan). Like Soviet citizens who have come to the top in other parts of Soviet society, they owe everything to the regime, and identify themselves with it rather than with whatever national group they may belong to.

Institutions of higher education and science are beginning to appear in the north, particularly in the Komi and Yakutskaya ASSR. There has been an Institute of Language and Culture (Institut Yazyka i Kul'tury) at Yakutsk since 1935, and a university since 1956, and branches of the Academy of Sciences at Yakutsk and at Syktyvkar, the capital of Komi ASSR, since 1947 and 1949 respectively. Various large all-Union scientific institutes have branches in the North, and some of these may act as local training centres for their particular discipline. One major institute, the Research Institute of Agriculture of the Far North (Nauchno-Issledovatel'skiy Institut Sel'skogo Khozyaystva Kray-nego Severa) has had its headquarters in the Arctic, at Noril'sk, since 1957.

The peoples continue to enjoy special treatment and concessions under Soviet law. Some of the taxation privileges are listed in the decree of the Central Committee of the party and of the Council of Ministers of the USSR dated March 16, 1957, a decree which is particularly con-cerned with providing incentives to economic development.[14] These concessions are granted to the Komi and Yakut as well as to the smaller peoples. The position with regard to military service is not quite clear. After a period of exemption, military service was introduced (it is said,

[14]V. N. Malin and A. V. Korobov, *Direktivy KPSS i sovetskogo pravitel'stva po khozyaystvennym voprosam*, Tom 4, 1953–1957 gody. (*Directives of the Communist Party of the Soviet Union and the Soviet Government on Economic Questions*) (Moscow, 1958) pp. 690–95.

at the request of the peoples themselves) in 1939. What is not clear is whether or not exemption has been granted again after World War II. On the whole, it seems unlikely that it has been, so that the northern peoples probably are still liable to military service.

This is the positive side, about which many Soviet accounts give much information. It is now necessary to try to determine just how effective these measures have been, and whether there is any evidence of neglect or repression. These are points on which there is less likely to be any information in the Soviet sources, although indirect indications may be found in them.

First, the occupations—hunting, fishing, reindeer herding, and farming—and in particular, the results of collectivization. It is not to be supposed that everything is perfect, as Sergeyev (p. 489) makes clear: "It would, of course, be wrong to say that the change-over of the small peoples to the new way of life happened easily and quickly, or that this process was already complete." The preamble to the decree of March 16, 1957 lists a great many shortcomings, which the rest of the decree sets out to try to put right. Some quite interesting deductions can be drawn from this decree. For instance, there is strong emphasis on encouraging hunting, fishing, and reindeer herding, evidently because there was a tendency to introduce and foster crop-growing and cattle-raising without due regard to the environment. This point was made in an article in *Pravda* by the Party secretary of Evenkiyskiy Natsional'nyy Okrug on December 10, 1956. He attributed the tendency to a slavish interpretation of the party-government decree on agriculture of March 9, 1955—a document which urges greater productivity in forceful terms, but does not speak of the northern regions. A second interesting feature of the decree of March 16, 1957 is its tacit admission that members of collectives require also a personal stake in the economy, if they are to work with a will. Thus the tax concessions already mentioned were made expressly in order to ". . . increase the incentives [*zainteresovannost'*] of collective farms and collective farmers," and another article of the decree permits more private ownership of reindeer. This point of incentives in connection with the reindeer industry had been made by Kovyazin in 1955 (pp. 15–16), and was repeated by Maslov[15] in 1960. The fact that the total number of domesticated reindeer in the country was still in 1961 almost the same as it had been in 1929 is certainly clear evidence that the new system is not especially successful. Yet reindeer continue to have great economic importance. They are a good source of local food in the North, producing 10,000

[15]Ye. P. Maslov, "Severnoye olenevodstvo" ("Reindeer Industry"), *Priroda*, no. 2, p. 53.

to 12,000 metric tons of meat a year.[16] They are also still very widely used for transport purposes. Although they are now being replaced by vehicles in regions where the roads permit this, they are invaluable for hunting and exploration parties. In 1957 geological parties employed 10,000 reindeer in Yakutskaya ASSR alone.[17]

More evidence that the basic economy of the northern peoples is not in every case flourishing is to be found in a book on the Evenkiyskiy Natsional'nyy Okrug by Kovyazin and Kuzakov published in 1963.[18] From this it emerges that in this particular region vegetable growing and dairy farming were encouraged, especially during World War II, and then were permitted to drop back to a low level (the sown area dropped by 78 per cent between 1945 and 1959, and the number of cattle dropped by 33 per cent between 1950 and 1958). But at the same time the traditional occupations were not doing very well either: hunting stations and fish canneries were closed down, although they were admitted to perform a useful function, and the yield of reindeer meat was about half what it might have been, because as many animals were lost through death or wandering as were slaughtered. A fall-off has recently been noted, too, in the number of hunters active in the North, according to a study of all seven national *okrugi*.[19] The reason suggested for this by the author of that study is that the hunters are discouraged by the low return they get for their efforts, the profits on their catch being used by the collectives to subsidize other branches of their economy.

Some nomadism remains, as was to be expected, mainly in connection with the reindeer industry. It is interesting that the same old argument about "way-of-life nomadism" and "production nomadism" still flourishes,[20] and those who seek to show that some "production nomadism" is necessary still have to defend their position. The feeling that nomadism is in some way improper persists, and serious thought

[16]V. N. Andreyev, "Nauchno-prakticheskiye rekomendatsii po proizvodstvu olen'yego myasa" ("Scientific and Practical Recommendations for the Production of Reindeer Meat"), *Problemy Severa*, Vypusk 6, 1962, p. 230.

[17]I. S. Gurvich, "O putyakh dal'neyshego pereustroystva ekonomiki i kul'tury narodov severa" ("Ways of Further Reconstructing the Economy and Culture of the Peoples of the North"), *Sovetskaya Etnografiya*, 1961, no. 4, p. 52 (English translation in *Soviet Anthropology and Archaeology* [New York, 1962]) vol. 1, no. 2 pp. 22–31.

[18]N. M. Kovyazin and K. G. Kuzakov, *Sovetskaya Evenkiya* (*ekonomiko-geograficheskiy ocherk*) (*Soviet Evenkiya* [*an outline of its economic geography*]), (Moscow and Leningrad, 1963).

[19]V. G. Konovalenko, "Zemel'nyye fondy natsional'nykh okrugov kraynego severa i ikh ispol'zovaniye" ("Land Resources of the National Districts of the Far North and their Use"), *Voprosy Geografii*, Sbornik 54, (1961) p. 26.

[20]Kovyazin and Kuzakov, *Sovetskaya Evenkiya*, pp. 175–78.

has been given to ways in which it might be mitigated, for instance by the use of portable houses, or by organizing relief herders who could be taken out to the herd by helicopter.[21]

It is relevant to consider here the employment policy of the government towards these peoples. As mentioned above, the industrialization programme of the 1930's and 1940's did not attract very many natives. But this programme was made possible to an important extent by the direction into northern areas of large numbers of forced labourers and other categories of unfree workers. In the 1950's, however, this source of labour diminished, and had to be replaced by workers from the south, who qualified for the higher rates of pay and other privileges which had long been used as incentives. This was expensive, and naturally the question again arose of employing local inhabitants. Opposing views have been expressed about doing this. The official attitude seems to be that it is a good thing, both for the immediate economic reason and because it brings the natives into closer touch with the Soviet system. Thus Sergeyev[22] sees "great cultural and organizational significance" in the tendency. And the decree of March 16, 1957 instructs local authorities to do all they can to attract natives into such undertakings, and to promote them wherever possible to responsible positions. On the other hand, the ethnographers appear to be against this. Gardanov and others[23] frown on such recruiting, on the strictly practical grounds that there are plenty of vacancies in positions which natives are better equipped to fill, such as reindeer herders. Similarly Gurvich[24] urges that if the natives abandon their traditional pursuits and lose their skills, the harm done to the economy of the North would be great, whereas if they were used as an industrial labour force, the gain would not be commensurate. It is not clear which of these two views is now dominant, nor how energetically the relevant section of the decree of March 16, 1957 is being implemented.

In the sphere of education, there seems no reason to doubt the im-

[21]Gurvich, *op. cit.*, pp. 53–54.

[22]"Nekapitalisticheskiy put' razvitiya malykh narodov severa," p. 409.

[23]V. K. Gardanov, B. O. Dolgikh, and T. A. Zhdanko, "Osnovnyye napravleniya etnicheskikh protsessov u narodov SSSR" ("Main Directions of Ethnic Processes among the Peoples of the USSR"), *Sovetskaya Etnografiya*, 1961, no. 4, p. 27 (English translation in *Soviet Anthropology and Archaeology*, vol. 1, no. 1 [New York, 1962], pp. 3–18).

[24]I. S. Gurvich, "Voprosy ratsional'nogo ispol'zovaniya traditsionnykh trudovykh navykov narodov Sovetskogo Soyuza" ("Questions of the Rational Use of Traditional Work Habits of the Peoples of the Soviet Union"), *Materialy I Mezhduvedomstvennogo soveshchaniya po geografii naseleniya (yanvar'–fevral', 1962 g.) (Materials of the First Interdepartmental Conference on the Geography of Population, January–February, 1962)*, Vypusk 5, 1961, p. 15.

pressive figures already quoted for the growth in the numbers of schools and of pupils, and for the diminishing number of illiterates (but one may perhaps note in passing that in the USSR literacy is sometimes defined in rather different terms from those used in the West). The work of the Institute of the Peoples of the North was continued by teacher training colleges at Leningrad and Khabarovsk, and by the northern faculty of Leningrad University, which also took over the scholarly side of the work. It may be added here that a movement was under way in the late 1950's to adjust the curriculum of the boarding schools, which were attended chiefly by native children, to include practical instruction in such things as reindeer husbandry, hunting, and fishing— the first attempt, apparently, to get across to schoolchildren the improved techniques in these fields, and the first attempt also to provide practical instruction (the "polytechnic" idea) on subjects appropriate to the north.[25] There is no evidence, unfortunately, on the effectiveness or standards of these or any other schools in the north.

A point of special interest is the extent to which the native languages continued to be used for instruction. The change-over of the alphabet from Roman-based to Cyrillic-based in 1937 opened the door, as was intended, to greater Russian influence. This could lead to the gradual replacement of the native languages by Russian, and in some cases this does seem to have happened. It is reported that the Chukchi living in Nizhnekolymskiy Rayon in Yakutskaya ASSR, and the Koryak of Koryakskiy Natsional'nyy Okrug both requested that their schools should go over to teaching in Russian, the former in 1950 and the latter in 1955–56,[26] and permission was granted. On the other hand the decree of March 16, 1957 calls for the publication of more fiction, political and scientific literature, textbooks, and instructional handbooks in the northern languages, so it is clear that by no means all the languages were moribund. But this issue is really part of the larger one of assimilation, which will be considered a little later.

The Soviet state paid special attention to devising, in the early 1930's, a system of local government by which the natives would play the greatest possible part in their own administration. This was the object of the national districts, and much importance was attached to it. Skachko,[27] a specialist in northern affairs writing at that time, strongly deprecated

[25]L. A. Faynberg, "Politekhnizatsiya shkoly na Taymyre" ("Polytechniza-tion of a School in Taymyr"), *Letopis Severa*, Vypusk 3, 1962, pp. 90–91.
[26]Gardanov, *et al.*, p. 25.
[27]A. Ye. Skachko, *Narody kraynego severa i rekonstruktsiya severnogo khoz-yaystva* (*Peoples of the Far North and the Reconstruction of the Northern Econ-omy*) (Leningrad, 1934), pp. 47–8.

the suggestion that socialism should be built on the basis of immigrant labour from the south. Any development of natural resources, he said, without involvement of the local population in the reconstruction of the economy is a method of capitalist colonization, having nothing whatever to do with socialism. Yet that is what happened. The process of industrialization could only be carried through by immigrant labour, and the result was that all the northern peoples found themselves in a minority in the administrative region in which they lived—in many cases, a very small minority. Clearly their "autonomy" could not be real in such circumstances. How, for instance, could the 5,000 Nentsy in the Nenetskiy Natsional'nyy Okrug retain the initiative when there were over 30,000 Russians living there too? Only the Yakut, of all the northern peoples, might be expected to, for, although not the majority, they were still the largest single national group in their own territory in 1959. But in fact it is most unlikely that there ever was any real autonomy of national minorities, even when the northern peoples formed the majority in the national districts, as they did in 1926; for there never has been in any other part of the Soviet Union. The term "autonomous" is misleading—no doubt deliberately so. For although the constitutionally established organs of government do exist and function, real power resides not in them but in the Communist party, which is a highly centralized body. It is also true that many of the largest undertakings in the territory of the autonomous and national districts— mining trusts, transport agencies, and so forth—have in any case been run straight from Moscow and have been quite independent of the local authorities. But although there is no real autonomy, in spite of an appearance to that effect, there are many members of the northern peoples filling positions in the local administration, and sitting as representatives in local soviets. In Taymyrskiy Natsional'nyy Okrug and Evenkiyskiy Natsional'nyy Okrug, for instance, where the northern peoples in 1959 numbered 10,433, or 23 per cent of the total population, it is reported that 46 per cent of the elected members of local soviets in 1957 were members of those peoples[28]—twice the proportion that might have been expected. Similarly for Yakutskaya ASSR in 1962. According to *Sovetskaya Yakutiya* of January 26, 1962, Yakut filled 65 per cent of the places on local soviets.

From this assessment of the Soviet measures affecting the economy, culture, and administration of the northern peoples, it will be seen that a charge of neglect on the part of the Soviet government is indeed hard to sustain. Even although the only source of information on the

[28]V. N. Uvachan, *Peoples of the Soviet North* (Moscow, 1960), p. 85.

subject is highly partial, the strongest impression is given that whatever faults have been committed, neglect is not one of them. Because of the ideological importance of treating minorities in the approved way, and because these particular minorities excited interest by their rarity, remoteness, and alleged ill-treatment under the Tsars, they have always received much attention. It would be easier to sustain a charge of pampering than one of neglect. The very few references to northern peoples in accounts written by ex-inmates of forced labour camps in the north—the nearest approach to independent observers—in fact tend to confirm this view.[29]

Repression is a somewhat different matter. Again, there is little evidence, but the record of the Soviet government in treating other minorities shows clearly enough that repression of the most ruthless kind is not something from which that government shrinks, if the reasons seem to it good. There was probably repression of particular groups at the time of collectivization—violence is in fact admitted by Sergeyev (pp. 354–58). Later, there was repression of a more refined sort directed against what were believed to be nationalistic tendencies. The Yakut historian Basharin was taken to task in a *Pravda* article on December 10, 1951 for having published a book on three pre-revolutionary Yakut writers in which he approved their Yakut nationalism. But this, it may be fairly objected, is the sort of attack which *Pravda* makes from time to time, countering widely different forms of intellectual deviation in very various groups of the population, and should not be taken as evidence of a specifically anti-Yakut attitude. On the whole it seems likely that there has been little physical or intellectual repression of northern peoples beyond that stemming from insistence on conformity and directed to all Soviet citizens. After all, the northern peoples are numerically rather weak, pose no threat to the country's security, and do not occupy territory over which Soviet sovereignty is ever likely to be contested, so it is hard to see what motive there could be for repression.

Finally, there is another question: that of assimilation of small groups into larger groups. By this means a people may entirely lose its national identity, but there can be widely differing views about the moral issues involved. First, the facts of the situation must be examined. There is plenty of evidence that assimilation has taken place, and is still taking place, in the north. Sergeyev (pp. 526–27) lists many instances. Some Mansi, Khanty, Tungus, Ket, and Sel'kup have become russianized. Other Tungus have merged with the Yakut, the Lamut, and the Yukagir.

---

[29]Vladimir Petrov, *It Happens in Russia: Seven Years Forced Labour in the Siberian Goldfields* (London, 1951), p. 258.

The Chuvantsy have been quite absorbed by the Chukchi and the Russians, many Kamchadal by the Koryak and the Russians, some Koryak by the Chukchi, others by the Lamut. Some Lamut have merged with the Yukagir, other Yukagir have become russianized. Most Aleut are russianized. Some Nentsy have been assimilated by the Komi. This list is not exhaustive. It is very likely that assimilation accounts for some, perhaps most, of the movement in population numbers between 1926 and 1959 (see Table II). In the aggregate, the peoples this chapter is concerned with increased by only 8 per cent over the thirty-year period, while the population of the country as a whole, adjusted for frontier changes, increased by 20 per cent; and if the Komi are left out of consideration, there is even a 2 per cent decrease. Taken severally, the increases and decreases are too large and too erratic to be attributable to natural causes, and they cannot all be due to mistakes in census enumeration. Of the many instances of assimilation noted, it is likely

TABLE II

POPULATION CHANGES IN THE NORTHERN PEOPLES, 1926–59 [30]

	1926	1959	Percentage increase or decrease
Lapps	1,720	1,760	+2
Nentsy	16,375	22,845	+40
Nganasan	867	721	−17
Entsy	1,445	350	−76
Komi	226,383	282,780	+25
Khanty	17,800	19,246	+8
Mansi	5,700	6,318	+11
Sel'kup	6,000	3,704	−38
Ket	1,225	1,017	−17
Dolgan	3,728	3,900	+4
Tungus	38,804	24,583	−37
Lamut	7,000	9,023	+29
Yakut	235,926	236,125	+0.1
Yukagir	443	440	−0.7
Chukchi	12,364	11,680	−6
Koryak	7,434	6,168	−12
Kamchadal	814	1,096	+35
Eskimo	1,294	1,111	−14
Aleut	345	399	+14
	585,667	633,266	

[30]M. G. Levin and L. P. Potapov, eds., *Narody Sibiri: Etnograficheskiye ocherki* (*Peoples of Siberia: Ethnographic Sketches*) (Moscow and Leningrad, 1956); *Itogi vsesoyuznoy perepisi naseleniya 1959 goda. RSFSR.* (*Results of the All-Union census of Population, 1959. RSFSR*). (Moscow, 1963), pp. 300–302; F. Lorimer, *The Population of the Soviet Union: History and Prospects* (Geneva, 1946), p. 56 (for Komi); *Trudy Instituta Etnografii im. N. N. Miklukho-Maklaya: Novaya Seriya*, Tom 84, 1963, pp. 33, 92, 94 (for Entsy and Dolgan).

that those with Russians involved most individuals, so that it is reasonable to speak of russianization as a significant fact, even although exact numbers are not known.

Soviet ideology unhesitatingly welcomes this process. The official position is put by Gardanov:[31] "The essence of present ethnic processes related to the consolidation and further development of socialist nations is expressed primarily in the disappearance of the particularity and isolation of small ethnic groups and their gradual assimilation into socialist nations." Merging is thus seen as a politically progressive phenomenon, but the rider is added that it must not be forced. It is admitted that in the north this process is far from complete. Sergeyev (pp. 521–28), applying this principle to the particular peoples with whom he is concerned, makes a detailed forecast of how each will develop. None of those he is considering may yet be called a "socialist nation" (while the Yakut and the Komi are said by other Soviet sources to have reached this stage). Six of them, however, are on the way to becoming such nations—the Nentsy, Khanty, Mansi, Tungus, Chukchi, and Koryak. Thanks to the creation of national districts and written languages, each is knitting together sufficiently to assert, with Russian help, its national consciousness. Below this level comes a second group, comprising the Sel'kup, Lamut, and Eskimo. These have some elements of a national culture, but not enough to permit them to achieve full national consciousness (the Sel'kup and Lamut, for instance, are too scattered to have achieved a single common language out of several competing dialects). Sergeyev sees their future as national minorities, who will use the Russian language for the absorption of socialist culture. It seems likely that the Lapps (with whom Sergeyev does not deal) would fall into this group. Finally, there are the remaining peoples— Entsy, Nganasan, Ket, Dolgan, Kamchadal, Yukagir, and Aleut—who are small in numbers and have no written language (the attempt to provide one for Ket was abandoned). These will not be able to become even national minorities, but will be assimilated. Sergeyev insists that the process is, by Leninist principles, basically progressive, and therefore approves the formation of multi-national collectives, such as a Nentsy-Entsy-Nganasan-Dolgan one in Taymyr, and a Yukagir-Lamut-Chukchi one in the north-east, which will hasten the assimilation. At the same time he declares that none of this has anything at all in common with a deliberate policy of assimilation, which is impossible in a socialist state. Gardanov,[32] however, admits that force had been used in the Soviet

[31]Gardanov, *et al.*, p. 12.
[32]Gardanov, *et al.*, p. 19.

Union to promote assimilation, and he deplores this. It is worth noting in addition that the concept "socialist nation" is not taken by Soviet social theorists to imply any very firm rejection of subsequent moves in the direction of assimilation. The main point to make is that the whole issue of assimilation is thought of as being quite unimportant.

LESSONS FOR CANADA

The object of discussing here the Soviet experience in administering northern peoples is, of course, to judge whether anything in that experience is likely to be helpful to Canada. Before any pointers in that direction are attempted, it is again necessary to stress the tentative nature of any deductions to be drawn from statements which it is virtually impossible to check.

In any attempt to compare or contrast the Soviet and the Canadian experience, it must be borne in mind that the whole subject looms much bigger in the Soviet Union than in Canada. The number of natives involved is greater, the area is greater, and the stage of economic growth now reached is more advanced; but more important than any of these are the ideological considerations. At times during the Soviet period the bringing of socialism to the northern peoples has been stated to be one of the main motives for undertaking the whole immense effort and expense of the northern development programme. This did not imply concern only for the well-being of the natives, but also concern that they should themselves participate in the building of socialism. There was a strong missionary feeling in the Soviet attitude. The economic importance of the traditional native pursuits is also much greater than is the case in Canada. Leningrad is still the most important fur market in the world, and a significant part of what is sold at the annual auction comes straight from northern hunters. Similarly the reindeer industry helps in a small but significant way towards solving the food problem for northern industrial settlements. All this has led to a directing of attention to the North, not only of the relevant government departments, but also of the public by means of the press. The North and its inhabitants have become known in considerable detail to large numbers of Soviet citizens. Any schoolchild knows where the Chukchi live or what the Nentsy do. This wide awareness must be helpful to the authorities in many different ways.

Of the various contexts in which the northern peoples encounter Soviet authority, only some are likely to hold useful lessons for Canada.

The unlikely ones may be disposed of first. The most unlikely is the process of collectivization, which no one in Canada is likely to copy. This was the work of missionaries fired by the spirit of the Inquisition. The advantages which have resulted from it—mainly technological improvements—could surely be obtained in a much milder way, and without any need to introduce the collective idea. The next most unlikely is the Soviet system of administration by national districts. It is an elaborate facade covering a very different reality. If Canada wished to attract her northern peoples into local government—in itself a laudable objective—she would scarcely wish to copy a system which was designed by persons whose aims and outlook were fundamentally different from those of citizens in a western democracy. Quite apart from its ideological presuppositions, the Soviet blueprint for administering minorities was devised to meet a total situation quite unlike Canada's. Finally, there is the question of tax and other concessions granted by law. In principle, these are points which might be usefully studied in Canada, where there is some feeling that concessions to one group imply discrimination against others, and are therefore undesirable; but in fact the fiscal and legal systems in the two countries are so dissimilar that it is not likely that a detailed study of methods would be practically helpful.

It would seem to be in the sphere of education, and educational facilities, that Canada might learn most from the Soviet Union. The Institute of the Peoples of the North and its successors, for which there is no counterpart in Canada, have played a key part. By providing higher education, they have fitted members of the northern peoples for many positions of responsibility, and especially for posts of teacher in local schools. The linguistic work done in connection with schooling is also most impressive. Of course, the reason why such a high priority was given to this subject, as the record of the Committee of the North shows, was that education was recognized, correctly, as potentially the most important of all political weapons. But this in no way detracts from the value of the lesson. Education of these peoples is a prerequisite for solving many problems, and not just political ones.

There remains the question of assimilation. On this issue there are widely differing attitudes. It may be held that the process should be prevented at all costs, merely discouraged, left to take its course, actively encouraged, or deliberately enforced. Furthermore, each of these positions may be held passionately as the only permissible attitude, or unemotionally as the least unsatisfactory under the circumstances, or at any intermediate level. The Soviet position, held warmly but not passionately, is that assimilation is never a bad thing, and should be actively encouraged in the case of certain small peoples. My own position, and it is probably not an uncommon one in the West, is that assimilation should be discouraged, since there is an obligation on more advanced peoples to do nothing which might harm the national culture of weaker, more primitive peoples. To those who hold this view, assimilation becomes acceptable only if it can be conclusively shown to be the only reasonable course left. No force, needless to say, must be used. But the Soviet Union believes in the primacy of economic factors, and therefore is interested first of all in making a useful citizen out of the northern native, and only secondly in preserving his national culture. All that has been done there has quite logically tended towards that end. This process of assimilation is essentially the same as the integration spoken of in Canada, and if that is the course which Canada, arguing from different premises, decides to be necessary, then there are lessons to be learnt from the Soviet experience: which peoples have responded best to the process, what precisely were the alternatives put before them, how long does it all take, and so forth. These are not questions which can be answered in this essay, but it can be made clear here that there is much relevant experience in the Soviet Union.

In summary, then, it may be seen that the Soviet Union has gone further than Canada, for reasons of history and geography, in her working out of relations with dependent northern peoples. The ideological motives behind most of the Soviet actions have no counterpart of comparable force in Canada—perhaps unfortunately, for they have provided a powerful stimulus. The actions themselves provide some useful lessons, particularly in the fields of education and integration. But study of the literature can provide only the most general pointers. Real lessons of practical value are likely to be learnt only when book knowledge is supplemented by a field investigation in the Soviet North.

The Administration of
Northern Peoples: Canada and Alaska

◄ MARGARET LANTIS* ►

FORTY PER CENT of Canada is not in its provinces—it is in the Yukon and North-West Territories—and large areas of two provinces, in northern Quebec and northern Labrador, are lands like the Territories. Although Alaska is now a state, it is similarly divided into two great areas: the southeast, south, and central parts, originally Indian territory, now dominated by characteristically United States towns, linked by roads and railroads and served chiefly by state institutions; and the west and northern parts, dominated by Eskimo villages in a treeless and trackless area (except for trails), served principally by federal government agencies. Canada too provides educational and medical services for the Eskimos in northern Quebec as well as in the North-West Territories. In short, the indigenous peoples of the vast tundra areas are, through our national governments, the responsibility of all of us born elsewhere in these two large North American nations.

The northern marginal lands are the despair of economists. In our modern national life weather flows out of the North and money flows into it. But who wants to buy Arctic weather, and at what a price! "Total government expenditures in the Northwest Territories rose from $12 millions in 1955 to $47 millions in 1959; . . ."[1] In more detail, in 1959–60, revenues from the North-West Territories were $6,631,304, expenditures $54,307,989 (a 15 per cent increase from the preceding

---

*Visiting Professor in Anthropology, University of Kentucky, Lexington, Kentucky.

[1]Diamond Jenness, "Eskimo Administration: II. Canada," *AINA Technical Paper*, no. 14, p. 91.

year), for the Yukon Territory $4,809,600 and $21,977,033, for the latter a $2 million decrease from the preceding year.[2] And expenditures continue to climb as more facilities and services are provided, for example, as more schools are built, and as prices rise.

It is difficult to separate from the total federal expenditures for the state of Alaska that portion directed to a northern area comparable to the North-West Territories. For the fiscal year 1963–64, perhaps $35 million of the more than $500 million appropriated for federal activities and construction in Alaska can be allocated to north and west Alaska. The population in this area (north of the middle Yukon River but curving southward to include the Yukon and Kuskokwim River deltas and Goodnews Bay along the east side of Bering Sea) we estimate as about 25,000, including all races. What the state of Alaska additionally spent on this region from its own appropriations, we do not have means of estimating. In 1960, when Canada was spending $54 million, the North-West Territories population was estimated at about 22,000 (all races). Before figuring the per capita expenditure, one should note that the $54 million covers also education, health, and some other services to the Eskimos of northern Quebec. One must add, therefore, the northern Quebec population of about 3,000. Although the estimates are crude, it appears likely that Canada by 1960 was spending a little more than $2,000 per capita annually in its northern marginal lands, while the United States currently is spending about $1,700 or slightly more, the exact figure being unknown. Of course not all this money was spent on the people. Mapping, geological, and biological surveys, and several other activities were intended for national as well as territorial benefit and even for international benefit, for example to facilitate transportation on so-called "over-the-Pole" routes.

Why do both Canada and Alaska spend so much money on so few people—even allowing for the above-mentioned interests—and still have such small development of the northern regions? The national pressures for development of the North, or lack of such pressures, are the same for both nations. Both are very large countries, with so much land that they do not yet feel sheer population pressure for land. Both have wealth enough that they are not seeking desperately for a firmer economic base or more diversified sources of revenue or scarce raw materials. Alaska is mining little of its available gold, for example, because the controlled price of gold is not high enough to pay current mining costs.

[2]Department of Northern Affairs and National Resources, *Government Activities in the North—1960* (Ottawa, 1963), p. 138.

Of course, if a diamond deposit could be found, either country probably would work it since diamonds never have been found in North America. But even the tin deposit near Nome is not being mined although the United States has no tin elsewhere. It evidently does not feel a sufficiently urgent need for it. Although both have oil and gas resources elsewhere, it is true that Canadian and US oil companies are conducting wide searches in the Arctic for additional oil deposits. These may not be essential today, but international trade and politics may make them essential in the future.

Until recently Canada and the United States both felt territorially secure enough that they did not need coastal defences in the North. Even now, Canada evidently feels less threatened by the USSR than does the United States. In the 1950's, with the development of jet planes and long-range missiles, one of the coldest areas became potentially one of the "hot spots" of the world, resulting in construction of the DEW Line (Distant Early Warning Line) and the Mid-Continent Line of radar bases and sites. These brought people, jobs, new types of equipment, new concepts of construction to both Arctic and sub-Arctic. This was not only an important military development: it was the widest spread economic development, actually and potentially.

Both countries because of their size and diversity do need shorter transportation routes. The Arctic's greatest asset is its location between the Old and New Worlds. Before the widespread use of jets, more communities in the Arctic benefited from northern airline routes. Some of the landing sites used by the large propeller planes now can be by-passed by the jets. But there are still possibilities for inter-continental transport.

Because of their wealth and progressiveness, both Canada and the United States feel that they can and must take care of their indigenous peoples. Nations like these do not want to appear neglectful of their native peoples, even though they find it difficult to provide a sound economy for them. They seem to have, actually, a greater concern for Eskimos than for Indians: the Eskimos have been viewed romantically as a very friendly people, uncomplaining under great hardships, a people who deserve help. There is little or no ambivalence in attitudes toward Eskimos since they never were the enemy who were fought, defeated, and whose lands were taken—all of this perhaps more pertinent to the United States than to Canada. Canadian advances to the West and North were not accompanied by a succession of "Indian wars" as in the States. In the latter, conqueror and conquered have had an uneasy relationship ever after.

SIMILARITIES BETWEEN CANADA AND ALASKA

It may not appear so at first glance but a detailed examination shows that the histories of Canada and the United States in the North have many similarities. The Arctic was not, for either country, a foreign-occupied territory. True, Russia owned Alaska but it never occupied and administered the area north of Bering Strait. Neither nation has had to undo or modify some other nation's political administration, official language, and system of education. Also, while the Eskimos were not everywhere a passive people, there was, as we have indicated, no continuing warfare with the aboriginal inhabitants. So there were not the effects of war to be overcome. Russia had the same advantage in northern and eastern Siberia: it did not have to contend with another world power for possession.

The people whom the pioneers encountered were remarkably homogeneous. Even the interior Indians belonged to one or another of only two great language groups—Athabaskan or Algonkian. They were not divided into small, quite different tribes, always at war with one another. In fact, neither Eskimos nor Indians of the North had "tribes" with any organization beyond that of village or small band. The only division was the fundamental one between Eskimo and Indian. Although both belong to the great Mongoloid group of races, they are different in race (or sub-race), language, and culture. Usually—not always—they occupied different habitats, one coastal and the other inland, and they were suspicious of each other. Even so, the history of exploration and early settlement in the North sounds very different from the European history of most of the tropics: no "subduing the natives," no treaty with one chief to get his help in fighting another chief. Not always necessary today but essential in the early days was mutual assistance between Caucasian and Eskimo or Indian in fighting the common enemy: weather and the scarcity of food and fuel.

The demographic and political situation of the American Arctic today is an expectable outgrowth of that early experience. First, in far northern Canada there are no native peoples on reserves, and in northern Alaska, although there is one large reservation (Venetie) in the Indian area, it is not occupied by "treaty Indians" and has little functional meaning, while such coastal or insular Eskimo reservations as Unalakleet, Wales (at Bering Strait), Little Diomede Island, and St. Lawrence Island serve chiefly to protect their wild food supply and on rare occasions to keep out white exploiters. There is no system of "Indian agencies" and "Indian superintendents," meaning white men's directorates of the few Alaskan reservations. There is little sense of "boundaries": the North has not yet been plagued with border wars.

Second, in Alaska there were no treaties with any of the indigenous peoples, and in Canada none with the Eskimos. As a result, there are no "allotments" of food or cloth or money in fulfilment of old treaty terms. In the North, all races receive equally Family Allowance (Canada), or Aid to the Blind or Aid to Dependent Children (US), and whatever other forms of financial assistance the national governments give. There was a time when the Canadian Family Allowance was given to unlettered Eskimos in goods rather than money. The trend now, however, is to payment by cheque; hence the trader is no longer required to serve as a government agent in distributing the allowance.

Third, another effect of the wide-openness of the Arctic is that all or virtually all the land is owned publicly. Unlike most Latin American countries, for example, there is no class of great landlords, of *patrons* between the government and the Indian mass. There are no tribal chiefs claiming ancestral rights to hunting territories. Vast stretches of land have no year-round inhabitants and are claimed by no one. Even the inhabitants of most settlements in the Arctic have no formal title to their place of residence. This is a potentially explosive situation, as recent developments in Alaska foretell. According to Public Law 85–508 of the Eighty-fifth Congress, 1958, "To provide for the admission of the State of Alaska into the Union," the new State was granted the right to select within twenty-five years 102,550,000 acres, principally for revenue, "from the public lands of the United States in Alaska which are vacant, unappropriated, and unreserved at the time of their selection. . . ." Since very few Eskimos and Indians in the North have entered any mineral or other claims according to United States law and the question of their aboriginal rights never has been legislated on or tested in the courts, and the land is vacant except for seasonal hunting parties, the state has become a competitor with some of its own citizens in claiming land. That is, though the land was considered theirs by some Eskimo and Indian groups, it had not been "appropriated." (In southeast Alaska, Tlingit and Haida Indians had received favourable judgment when they took their land claims case to court. For various reasons, it probably would be much harder to make out an Eskimo case.) In 1963, twenty-one villages in northern and interior Alaska, representing about a thousand residents, petitioned the United States Department of the Interior, asking that land around native villages be "frozen" and closed to state selection until aboriginal land claims could be settled.

The current oil boom in Alaska has made the original settlers, whose ancestors have occupied the region for at least 2,000 years—and perhaps 4,000 to 5,000 years—wonder whether they own their land in law. For the first time, there are great potential sources of revenue, the oil companies. The Eskimos do not want to keep them out but they want to make sure that they themselves get a good share of the income from oil leases. This they cannot do unless their claims to the land are recognized. Although land claims are not yet a political issue among Canadian Eskimos, it can be expected that the young people now in school will be quite aware of this and related issues by the time they are heads of families.

Fourth, the distribution of population in the Canadian North is more and more resembling that in Alaska, and in some other demographic characteristics the two areas now look much alike. Whereas Alaskan Eskimos for a very long time have had permanent village sites, especially at favourable locations on the coast, Canadian Eskimos have had few of these. (Iglulik is one such, periodically reoccupied through many centuries.) They tended to be dispersed in kin groups, the population widely and thinly spread, often on the move, and in winter, it seems, camped on shore ice as often as on land. Life was very insecure and mortality was high.

Today, population is increasingly concentrated at only a few points where trade, a little wage work, and public services are available, with great gaps between these places. This trend in the Canadian Arctic is already well established in Alaska north of Kotzebue Sound and the Kobuk River. South of this area, there still are many villages strung along the rivers and sea coast, although here too there tends to be withdrawal from the smallest settlements. Noticeable is the post-World War II development of trade and service centres in the 1,000 to 2,000 population range: Frobisher, Inuvik, Barrow, Kotzebue, and Bethel. Nome is now in that range although at one time much larger. A surprising number of villages now have 300 to 600 people, for example, Chimo, Great Whale River, Hooper Bay, and Kwigillingok, all of them with the same basic problem although as far apart as Ungava Bay and Kuskokwim Bay. The problem: an inadequate economy to support the population in accordance with the modern standards they have been taught. Nevertheless, with public financial assistance and public health care, both Alaskan and Canadian Eskimos are living well enough to have a high rate of annual increase: about 3.5 per cent, and in some localities even higher. On its present resource base, the Arctic easily can become over-populated, not of course in its whole area but at those few places where the population now is concentrated.

The total indigenous population consists of 28,650 Eskimos and Aleuts, according to the 1960 census of Alaska, and perhaps 5,000 Indians north of the Alaska Range, but there are only a few hundred Indians north of the Arctic Circle or north of the tree line. My characterization of the condition of these peoples has been based, however, on a smaller area and smaller population, given earlier, than the above. Moira Dunbar gives for Canada figures of 11,500 Eskimos and 50,000 Indians in the Arctic and sub-Arctic. Her sub-Arctic seems to be broader north to south and of course is much longer east to west than the comparable zone in Alaska. One must recall that many of those Indians are in the provinces, not in the territories. The number of Eskimo and mixed-Eskimo Greenlanders seems to be about 30,000. One can make as good a case for excluding the commercial fishermen of Bristol Bay and the Aleutian Islands, as I have done, as for excluding the commercial fishermen of southwest Greenland. In both areas, the people are living a life highly acculturated to the Scandinavian-American fishermen's variant of the dominant culture. Also, even though they live in treeless regions, they have in neither case Arctic tundra conditions on land or sea-ice for travel off-shore. In neither area are dog-teams now of much use.

Fifth, there is the problem of transportation. In both countries there is still no public land transportation beyond the tree line, although a road from Fairbanks to Nome is planned. This absence strongly affects population distribution, economic development, and public administration. Since Eskimos were oriented traditionally almost entirely to water and ice—even many of the caribou hunters sought their prey at river crossings or drove them into lakes—there has been nothing essentially new for them except the aeroplane. This indeed has brought them not only much greater contact with white officialdom but also with other Eskimos, and even with Indians at a few places. In both countries, medical patients are airlifted to hospitals in "southern" cities and young people are flown to boarding schools in intermediate towns. Natural barriers are surpassed; only the social barriers remain.

Historically, the Arctic of both nations first received attention because of their seas: the search for the North-West Passage and for the great whales. Now, national interest has shifted to the air for defence and transportation, to the land for economic development, chiefly in the search for exploitable minerals. The old world of the Eskimos, a world of water and ice, is not of much current use—a few fish here, a few walrus or polar bears elsewhere. For the future, there is the possibility of developing nuclear-powered submarine tankers or freighters, which would be a boon to the Canadian Arctic Archipelago, provided that sufficiently valuable cargo is found, but not a great help to the Alaskan Arctic coast.

Eskimos already have felt the lure and the pressure to become sedentary wage-workers. Now there are factors nudging them to obtain knowledge of and a concern for the land itself instead of the caribou, muskox, fox, and wolf which, like man, roamed over the land. Such a basic reorientation occurs only centuries, even millenia, apart in the history of a race.

Having looked at the similarities of Alaska and Canada, we should move on now to the differences between them; but before doing that, we might compare their agencies of cultural change in the Arctic. Then we should understand better the differences as well as the similarities.

AGENCIES OF CULTURAL CHANGE IN THE ARCTIC

Religion

Until recently, the only denominations maintaining missionaries among Canadian Eskimos were the Roman Catholic, Anglican, and Moravian churches, the last in Labrador only. In a few places, both Catholic and Anglican churches were represented, in other places only one or the other. As we shall see, at one time they provided educational and medical services partially subsidized by the federal government.

In Alaska, the Aleut areas of the southwestern part of the state, Sitka in southeast Alaska, and a few Eskimo villages as far north as the Kuskokwim Valley, but none in the Arctic, still have Russian Orthodox churches surviving from the days of Russian occupation, although they have long since lost any direct connection with Russia. Russian churches were located no farther north than their trade and administration penetrated.

When the dominant sects of the United States began to establish missions in Alaska, they decided not to compete with each other in the northern villages. As a result, until after World War II, while there might have been competing churches in centres like Nome and Bethel, most outlying villages were grouped in provinces, each with its prevailing denomination, Roman Catholic, Episcopal, Presbyterian, Moravian, a Friends church (not the better known Friends or Quakers), and Evangelical Covenant being the principal ones. Both in Canada and in the

United States, fundamentalist, evangelical sects such as the Pentecostal have disregarded the gentlemen's agreement regarding areas, and within the past ten years have started to compete vigorously with the older churches. There are now quite a few Alaskan Eskimo and Aleut lay preachers or lay readers (the writer would guess there are at least fifty but two-thirds or three-fourths of these men live south of the Arctic) and perhaps six or seven ordained ministers or priests, the Russian Orthodox, Moravian, Evangelical Covenant, Episcopal, and Presbyterian churches having done the most to develop such local leadership. Although catechists and other church leaders among Canadian Eskimo laymen are not unknown, there seems to be a smaller proportion of them in the total church membership. Certainly, in both countries a high proportion of the settled Eskimos are devoted church attendants. One might note, incidentally, that a study of the present status of churches in the Arctic is very much needed.

Schools

Even though a Presbyterian missionary provided the strongest force in the early development of education in Alaska, both the federal and the territorial systems of education early separated schools from churches. The federal system progressively withdrew subsidies to mission schools throughout the period 1895–1915.[3] While there have been a few parochial schools in Alaska, those outside the cities seem to have developed from orphanages. There are now no such schools in the Arctic. (Similarly, a few Canadian Eskimo orphans were sent to mission boarding schools at Fort Providence, Hay River, or Fort Resolution, far south in the Mackenzie Valley.) Finally, the cities have their own school systems, accepting all resident children, regardless of race, among whom there are some urbanized Eskimos and Indians.

The Alaska territorial school system for white children and mixed blood children living "a civilized life" was founded in 1905, while the federal schools were for "native" children. Until the 1940's and 1950's, therefore, a few towns with a mixed population had a dual educational system. Gradually the duplication was eliminated, and now all children attend whatever school their village has, whether state—succeeding the territorial system—or federal. The Bureau of Indian Affairs, of the Department of the Interior, provides the federal schools, which serve many although not all Aleuts, Eskimos, and Indians. This system includes, besides nearly eighty village day-schools, about two-thirds of

[3]Diamond Jenness, no. 10 (1962), p. 11.

which are in Eskimo communities, a boarding high school at Sitka, in southeast Alaska, with an enrolment of more than seven hundred, and a boarding grammar or grade school, also southeast, for children with inadequate or no homes. Young people are sent from all parts of the state to Mount Edgecumbe, the high school at Sitka, which was established in 1947. For special purposes, some youths are sent to "Indian schools" outside Alaska. From the beginning, children at all levels have been taught in English and without any form of picture writing or syllabics. Only a few early missionaries who could speak Eskimo and until quite recently only a few Eskimo teacher aides in the federal schools might instruct partly in Eskimo, but chiefly for the purpose of clarifying the English. The English language was not learned immediately, however. Today, at such Arctic coast villages as Port Hope and Wainwright, all residents except the aged speak English well, that is, within their range of experience and reading. One must remember, however, that these villages were in regular contact with American whalers for about fifty years and that when the whaling declined, their formal schooling began. By 1905, there were four schools on the coast from Bering Strait to Barrow.

Although there had been occasional Eskimo graduates of high schools before, since 1951 there has been a steady stream of graduates from Mount Edgecumbe. By now a few Eskimo youths have graduated from the University of Alaska. (No one knows how many have returned to live in their own or similar villages and how many have migrated to cities in or out of Alaska.) Despite this progress in education, the 1960 decennial census showed that the median school year completed for the non-white population as a whole was only 6.6. This was, however, an increase from less than two years median of schooling twenty years earlier. In northwest Alaska, including nearly all the Arctic region as the term is being used here, 11 per cent of the population twenty-five years old and over had had in 1960 no schooling, while at the other end of the scale 30 per cent had had more than grade school education. In the south-west region, 22 per cent had had no schooling by 1960, while 38 per cent had gone beyond grade school.[4] The former figure (22 per cent) is explained by the isolation and "backwardness" until recently of the Lower Yukon-Lower Kuskokwim region, which has the highest Eskimo population density, and the latter figure by the advancement of

[4]George W. Rogers and Richard A. Cooley, *Alaska's Population and Economy*, vol. 1, *Analysis*, Division of State Planning, Office of the Governor (Alaska, 1962) pp. 86-9, figs. 20 and 21.

the commercial fishermen of the Bristol Bay-Aleutian region. One of the biggest problems for the native peoples is revealed by these contrasting figures: whereas in 1960 only 1.2 per cent of whites in Alaska had less than five years of formal schooling, 38.6 per cent of non-whites were at this level.

The educational situation in Arctic Canada at first appears simple compared with that of Alaska: until 1949 there were no federal schools and no territorial system of education in the North-West Territories (there were federal schools for Indians in the Yukon Territory) and no provincial schools in northern Quebec or northern Labrador. Yet the Department of Northern Affairs and National Resources notes that "in 1949 eight different authorities operated schools in the north. Only three classrooms were operated by the Department." And these three had just begun to function, at Fort Chimo, Fort Brabant, and Fort McPherson. The different authorities presumably were those of the religious denominations and of the town of Yellowknife which had its own educational system. In a frank review, the department states,

Some schools operated for only four hours a day, four days a week, and 35 per cent of the teachers in such schools did not hold teaching certificates. Classroom visitations were infrequent. Film services and adult education classes were provided in only three communities. There was no vocational training program nor were there any teachers employed to teach hospital patients. There was little or no provision for any program of in-service training and there were no plans for using a curriculum, other than that of the Province of Alberta. Community libraries were almost unknown. There were only 117 Eskimo children attending school on a full-time basis.

More progress has been made in education in the Northwest Territories in the ten-year period between the 1949–50 academic year and the 1958–59 academic year than has been made in any other part of Canada. The number of Eskimos in schools has increased over 1,000 per cent and the number of federal schools has increased from 3 schools with 1 classroom each to a total of 51 schools with 182 classrooms. [This covers northern Quebec as well as North-West Territories.] The total enrolment in all schools has increased from 1,121 pupils in 1949, to 3,928 in September, 1958. In 1949, there were 103 pupils enrolled in the junior and senior high school grades. [Presumably, none or almost none of these were Eskimo.] By September 1, 1958, this enrolment had increased to 576 pupils. A gradual consolidation of the various types of schools began in 1954 and in 1955 schools formerly operated by the Indian Affairs Branch were transferred to the Department of Northern Affairs. In 1956, all mission school teachers became federal employees. . . . By 1960, there will be only two authorities operating schools in the Northwest Territories. . . . These will be federally-operated and municipally-operated schools. All schools now offer a full five hours of instruction daily for five days a week.

. . . by September 1, 1958, all northern teachers held at least a first-class teaching certificate or license.[5]

Visits by supervisors, in-service training, and other assistance to teachers similarly had been increased. In 1958, the first vocational school in the Northwest Territories was opened at Yellowknife, offering high-school level education.

Although not many Eskimos are yet sufficiently advanced to enroll, the few who can qualify are transported and maintained there by the federal government. As of January 1961, 46 Eskimos from the District of Mackenzie had reached grade seven or above.[6]

Despite difficulties, both Canada and Alaska have adult education programmes and, more successfully, films are distributed to the schools. Radio broadcasts in Eskimo, important in reaching non-English-speaking folk, are handled differently in the two countries: in Canada, such broadcasts—from Frobisher, Churchill, Yellowknife, and Inuvik—are government-sponsored; in Alaska, Eskimo language broadcasts are privately sponsored. The Canadian Broadcasting Corporation initiated its Northern Service in 1958.

Both countries have a problem not only in keeping Eskimo children in school—a greater problem in Canada because of their parents' hunting-trapping economy—but also in keeping southern teachers in the northern schools. More than a third of the teachers in North-West Territories schools resign at the end of their first year and another third at the end of their second year.[7]

Both countries have expensive construction programmes, necessarily expensive because of the Arctic's special requirements. In 1949, when there were thought to be 15,700 Eskimos in Alaska (a possible under-enumeration), there were 47 Indian Bureau and 8 territorial schools in Eskimo villages. Today, when the population is well past 20,000, there are not many more schools but more classrooms, and larger quarters for the added teachers. Also, Alaska has more old schools to be replaced. Canada has the advantage of having nearly all new ones, with, of course, new teacherages in its Eskimo settlements. In 1963, it had 37 federal schools in the North-West Territories and Northern Quebec Eskimo settlements for a population of about 11,500. Although a ratio based on total population is not as good as one based on school-age population (also based on number of schools rather than number of

[5]Department of Northern Affairs and National Resources, *Northern Education: Ten Years of Progress*, Education Division (Ottawa, 1960?) pp. 1–2.
[6]Diamond Jenness, no. 14, p. 123.
[7]*Ibid.*, p. 129.

classrooms), a comparison of the two national systems using a crude ratio of schools to population shows that each had a school for every unit of 290 to 300 people. The principal difference is that Alaska reached this level fifteen years earlier.

Two differences between the two governments' educational policies need mention. One, the use of a syllabic writing, has really been forced on the Department of Northern Affairs because Eskimos from King William Island to Hudson Strait and James Bay use it instead of the Roman alphabet. All other Eskimos use the latter. To reach the east-central group, the Eskimo language magazine published by the department uses syllabics, although use of this script perpetuates the educational and economic cleavage between eastern and western Eskimos. The other difference is more fundamental since it involves personal relations: Canada and Greenland have taken the lead in providing hostels for students and patients away from home. At Inuvik, there is

a large federal school with accommodation for 625 pupils, 500 of whom can live in the two hostels that flank the school building. The Anglican church operates one hostel, the Roman Catholic church the other; but the children share the same classrooms and possess a common playground. Alongside the federal school at Chesterfield Inlet is another hostel capable of housing 80 children. Here the government purchased the hostel building from the Roman Catholic mission, but left the operation of the hostel in the mission's hands.[8]

Except for a school at White Mountain a few years ago, the Indian Bureau in Alaska has not had hostels (dormitories), that is, boarding-schools, in the Eskimo areas. After fifteen years of discussion, the argument for federal high schools in northwest Alaska, which Eskimo youth can attend instead of going hundreds of miles away to the southeast, has been accepted and such schools are being built at Barrow and Kotzebue—however, without dormitories. The students are expected to live with local Eskimo families, as they have done at Bethel for several years. The agency now (1964) is asking Congress for funds to build a 150-pupil dormitory at Nome in connection with a new vocational school. It will be interesting to see how both countries handle this problem in the future. There are strong arguments against large hostels since they take young people away from home life at an important period in their development. On the other hand, most Eskimo families cannot board children other than their own, or even their own who are not working, unless they get bigger houses and more income. This is one of the difficulties of "progress" on the frontier.

[8]*Ibid.*, p. 137.

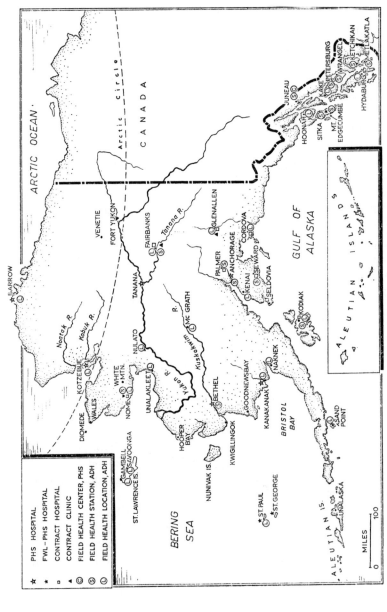

MAP 1. Location of US Public Health Service, Fish and Wildlife Service, and Alaska Department of Health facilities in 1959, and of villages cited in text. (Adapted from a map prepared by the US Department of Health, Education, and Welfare.)

Medical Care (See Map 1)

It should be recalled that, at the moment, we are reviewing agencies of change, of socialization of the individual and acculturation of the group, to see what the agencies have been and when they existed. We are not trying to survey all the needs for and effects of all agencies in the North.

Although there have been physicians elsewhere in the North-West Territories for short periods, the three long-time locations of doctors have been Pangnirtung on the east side of Baffin Island, Chesterfield Inlet on the west side of Hudson Bay, and Aklavik in the Mackenzie Delta, with no facilities between these widely separated places. Before World War II, the hospitals at all three places were mission operated and federally subsidized. Also, a few medicines were supplied to northern missions. Government vessels in the eastern Arctic could do little more than give first aid and could not give even that to many villages that they could not reach. It was not until the new deal for the Arctic came in after the war that, as in education, medical facilities and services were rapidly expanded.

In 1939 Canada's total medical expenses on behalf of the Eskimos amounted to $29,480, or a little over $4.00 per head of population; and of that $4.00, roughly $3.00 went to pay the salaries and living expenses of the four white doctors and five white nurses who composed the medical staff. . . . In the fiscal year 1961–62, according to an estimate . . . by the Northern Health Service of the Department of National Health and Welfare, Canada spent over $3,000,000, one hundred times the amount she spent in 1939. . . .[9]

By 1963, there were in northern Quebec and the North-West Territories fifteen nursing stations, several health stations where public health nurses could hold clinics but did not reside, and four hospitals: at Pangnirtung, Frobisher Bay, Chesterfield Inlet, and Inuvik. The two new ones, Frobisher and Inuvik, are government operated. Tuberculosis patients from the western Arctic were hospitalized in Edmonton and those from the Hudson Bay area were hospitalized at Moose Factory. (In the post-war period Health and Welfare has been given several Department of National Defence hospitals and has built others.) In 1946, X-ray surveys by specially outfitted government vessels were started. Most important, in recent years preventive medicine and health education have been started among the Eskimos. To help prevent the serious health conditions that have prevailed (high rates of tuberculosis,

[9]*Ibid.,* p. 143.

infant mortality, and accidents are the chief problems), Northern Affairs has undertaken a housing programme, annually shipping to the North materials for about 150 dwellings, which it gives to destitute Eskimos and sells to others at a low price. The latest development is a rudimentary training and payment of health aides to work in their own villages. The health care, Family Allowance and other financial help, a less hazardous life, and more education operate together to produce the rate of population increase mentioned earlier. This requires in turn a more productive economy, to support the population without high "relief" payments. But that is another story.

In Alaska until the 1950's the Bureau of Indian Affairs operated field hospitals at Juneau, Kanakanak, Bethel, Tanana, Kotzebue, and Barrow (all built after 1930 except the one at Juneau), while churches operated and supported two hospitals in the North outside the cities: at Nome and Fort Yukon. Roman Catholic orders operated most of the hospitals in the larger towns. As in Canada large hospitals were developed after World War II, one acquired from the Navy (at Edgecumbe) and another built at Anchorage. Both had many tuberculosis patients, but were not limited to the treatment of this disease.[10] Services by the Territorial Department of Health were minimal until 1945 when the Health Officer's position was made a full-time job.

By 1931, just before the duties of the Bureau of Education were transferred to the Bureau of Indian Affairs, its appropriation had included $824,000 for education, $319,000 for medical work and $26,000 for reindeer service.[11] Until that time and even continuing into the 1930's, many coastal villages distant from the field hospitals received medical attention only from Coast Guard ship's surgeons and a nurse on the Indian Bureau's own supply vessel, and only in summer, while remote interior villages did not receive even this much attention. The $319,000 was spent almost entirely for the government hospitals and for some contract care in private hospitals. One can imagine how much health education was possible.

In the late 1940's medical work began to accelerate. In 1949, the United States Public Health Service established the Arctic Health Research Center to investigate systematically the hazards to health in the North; the Territory developed a system of public health nurses who in due time supplanted the federal field nurses, except for those in one

---

[10]Department of Health, Education and Welfare, *Eskimos, Indians, and Aleuts of Alaska: A Digest*, Division of Indian Health, Public Health Service (Washington, D.C., 1963).

[11]Diamond Jenness, no. 10, p. 26.

region who assist in federal research projects; in 1954 territorial and national health agencies co-operated in launching a large TB case-finding and hospitalization programme, even sending Eskimo and Indian patients, chiefly the former, to three hospitals in the Seattle-Tacoma area; in the same year a programme was launched to train sanitation aides to work in their villages; and in 1955 all medical responsibilities were transferred from the Indian Bureau to the Public Health Service, in the Department of Health, Education, and Welfare. The latest development is the federal provision of materials to villages for construction of sanitation facilities.

In strong contrast with the 1931 total of a little more than one million dollars for both education and health services, the federal appropriation for fiscal year 1964 totals close to $15 million for education and construction and maintenance of schools (not including such things as "development of arts and crafts" and "relocation and adult vocational training") and nearly $14 million for Indian Health activities and construction, not including the Research Center, Coast Guard medical care, and numerous grants to the State Department of Health and Welfare, as to all states, for specific programmes like cancer control and water pollution control for the benefit of the general public.[12] Even though the Eskimo-Aleut population may have nearly doubled in the same period, with the Indian population increasing less rapidly, the nearly thirty-fold rise in expenditures reflects not merely the size and urgency of need but the size of national concern and feeling of responsibility as well as the national capacity to deal with the problems of the North.

Trade and Industry

The Canadian story on this subject has been relatively simple. It is the story of the Hudson's Bay Company, so well known—especially to Canadians—as not to require repetition here. The peak of Hudson's Bay Company expansion seems to have been reached before 1930, with a closing of many of its Arctic posts during the depression of the 1930's, when its chief competitor disappeared, and during the war. The whaling ships, which also had done some trading, had long ago ceased to visit both the eastern and western American Arctic, and in 1936 Revillon Frères withdrew from its field in the eastern Arctic so that thereafter the Hudson's Bay Company had a monopoly.

The people of the Mackenzie Delta did not have such limited trade contacts as did the Central Eskimos (roughly, those from King William

12Information from office of Senator E. L. Bartlett, Jan. 10, 1964.

Island to and including Baffin Island), and they seem to have learned more about the value of money. Their habitat provides muskrat so that from Indian and White trappers as well as traders they learned more than the trapping of white fox, which was virtually the only basis of any money economy in the eastern Arctic between the end of commercial whaling and beginning of the current arts and crafts business. Bartering fox skins for traps, ammunition, tea and flour was a simple business from which the Eskimos could learn little of modern economics.

In Alaska, there was no trade monopoly north of the Aleutians. There might be only one trader in a village, but if an Eskimo had enough initiative to go to a village outside his immediate area, he could deal with a different individual entrepreneur or the representative of a different company, and in some areas individual fur buyers visited the settlements, paying cash. Such competition did not necessarily bring low prices for goods. Here, as in Canada, high freight rates were the reason for—but on some goods, only the excuse for—very high prices for commercial products. Nevertheless, there was generally a *laissez-faire* situation, of which both buyers and sellers took advantage. For the local people, the greatest advantage was not economic but social and educational. Traders who were small businessmen, not company agents likely to be transferred elsewhere in a few years, were settlers, residents who lived in houses that they usually built for themselves. If they married Eskimo women, so much the better, as their children almost always were bilingual. From the traders and from a few long-term resident missionaries and teachers with families, the villagers could learn the everyday practical personal values of the North American white man's culture far better than they could learn it in formal classroom instruction —or than they can learn these values now from government teachers and administrators living in, for the Arctic, excellent housing that most of them individually could not afford to build. The latter are almost like the mine owner's and manager's families living on the hill while the miners' families live in the valley by the pit-head.

The only other source of information on everyday life was, for the local people, the transient single men—construction workers, military ranks, ships' crews and other transport workers. As one recent observer of life in the North has commented astutely, much of the Eskimo and Indian drinking, gambling, easy-go attitude toward money and personal responsibilities, and vocabulary has been learned from this class of transient whites, with whom they could associate more comfortably than with middle-class white officialdom.[13] Most traders were between

[13]Jacob Fried, "The Northwest Territories: A Survey of Emerging Communities" (Manuscript, 1963).

these two groups of whites, often taking advantage in small ways of their customers' ignorance of modern economics, yet having to be sufficiently responsible to be tolerated for many years as resident businessmen.

One of the greatest deficiencies of the Canadian central and eastern Arctic, in contrast with the Mackenzie Valley, Yukon Territory, and Alaska is that, except for Labrador, it has no true immigrants, no people from outside the Arctic who have brought their families to settle among the old inhabitants. Even the "old sourdough" prospectors and trappers have been lacking. Many of the long-term residents who have made the eastern Arctic genuinely their home have been unmarried missionaries. Helpful as they and other representatives of outside agencies have been, they have not been settlers on the frontier. The mining and oil companies' technologists and local superintendents may learn much about the region in which their companies happen to operate, yet they tend to form their own society, living a well-furnished life shipped in from the south, in both its material and non-material aspects. Closer to being true settlers are a few bush pilots and aircraft mechanics who are building an essential business in the North.

If, under modern conditions, whites cannot be brought into the Eskimos' world, then Eskimos must be brought into the white man's world. This does not mean necessarily that Eskimos must move to Winnipeg and Montreal, although this may be the desperate eventuality if no adequate employment in the North can be found. Classroom instruction in northern Alaska and Canada is based on the assumption that all citizens have a right to the same schooling and will have an opportunity to use it. Difficult as it may be to keep the children in school more than three or four months a year and to teach them the history and organization of institutions they have never experienced, these tasks are simple compared with the task of developing a society and an economy to fulfil the educational promise. The question that has bothered educators for many years has special force in the far North: what are we educating the children *for*?

For years a few Eskimo and northern Indian children have been brought south to live, always special cases such as orphans adopted by white missionaries, and a few Eskimo women have moved out with their Caucasian husbands. In Alaska there is now a programme to relocate in the other states any individuals and families classified as "natives," hence eligible for such Indian Bureau help, who want to move south and are qualified in language, work experience, and the like. In 1961, for example, 140 Eskimos were helped by relocation officers to find jobs and housing, and their transportation and initial living expenses were paid by the government. They have resettled not in the closest states but in developing states like California and even as far away as Ohio and Texas. (This is part of a national programme to move Indian volunteers to industrial centres from unproductive rural areas.) Some of the moves have been successful, others unsuccessful and unhappy experiences. In the latter cases, many of the "relocatees" have returned to Alaska as soon as they could accumulate enough money to do so. The programme, however, continues and is expected to increase. Although Alaskans have had advantages in that they have had opportunities to gain experience in a variety of jobs for many years—working in salmon canneries in the state (several hundreds are flown seasonally from the tundra villages to south Alaska fishing areas), formerly on river boats elsewhere, in gold mines somewhere else—it can be expected that in ten to fifteen years Canadian Eskimos, even in the eastern Arctic, will catch up with their western relatives and will be ready to move South. Already, in the movies that are distributed to all the schools, the children are getting a preview of the world that they probably will want to move into. Already a few young men are receiving intensive training in operating various types of machines, and in due time some Eskimos will be inducted into the field of electronics. The biggest problem will not be theirs but ours: how will we in the south receive them? If some of the Alaskans' experiences can be taken as an example, it can be predicted that social integration will be hard. The recommendation in a recent publication, therefore, should be considered seriously: to bring to the South small colonies of Eskimo families, which would be supported by work in river transportation and other occupations not entirely different from those they have known.[14]

Meanwhile, if the Eskimo people are to have something to live on besides government "welfare," they must be able to produce and sell things that are wanted outside the Arctic, since they must buy so much from outside their region. Guns and ammunition, canned milk and flour are not produced in the Arctic. These imperatives have spurred the development of a new agency of change: the co-operative. There are now sixteen government-sponsored co-ops distributed from the Mackenzie Delta to the east coast of Baffin Island. In 1960 there were only eight: six in the North-West Territories and two in northern Quebec.[15] In 1963 a conference was held at Frobisher to bring together for the first time representatives of all the co-ops and surprisingly, in view of transportation difficulties, nearly all were represented. Moreover, despite

[14]Diamond Jenness, no. 14, pp. 176–78.
[15]*Government Activities in the North—1960*, p. 93.

timidity in an unfamiliar situation, several of the Eskimo co-op officers were willing to express their ideas, whether or not these agreed with the views of their white advisers.

These Canadian co-operatives are chiefly production organizations: for catching and shipping fresh char, for making stone sculptures and prints, fur clothing and other handwork. They depend heavily on the Department of Northern Affairs for help in marketing their products, a service that they must have since their leaders do not yet know southern markets. Despite ups and downs, this northern co-operative movement has been generally successful. The next step probably is a buying as well as selling organization, and the third step is a credit union. Most Eskimos, like the Japanese, are adept at hand crafts, imitative, and quick to learn material things, yet showing their own particular style when given an opportunity. Despite the danger of fashion changes in any business based on specialty products (as trappers and traders learned when white fox and other long-haired furs went out of fashion), nevertheless, until basic industries such as mining and oil drilling come to their regions, Canadian Eskimos have little choice of occupations.

They should be encouraged to do what they can do best; then southern Canada as well as the Eskimos will be the richer. People who until two generations ago made every single weapon, implement, utensil, toy, ceremonial object, and boat that their families needed, and often made them ingeniously from inadequate materials, should be regarded more as craftsmen than as hunters and trappers. Both Canada and Alaska have been fortunate in having a few true leaders, white and Eskimo, private entrepreneurs and government representatives, who have developed the ivory carving and wood carving of the Alaskans and the stone carving of the Canadians, but more such people are needed to bring in more new ideas and marketing know-how in order to make good use of a skilful labour force.

In Alaska, village co-operatives (also government sponsored) were started a generation earlier, as much for purchasing as for marketing. (Reindeer-owning corporations, with individual reindeer owners holding shares, had also been promoted but, poorly conceived by both Eskimos and government officials, they have foundered.) By 1930, eighteen Eskimo villages had community stores; in 1950, there were thirty-three. In 1939, a federal revolving credit fund began functioning, from which loans in other parts of Alaska were given to Indian-owned canneries and other production enterprises but from which loans in the Eskimo area were given chiefly to establish the village stores. The record of repayment was good. The managers were local men chosen by their communities. In 1947, twenty-seven native village stores (20 Eskimo and 7 Aleut or Indian) were organized in a purchasing and merchandising co-operative, known as the Alaska Native Industries Co-operative Association, with headquarters in Seattle and with a manager from the Indian Bureau, who occasionally exercises a benevolent restraint on inexperienced store managers who order much more than their shipments of furs and craft products can pay for.

The co-operative movement in the North is part of two larger movements, one economic and the other social, both of which are essential: diversification of products and purchasing channels (the mail-order business has helped the latter) and experience in community organization. This leads to our next major topic.

Politics and Law

In both national jurisdictions, Eskimos are citizens, not members of tribes with which the government deals as with foreign nations. Administrative devices have been found at times to prevent their doing what other citizens could do: buy and sell liquor.[16] The motive here can be characterized as kindly paternalism. In other aspects of civic life, the lack of full citizenship functions for Eskimos probably can be attributed to simple neglect, the urgent need to do other things first, the lack of Eskimo demands for citizenship rights, and the opinion that they have not been politically mature enough to exercise their prerogatives. Their principal political disability in Canada has been lack of a vote. The illiteracy of many would be an obstacle to their voting even if the opportunity to do so were given. In Alaska, similarly, even though it has been legally possible to have all necessary election machinery in outlying villages, the establishment of election districts and the holding of elections, for representatives to the territorial (now state) legislature, for example, were accomplished slowly because the residents did not ask for them. If they had, their request could not have been granted in all cases because of the rate of illiteracy. Gradually, however, with the growth of education and political awareness, not only Eskimos in large villages like Kotzebue but also those in some of the smaller communities have been able and willing to exercise their citizenship rights. And there have been Eskimo as well as Indian members of the legislature for many years.

The situation in the Keewatin (central) and Franklin (eastern)

16Diamond Jenness, no. 14, pp. 36–7.

districts of the North-West Territories is somewhat different: there appear to be no elected representatives in the territorial or federal government.[17] For information on this subject, the reader is referred to Mr. Fingland's article, page 130. Whether the indigenous residents of northern Quebec vote in that province's elections is not clear. Probably they do not try to vote because they lack knowledge of political issues and perscnalities.

Nearly every student of modern community development in the Canadian Arctic—there have been some excellent reports—has described the lack of formal community organization among Eskimos. Centuries of life in small camps, with frequent moves from place to place, were not good preparation for modern organization. It is because earlier efforts to form village councils or other representative units have failed that the current co-operative movement is so significant.

Although no Alaskan Eskimo village until the 1940's had more than 500 people (in 1939, only 20 of the approximately 200 to 220 villages had more than 200 inhabitants apiece), the people nevertheless did have a sense of community and the rudiments of an organization. When, beginning in 1936, the Indian Bureau began urging the villages to organize and to elect councils, the larger, more active ones complied, until by 1950, thirty-two Eskimo communities had organized and had received charters from the government. This did not mean, however, that all the councils were effective functioning bodies. Organization, even among the more settled Alaskans, did not come easily. Nevertheless, experience was gained, until today there are mothers' clubs, locally run church organizations, and National Guard units (chiefly in coastal villages) besides the councils, even in villages where the Eskimo language still is dominant. The same kind of development can be foreseen in Canada if stability is achieved. However, if the people must constantly move around in order to gain a living, village organization will be slow.

An excellent means of giving people experience in organization— many would say the ultimate in organization in western society—is military service. This is an example of the way in which small fringe groups are affected by large national policies never developed for them. In the United States, Eskimos, like other citizens, are subject to military draft. Canadian Eskimos, like other citizens, are not drafted. In time, though, some young men will volunteer.

In regard to the police, the Royal Canadian Mounted Police is rightly visualized by the Temperate Zone citizen as an important institution in the North. For a long time lacking government teachers or other

[17]R. A. J. Phillips, "The Administration of Northern Canada" (1963) (Mimeo).

representatives of government, except on ships that came in to the Arctic only in the summer, the northern areas received from the Royal Canadian Mounted Police whatever government services could be given. The policemen's feats of dog-team travel, of assistance to the starving and the injured, and of tracking down murderers are legendary. Like the Hudson's Bay Company agents, they need no further description here.

In Alaska, police duties were not performed so vigorously and consistently. Until Alaska became a state and organized its own state police system, that is, while it was a federal territory, there were only US Marshals outside the cities, and they were stationed in only a few large villages. There still are US Marshals and US Commissioners, the latter to perform civil duties much like those of county judge and county clerk in other states where there is a county organization, which Alaska does not have; but the Alaska constitution provides for the formation of boroughs, a process that has just begun. By January 1964 eight boroughs had been formed, only one of which is in an area with considerable Eskimo population, namely Bristol Bay. Each borough absorbs existing school districts, utility districts, and other civil bodies, becoming a political unit like a metropolitan county. How the borough system will function in the outlying areas is not yet clear.

Finally, Arctic Canada and Alaska are alike in that one federal agency has wider and more important responsibilities for developing the North than any other: in Canada, the Department of Northern Affairs and National Resources; in Alaska, the Department of the Interior. For co-ordination of plans and activities, there are advantages in this; but there may develop in Canada what has already appeared in Alaska, namely, the local residents' feeling that they are not sufficiently free agents, that their whole welfare depends on a bureaucracy far away in the nation's capital. Since the granting of statehood, this feeling has lessened somewhat in Alaska, and it is hoped, with greater self-government for the North-West Territories, people there will not feel and will not become in fact too dependent on one federal agency.

For an under-developed, economically dependent, marginal area, there probably must be a period in which the officials of a department unconsciously develop a benevolent managerial and possessive attitude like that of superintendents of national parks and other national trusts. The Arctic *is* a national trust—with a difference: it is not merely land underlaid with great natural resources. It is also the home of some Canadian citizens who are just entering the national life. They present the anomaly of being among the country's oldest inhabitants and in speech and culture among the newest of New Canadians. Regarding the Eskimos, administrators are pulled and divided between two viewpoints which, at the extremes, can be stated as follows: Eskimos are actually relics of another era, to be maintained in their natural habitat. Or, Eskimos must be resettled in the industrially expanding areas like any other immigrants. The Department of Northern Affairs and the Department of the Interior are presented with no easy choice.

The former has done more than the latter in trying to co-ordinate the plans of all federal agencies that operate in the Territories. For the past ten years an interdepartmental co-ordinating committee, called the Advisory Committee on Northern Development, promoted especially by the Department of Northern Affairs, has been functioning. In Alaska, a Field Committee of the Department of the Interior tries to keep at least the varied Bureaus within that Department working together, but beyond that, there is no comprehensive co-ordinating body.

Similarities of Canada and Alaska have been reviewed. Let us now summarize the pertinent differences.

DIFFERENCES BETWEEN ALASKA AND CANADA

First, the eastern Canadian Arctic offers narrower economic opportunity, that is, there is less variety in the economy, than in the western Canadian Arctic and in Alaska, due to barrenness and, in some places, inaccessibility. There is a central coastal area northwest of Hudson Bay and east of Coronation Gulf, for example, that is hard to reach by sea from either west or east because of ice conditions. As with any single-industry region, its residents suffer not only from the decline of that industry—in this case, fox trapping—but also because they are unable to adjust readily to other occupations. The relative poverty of both land and sea (at their present stage of development) means that there are not as many bush planes serving it as in the Eskimo area of Alaska. East-west transportation and communication have been especially meagre, compared with the north-south. This situation has not been conducive to inter-area trade within the Arctic. Also, except for a few Eskimo families who for a generation or more have moved from one major area to another as employees of the Hudson's Bay Company or the RCMP, eastern Canadian Eskimos as a whole have only recently started to make major moves in search of employment or education.

As we have seen, to exist in an unproductive region, that is, unproductive at their level of technology, Eskimos had to live in small isolated groups. This life, in turn, was not conducive to local community organization. All these factors together explain why it was not until the government made large expenditures in the North during and following World War II, especially in construction of the DEW Line, that communications were developed, employment became more diversified, and the population began to clump in a few places. Although in Alaska the same processes were speeded by the same drive for northern defence in the past fifteen to twenty years, the processes were started there before World War II, because of greater accessibility and because of a slightly stronger economy.

Second, Canadian Eskimos have had less education, less use of English or French language, and less political participation, and they still have less autonomy than Alaskan Eskimos. The difference in education is due to a time lag in government policy: the missions were depended on to provide schooling for a longer time in Canada's North than in Alaska. Presently there is little difference between the two governments in their expenditures of money, time, and thought; but general realization by government of the magnitude of the job to be done in the Arctic—a few people always had known it—has come only recently. So long as it was thought that a few thousand dollars, instead of a few million, were adequate, the task of education could be given to private agencies.

Even more fundamental was an attitude toward the Arctic as a whole: it was not really a part of national life, hence did not need what the remainder of the nation needed. It would have helped if Boothia Peninsula or the west side of Baffin Island had had a gold rush, bringing in thousands of Canadians. Even though they did not stay, the Arctic would thereafter have been part of their experience. Without natural economic forces to bring the far northern peoples into a "one of us" or "part of us" relationship to other Canadians, universal education and representative government were not extended to the country's northern limits. It appears that finally a combination of forces did strongly influence the federal government to institute a comprehensive policy of Arctic development: pride aroused by competition with the other nations owning Arctic lands; improved communication and greater travel to and from and within the Arctic bringing much better knowledge of it; defence needs and natural resource needs at last bringing the attitude that "that region is a necessary part of our country." Last to come is the feeling that "an Eskimo is one of us."

ADMINISTRATION FOR DEVELOPMENT OF A DEPENDENT PEOPLE

To see Canadian administration in comparison with others, it is useful to list the reasons for caring for a dependent people, that is, a people who may or may not have attitudes of dependency but who are largely dependent for their livelihood on government programmes rather than private industry and their own efforts. (Most Eskimos still do some hunting, trapping, and fishing, yet obtain much of their cash support as well as schools and other services directly from the national government.) The commonest objectives in supporting such a people are: (i) to establish sovereignty over their land; (ii) to get labour for enterprises that need a labour pool, inside or outside the indigenous people's territory, or to get military conscripts; (iii) to get special skills or products that only these people can provide; (iv) to provide defence, military or non-military, perhaps only to occupy the territory with a friendly people, to prevent infiltration; (v) to meet current welfare standards, for humanitarian reasons.

The first objective has never been an important reason for providing services to Eskimos in either Canada or Alaska although RCMP posts were established at the eastern end of the Arctic Archipelago in the 1920's in order "to show the flag."[18] Once established, the police gave their usual services, but of course there were few people in those remote areas. As for Alaska, beginning about 1880 US revenue cutters were sent around its north-west coast to keep under control the whaling fleet's sale of liquor (or the ingredients for making spirits) to Eskimos as well as to show the flag, and possibly give support and protection to crews building a telegraph line to Europe by way of Alaska and Siberia.

The second reason—to get labourers or soldiers—has had almost no significance. Some whaling ships in the last two decades or more of the nineteenth century took Eskimo men and women aboard at various settlements along the Alaskan Arctic coast and carried them eastward to Hershel Island and even farther east on the Canadian coast, but this brought little government attention. In other words, the United States government was not working with a great industry in need of labour. Similarly in Canada there was nothing like the long-term well-established South African system of taking Negroes to work in the mines.

The third possibility has at various times become an actuality. In gold rushes and mining booms, Eskimos with dog-teams, Indians with

[18]Diamond Jenness, no. 14, pp. 29–31.

boats, local guides, people with skins for sale for warm clothing have not only been paid well but, congregating at the "hot spots," have come to the attention of missionaries and government officers and in due time have received their assistance. Eskimo dog-team drivers and guides have been sought and appreciated by scientific expeditions. Lately Eskimos working at DEW Line sites and bases have been helped to get village water supplies, building materials, and medical services, partly for humanitarian reasons and partly to ensure a healthy resident labour force more willing to work under local conditions than is imported labour. Before the development of air transport, Indians along the Yukon (in Alaska) and Slave-Mackenzie (in Canada) River systems worked cutting fuel wood for the river boats. Again, incidental services were received. The Canadian Indians lost their occupation when diesel boats and then aircraft came to the Mackenzie; the Alaskans lost theirs when first the Alaska Railroad and later the Alaska Highway and aircraft supplanted river traffic.

The strongest present impetus to give help, in the form of art and craft training, organization of producing co-operatives and organization of marketing, comes from the discovery of Eskimo artistic skills, or perhaps we should say, from the discovery of public demand for the kind of stone sculptures and prints that several eastern Canadian Arctic groups can produce. Beginning in the late 1930's, the Indian Bureau in Alaska similarly began organizing and promoting the Eskimo women's manufacture of skin clothing, an effort that paid off well during World War II. In another two generations such skills may be lost. While they exist, governments are wise to capitalize them, as they seem to provide a sound bridge between traditional craft work solely for home use and fully industrialized work requiring new skills. In other words, the old skills are applied to new materials or they produce new styles, and the finished product gets a much wider distribution requiring a kind of organization that is new to the craftsman. If nothing else is accomplished, this last is an important accomplishment.

The establishment of about two hundred National Guard units in north and west Alaskan villages since World War II is an example of the fourth motivation: defence. Issue of heavy military clothing, guns and ammunition has been undoubtedly more helpful to Eskimo guardsmen than it is potentially helpful to their nation. Certain types of education received as part of the Guard training is a benefit to both. The other important example of defence, the DEW Line, has been mentioned already.

The last objective—the humanitarian—is the most persistent motive, even though it has not always been consistent. Opinions as to what is best for the Eskimo people have varied; the willingness to spend money and thought on them has varied, and the results of humanitarian efforts have been spotty. Today, certainly, Canadians who know the situation in the Far North feel that their government must hurry to catch up with Denmark in Greenland and the United States in Alaska—not that either one of them is without deficiencies in administering to Eskimo welfare —and to catch up with the needs for education and a viable economy in arctic Canada.

The first objective today is to keep Eskimos and northern Indians alive, no small undertaking, the infant mortality rate being what it is. The second objective is to educate the youth, although no one is sure what kind of life they are being educated for. The third objective is to provide employment that will bring not only self-support but also self-respect. Of the three, the last is by far the most difficult to achieve. Eskimos, like all other people in today's world, need commercial goods; yet in some areas of both countries they have a family annual cash income of no more than $500; consequently they can exist only because they receive from the government direct subsidies of one kind or another. Eskimo children do not sit in school in their fur parkas—they must have cloth garments. Very few of their fathers still use kayaks—they use plank boats with either outboard or inboard motors. Their homes may have home-made furniture but they cannot have home-made alarm clocks, nursing bottles, and flashlights. Every year the list of needs grows.

The possibility of relocating Eskimos outside the Arctic has been mentioned. Most Eskimos undoubtedly would prefer to have employment within their own region; most Canadian officials having responsibility for Eskimo welfare seem to favour the latter alternative; and indeed, until this ethnic group learns more about the outside world and learns more English or French, it is ill equipped to compete outside the Arctic. Let us review briefly the local opportunities for the indigenous peoples of the North.

(i) Employment in transportation, weather observation, defence, and other public services requiring skilled and semi-skilled workers. For any of these, technical training is needed. In 1962, 135 Canadian Eskimos were taking vocational courses, and the goal was 400 students in 1963–64. Total school enrolment in 1962 was 2,397 Eskimos. (Some of the vocational training, such as carpentry, was aiming toward self-employment as well as public or industrial employment.)

(ii) Employment in primary production and processing of primary products. For such occupations as commercial fishing, the workers need to retain considerable knowledge of the local country as well as to receive new specialized knowledge of preservation and packing of the product. In the past two years, Arctic char, Atlantic salmon, whitefish, cod, and lake trout have been shipped out of the North-West Territories. "Several experiments were undertaken to process seal, whale, buffalo, and fish for sale to northern peoples with the object of finding ways of processing country food so that it would appeal to the people and could be easily transported from one area to another. One of the greatest problems in the north . . . is that the greatest concentrations of local food resources do not coincide with the population centres. The reactions of northern peoples to these foods was very positive. Plans are being made to establish small processing plants in several locations."[19]

(iii) Employment in handcrafts. For this, technical training is needed to adapt the old arts to modern forms.

(iv) Employment in professional services. Much as teachers and nurses, for example, are needed in the North, it will be a long time until more than a handful of Eskimos can qualify for such positions. Once the essential general education has been obtained, a beginning can be made by employing teachers' aides and nurses' aides, and in due time full professional training for the few who want it can be secured.

Meanwhile, probably the largest single category of steady wage employment for Canadian Eskimos is "janitorial-maintenance," while the largest category of non-wage employment still is hunting-trapping-fishing. Indeed, until it is obvious that new sources of employment are stable and long-term, Eskimos are foolish to give up their traditional occupations. In Alaska, again and again when government schemes and private enterprises have collapsed, local groups have had to return to seal hunting, caribou hunting, or fishing. There can be no doubt that the Department of Northern Affairs is working hard and with considerable ingenuity to get Eskimos into productive enterprises like fishing and stone-carving, and that the US Department of the Interior is working to get its northern "clients" into skilled wage-work. Inevitably, however, only a few of the projects of either agency will be successful.

Eskimos have much in their favour for both types of work. Their basic attitudes toward capital and work in aboriginal times were not so unlike those of the urban middle class as one might think. Land ownership by individuals meant nothing and amassed goods were not valued so highly as generosity, as sharing the natural products of one's efforts;

[19]Department of Northern Affairs and National Resources, *Government Activities in the North* (Ottawa, 1963), pp. 170–1.

also, goods were not valued so highly as the display of skill. A mobile people always seeking more productive and more secure locations could not accumulate many possessions even if their land had been richer. Their capital consisted of the instruments of production, such as harpoons, boats, and carving tools, and—most important—their nonmaterial possessions: skill, geographic knowledge, magical knowledge to produce the game animals, and religious power. Their capital was what they carried in their heads and their hands.

What capital does a white-collar worker have? What does he carry to his office? His education, personality, experience in a broad field of work. What does the skilled blue-collar worker offer? A few tools, training and experience in a specific type of work. Eskimos do not have the attitudes of husbandmen desiring acres and livestock or of businessmen seeking rights to mineral resources or trade outlets or industrial processes. Like the modern model of the technician and the professional man, they offer an alert mind, an adaptive personality, a willingness to try new types of work that their fathers did not know.

Not only for the sake of their conscience and their pride, urgently as these may demand action, but also for the future development of their country, Canadians must not allow Eskimos to stagnate in their present shack-towns, unequipped to live either entirely "on the land" or entirely in the modern Canadian economy. Eskimos are a valuable part of the Canadian heritage, a heritage that must not be wasted.[20]

[20]Trevor Lloyd, "The Future Colonization of Northern Canada," in *Canadian Population and Northern Colonization.* Symposium presented to the Royal Society of Canada in 1961. University of Toronto Press, 1962. For a recent and comprehensive account, see Charles C. Hughes, "Under Four Flags: Recent Culture Change among the Eskimos," *Current Anthropology,* vol. 6, no. 1 (1965).

The Administration of Northern Peoples: America's Eskimos—Pawns of History

◀ DIAMOND JENNESS* ▶

ALASKA, Canada, and Labrador are three Eskimo homelands in Arctic America which Nature carved out of our globe aeons before our first human ancestors descended to the ground from the trees of the forest and defied all other animals that roamed its surface. Time the Reaper marched endlessly on, and as he marched those first men multiplied and separated into races, most of which he mowed down with his scythe and buried in History's graveyard. On and on he marched, and the mists of antiquity covered his footsteps.

After a long interval he paused, and slowly drew back antiquity's misty curtains. The focus sharpened.

In the foreground the unsetting sun of an Arctic summer shone on a wide, clear stream which meandered through the soggy tundra of northern Canada to an ice-flecked sea. A score of men, women, and children leaped and splashed in the shallow water, frantically jabbing long, three-pointed spears into the frightened fish that swirled around them. Over their shoulders streamed masses of tangled black hair, half-concealing their round, sun-blackened faces and high, protruding cheeks faintly tinged with red; and across the tundra came echoes of their cries, strange utterances not known to the half-civilized world of that period, and to only a few thousand of its inhabitants today.

The background to this scene was a nearly land-locked bay; but far to the west, off a sandy strip of the Alaskan coast, moved a large row-boat

*Formerly Chief, Division of Anthropology, National Museum of Canada, Ottawa.

heavily laden with people, dogs and household goods. Three kayakers escorted it: one, balanced by his paddle, sat poised to hurl his harpoon at a seal whose head was emerging above the flat sea.

Opposite this Alaskan scene, away in Northern Labrador on the panorama's eastern edge, a line of hunters, crouching low in saucer-shaped pits, nervously fumbled their bows as they awaited the charge of a caribou herd which their wives and children were stampeding towards them. At right angles to the hunters, fencing them in on each side, stretched rows of stones capped with black turf—the dummy hunters erected to keep the herd from scattering. One animal, however, had already broken through the barricade and was galloping away to safety.

The mist swept in again, and Time moved on a few paces: by human reckoning he travelled four thousand years. And again he stopped to roll the mist away.

In this second panorama snow blanketed the ground so that it was impossible to distinguish land from sea. In the middle distance the snow was drifting, and its hard, sharp flakes lashed a fur-clad figure, bowed beneath a heavy pack, which was approaching a log trading-post somewhere on the western shore of Hudson Bay. Wearily the man stumbled along, for he had travelled far since dawn, and the snow was deep. He had almost reached the building when its door swung open, and a man and woman appeared, still loudly arguing over the packaged foods, the cloth, and other European goods they were carrying in their arms. Both stopped short at the sight of the traveller burdened with his winter's catch of furs; then broad smiles lit up their faces and they hurried forward to greet him.

On the panorama's western edge the blizzard had ended, and off Point Barrow, the northernmost tip of Alaska, little knots of seamen were streaming from an ice-locked whaling vessel towards a group of cabins whose roofs alone protruded above the concealing snow. A woman awaited them in a doorway, and behind the cabins three men huddled round a small drift-wood fire that wafted in its smoke an odour of moon-shine. Some thirsty white man had taught these Eskimos how to make a primitive still; and now it was operating at full capacity—one five-gallon petrol tin half-filled with molasses sizzling on the fire and feeding its counterpart, the condenser tin, buried in the snow four feet away.

Less foreboding was the scene far to the eastward, under Labrador's clear sky. There, bare-headed at the entrance to a little white-walled, red-roofed church, stood its Moravian pastor, his arm raised in salute to an Eskimo hunter who was dragging a small sled toward a newly-formed lane of open water in the frozen sea. The arm dropped suddenly and the mist, moving swiftly in, blotted all this second panorama from view.

Almost immediately the mist lifted again, for Time had moved onward only one step, one century. He had reached the present day, where historians are now studying his latest landscape.

The foreground reveals a small town in Arctic Canada adjacent to a medium-sized air-base. The meteorological station on the base still operates, although the last military plane that parked on its apron has disappeared over the horizon. Grouped together between the airfield and the harbour stand a government school, a hospital, one or two other public buildings, a few substantial homes and some smaller, prefabricated ones. Here also are two churches, rival lighthouses that confuse the stumbling wayfarer with their clashing beams. Near the water's edge is a smaller settlement—Lower Town —a collection of packing-box and galvanized-iron shanties that house Eskimos who do not qualify for, or cannot afford, the prefabricated homes of those brothers and cousins who have the good fortune to work for the governing white men. It is a warm spring day: the snow has melted from the rocks, and four men, sitting on a rounded knoll outside one of the shanties, listlessly carve small figurines of grey-black soapstone to sell to summer visitors, or to hand over to the local handicraft official, who will certify them as "Genuine Eskimo" and launch them on the curio market in southern Canada. A siesta atmosphere broods over the town. Now and then a low hum from the direction of the school hushes the murmur of the newly-freed streams; but the only noise, the only semblance of excitement, emanates from the liquor-parlour, where a white policeman tries patiently to pacify and steer toward his home a workless, despondent Eskimo, who has just drowned his idleness in successive mugs of canteen beer.

The scene from Alaska, in the west, resembles the Canadian. Here again is a small town, for everywhere in the American Arctic the "utilities and amenities" of civilization have forced the wandering Eskimos to agglomerate and attach themselves to fixed communities. There is an airfield, a cluster of government buildings associated with it, and, close by, a scientific research station. The Eskimo settlement visible a short distance away contains a church and a parsonage, a school, a nursing-station, a co-operative store, and those appendages without which no North American settlement is quite complete, a barber shop, an ice-cream parlour, a restaurant, and a gas-station; for even if there are no roads, tractors and marine engines require the ubiquitous petrol. The houses are of three kinds: comfortable dwellings well maintained, most of them occupied by whites; once comfortable dwellings in sorry disrepair; and wretched hovels. The centre of the settlement, which is exclusively Eskimo, nurtures a foul dump knee-deep in tin cans, animal bones, and other waste. Prosperity had visited this town less than ten years before, lingered long enough to sign her name on a gas pipeline, and departed, leaving a demoralized army of unemployed and unemployable. Yonder are some of the former workers, helping to unload the civilian plane that has just landed on the runway—the plane which brings the family allowances and other government subsidies that keep the settlement from disintegrating.

In the east a small dory is putt-putting under a perpendicular, multi-coloured cliff on Labrador's rocky coast. It stops about a hundred yards from shore, and the lone fisherman, dropping overboard his long line, settles down to jig for cod. There is no waiting: hardly has his line sunk to its full length than he pulls it up again, two large fish wriggling on its treacherous hooks. Hour after hour he continues to haul his catch into the small boat, which now lies low in the water, weighed down by its slippery freight. A gray cloud-bank spreads and obscures the sun, and a chilly east wind stirs up the waves into a menacing chop; but still he fishes. Three miles away, sheltered in a small bay, stands his cabin: he can see, or imagines that he sees, his wife moving among the lines of fish hung up to dry on three sides of the building, and his two children climbing the slope above, directly beneath the mast of the radar station on the mountain top. He had helped to build that station not many years before, when impatient white men suddenly arrived in the neighbourhood and clamoured for day-labourers. Life had been hard and often lonely before its construction, and it was hard and lonely again now; but his spirit could rise above its hardships and perils so long as nature kept her cruelty within bounds and civilization's markets offered reasonable prices for his cod.

Nature, however, is fickle, and the movements of civilization even more fickle. Today from all three regions—from Alaska, from northern Canada, and from Labrador, comes a cry for the steady wage-employment which alone can provide security, the necessities of life and a few of its comforts. From the more vocal parts of those regions comes also a cry for the education and the training that today are indispensable for secure employment. The old Eskimo way of life is no more. It has gone for ever, just as have gone for us the days of the ox-cart and the stage-coach, the flail and the threshing-floor, the spinning-wheel and the tallow candle. Civilization has caught both ourselves and the Eskimos in its dragnet, along with a variegated assortment of peoples in undeveloped Africa, Asia, and South America. Two hundred, even one hundred years ago the Eskimos could easily have bridged the gap that divided their way of life from our own: but the dawning age of automation has widened the chasm, so that the bridge it now needs must be longer and stronger. Among ourselves the gap between grandparents and grandchildren is still narrow, and most of us can leap over it quite easily; yet it has already become too wide for thousands and tens of thousands of our young people, and many not only fail to cross it, but fail even to make the attempt.

Scientists may vehemently dispute the inheritance of acquired characteristics and its possible mechanisms, but they cannot deny that man's physical and social environments influence his somatic and psychic traits, and that some of their effects, for example, skin colour, and musical ability, pass on to his descendants. Just as the caribou, the hare, and the ptarmigan have learned to change their coats seasonally to help them withstand the Arctic's rigorous climate—the ceaseless sunshine of its brief summer and the darkness and cold of its long winter—so likewise the Eskimos, during the millenia they have lived in the same region, have developed special characteristics which have helped them in the struggle for existence and contributed to their survival. It is true that

nature has undergone many swings and fluctuations during those millenia, but of a minor character only: North America's climate remains
very much the same today as it was ten thousand years ago, when the
massive ice-sheets that had covered half its surface were shrinking, and
man and animals could freely wander from the equator to the Arctic
Ocean. And certain adaptations made by the Eskimos during those long
past years, consciously or unconsciously, can be just as useful to them
in our mechanical age, even if they should move out of the Arctic, even
if they should abandon, as most of them already have abandoned, the
manners and customs of their ancestors.

Very noticeable among these successful adaptations are a profound
resignation to the venomous barbs of fate, and a defiant cheerfulness, an
exceptionally keen sense of humour, that belittle and even mock fate's
malignities. Where an Arab would humbly bow his head and murmur
kismet "it was fated," the Eskimo of Canada's far north mutters *ayor-
narktok* "it can't be helped; there is nothing one can do about it"; and
he carries on as usual. The Arab courts certain death without hesitation
because he believes that it will open for him the door to the Garden of
Delight within the Gates of Paradise; but the Eskimo meets death no
less fearlessly—in his old age he often seeks it—although his ancestors
depicted for him an afterlife peopled, like Homer's Hades, with gibber-
ing ghosts. And when the trail to the night's camping-place seems endless, and the bitter cold half-numbs his weary limbs, a simple joke will
kindle a smile on his drooping face and lighten his feet for the next three
miles. It was this quiet courage, this day to day cheerfulness, this bub-
bling sense of humour, which gave him the strength to withstand and
even enjoy the continuous struggle against the toughest environment that
man has ever encountered, and overcome.

Courage, cheerfulness, ingenuity, all races of man possess these qualities in varying measures: but very few have learned, as fully as did the
Eskimos, another lesson that life is now insistently pounding, or striving
to pound, into our sluggish minds on pain of human extinction—the
lesson of social tolerance, or, as the Bible felicitously expresses it, "Thou
shalt love thy neighbour as thyself." In a world whose human population,
if it continues to increase at its present rate, will find not even standing
room a century hence; a world where already population pressure has
combined with the disruptions caused by automatic machinery to intensify the ever-present strains on family life, the revolts of youth, race
tensions and international strife; in a world, too, where science has now
given us the power to "shatter this sorry scheme of things" with nuclear

blasts, to destroy all vestige of life with radio-active fall-out; in such a world man must either replace nature's law of the jungle by the law of reason and learn to live harmoniously with his fellowman, or else follow the mammoth and the dinosaur into oblivion.

The Eskimos learned the first exercises in this lesson long centuries ago. Isolated in the Arctic, they discovered how to live together for months on end in tiny one-roomed huts, unvisited by the sun from mid-November until mid-February—in some districts even longer; they discovered how to share without complaint dark weeks of famine and of cold, when fierce blizzards prevented even the hardiest and most skilful hunters from tracking down the breathing-holes of the seals and obtaining fresh meat and blubber to relieve their hunger and to light and warm their freezing homes. "One for all and all for one" became their motto; and we must adopt the same motto if we wish to survive. Hitherto we have recognized only the law of the jungle, where

> Big fleas have little fleas
> Upon their backs to bite 'em;
> And little fleas have lesser fleas,
> And so *ad infinitum.*

On that law we built our ruthless civilization, which today stands trial on capital charges and may shortly face a firing squad. For our scientists and engineers have brought us to a perilous cross-road where every race and every people must join hands with every other if mankind is to go forward. The law of the jungle now works against us.

Until the end of the Second World War Canada neglected her Eskimos; she scorned to join hands with them in mankind's forward march. She said to herself "I am not my brother's keeper"; and she tried to keep them isolated in their wilderness. Her missionaries warred with one another for the privilege of teaching them discordant doctrines, and of educating them to a level where they could sign their names on a money receipt and read the numbers in church hymn-books; and both government officials and commercial companies hired a few individuals for menial tasks, and promptly dismissed them as soon as those tasks ended. In hunting and trapping the Eskimos proved as skilful as our hardiest frontiersmen; in fishing they held their own against the veteran fishermen of Newfoundland. Their employers at the nickel mine in Hudson Bay (which closed, unhappily, in 1962) accounted them capable workmen; and when two battalions of Eskimos enlisted for the defence of Northern Alaska during the Korean War, senior US army officers rated them "the most alert, most intelligent, and most patriotic" soldiers in the region.

Yet right down to the middle of this twentieth century, after a hundred years of close association and the travail of two world wars, Canada refused to accept them as fellow-marchers on life's journey or to offer them a place in her society. She—or some of her citizens—recognized their intelligence and their abilities; she acknowledged that they possessed special traits which had served them well in earlier centuries; but instead of putting to work their abilities, instead of profiting by their special traits, she used them as a central African tribe used the tractors it had acquired from America—she allowed them to corrode in idleness because she could not make up her mind what to do with them.

In Northern Alaska the United States has been groping in similar darkness, unable to discover how to make possible an acceptable living in a region of so few resources, how to bring prosperity to Eskimos who have so lately emerged from the stone age. She can help to feed and clothe them, as she does the Arab refugees in Gaza; she can minister to their health, and furnish them with better homes than they knew in pre-European times. But far more than this is needed to unlock for them opportunities equal to those of other Americans, to lift them out of their present degradation, physical and mental, and make them useful, respected, and contented citizens of the richest nation in the world.

It is with the less numerous Eskimos of Newfoundland that fate has dealt most gently. Their home in northern Labrador lies much nearer than Arctic Canada and Arctic Alaska to the main streams of the world's activities, and its shores are easier to approach. The abundance of cod off those shores attracted numbers of white fishermen whose way of life closely resembled their Eskimo neighbours'; and when two peoples live side by side, share the same occupation and endure the same hardships, their common humanity usually penetrates through the superficial layer of race and language and inhibits any rank growth of racial intolerance. So many fishermen settled in northern Labrador and married Eskimo women that Newfoundland never looked upon the local natives as another "white man's burden," as Canada regarded her Eskimos during the first half of the twentieth century.

Fate smiled benignly on the Labrador Eskimos, again, when she spared them the misery of religious strife. During the decades when the region seemed useless and the world of commerce passed it by, Moravian missionaries, passively supported by the Newfoundland government, made themselves guardians of its unsophisticated inhabitants and tried to quarantine them from the evils which every civilization drags in its train. Through prudence and foresight they discouraged the intrusion of any rival mission that might have confused their converts and stirred up social unrest; and they armoured their wards against subversion by giving them an education equal or superior to that of the whites who settled among them, or with whom they came into contact. Even after the Moravian's isolating wall collapsed and the Newfoundland government took upon its own shoulders all responsibility for the education and welfare of its Eskimos, fate still smiled benignly; for Newfoundland never doubted that she *was* her brother's keeper, and she gave to northern Labrador administrators who knew its people intimately, and were willing to labour all their lives for the region's advancement and its closer union with the rest of Newfoundland. Today its economic and human resources are still not fully utilized; its Eskimos, though equal under the law with other Newfoundlanders, still encounter racial prejudice strong enough to delay their total integration. But the fusion of aborigine and white is proceeding rapidly and painlessly, and in one more generation should be virtually complete.

The future of the Labrador Eskimos, then, seems assured. But what of those in Canada, and in Alaska?

In both countries their numbers are growing, thanks to the care they receive from the Health and Welfare services of the Canadian and United States governments; and in both countries, too, their already marginal living standards are sinking to sub-marginal depths, swelling year by year the unending cost of the various "assistance" programmes on their behalf and increasing the load on each nation's tax-payers. The resources of the far north are too limited to provide today's populations with incomes, in cash and kind, on which they can even survive, and the education and training that might enable them to compete for employment in the industrial south have failed to materialize for the present generation of Eskimos, and may come too slowly for the next. So both the Alaskan and the Canadian Arctic are depressed regions, as depressed, though in a different way, as are the deserts of Somalia and the jungles of the Amazon basin.

What is the solution? Already, by her own road, racial integration—the road she has successfully followed in Labrador and Greenland—Nature has led us far along the first stage to our goal, even though, like old soldiers, we ourselves have closed our eyes to Time's changes and are attempting to wage this century's struggles on last century's battlefield. We speak of Canadian Eskimos and Canadian Indians as if they are still the Eskimos and Indians of frontier days, Canadians now only because they continue to share what has become our territory. But where are their old cultures, the dress, the manners, and the customs that marked them off from other peoples, the varied patterns of their tribal societies and the religious beliefs they held before we Europeans wrenched them out of the stone age and plunged them into a "Christian" civilization that was daily becoming more mechanized? Numberless professional and business men in Montreal, Toronto, and other cities carry a percentage of Indian blood in their veins, the majority without knowing it, and a handful of them, perhaps, can speak one or other of the many Indian languages; but where will we find a genuine Indian who still lives the life of his forefathers, still cherishes their traditions and inherits their outlook?

Eskimos of pure blood may survive today in a few remote corners of the Arctic, but nowhere in either Canada or Alaska, I suspect, does there exist a pure-blood Indian. The true Indians, the true Eskimos, have passed into history, to join the Romans of Italy (*pace* Mussolini), the Visigoths of Spain, the Vikings of Norway, and the Normans who conquered and settled in England. Even in our neighbour Greenland, the new self-governing province of Denmark that sends two deputies each year to the parliament in Copenhagen, there are no true "Eskimos," only Greenlanders and Danes: its inhabitants would resent your calling them Eskimos, though Eskimo remains the island's official language, and the majority of its people possess high cheek-bones and other features that betray their part-Eskimo ancestry. Are we not duping ourselves, then, when we persistently talk about, and even legislate for, "Canadian Eskimos" and "Canadian Indians"? Or ought we to carry our peculiar logic one step further, rename our fellow-citizens in Quebec "Canadian French," those in Ontario "Canadian English," and call our hardworking Mennonite and Ukrainian farmers on the prairies "Canadian Russians"? Perhaps our legal luminaries, and our legislators in Ottawa, can enlighten us on the meanings of these words "Eskimo" and "Indian" in twentieth-century Canada?

In 1939, after several years of deliberation, the Supreme Court of Canada decided that, in the British North America Act of 1867, the term "Indians" included the "Eskimos" of Quebec. It failed to mention that within the boundaries of the Province of Quebec as constituted in 1867 there were no Eskimos. Also it made no pronouncement about the "Eskimos" of regions outside Quebec, but left them silently rotating in outer space.

If, however, all Canada's Eskimos are to be considered Indians, as is widely assumed, who are the "Indians"? In 1951 the federal parliament for ever set to rest any doubts that may have lingered on that question. Realizing that the "Indians" were no longer the tomahawk-wielding warriors or prairie-buffalo hunters of Champlain's day, it amended its Indian Act to read "An Indian is a person who, pursuant to this act, is registered as an Indian or is entitled to be registered as an Indian"; and it then clarified this statement by adding, "This act does not apply to the race of aborigines commonly referred to as Eskimos" (Statutes of Canada, 15 Geo. VI, c. 29, 1951). May a troubled citizen, who has failed to trace his origin back to Noah's Ark, respectfully approach his representative in parliament and enquire: "Am I an Indian? And are you?"

In today's Canada we no longer contend with any real racial problem, but only with a spurious one that we ourselves have blindly created and now perpetuate. Yet we must not dupe ourselves twice over. This spurious problem, as I hinted earlier, is a part of a much larger and graver one with which Canada must strenuously wrestle, a non-racial problem that confronts every one of us, "Eskimos," "Indians," and "whites" alike. It is the problem of Canadian citizens who, regardless of their origin, lack both the education and the opportunity to pull their weight in the always uphill struggle for national progress and nation-wide prosperity. They include nearly all our so-called "Eskimos" and "Indians"; include, too, the thousands of Métis in our northern prairies, descendants of hardy Quebec voyageurs and Indian women who are as destitute and depressed as the "Eskimos." And in the same army of unfortunates we must number the tens of thousands of underemployed, unemployed, and frequently unemployable citizens of white descent who are too ill-educated and ill-trained to hold any but menial jobs, and who lack the intelligence, the basic knowledge, or the will to be trained for more demanding and more permanent tasks.

That is Canada's great problem today, perhaps her greatest. Our frenzied, rapidly automating world has little time or mercy for the incompetents, the misfits, and the voluntarily or involuntarily unskilled. Yet their numbers are multiplying fast; and as long as we think and behave as human beings we cannot, like worker bees, drive these fellow-creatures outdoors to perish at the first cold breath of winter. It is not an "Eskimo" problem, nor an "Indian" problem, but one which should weigh heavily on every Canadian: and it is not confined to Canada alone, but with the spread of automation is steadily engulfing the whole world. Until now its solution (or solutions, for there must surely be more than one) has evaded us, and the remedial measures we should apply in Canada may not be suited to other nations. Yet some remedy we must apply, and quickly, if our country is not to drop behind on mankind's forward march. And the search for the measures that best fit our needs will tax the combined talents and energies of us all.

Administrative and Constitutional Changes in Arctic Territories: Canada

◄ F. B. FINGLAND* ►

ALL THREE Arctic lands of the western hemisphere, Alaska, the Canadian Yukon, and Greenland, have been dependencies of Europe and are inheritors of European political traditions. These traditions have survived in the Arctic in spite of radically different physical and cultural circumstances, and, as in their original European milieu, they have found expression in representative institutions. Only in Canada, out of the sheer magnitude of its Arctic territories and the sparseness of their population, can a northern legislature be found which is not wholly based on universal suffrage. In Greenland all men and women over the age of twenty-one are eligible to vote for the Greenland National Council and two members are elected to the Danish Folketing on the same footing as members from Denmark. Alaska's position is very much the same. Members of the State Congress, as well as representatives elected to the Congress of the United States, are chosen by direct universal franchise. Although Canadian practice does not differ fundamentally from that of its neighbours, with each of its territories represented in the House of Commons by a member selected by popular vote and a fully elected council in the Yukon, it is nevertheless one of the anomalies of Canadian democracy that the Council of the North-West Territories is still partially appointed and has no elected representation outside the Mackenzie District.

Self-government in the original Canadian territories developed largely in response to the spread of European settlement and the growth of

*Department of Northern Affairs and National Resources, Ottawa.

population. Local political considerations were not without their influence, especially the first Riel uprising which accelerated provincial status in Manitoba, but these have been exceptions rather that the general rule. European settlement concentrated on the arable lands of the west in preference to the more formidable geographical and climatic circumstances of the Yukon and the North-West Territories. To people with techniques relatively familiar to them in the agrarian communities of Europe from which they came, the prairies presented a renewable resource capable of exploitation with very little initial capital investment. As an economic base, agriculture was conducive to the rapid growth of population which in turn made it possible for self-government to flourish. North of the sixtieth parallel, on the other hand, climate and soil conditions have been obstacles to large scale settlement and these make it unlikely that provincial status can be attained in the traditional way. Large-scale economic development is dependent upon non-renewable resources requiring immense capital investment. The relative sparseness of European settlement makes it necessary to adapt political institutions to meet the needs of the indigenous Indian and Eskimo people, different culturally and linguistically from the majority of their countrymen, and separated from them physically by vast distances and limited communications. As a result, self-government in the territories entails some form of compromise with distance, climatic environment, difficulties of resource development, and cultural disparity unlike anything in modern Canadian experience.

By inhibiting the development of provincial institutions in the North these factors have created an awkward dilemma for Canada. Citizens throughout the territories are free to participate in the election of members of Parliament on the same footing as all other Canadians, and through Parliament to exert an influence on the federal government much the same as everyone else.[1] But because executive responsibility for territorial affairs rests with the federal government, control over local affairs is in practice shared with federal voters in the provinces. The elected or partially elected councils give an impression of equality which is deceptive. There are parallels between the territories and the provinces in their fields of legislative jurisdiction and in the apparent dichotomy of executive authority between federal and territorial governments, but they do not reflect the territories' true constitutional position.

[1] The first northern Member of Parliament came from the Yukon in 1902. The Yukon electoral district became the riding of Yukon-Mackenzie River in 1947 when it was enlarged by the addition of the Mackenzie District west of the 109th meridian of longitude. In the general election of 1953 it was divided into two constituencies, Yukon and Mackenzie River, and in 1962 the latter was absorbed in a new constituency embracing the whole of the North-West Territories.

Provincial powers are cognate with those of Parliament, having a common origin in the British North America Act, whereas the territories are derivatives of Parliament and are ancillary to it. The spheres of jurisdiction of the provincial legislatures are exclusive in relation to Parliament and only in special circumstances can Parliament encroach upon them. The territorial councils have no such entrenched position; Parliament is free to give them as much or as little power as it may determine. The absence of an executive responsible to locally elected legislatures also represents a missing link in territorial affairs which is augmented in the North-West Territories by the absence of elected representation from the Keewatin and the Franklin Districts. The councils in both territories have no means of directing the implementation of their legislation nor can they impose their will on an executive which is answerable only to Parliament. The missing link is responsible government.

This situation is consistent with the historical pattern of Canadian constitutional development. Before the achievement of responsible government in the colonies of British North America, the assemblies exercised legislative powers delegated to them by the Parliament of the United Kingdom. Executive authority rested with the governor in each colony who was responsible to his superiors in England. The dilemma posed by the demand for responsible government is evident in the comments of successive colonial administrators who could not reconcile the divisibility of sovereignty with the continuation of allegiance to the Crown. Yet the responsible government that they feared would lead to "inevitable independence" proved in the end to be the very means by which the connection with the Crown was maintained. With Confederation virtually all the local responsibilities of the Imperial government in Canada were transferred to the new Dominion, and thereafter the development of provincial status in the west placed the federal government in much the same position as had been occupied by the Imperial government in relation to the colonies. In the light of this change, the evolution of responsible government in the old North-West Territories before 1905 may be seen as a continuation of the earlier struggle in Nova Scotia and the Canadas. There are also similarities between the way forms of government evolved in the colonies and in Alberta and Saskatchewan which have a bearing on contemporary constitutional problems in the territories. In each case there have been three main phases. In what was formerly New France, after the Proclamation of 1763, legislative and executive authority were concentrated in the governor and his appointed advisors, just as in 1870 they were combined in the lieutenant-governor and council of the North-West Territories.

This period was followed by a clear distinction between executive and legislative functions and the introduction of popularly elected legislatures. In the last phase responsible government makes its appearance; the practice of selecting the executive from the elected legislatures with the governor submitting to the will of the executive as long as it can retain the confidence of the legislature.

THE BACKGROUND: NORTH-WEST TERRITORIES

The emergence of this pattern in the old North-West Territories is most immediately relevant for the Yukon and North-West Territories of today because their constitutional development is expected to culminate eventually in a form of government comparable to the provinces that evolved on the prairies. As a result it is useful to review briefly the growth of provincial government in the west. When the possibility of uniting the Hudson's Bay Company lands and the North Western Territory with Canada was first given statutory expression in the British North America Act, there was nothing in the statute to indicate how they were to be governed. The act made it lawful to unite these territories with Canada, but it made no mention of the political institutions to be established or the extent to which the Canadian Parliament could legislate on such matters. In an attempt to remedy this situation, an act of the Imperial Parliament was passed in 1868 which, in effect, amended the British North America Act to permit "the Parliament of Canada . . . to make, ordain, and establish within the Land and Territory so admitted . . . all such Laws, Institutions and Ordinances, and to constitute such Courts and Officers, as may be necessary for the Peace, Order and good Government of Her Majesty's Subjects and others therein."[2] The following year, as a prelude to the admission of the new territories, Parliament passed an act for the temporary government of Rupert's

[2]Rupert's Land Act, 1868, 31–32 Vict. (UK), c. 105, s. 5. This act applied only to Rupert's Land and not to the North Western Territory. Parliament had no authority to enact laws for the government of the North Western Territory until the Imperial Order-in-Council bringing both Rupert's Land and the North Western Territory under Canadian jurisdiction came into effect on July 15, 1870. See W. H. P. Clement, *The Law of the Canadian Constitution*, 3rd ed. (Toronto, 1916), pp. 849–50.

The distinction between the North Western Territory and the North-West Territories should be noted. The North Western Territory was that part of continental British North America not contained in Rupert's Land or the Colonies. Its boundaries were never accurately determined. The term "North-West Territories" was first used in the British North America Act of 1871 to describe both Rupert's Land and the North Western Territory. See R. G. Robertson, "The Evolution of Territorial Government in Canada," in J. H. Aitchison, ed., *The Political Process in Canada* (Toronto, 1963), p. 140n.

Land and the North Western Territory which gave the governor-in-council authority to appoint a lieutenant-governor and a consultative council of seven to fifteen members. The lieutenant-governor was charged with the responsibility of administering the territories according to instructions received from Ottawa from time to time, and if so empowered by the governor-in-council, to perform legislative as well as executive functions. It is significant that no provision was made for the election of council members and that the council's functions were restricted to assisting the lieutenant-governor in the administration of the territories, a state of affairs contrasting sharply with local demands for an elected legislature.

Subsequent events are well known; in 1870 Rupert's Land and the North Western Territory became part of Canada by an Imperial Order-in-Council and, as a result of the Red River uprising, it became necessary almost at once to establish the new Province of Manitoba. To add to these troubles, doubts were expressed about the competence of Parliament to pass the Manitoba Act and the Temporary Government Act. Although confirming legislation was not considered necessary by either the Canadian government or the British law officers of the Crown, an amendment to the British North America Act was passed by the Imperial Parliament in 1871 to remove any remaining misconceptions and to ensure that Parliament was clothed in future with adequate authority to "make provision for the administration, peace, order and good government of any territory not for the time being included in any Province."[3] Ironically the amendment also vindicated those who had defied the extension of Canadian dominion in the west because, in a sense, the Manitoba Act represented a victory for popular government, even though its effects were limited. The province was deliberately confined to a small geographical area, and the terms of the Temporary Government Act, re-enacted in 1871 as the North-West Government Act, remained in force throughout the rest of the territories without change until 1875. Indeed the territories were considered of so little importance during these years that the position of lieutenant-governor was simply bestowed on the Lieutenant-Governor of Manitoba. The first council, consisting of eleven members out of a possible total of fifteen, were not appointed until December 1872. In 1873, the maximum size of the council was increased from fifteen to twenty-one, but no more than eighteen members ever held office at any one time. The same amendment also revised slightly the consultative aspect of the council's position by requiring the lieutenant-governor to legislate "by and with the consent of the Council,"

[3]BNA Act, 1871, 34–35 Vict. (UK), c. 28, s. 4.

thereby indicating a shift in emphasis towards a purely legislative role. The North-West Territories Act passed in 1875 was intended by the Mackenzie administration as the opening of a new chapter in the history of government in the West, as indeed it eventually became, as much in spite of its deficiencies as because of its liberalism and ingenuity. The new act came into effect on October 7, 1876, and perpetuated the mixed legislative and administrative powers of the council. Initially the council was to consist of not more than five members appointed by the federal government but this number was later increased to six. For the first time there was provision for the election of members, and their numbers were to increase as the population grew. It was a change which clearly depicted the council primarily as a legislature rather than an executive body. By 1884 the elected members outnumbered the appointed members, and finally in 1888, the council was replaced by a legislative assembly with twenty-two elected members and three legal experts appointed by the governor-in-council. Save for the appointed legal experts, the amendment of 1888 finally conceded the principle of a fully elected legislature, and from this time on the movement for responsible government and provincial autonomy quickly gained momentum.

Changes in the role of lieutenant-governor also illustrate this trend as well as simultaneously revealing a shift in emphasis from the concept of a "colonial" governor to that of a provincial viceroy. The Order-in-Council of February 12, 1873 made it mandatory for the lieutenant-governor to sit with the council and this requirement was repeated in the North-West Territories Act of 1875. With the introduction of a legislative assembly in 1888, provision was made for the appointment of a speaker to act as presiding officer, and thereafter the lieutenant-governor assumed a role similar to that of his counterpart in the provinces. But the situations were not identical because a provincial lieutenant-governor could assent to bills or withhold his assent as well as reserve bills for the consideration of the governor-in-council, whereas the Lieutenant-Governor of the North-West Territories at this stage could only assent to bills or reserve them for review by the governor-in-council; he could not exercise the customary monarchial prerogative of withholding his assent. One innovation in the act of 1888 with a significant bearing on recent events in the Yukon was the provision for the lieutenant-governor to select four elected members from the legislative assembly to serve as an advisory council on finance. The lieutenant-governor was required to preside at all sittings of the advisory council, and he could vote as a member as well as cast a deciding vote in the event of a tie. Although the advisory council was originally designed to answer criticism about the absence of a legislative council, it represents a first attempt at the rudiments of a cabinet system, and as such, is a landmark in the development of responsible government.

It was not long before a concerted effort was made by the members of the advisory council to convert it into an executive body. To this the Macdonald government was adamant in its opposition, and in the North-West Territories Amendment Act of 1891 it retaliated by giving the lieutenant-governor power to dissolve the legislative assembly. Nevertheless the act of 1891 was a step forward. The three appointed legal experts were dropped from the assembly and its powers were extended to cover virtually all matters within the legislative competence of the provinces under the British North America Act except that of borrowing money. The amendment also made reference to the expenditure of funds by the lieutenant-governor on the advice of the legislative assembly "or any committee thereof." The assembly took immediate advantage of this opening by establishing an executive committee of not less than four members to be chosen by the lieutenant-governor "to aid and advise in the government of the territories, so far as the same [was] vested in the Lieutenant-Governor and the Legislative Assembly of the Territories or any act of Parliament, or Order-in-Council of Canada."[4] This was followed by a transfer to the executive committee of all authority respecting territorial legislation previously exercised by the advisory council. When in 1892 the minister of justice expressed the opinion that the assembly had given the executive committee powers beyond those contemplated by the act of 1891, a new ordinance was passed, this time providing for the appointment of the members of the advisory council by the assembly instead of the lieutenant-governor. Despite the obstacles placed in its way, the executive committee continued to insist that the lieutenant-governor take its advice on the administration of territorial ordinances as well as on financial matters, and finally in 1897 full responsible government was conceded.

In 1905 the Provinces of Alberta and Saskatchewan were admitted to Confederation. In the same year, a new North-West Territories Amendment Act was passed to provide for the government of what was left of the old North-West Territories. The Provinces of Alberta and Saskatchewan had left the North-West Territories little more than a truncated remnant, even though the Arctic islands had been added in 1886, and the Territory of Keewatin was included in 1906. According

4Ordinance No. 1, 1891–92, s. 1, quoted in L. H. Thomas, *The Struggle for Responsible Government in the North-West Territories, 1870–97* (Toronto, 1956), p. 204.

to the act of 1905 there was to be a chief executive called a commissioner, and a council of not more than four members appointed by the governor-in-council. The legislative powers of the commissioner and council were to remain the same as those vested in the lieutenant-governor and the legislative assembly at the time the Provinces of Alberta and Saskatchewan were created. In 1921 the council was increased to six members, one of whom was to be a deputy commissioner with power to act on the commissioner's behalf during his absence. There was obviously a lack of urgency about territorial matters during these years, attributable largely to the exclusion of the most populous areas in 1912 when the Provinces of Ontario, Quebec, and Manitoba were extended northwards to their present boundaries. By the thirties mining activity began to produce small flourishing communities, and slowly the Territories threw off their lethargy. The Second World War was a major stimulus to the economy, and as a result, the population gradually began to increase. The first resident of the North-West Territories was appointed to the council in 1946, and in 1951 provision was made for three elected representatives from the Mackenzie District bringing the membership up to a total of nine, including the deputy commissioner. In 1954 the number of elected members was increased again, making the division between appointed and elected members five to four respectively, as it has remained to the present day.

THE BACKGROUND: YUKON TERRITORY

The Yukon was first defined as a separate geographical entity when it was made a Provisional District of the North-West Territories in 1895. In 1897 a Judicial District was formed to permit more effective control of the flood of people which poured into the region upon the discovery of gold in the Klondike the preceding year. By 1898 the population had reached such proportions that some form of local government could no longer be postponed, and a new territory was created by act of Parliament on June 13, 1898. Under the terms of the Yukon Territory Act the government of the Territory was to consist of a commissioner and a council of not more than six members appointed by the governor-in-council "to aid the Commissioner in the administration of the territory. . . ." The designation "commissioner," which previously had been applied to the senior federal officer in the Yukon, persisted in the new act as the name for the chief executive of the Territory, and in 1905 it also replaced the term "lieutenant-governor" in the North-West Territories. In 1899 the act was amended to increase the total possible membership of the council to seven by the addition of two elected members, and in 1902 provision was made for three more elected members bringing the membership up to a total of ten. During these early years the commissioner sat with the council and presided over it in much the same way as the lieutenant-governor in the North-West Territories prior to 1888. When a fully elected council was constituted in the Yukon in 1908, it was reasonable to assume, as a result of a phenomenal increase in population, that the Territory would continue to grow and in all likelihood would pass rapidly through the same stages of constitutional development as had taken place in the North-West Territories during the previous twenty years. Thus the commissioner was expected to give up his position as chairman of the council and assume a role more in keeping with that of a provincial lieutenant-governor. The effect of this was to leave the council without leadership, and to fill the vacuum, and incidentally bring the council more closely in line with provincial practice, the position of speaker was introduced. These developments were embodied in the amendment to the Yukon Act of 1908. Formal provision was made for a speaker, and the council was henceforth to sit separately from the commissioner. The commissioner at this stage was placed in much the same position as the lieutenant-governor of the North-West Territories in 1888, except that no provision was made for an advisory council.[5] Unfortunately the continued expansion did not materialize, but no attempt was made to reverse the steps which had already been taken toward responsible government. A brief effort at retrenchment took place in 1918 when the Yukon Act was amended to enable the governor-in-council to abolish the elected council and substitute an appointed council of two or more members, but during the following year there were second thoughts about complete abolition, and the ten-member council which had remained in existence was replaced by an elected council of three members. From this time on there were no major changes until the construction of the Alaska Highway and the Canol pipeline during the Second World War brought a new upsurge of population and prosperity. In 1951 the size of the council was increased to five elected members and in 1953 the old act and its amendments were replaced by an entirely new statute.

[5]In 1904 an attempt was made in the Council of the Yukon to establish an advisory board, of which a majority was to consist of elected members, but it was defeated. See *Journals of the Yukon Council*, July–August, 1904, pp. 26–7.

ADMINISTRATIVE STRUCTURE AND PRACTICE

The governmental framework of both territories is basically the same. In the Yukon Act and the North-West Territories Act, Parliament has made provision for a council for each territory with legislative powers comparable to those of a provincial assembly. These acts also provide for the appointment of a commissioner for each territory under whose direction the territories are administered according to instructions from the Minister of Northern Affairs and National Resources or the governor-in-council. The government of the territories differs from that of the provinces in two major respects. As already indicated, the powers of the councils are simply a delegation of Parliament's legislative authority which can be amended or withdrawn at any time and the administration of territorial legislation remains, in the last analysis, in the hands of the federal government. In the provinces the enactments of the legislature are administered by an executive which is itself part of the legislature and is answerable to it, whereas in the territories there is no formal link between the administration and the councils. In practice, the commissioners recognize a responsibility to keep the councils informed and to consult them on major matters of policy, but there is no constitutional obligation to do so. The statutory channel of responsibility lies exclusively between the commissioner, a federal civil servant, and his superiors in Ottawa.

The effect of this arrangement is to place the federal government in the position of having to perform for the territories all the functions that would normally be carried out by a provincial administration. In fulfilling these responsibilities, the federal government has distributed the specific duties involved among its constituent agencies according to their normal federal fields of specialization. For example, the overall management of health and hospitalization is assigned to the Department of National Health and Welfare, the Minister of Justice is Attorney-General for both territories, and other departments such as Fisheries, Mines and Technical Surveys, and Citizenship and Immigration (Indian Affairs Branch) become involved where their activities have a bearing on the administration of the north. By far the largest role is reserved for the Department of Northern Affairs and National Resources. It has a statutory obligation to co-ordinate the activities of all agencies of the federal government, including those with strictly federal responsibilities like the Department of Transport and the Department of National

Defence, as well as those which comprise, through a multitude of complex interdepartmental relationships, the equivalent of what would otherwise be a provincial administration. This co-ordinating function is exercised through the Advisory Committee on Northern Development consisting of representatives of each of the agencies concerned, and the Northern Administration Branch which, in addition to discharging the department's special responsibilities in connection with Eskimos, superintends the direction of territorial affairs.

Although the actual functions of the Northern Administration Branch are virtually identical in each of the two Territories, the organizational framework is quite different. The Yukon has its own financial administration legislation and territorial consolidated revenue fund for which there is no equivalent in the North-West Territories. The latter has no Financial Administration Ordinance and all supply for territorial purposes is appropriated from a special North-West Territories Revenue Account in the Consolidated Revenue Fund of Canada. The Yukon is also more autonomous in its public service. Except for the operation of the liquor system, which has been manned by employees hired by the commissioner under contract, the administration of territorial affairs in the North-West Territories has been in the hands of federal civil servants.[6] In the Yukon the administration is divided into two parts, both subject to the direction of the commissioner, consisting of those who are employed by the Department of Northern Affairs and are federal civil servants and those who are employees of the government of the Yukon Territory hired according to a territorial Public Service Ordinance. The Northern Affairs staff comprises only a fraction of the whole administration. Apart from the commissioner himself and his immediate staff, the only other departmental employees are those engaged in the administration of land, timber and mineral resources. All other territorial functions, except those assigned for special reasons to other agencies of the federal government such as Justice and Health, are administered by the territorial public service.

The public service of the Yukon is divided into departments in the customary way, each with its own field of responsibility and lines of communication to the commissioner through a department head.[7] In practice, not only are the department heads responsible for the conduct

[6]A Public Service Ordinance for the North-West Territories was passed in June, 1965.

[7]One important difference is that departments are not established by statute. Only the Department of the Territorial Treasurer is provided for in this way, and then only as an adjunct of the Financial Administration Ordinance.

of their respective departments, but they are also expected to act as advisers to the commissioner on policy matters. In conjunction with the commissioner's immediate staff, the department heads act, in effect, as an informal territorial cabinet. Normally the individuals concerned do not operate as a group. Individual officers are consulted as the commissioner sees fit, and when they are consulted as a group particular individuals may be included or excluded as the circumstances warrant. Only the Yukon Legislative Programming Committee operates as an identifiable executive body.[8] It performs a key function as co-ordinator and adviser to the commisioner on administrative matters giving rise to a need for legislation, and its membership is fairly uniform. Nevertheless its meetings are irregular and it does not concern itself with operating strategy unless the commissioner asks it to do so.

Apart from the formation of such new departments as Travel and Publicity, the Regional Library System, and the Department of Housing and Area Development, the basic structure of the government of the Yukon has not changed significantly in recent years. The same cannot be said of the North-West Territories which has undergone a series of major changes during the last two decades. From the beginning the administration of the North-West Territories has been virtually synonymous with the evolution of what is now the Department of Northern Affairs and National Resources.[9] When Rupert's Land and the North-Western Territory first became part of Canada they were made the responsibility of the Department of State which already had jurisdiction in matters concerning Indians and Ordnance lands, but in 1873 these areas of activity were transferred to the new Department of the Interior. As the West developed, the department was gradually divested of such specialized functions as Indian affairs, the Geological Survey, and the North-West Mounted Police, leaving it largely the resource-administration organization it remained until after the Second World War when Eskimo affairs and problems of sovereignty in the far north began to take on new significance. Its expansion and decline over the years reflect the ups and downs of resource activity in the north. The gold

[8]This committee is not to be confused with the Legislative Programming Committee of the Department of Northern Affairs which sits in Ottawa. Its main function is to review the legislative requirements of both territories and maintain liaison with the Department of Justice in connection with the preparation of bills. The recent appointment of a Senior Advisory Counsel in the Yukon is a step towards eventual autonomy in the preparation of all bills for the Yukon Council.

[9]What follows is based on R. T. Flanagan, "History of the Department of Northern Affairs and National Resources" (1963) (unpublished manuscript in the library of the Department of Northern Affairs, Ottawa).

rush in the Yukon produced the first resident administration in what are now the territories with the arrival in the district of a gold commissioner and his staff in 1897. Between 1905, when the Provinces of Alberta and Saskatchewan were formed, and 1920, the year after the discovery of oil at Norman Wells, there was little resource activity, and the comptroller of the Royal North-West Mounted Police was also commissioner of the North-West Territories. The twenties represent a period of awakening interest and expansion. In the first year of the decade the deputy minister of the Department of the Interior was made commissioner, and to keep pace with developments following the discovery of oil and the extinction of Indian title, timber, land, and mining offices were opened at Fort Smith, Fort Resolution, and Norman Wells in 1921. A significant new chapter opened for the department in 1928 with the transfer of responsibility for Eskimos from the Department of Indian Affairs, but coming just as the decline of the thirties was about to begin, this change had little immediate effect. The economy drive of the thirties, following closely on the heels of the transfer of natural resources to the prairie provinces in 1930, brought about a substantial reduction in the size and activities of the department.

In many ways the modern era of northern administration can be said to begin in 1936 with the creation of the new Department of Mines and Resources to embrace what had previously been four departments, the Department of Mines, the Department of the Interior, the Department of Indian Affairs, and the Department of Immigration. The Bureau of North-West Territories and Yukon Affairs, which was the forerunner of the present Northern Administration Branch of the department, was made part of the Lands, Parks, and Forests Branch of the new department. The Second World War imposed a moratorium on northern development but this was more than compensated for by the rapid post-war expansion arising out of the government's efforts to maintain Canadian sovereignty throughout the far northern reaches of the country and to bring to the isolated peoples of the territories a standard of health, welfare, and educational services as close as possible to those available to Canadians elsewhere. The first step in this direction was the transfer of responsibility for the health of Indians and Eskimos to the Department of National Health and Welfare in October 1945. Almost simultaneously a concerted effort was made for the first time to construct a network of government schools throughout the North-West Territories. In January 1950 the Department of Mines and Resources was replaced by the Department of Resources and Development, and in the following year the reorganization of the branches brought about the formation of a Northern Administration and Lands Branch consisting of two divisions, a Northern Administration Division responsible for all non-resource activity, and a Lands Division responsible for non-renewable and timber resources.

In 1953 Parliament replaced the Department of Resources and Development with the present Department of Northern Affairs and National Resources. The change was aimed mainly at outlining more fully the department's responsibilities in the north, particularly its co-ordinating function which had become increasingly desirable as the federal government's activities increased. The Northern Administration and Lands Branch was organized into three divisions, the Territorial Division responsible for the direction of territorial affairs, the Arctic Division in charge of matters relating to Eskimos and the Lands Division which continued to handle non-renewable and timber resources. At the same time an Eskimo Loan Fund was established to assist Eskimos to purchase supplies and equipment for projects they could not finance themselves. The Advisory Committee on Northern Development was organized in 1954, and in the following fiscal year a new Education Division was added to the Northern Administration and Lands Branch in response to the need for a larger, more specialized school administration. It was at this time that the branch also embarked on a major new departure by recruiting Northern Service officers to handle local administration in remote areas. This programme brought into the department a wide variety of skills and experience which made it possible to build up an organization quickly in the northern and eastern outposts of the North-West Territories.

It became evident during these years that the administration of the North-West Territories, if it were to continue to function efficiently, could not remain indefinitely in Ottawa. There had been a simple form of local organization in the Mackenzie District under the control of a district administrator at Fort Smith, which was adequate as long as his duties and those of the sub-district administrators at Hay River, Yellowknife and Aklavik did not go beyond problems involving municipal government, liquor administration and minor aspects of resource development. But it was clearly no longer suitable as the organization spread into the eastern Arctic and responsibilities were added which required the attention of qualified professionals. In the fiscal year 1958–59 a start was made on a major programme of decentralization and reorganization. A branch directorate was formed consisting of the director, the two assistant directors and a small secretariat section. The Arctic Division was replaced by two new divisions, the Industrial Division, aimed at stabilizing and improving the Eskimo economy by means of better resource utilization and the development of new sources of income, and the Welfare Division, to provide social services as well as the additional special assistance needed by the Eskimo people as their contact with modern technological society increased. The administrative services of the branch were placed on a par with the other divisions. In the field, the North-West Territories was divided for administrative purposes into two districts, the Mackenzie and the Arctic, with headquarters at Fort Smith and Ottawa respectively. Mackenzie District was divided into regions based at Fort Smith, Yellowknife, and Inuvik, and Arctic District into regions based at Churchill, Frobisher Bay, and Ottawa; these were further divided into areas centring on the more important settlements of each region. According to the new arrangement the administrator at each level was provided with all necessary professional support staff and they answered through him to the next level by means of a common channel of communication running from the area administrators through the regional and district administrators to the director. Thus the old pattern of field staff reporting to the divisions and then to the director was reversed, the divisions taking on a relationship with the director similar to that of the administrator and his section heads at each level of the field organization.

Recent administrative changes have derived much of their impetus from the proposal to divide the North-West Territories and create two new Territories of Mackenzie and Nunassiaq. Although the decision to divide the North-West Territories administratively into Arctic and Mackenzie Districts was not made at the time with a view to their immediate political division, the idea of two new territories appeared to follow logically from previous developments. Decentralization was a prerequisite of any form of territorial government on the Yukon model, so that the decision to undertake a full-scale constitutional renovation advanced even further a number of administrative changes which hitherto had been regarded only as long-term objectives. The organization of a separate territorial public service and the appointment of a resident commissioner were both cases in point. The position of commissioner was detached from that of deputy minister of Northern Affairs and National Resources in 1963, in anticipation of its ultimate transfer to Fort Smith, and the question of a territorial public service, which had been a recurring topic of discussion ever since the territorial government took over the operation of its liquor system from the government of Saskatchewan in 1950, was settled when the proposal to introduce the necessary legislation was approved in principle by the council in 1964.

FEDERAL-TERRITORIAL FINANCIAL RELATIONS

The financial relations of the federal and territorial governments are one of the least known and yet one of the most important chapters in the recent history of the North. Indeed they are the real key to the constitutional future of the territories, for without adequate financial resources there can be no hope of attaining provincial status. Recognition of the need for a formal approach to the problem arose initially out of two circumstances, the huge increase in government expenditures in the North following the Second World War and the example of Federal-Provincial Tax-Rental Agreements.

Until 1948 the government of the Yukon Territory received financial assistance from the federal government in the form of annual payments in varying and unpredictable amounts. No grants were paid between 1943 and 1947 because liquor revenues, which formed the mainstay of territorial finances, had been sufficient to meet all expenses. By 1947 post-war expenditures had reached a level that could no longer be sustained from liquor revenues, and the commissioner was obliged to apply to the federal government for assistance. As a result, the sum of $170,000 was paid to the territorial government as an interim measure pending the adoption of a better system of meeting the territory's requirements. Discussions in 1948 between the Department of Finance, the Department of Mines and Resources, and the Commissioner of the Yukon resulted in an agreement between the two governments for the four-year period 1948 to 1952 along the lines of the current Dominion-Provincial Tax Rental Agreements. The agreement provided for a guaranteed payment from the federal government of $89,365 per annum subject to the same formula for upward adjustment based on increased population and gross national product per capita as in the provincial agreements. In return the territorial government agreed to refrain from imposing personal income taxes, taxes on corporations and succession duties, and also to increase and maintain certain taxes which would increase or sustain local revenues.

Prior to 1952 there was no formal financial relationship between the federal government and the government of the North-West Territories.

Many functions allocated to the territorial government were actually performed by the federal government with financial responsibility being determined "frequently by expediency, rather than by established policy."[10] The explanation for this lies in the fact that territorial revenues were derived solely from the sale of liquor and these were increasingly unequal to the growing financial burdens of the territorial government. By 1952 the situation was clearly unsatisfactory, and with the expiry of the agreement between the federal government and the Yukon, a systematic review of the financial position of both territories was undertaken by a federal Interdepartmental Committee consisting of representatives from the Department of Resources and Development, the Department of Finance and the Bank of Canada. The terms of reference of the committee included wide powers to examine and make recommendations on the revenue-producing capabilities of the territorial governments and their municipalities in relation to the functions allocated to them. The committee studied not only the appropriateness of the level to which a particular function was currently assigned but also the level at which the function was in fact being administered. The practices in effect in the provinces were used as a standard for comparison, although the committee was careful to point out that provincial practices were not necessarily suitable for the territories in every case. Since the relation between provincial functions and financial capabilities were also periodically under review, prevailing social and economic conditions in the territories were considered a better basis for arriving at suitable levels of financial and administrative responsibility. It is significant that in referring to the possibility of drawing comparisons between the territories and the provinces, the committee avoided "making the specific assumption that the [territories] must eventually attain provincial status."[11]

The 1952 reports of the Interdepartmental Committee represent what has since become a regular feature of federal-territorial relations. The 1952 report on the Yukon was not as sweeping as the report for the North-West Territories because the agreement entered into in 1948 had already helped to establish a more orderly approach to the problems concerned. Nevertheless the committee did make specific recommendations for amendments to the Yukon Act to give the council legislative power in matters concerning hospitals and the construction and main-

[10]Interdepartmental Committee on Federal-Territorial Financial Relations, *Report on the Northwest Territories, 1952* (Ottawa, 1952), p. 3.

[11]Interdepartmental Committee on Federal-Territorial Financial Relations, *Report on the Yukon Territory, 1952* (Ottawa, 1952), p. 3.

tenance of roads. No changes were suggested in the allocation of taxing powers because it was the view of the committee that these were generally commensurate with the distribution of administrative responsibility, but a number of specific suggestions were made to have existing federal-provincial programmes, such as hospital construction grants, apply to the territory. The North-West Territories report indicated that the committee was breaking new ground to a much greater extent than it had in the case of the Yukon. Until 1950 there had been no Appropriation Ordinances, as such, and expenditures were made from the Liquor Fund of the North-West Territories "for territorial purposes" either on the authority of the Territorial Council or in federal appropriations for the Department of Mines and Resources. As a result the committee recommended a general reallocation of financial and administrative responsibilities based on the underlying belief that to as great an extent as practicable, the cost of government services should be borne by the government assuming responsibility for carrying them out.

Following the committee's review in 1952, agreements were entered into between the federal government and each of the two territorial governments for the five-year period commencing April 1, 1952 and terminating on March 31, 1957. In 1957 the practice adopted in 1952 was renewed. A committee was appointed by the deputy ministers of Finance and Northern Affairs and National Resources with terms of reference, as in 1952, that included both financial relations and the allocation of functions between the federal and territorial governments and the municipalities. The pattern established in 1952 was also followed in the committee's method of arriving at the basis for annual payments from the federal government. Projections of estimated revenues and expenditures, taking into consideration recommended adjustments in the allocation of functions and levels of taxation, were used to arrive at an average annual budget for each territory for the following five-year period. Subject to variations consequent upon changes in population and gross national product and the application of accumulated territorial reserves, the resulting average annual deficit became the sum payable each year by the federal government. From the point of view of the federal government this formula had a distinct advantage over other possible methods of computing the amounts of assistance necessary. It meant that in the first years of an agreement the territorial governments would be receiving more than their estimated requirements, but in the last two years, the period for which the five-year estimate was most difficult, they would be receiving less. Consequently it was implicit in each new agreement that the territorial governments must use their financial resources with caution and responsibility. Added to this, in the 1957 reports, was a more careful adjustment of financial responsibility betwen the federal and territorial governments for expenditures attributable to Indians and Eskimos and for such matters as road maintenance which involved both a federal and a territorial as well as a municipal interest.

The new agreements entered into in 1962 form the basis of current federal-territorial relations and are largely an extension of previous arrangements. The 1962 committee recommended that formal agreements be entered into between the federal and territorial governments for the provision of police services similar to those in effect with most of the provinces, and this has been done. The cost to the territorial governments was included in their estimated expenditures for the five-year period so that the added burden has been offset by a corresponding adjustment in the average annual budget. Normally changes in policy of this kind are no problem as long as the anticipated increase in expenditures are known and are provided for at the time the average annual budget is prepared for each new agreement. The real difficulty arises when substantial new costs are incurred by the adoption of policies introduced part way through the term of an agreement. Sometimes these changes can be foreseen, as was the case with hospital insurance when the 1957 committee recommended that appropriate adjustments be made in the federal payments if such a scheme came into effect. On the other hand, new proposals can emerge, like the territorial public service for the North-West Territories, for which no provision was made in the five-year estimate of expenditures, and in order to finance the additional costs, the territory concerned must resort to increased taxes or revise its programme of expenditures.

THE ADVISORY COMMITTEE ON FINANCE

So far the proposals to alter the institutional structure of the government of the two territories has had little impact on federal-territorial financial relations but they have had a dramatic effect on contemporary thinking about the constitutional future of the north. Unlike the North-West Territories, where the basic issue has been the formation of two new territories and the composition of their respective legislatures, the most important problem in the Yukon has revolved around the question of how to integrate the executive with the legislature as a first step towards responsible government. In seeking a solution, recent experience in the North-West Territories provided a partial answer. There it had been customary for the commissioner to sit with the council and act as its chairman, and over the years, a close, harmonious, working relationship ensued. The long separation of commissioner and council in the Yukon had given rise to a separation of executive and legislature not unlike the position of the governor and congress of a state in the American Union. Obviously this situation had to change if the form of government in the territory were to follow the traditional British pattern of integrated executive and legislature in effect in the provinces. To bring about a closer relationship between the territorial administration and the council, therefore, two major changes were made in the Yukon Act in 1960. The section which prohibited the commissioner from sitting with the council was repealed, making it possible for him to offer immediate assistance and advice as the occasion warranted. Conversely, provision was made for greater participation by members of the council in the performance of executive functions by the establishment of an advisory committee on finance. The committee was similar in many ways to the advisory council on finance established in the old North-West Territories in 1888, but the arrangements in the Yukon were not as explicit as in the North-West Territories, especially in defining the relationship between the advisory body and the commissioner. The Yukon Act amendment states, "there shall be an Advisory Committee on Finance consisting of three members of the Council to be appointed by the Commissioner upon the recommendation of the Council" and "the Commissioner shall consult with the Committee in the preparation of the estimates of the expenditures and appropriations required to defray the charges and expenses of the Public Services of the Territory for each fiscal year" (8–9 Eliz. II, c. 24, s. 3) but otherwise, it left the commissioner and the council to work out the details of how the committee was to proceed.

The members of the new advisory committee were recommended to the commissioner by the council at the third session in 1961. During the council's discussions the commissioner outlined briefly how he thought the committee should function. At first he was not greatly in favour of the advisory committee; he thought it was premature and would encroach on the field of administration which he considered exclusively his responsibility. But these fears proved unfounded. The wording of the amendment provided only for an "advisory" committee which could not be construed to mitigate his responsibility for the day-to-day administration of the territory. There were also certain advantages, as he became aware, because in future, when the estimates of the territorial government were presented to the council, he believed "the Advisory Committee would answer the questions in the main rather than the Commissioner."[12] The commissioner took the view that his role was to reconcile the wishes of the members of the financial advisory committee with the policy of the minister of Northern Affairs and National Resources and to make sure that the territorial estimates, as finally presented to the council, kept within the terms of current financial arrangements between the territorial government and the government of Canada. In its instructions on the procedure to be followed in his relations with the advisory committee on finance, the Department of Northern Affairs pointed out that only the commissioner had the legal authority to present estimates to the council. Although complete agreement between the commissioner and the committee on the estimates to be presented would always be desirable, it was recognized that a situation could arise in which the commissioner and the committee disagreed on specific items. In cases of this kind it was to be understood that all the chairman of the committee could do was report the situation to the council and it would then be the council's responsibility to make a decision. It was not made entirely clear by the department, however, that under these circumstances the council had the legal right to reject an appropriation recommended by the commissioner, but it was powerless to insert an item in the estimates unless first recommended by the commissioner. To conclude its recommendations to the commissioner, the council suggested that membership on the financial advisory committee should rotate "as it would help temper the Councillors for Government in the Yukon Territory."[13] A resolution was passed calling for the committee to draft its own constitution and submit it to the council for ratification at the following session. Although the activities of the committee were reported to the council in detail after the first session in 1962, its constitution was never ratified by the council. In addition, the members of the committee were not formally appointed by the commissioner until July 1963, so the first committee actually sat and performed its duties without being officially designated.

The first session of the advisory committee on finance was held in Whitehorse on January 19, 1962. The rules which were adopted recognized the responsibility of the commissioner for calling meetings of the committee, but provision was also made for the chairman, on the advice of the other members of the committee, to notify the commissioner

12Yukon Territorial Council, *Votes and Proceedings*, 3rd sess., 1961, p. 151.
13*Ibid.*, p. 153.

that a meeting ought to be held. In his report to the council at the first session 1962, the chairman of the committee explained that the rules had been drafted in such a way that the council could continue with the same committee if it wished, or it could appoint another committee at the end of one year. The latter alternative seems to have prevailed. Two of the three members of the first committee retired at the fall session 1962 and were replaced by two other members of the council who had not yet participated, and the practice has continued.

It is still too early to determine how successful the experiment of an advisory committee on finance has been. A new commissioner was appointed shortly after the committee met for the first time, and this made it somewhat easier for the council to accept the change. But in some respects the committee has not accomplished all that had been hoped. It was originally expected it would become sufficiently familiar with the details of the territorial government's estimates prior to the sessions of the council that a second detailed examination would not be required by the council itself. As it functions at present, the committee reviews the estimates prepared by the departments and consults the commissioner and other senior officials of the administration as it deems necessary. Yet when the estimates are submitted to the council, the administration is faced once more with the responsibility of explaining its estimates in detail even though it has done so already for the advisory committee on finance. Gradually this may change as the advisory committee becomes more familiar with the way the administration functions and as the council learns to rely on the committee for an adequate analysis of the appropriations. In spite of the absence of complete understanding about the functions of the advisory committee on finance, there is a growing awareness that the committee is intended to become eventually an embryonic cabinet. As the member for Mayo stated in November 1961 "this was a step towards a more responsible form of government . . . ."[14] Nevertheless it is still evident that the council's desire for greater participation in the conduct of the territorial government's affairs is not fully realized. An element of dissatisfaction remains which will not likely disappear until the members of the advisory committee can assume responsibility for some aspects of administration. The principle of rotating the members of the committee is not conducive to the formation of a shadow cabinet because there is not sufficient continuity. Moreover the members of the council have not come fully to grips with the problem of executive authority. They wish to influence the territorial government but they are not prepared to take over the

14*Ibid.*, p. 153.

reins of government completely. In the long run, however, it is likely that the temptation to play a greater part will prevail, and the advisory committee on finance will prove ultimately to be the mechanism by which executive authority is harnessed to responsible government.

On the whole the amendment of 1960 which removed the statutory bar to the commissioner sitting with the council has not been an unqualified success. By enabling the commissioner to sit with the council without abolishing the position of speaker, a duality of leadership has developed. The functions of the speaker have become too deeply entrenched in the proceedings of the council to be dispensed with at the stroke of a pen and it is now very difficult for the commissioner to insist upon his right to sit with the council when the custom has always been for him to remain aloof from its day-to-day activities. A further complication is a vague, undefined feeling among the members of the council that they represent the only democratic element in the government of the territory because the commissioner and all his associates, in whose hands actual responsibility lies, are appointed civil servants who do not necessarily reflect the attitudes and needs of the people. Obscure and unformulated though they may be, these attitudes represent a challenge for the future, for latent within them are the seeds of fundamental democracy upon which responsible government is ultimately based. It may be questionable whether the territory is yet in a position to produce representatives capable of directing its affairs. This is an argument often heard throughout the North. But it is an argument that cannot withstand continual popular pressure for control over a long period of time. In a democratic context consistency will likely prevail, and the people of the territory will assume responsibility for the direction of their affairs.

THE NEW TERRITORIES

Recent proposals for the North-West Territories have envisaged changing its name to the Territory of Mackenzie and substantially reducing it in size. The remainder of the North-West Territories would become the new Territory of Nunassiaq. The council and the administration of the North-West Territories have been preoccupied with these changes since January 1960 when a number of suggestions concerning the constitutional future of the Territories were first put forward by various members of the council. For several years the council had been following the gradual transfer of administrative functions of the Northern Administration Branch of the Department of Northern Affairs and National

Resources from Ottawa to the Mackenzie District, and these changes aroused an interest in the possibility of further constitutional changes which would enable the people of the Territories to participate more directly in the handling of their own affairs. Since 1957, when the council met for the first time in the eastern Arctic, there had been occasional reference to the possibility of broadening the representative base of the council, but no action was taken. At the summer session of the council in 1957, a paper was submitted by the administration setting out the factors to be considered in extending elected representation on the council to the Franklin and Keewatin Districts, but it was decided that it would be impractical to make such a change at that time. By 1960, however, the council had met again in the eastern Arctic, and their interest in the country and its people was now thoroughly aroused. Furthermore, there had been substantial improvements in transportation and communications throughout the Arctic during the late fifties, accompanied by a huge increase in governmental activity of all kinds. So impressive were these changes that in the short period between 1957 and 1960, the council completely reversed its attitude towards the feasibility of representation from the Keewatin and Franklin Districts, and one member went so far as to say "that the Territory should advance step by step toward responsible government and provincial status by increasing the number of elected representatives and changing the composition of the council gradually from a majority of appointed members to a majority of elected members."[15]

But impressive strides in the development of the eastern Arctic were not entirely responsible for this change in attitude. For the elected members of the council, their visits to the eastern Arctic had revealed how great the differences were between the Mackenzie District and the true Arctic. It seemed that as long as the Mackenzie District was tied to Franklin and Keewatin they could only retard the economic progress of the Mackenzie Valley. This view was reflected in the administration's suggestion at the second session of the council in 1960 that the establishment of two separate territories was justified by the difficulty of developing policies and legislation capable of meeting the needs of such a large and varied region. The two main reasons for a separate Mackenzie Territory have since been put forward as those which would "provide a more manageable and homogeneous area than the present extensive Territories" and "permit the greater exercise of local responsibility in Government, by grouping the most populated and articulate part of the Territories so that it might advance in self-government and other ways

[15]Council of the North-West Territories, *Votes and Proceedings*, 18th sess., p. 1.

without waiting for the rest of the North to catch up."[16] In 1960, however, the council's conclusions were still cautious and tentative, and not without a strong realization of the historical consequences that could flow from their deliberations. Sitting as a committee of the whole, it concluded in summary that:

(1) For the time being it was not desirable to provide for representation directly from the eastern arctic on the council;

(2) A new territory embracing most of the present Mackenzie District and related areas in the western arctic was desirable but further study of this proposal was required;

(3) Following the establishment of the new territory, the Council formed to administer the remaining areas of the North-West Territories should be an appointed body initially;

(4) The Council of the new Territory of the Mackenzie should for some time at least include appointed as well as elected members;

(5) Continuing consideration should be given to the division of executive functions in the Territories between the Federal and Territorial Governments.[17]

The question of dividing the North-West Territories was not dealt with again in an extensive way until the summer of 1961. The purpose of this review was to work out the exact nature of a new Mackenzie Territory, leaving the remainder of the Territories to be considered at a later date. As the paper presented to the council pointed out, incidentally revealing the extent to which administrative changes in the Northern Administration Branch in the late fifties had influenced the council in deciding to pursue further constitutional development, the Mackenzie Territory was to be defined in such a way that areas which could not be readily administered from the Mackenzie District as well as those with special or essentially different requirements were excluded. The main criteria upon which a distinction between eastern and western territories was to be based were transportation and communications, ease of administration and fundamental differences of economy. As the commissioner pointed out:

The matters coming before the present Council affected mainly the Mackenzie District and were entirely different from those that concerned the people in the Eastern Arctic. The division of the present North-West Territories would be, in part, a recognition of these differences and would allow the Council of each area to dwell on the matters most closely affecting its residents.

At the moment, there was no way of having any effective election in the eastern part of the Territories because communications were still far behind those of the Mackenzie District. Further, the level of education and sophis-

[16]Council of the North-West Territories, Sessional Paper No. 5, 1964 (second session), p. 1.

[17]Council of the North-West Territories, *Votes and Proceedings*, 19th sess., p. 80.

tication among the Eskimo population had not reached the point where more than a small minority understood what was meant by an election and representation . . . It would be doing the Eskimo people no service if they were rushed into political responsibility before at least a few of them were able to understand what it was all about and take part as equals with other elected or appointed representatives.

If an Eskimo were appointed to give special representation to Eskimos in the Eastern Arctic, there was the danger he would be looked upon as someone selected to put forth the view of the Administration.[18]

Although not without demur on the part of some members who were of the opinion that further constitutional development was premature or that it could be accomplished by means other than the division of the North-West Territories, the council finally agreed at the summer session in 1961 to have the administration definitely proceed with plans for a new Mackenzie Territory with a resident commissioner and a council of nine members. One significant change in the composition of the council was the proposal to have it comprise five elected members and four appointed members with the deputy commissioner an elected member, thereby reversing the current arrangement of five appointed members and four elected members with the deputy commissioner an appointed employee of the Department of Northern Affairs and National Resources.

In January 1962, the council considered the form of government for the part of the North-West Territories that would remain after the formation of the Mackenzie Territory. Here the council was breaking new ground. There had never been representation from the eastern Arctic on the council of the North-West Territories, and special pains were taken to make sure all the factors were clearly presented. It was assumed that the government of the new Arctic territory would follow the pattern of territorial government established in the past. Using this as a guide, it was readily agreed that the chief executive of the new territory should be a commissioner resident in Ottawa, and that the council should include representatives from the territory itself, whether elected or appointed. It was suggested that the problem of electing members to the council would be complicated by the fact that Eskimos, for the most part, did not understand the principles involved in electing representatives, and most of the geography of the territory made it impossible for a candidate to campaign effectively. With these considerations in mind, it was decided that the new council should consist of seven appointed members, of whom one was to be deputy commissioner and three were to be residents of the territory. Some discussion centred upon the desirability of making

[18]*Ibid.*, 21st sess., pp. 12–13.

it a requirement that representation on the new council include at least one Eskimo, but this idea was abandoned because of the dangers inherent in any sort of distinction based on race. Doubts about the wisdom of a wholly appointed council seem to have persisted after this decision was made because the resolution asking the Minister of Northern Affairs and National Resources to implement the decisions that had been taken referred optimistically to the possibility of elected institutions. The resolution repeatedly mentioned "appointed or elected" members, and after suggesting that initially all members should be appointed by the governor-in-council, it went on to recommend elections "as soon as it becomes practicable to establish constituencies."[19]

Some of these misgivings may have been communicated to the minister. In any case, it was highly unlikely that the cabinet could accept the principle of a fully appointed council after having extended elected representation in the House of Commons throughout the Arctic as recently as 1962. This was borne out by the fact that in January 1963, the Council of the North-West Territories was asked by the administration to recommend the size and location of two constituencies which would be suitable for the return of elected members to the new council of Nunassiaq. The main question to be decided was whether there should be two small constituencies, each with an elected member, with the remainder of the territory represented by an appointed resident member, or whether the entire territory should be divided into two constituencies, with the appointed member having no specified area to represent. It was the view of the council that the only areas where candidates could reach the population and be known to the local people were the southern portions of the District of Keewatin and Baffin Island. These were recommended by the council, and the principle of two elected members from these constituencies was incorporated in the legislation presented to the House of Commons.

The first official pronouncement of the federal government's decision to adopt the council's recommendations was made in the Speech from the Throne in September 1962. The change of government in Ottawa the following April did not alter the proposals, but after the bills were introduced in the House of Commons on July 8, 1963, the two northern members pressed to have them considered by a broader cross-section of opinion.[20] Although the council had decided in July 1961 to ask the

[19]*Ibid.*, 22nd sess., app. A, p. 113.

[20]Both governments were prepared to introduce the legislation on the grounds that it was the wish of the council to have it passed. See House of Commons Standing Committee on Mines, Forests, and Waters, *Minutes of Proceedings and Evidence No. 2*, Friday, December 6, 1963, p. 98.

general public for comment about the proposal to divide the Territories, and the question was aired extensively throughout the Mackenzie District, it was finally decided to refer the bills to the Standing Committee of the House of Commons on Mines, Forests, and Waters. A number of residents of the Territories appeared before the committee, including the elected members of the council who already had had an opportunity to see the bills when they were reviewed and approved by the council following first reading in the House of Commons. It is regrettable that the committee's terms of reference did not enable it to continue its examination of the bills after parliament was prorogued in December 1963. In its report to the House of Commons, the committee recommended that its terms of reference be renewed at the following session and that the evidence already taken be given further consideration, but when the bills expired at prorogation there was clearly little point in pursuing the matter.

Most of the argument presented to the standing committee in favour of dividing the Territories consisted of the familiar points about their unwieldy size and the relatively undeveloped eastern Arctic holding back the more advanced Mackenzie Valley. But there was also opposition, and the criticism of those appearing before the committee, combined with indications of mounting apprehension within the Territories, contributed to the view that the issues should be given further consideration. Consequently when the commissioner informed the new council at its first session after the territorial election in late 1963 that it was understood the minister intended to ask Parliament to have the standing committee continue its examination of the bills, the members tended to concentrate on questions other than the more highly charged controversy over the new territories. Only one member felt compelled to raise the matter formally by introducing a motion which, if passed, would have asked the minister to refrain from implementing the policies contained in the bills. But nothing came of it; the motion was referred to the committee of the whole where it expired without debate.

The council evinced more anxiety about the lack of elected representation from the eastern Arctic. "There was a general opinion that it is inappropriate for Canada to have any part of her country not represented by an elected member either in a Federal or a Territorial riding."[21] Probably the consensus of opinion was captured best by one of the appointed members in a resolution introduced but not passed, in which he sought the council's approval for a proposal to increase elected

[21]Council of the North-West Territories, *Votes and Proceedings*, 27th sess., 1964, p. 37.

representation so that members could sit on the council from the eastern Arctic. By continuing the principle of appointed members and calling for a resident commissioner, the resolution represented an attempt to find enough middle ground to bring about a measure of constitutional progress without arousing the controversy that surrounded the question of dividing the Territories. The climate of opinion was clearly conducive to the adoption of a policy that avoided the issue of division, and this attitude was reflected in the statement of the Minister of Northern Affairs that the government would drop the proposal to create new territories, and instead, would seek an amendment to the North-West Territories Act to give the eastern Arctic elected representation on the council.[22]

Without clear guidelines for the future, there has been an atmosphere of uncertainty about the constitutional prospects for the North-West Territories. The abortive bills to establish new territories and the discussion that surrounded them left an opening which, in the absence of any other foreseeable alternative, the council tried to fill by itself. At its session in November 1964 it recommended that the federal government appoint a "Judicial Commission" to investigate the future of the North-West Territories "including political, economic, educational and industrial aspects, the structure of a territorial government, the methods and interrelationship of the Federal Government activities, etc."[23] A commission of this kind has now been appointed, and in spite of the delays implicit in such an investigation, it should make available a body of fact and opinion upon which firm decisions can be based.

CONCLUSIONS

The real key to the constitutional future of both territories is the criterion by which eligibility for provincial status is determined. There are basically two alternatives; whether the constitutional powers of new provinces can be reduced to fit the humbler tax base of the territories, or whether financial resources can be enhanced to the point of sustaining conventional provincial responsibilities. The argument for constitutional consistency is based on the principle that the residents of the territories are entitled to the same rights and autonomy in the conduct of their affairs as those living in the provinces. In support of this claim, which represents, in effect, a demand for immediate change, it is alleged that provincial status would mean little or no additional expense to the federal

[22]*Ottawa Journal*, January 18, 1965.
[23]From text of Resolution supplied by Territorial Secretariat.

government because, in either case, it is obliged to maintain a minimum level of public services. On the other hand, the proponents of financial capability insist that the only true measure of eligibility for provincial status is the extent to which locally-produced revenues are sufficient to meet provincial expenditures. Economic progress may ultimately narrow the gap to the point where it will be realistic to consider provincial status, but this is not within the realm of possibility at the moment. A particularly cogent argument on this side of the debate is the fact that as the territorial governments assume more of the responsibilities normally performed by a provincial government, they are actually contributing to the disparity between local revenues and expenditures, and are thereby frustrating their own progress.

Immediate provincial status can be attained one way or another only if there are significant innovations in the present style of federal-provincial relations. Limiting the powers of new provinces raises objections in principle and creates as many problems as it solves, but some sort of special financial arrangement based on the precedent established by Newfoundland when it came into Confederation may be an avenue worth exploring. There are a variety of ways such a change might be accomplished; by special tax concessions, block grants for specific purposes, or jointly-formulated cost-sharing schemes. But none of these are as comprehensive as a system of fixed payments based on need determined at regular intervals. This formula is the present method of underwriting territorial finances, so that relatively few alterations would be necessary to adapt it to provincial status. As a special arrangement for the territories, and possibly as a basis for discussion for other less affluent provinces, it might well form part of a general reassessment of federal and provincial fiscal and legislative powers.

Administrative and Constitutional Changes in Arctic Territories: The USSR

◄ NEIL C. FIELD* ►

THE PAST HALF-CENTURY has witnessed significant changes in the administration of the Soviet Union's northern territories. This essay will review the evolution of the present territorial pattern and forms of administrative organization, with a view to assessing those factors which have guided their emergence and the features which have tended to distinguish them from those of the more developed regions to the south. What we are concerned with is the degree to which the Soviet government has judged its northern territories to be sufficiently unique as to require special forms of administration and the way in which it has attempted to cope with this problem. In the discussion which follows, we will find that the Russian approach, at least in the sphere of political organization, has more in common with the treatment afforded the northern mainland of Eastern Canada than with the territorial structures of the Canadian Northwest. There have never been in the Soviet North special territorial units, such as the Yukon and North-West Territories, fundamentally different in kind from those in the rest of the nation. The least developed areas of the North have rather been treated as extensions of territorial units rooted in the more populous regions of the South. The situation then is comparable to that of northern Ontario and Quebec. Evolution, in an administrative sense, may be viewed as the gradual emergence of self-contained

*Department of Geography, University of Toronto.

northern territorial units, divorced from their previous base in the south; or, put another way, of the North seeking its own individual identity within the administrative sphere. Evolution in these terms may be compared with the move towards self-government and, ultimately, provincial status in the Canadian Northwest. The original framework has been different, but the paths of change will eventually meet. And it is to the same basic factors, economic and attendant population growth, that the winds of change are sensitive.

Although the Russians have been in the European North since at least the eleventh century and in the Siberian North since the seventeenth century, it has only been during the Soviet period, and particularly since the early 1930's, that the northward movement has assumed substantial proportions. Over the past four decades the population of what we might broadly describe as the USSR's northern territories has more than tripled, rising from one and one-half million in the early 1920's to a current level of about five million. Throughout this period the European North, more favourably endowed both in terms of climate and accessibility, has continued to retain about 70 per cent of the population of the Soviet Northlands. Developments in the more sparsely populated Asiatic North have nevertheless been impressive. A significant side-effect of the northward movement has been the continued dilution of the indigenous northern peoples by immigrants from the south. The indigenous groups, which accounted for at least one-half of the northern population at the outset of the Soviet period, have remained almost stationary in number and now constitute less than one-fifth of the total. It is against the background of these developments that administrative changes affecting the USSR's northern territories must be assessed.

A discussion of administrative problems and structure in the Soviet North must, of necessity, be broader in scope than that involving the Canadian Northlands. In addition to the analysis of territorial divisions and their administration in a political sense, consideration must be given to the field of economic administration and to the territorial organization of the major regional planning divisions. Nor can the analysis be restricted to the zone of the true Arctic; we must consider instead the more extensive belt of forest and tundra which lies beyond the margin of close agricultural settlement and which can be loosely defined as the Northlands. The analysis of administration, as it relates to the indigenous peoples of the North, has been largely confined to territorial patterns and related matters.[1]

---

[1]For a fuller discussion of the USSR's treatment of the native peoples, the reader is referred to the article by Terence Armstrong on p. 57.

In the present essay attention is focused first on the "administrative-territorial divisions" of the Soviet North. These units might be thought of as political divisions, in that they are administered by locally elected bodies and provide the framework within which electoral districts are defined for higher legislative bodies at both the republican and national levels. Although the elected councils, or Soviets, administering these divisions have jurisdiction over some forms of economic activity, such as trade, and take a general interest in the economy of their area, they are not directly engaged in the administration of most types of economic enterprise. Their functions and budgetary responsibilities are limited in the main to cultural and political affairs and to activities such as law enforcement. Indirectly, however, the network of administrative-territorial divisions has been of considerable significance in the sphere of economic administration. The political units served as the basic areal building blocks through which the now defunct economic administrative regions were constituted. The shape and pattern of the political divisions continue to influence the configuration of the major economic planning regions.

In the analysis of economic administration and planning two questions invite attention: (1) the extent to which unique forms of management have been employed in the North, and (2) the extent to which northern territories have been divorced from the South in Soviet schemes of economic regionalization. Some consideration must also be given to the special labour legislation which has been enacted with regard to the North. Although it falls beyond the scope of this essay, both the magnitude and system of benefits designed to deal with the labour problems of the Soviet North invite detailed comparison with North American practice.

In the analysis which follows, it has been deemed necessary to provide some background information on the Soviet system of territorial division and economic organization for readers unfamiliar with basic administrative structures in the USSR. It is only within this framework that northern patterns and forms can be meaningfully assessed. Wherever appropriate, background material of this type has been assigned to the footnotes.

ADMINISTRATIVE-TERRITORIAL DIVISIONS OF THE SOVIET NORTH

With the possible exception of the national *okrug* type of unit, which has been reserved primarily (though not exclusively) for the minor native peoples of the Far North, the same basic system of administrative-territorial division has always been followed in partitioning the northern regions of the USSR as in the territorial subdivision of the remainder of the nation.[2] Nor has the internal governmental structure of the divisions been unique.

In view of the preponderance of autonomous republics and national *okrugs* in the North, however, the problem of political representation of the titular group, not only in the local Soviet but also in the Soviet of the Nationalities, deserves some comment. Although the problem

[2]The first-order administrative territorial divisions within the USSR are the union republics, of which there are currently fifteen. The Russian Soviet Federated Socialist Republic (RSFSR) is by far the largest and encompasses about three-quarters of the total area of the nation including all of the North. Second-order territorial units within the republics are of two types: national divisions, which provide an element of political recognition and cultural autonomy to minority ethnic groups, and non-national administrative units including both *oblasts* and *krays*. The nationality-based hierarchy of administrative units, below the level of a union republic, includes in descending order of importance the autonomous republic (ASSR), autonomous *oblast* (AO), and national *okrug* (NO). The autonomous republics, representing the largest national minorities within a republic, from the standpoint of territorial jurisdiction occupy a position comparable to that of *oblasts* and *krays*. Autonomous *oblasts*, at least within the Russian Republic, are subordinated to the *krays* within which they are located. National *okrugs* are in all cases located within and subordinate to an *oblast* or *kray*. National units of the ASSR, AO, and NO types are never located within or subordinate to one another. *Krays* and *oblasts* are, for all practical purposes, identical in terms of their administrative function and organization. The distinction between them cannot be clearly defined. *Krays* were originally intended as a higher order unit and had subordinate to them either a regular *oblast* (normally in a remote area) or an autonomous *oblast*. However, none of the six *krays* in the RSFSR any longer contains a regular *oblast* and one does not even contain an autonomous *oblast*. All of the foregoing types of divisions are further subdivided into *rayons*, which in the territorial hierarchy can be equated with the North American township although they are more comparable to a county in terms of area and population.

Krays and *oblasts*, as well as the autonomous *oblasts* and national *okrugs*, are administered by councils or "Soviets of working people's deputies" elected for two-year terms. *Rayons* at a lower level have similar councils. Autonomous republics have a more elaborate governmental structure, with a Supreme Soviet and Council of Ministers, similar in appearance to that of the full-fledged republics. However, the administrative responsibilities of the governing bodies of the autonomous republics extend no further into the economic field than do those of the *krays* and *oblasts*. In addition to a greater measure of autonomy in the cultural sphere, the nationality-based divisions receive political recognition through their representation in the Soviet of the Nationalities, the second chamber of the Supreme Soviet of the USSR. Union republics are each represented by twenty-five deputies, autonomous republics by eleven, autonomous *oblasts* by five, and national *okrugs* by one. The first chamber of the Supreme Soviet, the Soviet of the Union, provides for representation on a per capita basis, the nation being divided into electoral districts each with a population of about 300,000.

is by no means restricted to the North, it is perhaps of particular significance in this area in view of the dilution of the indigenous population by Russians and other immigrants. The titular groups no longer constitute a majority in any of the national territorial divisions of the North, and in many of these units they account for less than one-quarter of the population. No constitutional restriction, with regards to nationality, is placed on the franchise or on eligibility for election to either local government bodies or to the Soviet of the Nationalities. However, under the Soviet system of selecting in committee from amongst those nominated only the "one best candidate" to stand for election, preference could be given to representatives of the indigenous group. Unfortunately, almost nothing is known regarding this aspect of Soviet policy and it may, in fact, vary from one area to another.[3] The selection of deputies from national *okrugs* for the Soviet of the Nationalities would be particularly sensitive since only one representative is provided from each division. Although preference could reasonably be given to the titular group in elections to the Soviet of the Nationalities, it is difficult to visualize how fair representation could be provided for the Slavic majority on governing bodies of national *okrugs* and autonomous republics without sacrificing a large measure of the autonomy initially granted to the indigenous population.

Throughout the Soviet period, the administrative-territorial units encompassing the North have been reshuffled and revised on numerous occasions. The most radical and frequent shifts took place during the

[3]Figures have been reported for a few of the nationality-based territorial divisions of the North, which indicate representation on local Soviets by the indigenous groups in numbers significantly in excess of their share of the population. These cases, however, may not be representative. Moreover, where the analysis is based on all Soviets, including those of rural *rayons* and small settlements, the composition of the governing body of the larger division (for example, the ASSR) is not revealed. No analysis, to the author's knowledge, has ever been made of the composition of representatives in the Soviet of the Nationalities. Only the name and occupation of deputies to the Supreme Soviet are reported and many of the indigenous people of the North are likely to have acquired Russian names. At least a partial Russianization of names is very common. Recognizing the fallibility of the approach as a guide to nationality, and with appropriate warnings regarding the inferences that could be drawn, an examination by the author of the 1958 and 1962 election results for the Soviet of the Nationalities is perhaps worth reporting. For the seven national *okrugs* of the North, over the past two elections, six of the deputies bear Russian names while the remaining eight appear to be definitely of non-Slavic extraction. For the three autonomous republics not more than ten per cent of the names reveal roots or other forms that can be classified as non-Russian. However, one of the names classified as Slavic is known to belong to a Komi and many of the others may fall in a similar category.

first two decades of Soviet rule. The instability of the territorial structure cannot, however, be viewed as a phenomenon peculiar only to the North. Administrative divisions have been in a similar state of flux, in response to economic changes and other factors, throughout the nation. Although changes in the network of northern divisions have been relatively few in number since the late 1930's, it is doubtful that the evolutionary process has yet worked itself out. At least one or two additional developments can be anticipated over the next decade. In forecasting these developments, the past serves as a useful guideline to the future. It is appropriate therefore to review not only the present pattern of territorial divisions, but also the way in which it has emerged and the general factors which have governed its evolution.

The Present Territorial Pattern

All of the Soviet North falls within, and is subordinate in terms of political administration to, the Russian Republic. The current network of second-order territorial divisions (*krays*, *oblasts*, and ASSR's) in the North, together with subordinate national *okrugs*, is shown in Map 1. One of the relatively distinctive features of the North is the predominance of administrative units of the national type. Together, the autonomous republics and national *okrugs* occupy about four-fifths of the territory north of the sixtieth parallel, including the entire Arctic littoral from the White Sea to the Pacific. The extensive territorial recognition granted to the indigenous population of the North reflects again the recency of Russian settlement in the area. When territorial divisions were first outlined for nationalities such as the Komi and the Yakuts, the titular groups constituted 80 to 90 per cent or more of the population of their respective areas.

The European North is currently divided amongst four major divisions, with the Nenets NO occupying the tundra belt between the White Sea and the Urals subordinate to Arkhangelsk *oblast*. All of the administrative divisions of the European North might be thought of as self-contained northern units. Murmansk *oblast*, embracing the Kola Peninsula, and the Karelian ASSR immediately to the south lie on the Baltic Shield, while Arkhangelsk *oblast* and the Komi ASSR share the much larger sedimentary plain to the east.

Beyond the Urals, where settlement and economic development have not progressed as far, the evolution of self-contained northern administrative units is still in the incipient stage. The two national *okrugs*

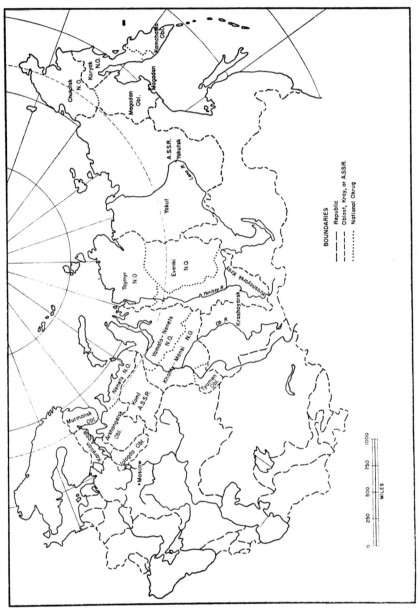

BOUNDARIES

——— Republic
— — — Oblast, Kray, or A.S.S.R.
.... National Okrug

Koryak N.O.

Chukotsk N.O.

Kamchatka Obl.

Magadan Obl.

Yakut A.S.S.R.

Taymyr N.O.

Evenki N.O.

Lena R.

Yenisey R.

Krasnoyarsk Kray

Yamalo-Nenets N.O.

Khanty-Mansi N.O.

Ob R.

Tyumen Obl.

Nenets N.O.

Komi A.S.S.R.

Murmansk Obl.

Karelian A.S.S.R.

Arkhangelsk Obl.

Vologda Obl.

• Moscow

0   250   500   750   1000

MILES

MAP 1. Political administrative divisions of the Soviet North, 1964.

encompassing the northern part of the West Siberian Lowland are both subordinate to the Tyumen *oblast*, with administrative headquarters in the southern closely-settled portion of the plain traversed by the Trans-Siberian Railroad. The same pattern is repeated in the Yenisey basin, centred on the Central Siberian Plateau, where the two national *okrugs* are subordinate to Krasnoyarsk *kray*. In the Lena basin of eastern Siberia, now occupied by the Yakut ASSR, a self-contained northern division existed even under the czars. In part this can be attributed to the more favourable agricultural environment of the middle Lena lowlands and to the much larger indigenous population which the area supported; in part it may reflect the less developed character of the territory immediately to the south and the lack of a direct connection, comparable to those of the Ob and Yenisey basins, between the north-south river routes and the Trans-Siberian Railroad. On the Pacific littoral, the Chukotsk NO is subordinate to Magadan *oblast*, while the Koryak NO occupying the northern half of the Kamchatka Peninsula falls within Kamchatka *oblast*. The creation of Magadan *oblast* in the far northeast is undoubtedly the most significant recent development in the evolution of the USSR's northern territorial framework.

The Arctic archipelagos of the Soviet Union, being much less extensive and more dispersed than those of the Canadian Arctic, have never been united within a single administrative unit. Rather, they have been attached individually to the adjacent territorial units of the mainland. Thus, in the extreme west, Novaya Zemlya and Franz Josef Land fall under the jurisdiction of Arkhangelsk *oblast*. Severnaya Zemlya, north of central Siberia, is a part of the Taymyr NO, while the New Siberian Islands further east are included within the Yakut ASSR. Wrangel Island north of the Chukotsk Peninsula falls within the Chukotsk NO.

Evolution of the Territorial Pattern

Although some of the reshuffling of territorial units during the first two decades of Soviet rule was of a short-lived and experimental nature, a resumé of the changes which have occurred does bring to light certain principles which have influenced the shaping of the pattern and which are likely to govern future developments. It is appropriate to begin with the territorial framework of the late czarist period from which the present network of divisions has evolved.[4] In the Asiatic North in

[4]The major territorial units of the Russian Empire were the *guberniya* and *oblast*, with the latter term being reserved for divisions in eastern Siberia, Central

particular, the pattern still bears a close resemblance to that of the pre-revolutionary period with its fourfold division equating, in rough outline, to the major drainage basins and physiographic provinces of northern Siberia. In its appeal to the national minorities, the Soviet regime wasted little time in introducing its new system of ethnic-based territorial divisions. In the North, autonomous units were established for the three major indigenous groups, the Karelians, Komi, and Yakuts, in 1920–22. Recognition of the minor, and more primitive, "little peoples of the North" was less urgent and the present system of national *okrugs* did not take shape until 1929–30. Two stages in the evolution of the territorial net (1914 and 1926) are portrayed in Maps 2 and 3.

The European North

Prior to World War I a single great division, the Arkhangelsk *guberniya*, stretched across the extreme north of European Russia. Although its southern margin lay further north than the present-day boundary of Arkhangelsk *oblast*, it encompassed in the west the northern half of Karelia as well as the Kola Peninsula. To the south lay the Olonets *guberniya* in the west and the much larger Vologda *guberniya* in the east.

The territorial divisions of the European North were radically revised by the new Soviet regime shortly after it assumed power. The new pattern which emerged can be seen in Map 3. In the Pechora region, the eastern parts of Arkhangelsk and Vologda *guberniyas* were carved off in 1921 to form the Komi AO, while the Karelian AO in the west was constituted in 1920 from the western portions of Olonets and Arkhangelsk *guberniyas*. With the acquisition of additional territory in 1923, the Karelian AO was elevated to the rank of an autonomous republic, but the Komi AO did not attain similar status until 1936. The year 1921 also witnessed the creation of a new division, Murmansk *guberniya*, on the Kola Peninsula. In the central region, to the south of the much reduced Arkhangelsk *guberniya*, what remained of the Olonets and Vologda divisions was divided into two new *guberniyas*, Vologda and the North Dvina.

Asia, and the North Caucasus. In size and number they may be considered the forerunners of the present-day *oblasts*, *krays*, and autonomous republics. Distinctive types of divisions for ethnic minorities were not employed. About half of the *guberniyas* and *oblasts* were grouped within nine larger divisions known as general-*guberniyas*. The term *guberniya* was retained for a period after the revolution, but the governors and their administrative organizations were replaced by Soviets.

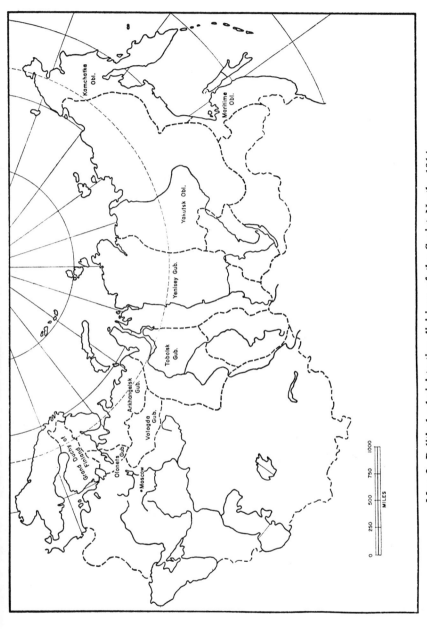

MAP 2. Political administrative divisions of the Soviet North, 1914.

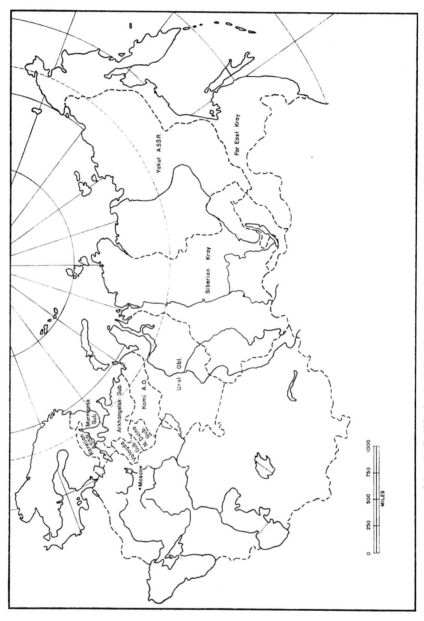

MAP 3. Political administrative divisions of the Soviet North, 1926.

The next fifteen years saw a gradual retreat from the 1920–21 fragmentation of the European North and a reconsolidation of administrative-territorial units. Settlement of the Kola Peninsula had begun under the exigencies of World War I with the founding of the ice-free port of Murmansk and the construction of a crude railroad north from Leningrad. Both the railroad and port facilities were improved during the early 1920's in an attempt to stimulate the development of resources and colonization of the region. By 1926, however, the population of Murmansk *guberniya* had reached a level of only 23,000, whereas administrative units of comparable rank elsewhere in the nation ranged in population from a minimum of almost one-half million to several million. Accordingly, the Murmansk division was abolished in 1927. The Kola Peninsula was transformed into a detached *okrug*[5] of the Leningrad *guberniya*, rather than of the Arkhangelsk *guberniya* across the White Sea with which it had no overland communication. It was not until 1938, when the population of the Kola area had risen to almost 300,000, that the peninsula regained its status as a fully independent *oblast*. At the same time it was ceded the Kandalaksha area, which previously had been the northernmost *rayon* of the Karelian ASSR.

The subordination of the Kola Peninsula to administrative authority centred in Leningrad was followed two years later, in 1929, by the creation of the Northern *kray* which encompassed all of the European North to the east of the White Sea and Karelia. Both the Komi AO and the newly established Nenets NO were subordinated to the *kray*. The eastern half of the Nenets *okrug* was carved out of territory which had belonged to the Komi AO, although additional territory in the forest zone along the Pechora in the northwest was transferred to the Komi division to compensate for the loss. With the promotion of the Komi region to the rank of an autonomous republic in 1936, it was separated from the *kray* and, for a period of one year, what remained of the *kray* was renamed the Northern *oblast*. In 1937 the Northern *oblast* was itself split into two units, Arkhangelsk and Vologda *oblasts*, with boundaries almost identical to those of the present day. One subsequent boundary adjustment in the extreme northeast deserves some mention. After the opening of the Pechora Railroad to Vorkuta during World War II, coal mining and associated industrial activity spread northward

---

[5]A substantial number of *okrugs* were formed during the late 1920's to serve as intermediate territorial links between *oblasts* or *guberniyas* and their constituent *rayons*. Most of these non-national *okrugs* had been abolished by the end of the 1930's and the last disappeared about 1950.

across the territorial line of the Komi ASSR into the Nenets NO. In 1960 this small, but industrially significant, slice of territory was turned over to the Komi ASSR. The stated purpose for the transfer was to consolidate all mining centres of the Vorkuta coal basin within a single territorial division. The ethnic balance of the Nenets administrative unit, as far as known, played no part in the decision.

The only substantial change involving territorial units in the European North since the late 1930's has been the elevation in 1940 of the Karelian ASSR, enlarged through the acquisition of territory from Finland, to the rank of a full-fledged republic. With a population at the time of its creation of only about one-half million, and with Russians constituting at least two-thirds of the total, the Karelo-Finnish SSR met none of the stated requirements for status as a union republic. Whether the formation of the republic was intended simply to assuage the Finnish population of the incorporated areas, or to serve as a possible springboard for further territorial demands, is not known. In any case, by the 1950's, the existence of the republic was clearly an enigma. In 1956, without forewarning or explanation, it was downgraded to its former position of an autonomous republic for the Karelians.

The Asiatic North

Although numerous changes have been made during the Soviet period in the boundaries and subordination of administrative units in northern Siberia, the territorial net still retains many of the features of the pre-revolutionary period. The sparse population of the region, the lack of east-west road or rail links, and the dominant role of the north-south water arteries in the transportation economy have discouraged any radical shift in the configuration of the territorial system.

Prior to World War I the northern part of west Siberia fell within the Tobolsk *guberniya*. The latter equated in general outline with the contemporary *oblasts* of Tyumen and Omsk, though the boundaries were by no means completely coincident. The remainder of west Siberia to the southeast all fell within the Tomsk *guberniya*. To the east lay the Yenisey *guberniya*, the forerunner of Krasnoyarsk *kray*, and in the Lena basin, the huge Yakutsk *oblast*. All of central and eastern Siberia, including the Yenisey *guberniya* and Yakutsk *oblast*, was administratively subordinate to the Irkutsk general-*guberniya*. The administrative divisions of the Far East were similarly grouped within the Pre-Amur general-*guberniya*. Throughout most of the late Czarist period, all of the Pacific littoral from Chukotka to Vladivostok fell within the Maritime *oblast* with headquarters in the south at Khabarovsk. It was only shortly before World War I that a separate division, Kamchatka *oblast*, was created to encompass all of the northern sector of the Far East.

In contrast to the fragmentation in the European North, the trend in the Asiatic North during the first decade of Soviet rule was towards huge territorial units tied firmly to the south. In the 1920's all of western and central Siberia was divided between two enormous units, the Urals *oblast* and the even larger Siberian *kray*. The latter embraced not only central Siberia in its entirety, but also most of the southern developed sector of the west Siberian plain, including the Omsk region of the former Tobolsk *guberniya*. The northern portion of the Tobolsk division was transferred to the Urals *oblast*.[6] In the Lena basin of eastern Siberia, the Yakut autonomous republic was established in 1922 on the territory of the former Yakutsk *oblast*, with only minor boundary revisions in the south and east. After the revolution Kamchatka *oblast* disappeared on the Pacific littoral, as did the more southerly subdivisions of the Pre-Amur general-*guberniya*. The short-lived Far Eastern Republic, which arose in the wake of the revolution, became the Far Eastern *oblast* after its incorporation into the RSFSR in 1922 and was renamed the Far Eastern *kray* in 1926.

The year 1930 witnessed the formation of the six national *okrugs* in the Asiatic North. At the same time the process of fragmentation of the first-order territorial units of Siberia began with the subdivision of the Siberian *kray* into a West Siberian and East Siberian *kray*, the latter including all of central Siberia. However, it is only with the fate of the northern territories that we need here be concerned. With the break-up of the Urals *oblast* and East Siberian *kray* in 1934, there emerged a pattern of territorial subordination in the northern parts of the Ob and Yenisey basins closely approximating that of the old Russian Empire. In western Siberia, the north was once again placed under the jurisdiction of a centre in the agriculturally-oriented southern fringe of the plain. The boundaries of the new Omsk *oblast* conformed closely to those of the pre-1914 Tobolsk *guberniya*. In central Siberia, Krasnoyarsk *kray* appeared as a self-contained administrative unit on the

---

[6]Thus began a see-saw process in which the northern tracts of west Siberia have been alternately linked with the more densely settled agricultural part of the plain to the south and the industrialized Urals region to the southeast. The problem of selecting the most effective link first arose in the revision of administrative-territorial divisions. More recently it has been reflected in the grouping of administrative divisions into major economic regions for planning purposes and in the 1962 consolidation of the economic administrative regions.

territory of the former Yenisey *guberniya*. Kamchatka *oblast* was also reconstituted in 1932 but remained subordinate to the Far Eastern *kray*. The new *oblast* included within it the two national *okrugs* of the northeast, but did not extend southward along the Okhotsk coast as had its pre-1914 forerunner. The Magadan-upper Kolyma region, in which development was just beginning, remained under the direct jurisdiction of the Far Eastern *kray*. The division of the Far Eastern *kray* into the Khabarovsk *kra*y and smaller Maritime *kray* in 1938 did not affect the territorial structure in the northeast, all of which remained subordinate to the *kray* council in Khabarovsk.

Since the mid-1930's there have been only two major changes affecting the administrative-territorial divisions of the Asiatic North. The first, in 1944, was the splitting off of Tyumen *oblast* from Omsk *oblast* in western Siberia. Although the administrative centre at Tyumen was tied to the railroad belt in the south, it was at least grounded in the forest zone and more northward in its outlook than any of its predecessors. Of greater significance in the evolution of northern territorial units was the creation in 1953 of Magadan *oblast* in the northeast, where substantial settlement and economic development had taken place over the previous two decades under the Dal'stroy mining empire. Three years later, Kamchatka *oblast* was also freed from administrative subordination to Khabarovsk *kray*. In the formation of Magadan *oblast*, the Chukotsk national *okrug* was transferred to its jurisdiction from that of Kamchatka *oblast*. In the process, the Koryak national *okrug*, which remained under the jurisdiction of Kamchatka *oblast*, was forced to cede a sizable parcel of its former territory to the new division centred on Magadan. The shift in subordination of the Chukotsk region to Magadan can be attributed to the parallel features of their mining economies and to the control which Dal'stroy had exercised over the combined area.

Although many of the revisions affecting administrative-territorial divisions in the Asiatic North can be described as regroupings of previously existing units, there are few boundaries which have not undergone some alteration in the process. The territorial line between the west and central Siberian divisions, which now follows the watershed divide between the Yenisey Basin and the rivers draining to the Ob Gulf, is a case in point. In the past, the boundary of the central Siberia division over-lapped even further onto the west Siberian plain; each regrouping of the territorial units has been accompanied by some alteration, usually involving an eastward shift, in the line. In east Siberia, about one-quarter of the original territory of the Yakut ASSR has been stripped away and handed to neighbouring divisions since the 1920's. By far the largest losses have been incurred on the eastern periphery, but some territory has also been ceded in the west and south.

One final development which should be noted was the transfer of Norilsk, in 1953, from the administrative jurisdiction of the Taymyr NO to the status of an urban centre directly subordinate to the council of Krasnoyarsk *kray*. Norilsk, which was founded as a nickel-mining centre in the 1930's, has subsequently expanded into an industrial city of over 100,000 population and is now the largest urban centre in the Asiatic North. Its population is over three times that of the national *okrug* within which it is located. Although the separation of Norilsk from the remainder of the *okrug* was in keeping with the general Soviet practice of subordinating smaller urban centres to *rayons*, larger ones to units of *oblast* or comparable rank, and the very largest directly to a republic, the policy is of special interest when applied to a large concentrated Russian enclave within an otherwise sparsely populated national *okrug*. Even so, the population of the *okrug* remains predominantly Russian, as does its administrative centre Dudinka, which serves as the outlet for Norilsk on the Yenisey.

Prospective Changes in the Territorial Pattern

From the foregoing review it is clear that the long-term trend, with increasing economic maturity, is towards the formation of independent administrative divisions across the entire North. The threshold for the creation of an administrative unit of the *oblast* type under northern conditions, to the extent that it can be judged from the emergence of Murmansk and Magadan *oblasts* and the severance of Kamchatka *oblast* from Khabarovsk *kray*, would appear to be about 200,000 to 300,000 population. In the southern parts of the Russian republic, *oblasts* are rarely constituted with a population significantly below the one-million level and many are several times this size. Since electoral districts for the Supreme Soviet cannot transect *oblast* boundaries and are defined, as closely as possible, on the basis of population groupings of 300,000, the minimum threshold suggested above has some constitutional basis.

The creation of Magadan *oblast* has set the stage for the organization of similar divisions in western and central Siberia, the last segments of the North remaining to be severed from territorial units based in the South. Active agitation for such a development has in fact already begun. The formation of two new *oblasts*, centred on the lower Ob and lower Yenisey, was proposed by at least several participants at the 1963 plenum of the Interdepartmental Commission on Problems of the North.[7] A self-contained northern *oblast* in central Siberia would presumably encompass not only the Taymyr NO with its major urban enclave at Norilsk, but also the Evenki NO on the plateau to the south and the adjacent part of Krasnoyarsk *kray* extending northward along the Yenisey valley to Igarka. One can only estimate the population which is now contained within this region, but it would not be far off 200,000, in contrast to less than 20,000 at the outset of the Soviet period. The population in the northern part of west Siberia, encompassing the Yamalo-Nenets and Khanty-Mansi national *okrugs*, by 1963 had reached 225,000 and would exceed one-quarter million if the line were drawn to include the old centre of Tobolsk in the south which lies outside the *okrugs*. That a new *oblast* will eventually emerge in this area appears certain. Whether it will be focused administratively on the river port of Tobolsk in the south, connected to the Trans-Siberian at Tyumen by road, or on a centre further north is a matter for conjecture. The post-war extension of the Pechora railroad across the Urals to Salekhard and the current construction of a new line from the northeastern railhead in the Urals to the gas fields of the lower Ob cannot help but detract from the gateway function which Tobolsk has fulfilled for the northern *okrugs* of west Siberia. Whether an *oblast* could be formed out of two national *okrugs* without an outside base for administrative subordination, such as Tobolsk would provide, is a constitutional problem to which there is no clear answer.

Although boundaries of administrative divisions have been subject to frequent alteration for economic or other reasons, there has been no obvious attempt to redefine the territories of autonomous republics and national *okrugs* in order to preserve their ethnic balance. If ethnic units are to provide an effective framework within which the indigenous groups can exercise a measure of local self-government, such a policy may eventually have to be instituted. The creation of northern *oblasts* could lead to a reduction in the territory assigned to national *okrugs* under their jurisdiction and to an erosion of territory around the margins of adjoining autonomous republics. Boundaries of the nationality-based territorial divisions, as a review of past changes makes clear, are by no means inviolable. All three of the autonomous republics in the North, as well as several of the national *okrugs*, have been required to yield territory at one time or another to adjacent units. Indeed, there is nothing

[7]*Infra*, pp. 188–89.

in either the Soviet constitution or the constitutions of its constituent republics to guarantee such boundaries against revisions imposed from above. Only the territory of a union republic is protected by the federal constitution from alteration without its consent; and even at this level it is difficult to visualize such consent being withheld.

ECONOMIC ADMINISTRATION IN THE NORTH

Although extensive tracts of the North have been treated as appendages of political divisions grounded in the South, the basic system of political administrative units has always been similar to that employed in the more developed parts of the country. It was rather in the field of economic management that the need for unique approaches to the problems of northern administration manifested itself most clearly. It was only in the post-Stalin era and, in particular, after the introduction of the *sovnarkhoz* system in 1957 that the forms of economic administration in the North were brought essentially into line with those in the South. With the breakdown of the *sovnarkhoz* system in late 1965 and the return to the branch system of economic administration a need may again arise for modified organizational forms in the North.

The Pre-1957 Period

Prior to the late 1950's economic management in the USSR was centralized in national and republican ministries (originally known as People's Commissariats), each responsible for all enterprises falling within a particular branch of economic activity such as ferrous metallurgy or railroad transport. It was only in the North that the forms and methods of economic administration deviated significantly from this pattern. It was clear from the beginning that a more integrated system of territorial management, responsible for all types of activity within a defined area, was required for effective resource development under the special conditions encountered in the North. More specifically, these conditions included: (*a*) a sparse population, concentrated in widely spaced clusters; (*b*) extreme problems of logistics stemming from the remoteness of the area, the seasonality of water transportation, and the lack of local service industries; (*c*) unique technical problems such as those presented by permafrost; and (*d*) special problems of the labour force.

In the North, the Soviet planning slogan of "proportional development" acquired special significance. Across the southern "railroad belt," if one ministry failed to complete its facilities within a developing production complex according to plan, materials could always be brought in from elsewhere on fairly short notice. In an isolated northern development, with supplies moving in only once a year, a missing link of this sort could prove disastrous. Moreover, the Soviet economic system, with its emphasis on gross production targets, was such as to encourage ministries to neglect facilities and to create bottlenecks in areas such as the North if their overall plans were in jeopardy. The high cost of northern projects ensured that they would be amongst the first to be sacrificed. A further consideration was the duplication that would arise if each ministry was required to maintain a staff of specialists familiar with the unique problems of logistics and construction in the North. A single territorial management could likewise lead to greater flexibility in the use of labour by shifting workers from one activity to another in accordance with peak demands. The number of seasonal labourers that had to be brought in during the summer months might thus be pared. This type of organization, under the supervision of the Ministry of Internal Affairs (MVD), was undoubtedly more suitable also in dealing with the enormous number of forced labourers who constituted the bulk of the northern work force during the 1930's and 1940's.

Thus it was that there developed in the North special types of economic organizations responsible for all, or a large share of, the economic activity within a designated area. Although the primary function of each organization could usually be described as either industrial or transportational, all forms of associated resource development and service activity fell under its unified management. In essence, the empires of these agencies may be likened to the company towns of the Canadian North, but on a much grander scale. As a group they have generally been referred to as territorial combines or trusts, but the two largest and most important were designated as Chief Directorates. Our knowledge of the operation and administrative subordination of many of the combines is limited by the extreme secrecy which has enshrouded, at least until recently, almost all developments in the Soviet North. Most of them appear to have fallen under the jurisdiction of the Ministry of Internal Affairs. Virtually all of the major resource developments in the North during the Soviet period were undertaken and managed, at least initially, by organizations of this type. However, it is the Chief Directorate of the Northern Sea Route and the Chief Directorate of Construction of the Far North, better known as Dal'stroy, which stand out above all others in assessing the history of Soviet development in the North.

In Soviet practice, particular stress was placed upon the territorial combine as the most appropriate form of management during the early stages of development in an area. Although the life-span of some extended over a period of several decades, others lasted for much shorter periods. As the economy of a region matured and transportation facilities improved, other forms of management similar to those employed in the more developed areas of the south tended to replace the combine organization. With the break-up of a combine, its assets were transferred to a series of appropriate ministries. However, it was not until the death of Stalin in 1953 and the subsequent release of most, if not all, of the forced labourers in the North that the majority of the northern combines were subordinated to appropriate economic ministries. Even then, it is by no means clear that the scope of their activity was substantially reduced. In some instances the entire combine appears to have been transferred to a single ministry. In any case, the changes between 1953 and 1957 were short-lived. The latter year was marked by the liquidation of the ministries to which the combines had been subordinated and the introduction of a new regional system of industrial management across the nation as a whole.

The first of the northern combines was The Transport-Industrial and Colonization Combine of the Murmansk Railway, organized in 1923. Although the Murmansk Railway had begun operation in 1916 under emergency conditions of the war, it was never properly completed and fell into complete disrepair during the civil war. The functions of the combine were to complete the construction of the railway and the port of Murmansk, to develop resources in the area served by the rail line, and to colonize the region. Particular emphasis was placed on the development of the forest industries and fisheries. Two subsidiary enterprises were organized under the management of the combine to deal with these activities, and some 12,000 square miles of forest land were placed under its jurisdiction. Geologic exploration also fell within its responsibilities. After the primary construction tasks had been completed and the associated resource industries were firmly established, the combine was liquidated and its activities distributed amongst various ministries. A second early combine, which operated from 1928 until 1943, was The Kamchatka Trust (or AKO), with responsibility for economic development in the Far Northeast, including part of the territory which later came under the control of Dal'stroy. It played an important role in the fisheries, lumbering, agriculture, and transport activities of the region. Other major organizations of this type included the Vorkuta and Ukhta Combines in the North European USSR and the Norilsk Combine in central Siberia. All three were finally subordinated to individual ministries (the ministries of the Coal Industry, Oil Industry, and Non-Ferrous Metallurgy respectively) during the 1950's. The Norilsk Combine had controlled not only mining and metallurgical enterprises in its territory, but also the railroad to the Yenisey, port facilities at Dudinka, and a number of agricultural units serving the urban population. The entire city of Norilsk appears to have fallen under its administration. What part of this empire may have been shed with its subordination to the Ministry of Non-Ferrous Metallurgy is not known, but the writer's impression is that it remained relatively intact.

Two combines have been associated in the past with maritime shipping in the Soviet Arctic, although by far the best known and most important was the Chief Directorate of the Northern Sea Route. In 1921 the Committee of the Northern Sea Route was created and given responsibility for shipping on the Kara Sea. In 1928 it was transformed into a transport-industrial trust under the name Komseveroput, subordinate to the People's Commissariat of Foreign Trade. Its sphere of operation was broadened to include development of the Ob and Yenisey North on which the shipping activity hinged. Of particular importance in its administration was the development of the timber industry and associated river traffic as far south as the Angara, but fisheries, fur trade, agriculture, and mining enterprises all played some part in its activity. It was finally broken up completely at the end of the 1930's. In the meantime a new organization, The Chief Directorate of the Northern Sea Route (Glavsevmorput or GUSMP) had come into being in 1932 and, prior to the final liquidation of Komseveroput, appears to have subsumed many of its activities. Glavsevmorput's primary function was the development of a through shipping route across the Arctic seas. Over the next few years its responsibilities were greatly increased and by 1936, at the zenith of its power, it had brought under its administration an empire spanning the entire Arctic and embracing an impressive array of economic, scientific, and cultural activities. Its importance can be partially judged by its subordination directly to the Council of Ministers of the USSR. A list of its activities, in addition to maritime shipping, would include river navigation in the Asiatic North, ship building and ship repair, coal mining, geological surveys, and the operation of a network of more than a hundred polar stations, several graphite mines and fish processing plants, and a substantial number of subordinate agricultural enterprises. In 1935, after the liquidation of the Committee of the North,

Glavsevmorput also acquired responsibility for the provision of economic and cultural services for the native peoples of the North; the following year, it took over all trade and procurement activities within its territory, which in Siberia extended south to the sixty-second parallel. Following the disastrous shipping season in 1937, when a large number of vessels were trapped in the ice and forced to winter at sea, Glavsevmorput was forced to shed many of its subsidiary activities and to concentrate on those directly related to the operation of the sea route. In 1953 the Chief Directorate of the Northern Sea Route was subordinated to the Ministry of the Merchant Fleet. Over the next decade other branches of this ministry, including the Murmansk and Far East Steamship Agencies, began to play a more active role in Arctic shipping. In 1963 Glavsevmorput was dissolved completely. With its final liquidation, hydro-meteorological services in the Arctic were transferred to the Chief Directorate of Meteorological Services of the USSR.

If *Glavsevmorput* was the most famous of the northern combines, Dal'stroy undoubtedly deserves the distinction of having been the most mysterious. Organized in 1931 for the development of gold, and later tin, mining in the Far Northeast, it was directly subordinate to the Ministry of Internal Affairs and appears to have relied almost exclusively on forced labour. The construction and operation of the Kolyma Highway from the newly-founded town of Magadan on the Okhotsk coast to the gold fields of the interior was one of Dal'stroy's major functions. A wide variety of service activities, including agricultural enterprises, developed under its management. It was on the territory of the Dal'stroy empire that the new Magadan *oblast* emerged in 1953. With the break-up of the forced labour camps following Stalin's death and the curtailing of the powers of the MVD, the Dal'stroy empire appears to have been transferred to the Ministry of Non-Ferrous Metallurgy. However, at least some of its subsidiary enterprises in the light industry category were turned over to the jurisdiction of the new *oblast* council.

The Post-1957 Period

The sweeping upheaval of 1957 in the economic management apparatus of the USSR was nationwide in scope. The decision to decentralize the organs of management led to the abolition of many of the central ministries and to the creation of a network of economic administrative regions (EAR's), each managed by a local economic council or *sovnarkhoz* responsible for the administration of most types of industrial and construction activity (but not agriculture) within its territory. The new system was intended to strengthen the day to day operation of enterprises, as well as planning activity, by concentrating decision-making authority in the hands of officials familiar with local conditions. It was hoped, in addition, that the integrated territorial approach to industrial administration would stimulate, wherever profitable, a higher level of regional self-sufficiency with a concurrent reduction in inter-regional transportation outlays. At first the economic administrative regions were made to correspond with individual *oblasts, krays,* and ASSR's. There thus arose in these units two parallel organizations, the elected political council or Soviet and the appointed economic council or *sovnarkhoz.*

Within a few years, a reaction to the 1957 "reform" had set in. Serious problems had arisen in co-ordinating the activities of the regional councils and many appeared to be taking the slogan of regional self-sufficiency too literally, with little regard to cost; in short, to have become too parochial in their outlook. Accordingly, there was soon a pronounced shift back towards more centralized control from Moscow. One of the first steps was the consolidation in 1962 of the network of about one hundred economic administrative regions into forty-seven larger units.[8] In the North the consolidation programme led to a number of interesting territorial linkages. Wherever possible, an effort was made to preserve

[8]A brief outline of other changes in economic administration should be included. They are relegated to a footnote here since they were national in scope and, although affecting the North, were not peculiar to that area.

In addition to the amalgamation of the economic administrative regions into larger units, there was established a master co-ordinating *sovnarkhoz* in each of the three largest republics and, at an even higher level, a *Sovnarkhoz* of the USSR. At the same time, construction activity was removed from the *sovnarkhoz* system and placed under the management of independent construction agencies in each of the EAR's, responsible at the national level to a new State Committee for Construction Affairs (Gosstroy). There were also created, within the individual EAR's, Councils for Co-ordinating the Development of the National Economy. The latter bodies were responsible for long-range planning, including policy decisions regarding new resource developments, and served as a co-ordinating link between the regional construction agencies and the *sovnarkhoz.* Although the *sovnarkhoz* contributed to the planning process by proposing production targets and other goals, their primary function was the management of enterprises and putting the plans into effect. Economic plans were co-ordinated at the national level by the USSR State Planning Committee, better known as Gosplan. Within Gosplan a series of state committees for branches of industry were established, each responsible for co-ordinating the production plans of the forty-seven *sovnarkhoz* for a particular type of industry. In a sense these branch committees represented a partial reincarnation of the pre-1957 ministries, although the centralized authority which they exercised was restricted to the planning field. They served, however, as a counterbalance to the integrated regional approach of the *sovnarkhoz* system. Agriculture and transportation remained under the jurisdiction of central ministries, while the electric power, gas, and certain defence industries were controlled by State Production Committees which differed

the identity of the North in the grouping of administrative-territorial divisions under a single *sovnarkhoz*.

The European North was organized into three economic administrative regions, the largest being the Northwestern EAR which encompassed Arkhangelsk *oblast* and the Karelian ASSR with their related forest-oriented economies. Murmansk *oblast* and the Komi ASSR, in view of their different industrial problems, were retained as independent economic administrative regions. Though not qualifying for such status on economic grounds, there was simply no other unit to which they could logically be attached.

In the Asiatic North, Tyumen *oblast* was included with Sverdlovsk *oblast* to form a Central Urals EAR, administered from the *sovnarkhoz* headquarters in Sverdlovsk. Subordination to an industrial centre in the Urals, rather than to the West Siberian *sovnarkhoz* focused on Novosibirsk, reflects at least in part the importance attached to the natural gas deposits of the lower Ob as a potential source of energy for the Urals. The association was reminiscent of the political administrative pattern of the 1920's. In central Siberia, Krasnoyarsk *kray*, together with the small Tuva ASSR on the border with Mongolia, was delineated as an EAR with the *sovnarkhoz* seat in the south at Krasnoyarsk. One of the most interesting developments was the creation of a self-contained northern economic administrative region, the Northeastern, grouping the Yakut ASSR and Magadan *oblast*. The two divisions share common development problems, in terms of the emphasis on the mining industry, and the former Dal'stroy empire did overlap into the northeastern corner of the Yakut ASSR. At the same time, there has been in the past virtually no overland communication betwen the two territories.[9] Their consolidation under a joint economic council was expected

---

from ministries only in name. All three of the national co-ordinative bodies referred to above (the *Sovnarkhoz* of the USSR, Gosstroy, and Gosplan) were subordinated to a Supreme Council of the National Economy (or Supreme *Sovnarkhoz*) of the USSR Council of Ministers.

[9]In Yakutia, the central lowlands have been supplied by way of the Lena River route, while the southern Aldan mining district has been served by the Yakutsk-Amur highway extending northward some 450 miles from the station of Never on the Trans-Siberian Railroad to Tommot. The remaining several hundred miles between Tommot and Yakutsk is traversed by only a winter road. Magadan, on the Okhotsk coast, has served as a maritime gateway for the southern part of Magadan *oblast*, with the Kolyma highway extending inland to the mining centres. It is only the first 450-mile section of the Kolyma highway which can be classed as a fully operational all-weather road. The next 450-mile section to Khandyga on the Aldan River, though reportedly functioning on a year-round basis, requires further construction. Khandyga at the end of the highway is connected to Yakutsk several hundred miles to the west by only a winter road or by the Aldan-Lena river route.

to hasten the development of a through all-weather highway linking Magadan, Yakutsk, and the Trans-Siberian Railroad and to lead to the emergence of the Yakut region as a source of timber and agricultural products for the mining centres of Magadan *oblast*. For the more distant future a railroad has been proposed across this territory, following much the same route as the projected highway via Yakutsk to Magadan but connecting in the south with the long-projected Baikal-Amur line rather than the Trans-Siberian. An interesting feature of the Northeastern EAR was the selection of Magadan, and not Yakutsk, as the seat of the economic council. The remaining part of the northeast, Kamchatka *oblast*, was attached to the Far East EAR which encompassed the island of Sakhalin and the Maritime *kray* with headquarters in the south at Vladivostok. The separation of Kamchatka from the remainder of the northeast was not surprising in view of the differences in its resource base and its essentially maritime outlook.

The liquidation of the remaining northern combines during the 1953–57 period, or at least the subordination of them to a ministry concerned with their primary activity, brought the system of economic administration in the North more into line with the national pattern. The introduction of the *sovnarkhoz* system throughout the entire country in 1957 was a further step in this direction. In a sense, the integration of all forms of industry under a single regional management, the *sovnarkhoz*, might be regarded as an extension of the northern combine system to the remainder of the nation. In some areas of the North, particularly Magadan *oblast*, the *sovnarkhoz* inherited a ready-made management structure organized on a territorial basis. In its broader features, the system of economic management in the North could be said to equate with that in the South.

At the same time, a detailed examination would reveal features in the internal organization of the *sovnarkhoz* that perpetuated some of the former differences between economic administration in the North and the South. Unified territorial management was carried one step further in some of the northern areas. Whereas transportation facilities in the south remained under ministerial control following the decentralization of industrial and construction activity in 1957, the *sovnarkhoz* in the Asiatic North retained the control over intraregional transportation facilities, such as the Norilsk–Dudinka railway and the Kolyma highway, exercised by the former combines. And while the management of construction was transferred after 1962 from the *sovnarkhoz* to special construction agencies in each EAR, no such fragmentation of management appears to have taken place in the Northeast region or, as far as known, in the Komi ASSR. A further contrast could be seen in the branch sections, or "micro-ministries," into which each *sovnarkhoz* in the south was divided. In some of the EAR's where northern combines previously existed, there was a tendency for the *sovnarkhoz* to retain more of a territorial form of subdivision in their internal organization. Presumably the same logistical and other factors which led to the creation of the combines could be used to justify such a structure, particularly in an area such as the Norilsk region which remained far removed from the seat of the economic council. More important, perhaps, was the fact that the type of industrial activity to be supervised within any one subregion of the North was less diverse than in the more developed and industrially complex South.

In late 1965 a sweeping new shake-up was announced in the sphere of economic management. At the time of writing the national network of economic administrative regions is being dissolved and the former system of centralized ministries re-established. Under the new system individual enterprises are to enjoy a greater measure of independence than in the past, and profit is to become the key measure of their performance. It is too early to tell how these changes will affect administration in the North. The branch principle of industrial management has never been as well suited to the conditions of this region. Moreover, with the increased emphasis on profit the new ministries can be expected to give low priority to their marginal activities in the North. Special procedures for dealing with the area will surely be required. It is not yet possible to predict, however, the form which they may take.

*Major Economic Regions and Long-Range Planning in the North
(Map 4)*

Prior to the introduction of the economic administrative regions in 1957, there had existed in the USSR a network of *major economic regions* which was employed by Gosplan for long-range planning and statistical accounting purposes. These regions were no more than intellectual constructs and were not, until recently, administered or represented by any sort of an elected or appointed body. It has only been since 1961 that planning commissions have been established in each of these regions. In the planning hierarchy, they served as an intermediate territorial link between the economic administrative regions and the republic and national organs of Gosplan. There has been no indication that the planning commissions of the major economic regions are to be dissolved in the return to the branch system of industrial

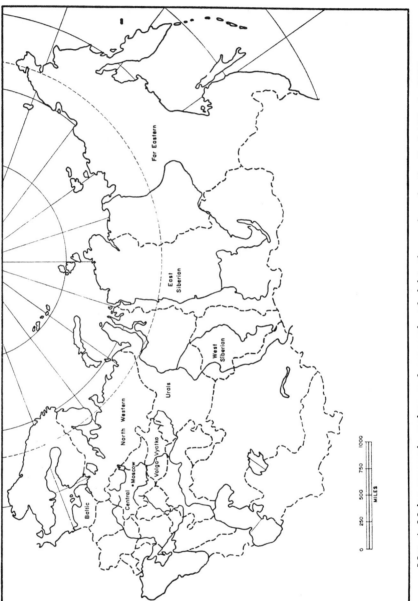

MAP 4. Major economic regions and economic administrative regions in the Soviet North, 1964.

management. Indeed, the future could see a strengthening of their role in the planning process.

The network of major economic regions, of which there are currently eighteen, has been subjected to some revision in recent years, but it is only with changes involving the North that we need here be concerned. The North has never been singled out as a unified economic zone in the delineation of these regions. Moreover, it would have been impossible to do so, since the planning divisions are simply groupings of administrative-territorial units some of which are still grounded in the South. The North is currently partitioned amongst four major economic regions, each of which includes as its core a more developed region in the South. All of the European North falls within the Northwest Region, with its centre at Leningrad. Prior to 1961, when the major economic regions gained new significance through the creation of planning commissions, a separate major economic region known as the North and encompassing the Komi ASSR, Arkhangelsk and Vologda *oblasts*, had been distinguished in the European part of the country. The Shield region of Kola-Karelia was always included within the Northwest Region focused on Leningrad. The Asiatic North, at least since the 1930's, has been partitioned amongst three major planning regions. However, significant changes in their configuration have been effected since 1960. In 1961, Tyumen *oblast* was transferred from the West Siberian major economic region to that of the Urals, an orientation which was further confirmed in the consolidation of the economic administrative regions the following year. The remainder of Siberia, both North and South, is divided between the East Siberian and Far Eastern major economic regions. With the amalgamation of the Yakut ASSR and Magadan *oblast* into a single economic administrative region, Yakutia was transferred to the Far Eastern regional planning division.

Thus in the delimitation of macro regional planning units, the North has never been treated as a distinctive region or series of regions. The major economic regions, built up from groups of administrative-territorial divisions, have always treated sections of the North as appendages to the more developed zones of the South. The only exception was the northeastern part of the European plain, which has now been absorbed into the Northwest Region. In part the treatment which the North has received for long-term planning purposes stems from the nature and configuration of the basic territorial building blocks from which the planning regions are constructed. At the same time, it reflects the lack of any real functional unity and East-West communication across the enormous expanse of the northern territories. There is, as yet, almost no interregional flow of goods between the various subregions of the North and links of this type will be a long time in developing. The northern part of central Siberia is entirely cut off from east Siberia in terms of land transport, as is the northern part of west Siberia from the Yenisey basin. Even in the European North, with its skeleton rail net, there is little economic integration or movement between the Baltic Shield of Kola-Karelia and the plain of the Arkhangelsk and Komi divisions to the east.

That the North does have unique problems and an identity of its own, which could justify its consideration as a separate planning unit, has nevertheless received some recognition through the recent creation of an Interdepartmental Commission on Problems of the North. The function of the commission, which operates under the joint auspices of Gosplan and the Academy of Sciences, is to co-ordinate the research and planning activities of all bodies concerned with the North and, of particular significance to us here, to develop a general scheme for the long-range development of the region. It represents then a type of regional planning organization superimposed on, and cutting across, the planning commissions of the major economic regions. However, its functions would appear to be more advisory in nature than those of the planning commissions; it does not participate directly in the shorter-term and more detailed planning process.[10]

It is worth noting that at the first plenum of this commission in 1963 several delegates, including the representatives of the Chief Directorate of the Northern Sea Route, the Arctic and Antarctic Scientific Research Institute, and Gosplan of the RSFSR, all spoke in favour of creating a special national organization responsible for the North as a unit. What

[10]The history of the Interdepartmental Commission is rather complex. It can be traced back to 1954 when a Commission on Problems of the North was created within the Academy of Sciences to co-ordinate the activity of various institutes of the Academy which studied problems relating to the economic development of the North. In 1962, following a series of organizational changes affecting Gosplan and the Academy of Sciences, it became an Interdepartmental Commission jointly sponsored by a branch of Gosplan, known as the Council for the Study of Productive Forces, and a parallel body of the Academy of Sciences, known as the Scientific Council on Problems of the Distribution of Productive Forces of the USSR. The chairman of the Interdepartmental Commission is the director of the Gosplan Council for the Study of Productive Forces. Representatives from a wide variety of local and national organizations, besides Gosplan and the Academy of Sciences, participated in the first plenum of the new Commission held in 1963. The Interdepartmental Commission was initially organized into three sections dealing, respectively, with the study of the natural environment, transportation, and the peoples of the North. However, additional sections were planned and at least some consideration was being given to the creation of regional as well as topical branches.

they had in mind was a state committee similar to those which had been established under Gosplan for branches of industry, or even a full-fledged ministry, which would be responsible for co-ordinating economic activity in the North. The territorial jurisdiction of such an organization would have run counter to that of the EAR's and major economic regions. Much of its work would have duplicated or even interfered with that of the management and planning organizations of the economic administrative and major economic regions. The proposal at that time was unrealistic and does not seem to have elicited widespread support. It reflected the frustration of northern specialists with the system of major planning regions and, in some areas, economic administrative regions which treated sections of the North as minor appendages of the southern territories. The suggestion, one might infer, was intended as a "second-best" solution to the impasse which confronted those seeking a more unified and distinct approach to planning and economic management in the North. More logical would have been the creation of a network of self-contained northern economic administrative regions and the grouping of these into one or more major economic planning divisions. This was impossible for the Asiatic North until independent *oblasts* had been established in the northern parts of western and central Siberia. It is significant that the advocates of a "state committee for the North" at the 1963 plenum also agitated the most vigorously for the creation of new *oblasts* on the lower Ob and lower Yenisey.

With the return to the branch system of industrial management the argument for a special organization to oversee activities in the North will become more cogent. If its responsibilities were limited to the planning sphere, such a body could operate under the auspices of either the national Gosplan or the subsidiary Gosplan of the Russian Republic. It could co-ordinate activities not only of the various ministries operating in the North, but also of the four planning commissions of the major economic regions whose territories extend into the North.

Labour Legislation

Under the special labour legislation which has been enacted for the North, higher wages and other benefits have been established within specifically defined zones. The original legislation of 1931–32 was amended in 1945 and was again revised in 1960. It has acquired increased significance since the death of Stalin and the breakdown of the forced labour system, which accounted for so large a share of the northern work force during the 1930's and 1940's.

In the original legislation of 1931–32, the zone of the Far North for which higher wage rates were set was defined on the basis of ethnic criteria. It corresponded with the areas inhabited by the so-called "little peoples of the North"; that is, with the national *okrugs*. In 1945, the region of the Far North was redefined and a second belt, with somewhat lower benefits, delimited. The second zone is referred to as "remote localities identified with (or equivalent in status to) regions of the Far North." Under the 1945 legislation the territory of the first zone, the Far North, was substantially reduced. Areas such as the Taymyr national *okrug*, where most of the Russian population lived in the city of Norilsk, were transferred to the second belt. At the same time, the island of Sakhalin and the Kurile Islands, with a less harsh environment, were added to the area described as the Far North. The higher wages which this implied were intended, undoubtedly, to stimulate Russian colonization of the territory which had just been acquired from Japan.

The 1960 legislation, which is currently in force, deserves more detailed consideration. The new boundary established for the Far North falls approximately along the Arctic Circle from the Finnish border as far east as the Yakut ASSR. In the European sector, the Far North is defined then to include only the tundra belt encompassing the Kola Peninsula, the Nenets NO, and the coal mining district around Vorkuta in the extreme northeast of the Komi republic. Beyond the Urals, the line runs eastward from Salekhard near the mouth of the Ob, crossing the Yenisey about a hundred miles upstream from Igarka. In the Yakut ASSR the boundary drops south to take in the diamond mining centres of the Vilyui basin, but crosses the Lena near its confluence with the Aldan, leaving the city of Yakutsk in the secondary zone of lesser benefits. The line finally reaches the coast just below the settlement of Okhotsk. All of Magadan *oblast*, as well as the Kamchatka Peninsula and the northern part of Sakhalin Island, are thus included within the Far North. The boundary delimiting the secondary belt of lesser benefits in the European North runs from the White Sea coast, northeast of Arkhangelsk, diagonally across the Komi ASSR, passing just west of the Ukhta oilfields. Thus the Karelian ASSR, the major share of Arkhangelsk *oblast*, and the southwestern half of the Komi ASSR, including the capital at Syktyvkar, have been excluded from even the secondary zone. In west Siberia the zone of lesser benefits includes the remainder of the two national *okrugs*, while east of the Yenisey it encompasses everything north of the settled belt along the Trans-Siberian Railroad.

The wage increments granted under the special northern labour legislation are supplemental to the regional coefficients which have been established for salaries throughout the USSR. The supplements are calculated on a percentage basis and are paid only on the first 300 rubles per month of regular salary. They are not to exceed a maximum of 80 per cent of the basic wage in regions of the Far North and 50 per cent of the basic wage in the secondary zone. However, with the higher regional coefficients forming the base, the average wage for the Far North and the secondary belt has been reported to be two to two and one-half times higher than in the Central Region around Moscow. The same source reports a cost of living differential of about 66 per cent between the Far North and the Moscow area.[11]

The significant feature of the northern wage increments is the fact that they are geared to the length of employment of a worker in the North and are additional to any regular length of service emoluments. The sliding scale has been introduced in an effort to cope with the high turnover of labour in the North and the considerable expenditures required to move families into and out of the area. Throughout the Far North, the wage increment is 10 per cent of salary upon completion of the first year of work and an additional 10 per cent for each subsequent year. The Chukotsk and Koryak national *okrugs* in the extreme northeast and the Arctic archipelagos have been singled out for even more favourable treatment, with the 10 per cent supplements being added every six months. In the second zone of "areas identified with the North," the 10 per cent increments are granted every two years.

Amongst the other benefits covered under the northern labour legislation the most important are undoubtedly those relating to annual leave and pensions. Workers in the Far North receive an extra eighteen working days of leave per year, in addition to the normal vacation period, while those in the secondary zone receive an extra twelve days. Leave can be accumulated for a period of up to three years and, one year in three, the cost of travel to and from the place where the leave is spent is paid by the employer. In computing length of service for retirement or disability pensions, each year of work in either the Far North or the secondary zone is counted as one and one-half years of service.

CONCLUSIONS

By North American standards, resource development and population growth in the Soviet North over the past several decades have been

[11]N. I. Shishkin, "O Sozdanii Postoyannykh Kadrov v Severnykh Raionakh Strany," *Problemy Severa*, no. 6, 1962, pp. 18–24. The average wage would also be affected by the occupational structure.

impressive. With improvements in transportation and increasing accessibility, special forms of economic administration, deemed essential in the early stages of development, have given way to management systems more closely approximating those of the South. With the introduction of the *sovnarkhoz* system in 1957, the normalization was essentially completed. The 1957 changes, however, could not be attributed to forces originating in the North. It was rather in the South that the major upset occurred.

With the reintroduction of the branch system of industrial organization, at least some differences in administrative structures may again emerge between North and South. It seems unlikely that a special ministry, or even a series of major territorial combines, would be established to manage all activities in the North. Within individual ministries, however, enterprises operating in the North are apt to engage in a broader range or supporting activities than would be normal in more accessible regions. Above all, one might anticipate the creation of a special department within Gosplan to co-ordinate the work of ministries and regional planning commissions whose jurisdiction lies only partially in the North.

The trend, with increasing economic maturity, has been towards the evolution of independent northern administrative-territorial units. The anticipated emergence of new *oblast* divisions in the northern parts of western and central Siberia would mark the final severance of political subordination to southern-based units and would open the way for new linkages in the sphere of regional planning. The emergence of a major economic planning division encompassing all of the Asiatic North is not difficult to visualize. Given such a development, the European North might also be separated from the planning region focused on Leningrad. A system of northern economic regions directly subordinate to a higher planning body for the North as a whole would then be possible.

Recognizing the Soviet propensity for experiment in economic regionalization and the intrinsic appeal of a more integrated approach to the North, evolution in this direction would appear likely. At the same time, much can be said in support of the present system of alignments. Although the subregions of the North share many common problems, the major lines of communication will continue, as in Canada, to run north-south. It is only natural to assume that Magadan will always be linked more closely with Vladivostok than with cities in the European North.

Of perhaps one thing we can be certain, and this is the inevitability of further change both in territorial arrangements and modes of administration. The ease with which boundaries can be shifted in the USSR lends a permanent element of instability to its territorial patterns. The North, moreover, will continue to be affected by developments at the national level. The branch system of economic management has never been as well suited to the conditions of the North. The latest upheaval in the administrative organs serving the nation's economy will lend greater urgency to the recognition of the North as a distinct region and may spur the realignment of boundaries and territorial groupings to facilitate a more unified approach to its problems of administration and development.

Sovereignty in the North:
The Canadian Aspect
of an International Problem*

◄ GORDON W. SMITH† ►

THE QUESTION of sovereignty in the polar regions is one that for years has fascinated international lawyers and bedeviled statesmen. The main reason is obvious enough: the unique physical, climatic, and demographic characteristics of the polar regions seem to forbid the application of normal rules of international law and to defy the creation of others. The issues involved are thus basically legal, but they are also political and diplomatic. Some are now of only historic and academic interest, while others are still significant. Until fairly recent times the major concern was with sovereignty over land territory, but, in the Arctic at least, this matter appears now to be essentially settled, and other questions involving territorial waters, ice islands, undersurface navigation of submarines, and airspace have come to the fore. In the Antarctic, the land issue has not been permanently resolved, but the interested states have by treaty put this and other problems "on ice" for a period of at least thirty-four years. The following pages attempt to summarize the Canadian aspect of the historic and the current issues.

*This paper was completed in the fall of 1963.
†Lecturer in History, University of the West Indies, Trinidad; formerly Professor of History, Collège Militaire Royal, St. Jean, Quebec.

CANADA'S ACQUISITION OF SOVEREIGNTY OVER HER NORTHERN
TERRITORIES‡

Some Legal and Historical Background

International law recognizes a number of basic modes of acquiring
territory. Oppenheim's classification, perhaps the best known, includes
five: cession, occupation, accretion, subjugation, and prescription.[1] In
addition, the supplementary doctrines of continuity, contiguity, the hinterland, and the watershed have sometimes been invoked in support
of territorial claims, and under certain circumstances may have weight.
Papal grants, important in earlier times, have fallen into disuse; but
discovery, although rather unlikely now on this planet, has been considered even by modern authorities to give an "inchoate" or temporary
title, which must be perfected subsequently by other means. There is
also that curious principle or theory of sectors, which has been put
forward specifically for the polar regions. Without going into detail, it
would appear that of the foregoing, the ones most likely to be invoked
in Canada's case, validly or otherwise, are cession, occupation, prescription, contiguity, discovery, and the sector principle.

One well-known authority on the subject says that acquisitions of new
territory were based mainly upon papal grants up to the sixteenth century, upon priority of discovery for the next two hundred years, and
thereafter upon effective possession. He adds that effective possession
was first advocated in theory and later required in fact.[2] His division
may be too categorical. Another authority suggests that effective possession has always been important,[3] and, as just noted, discovery may still
give at least an inchoate title. Also, although effective possession was
laid down as a requirement at the Berlin Conference on Africa in 1884–
85 for the acquisition of new territories in that continent,[4] a series of

‡This section is based upon a paper delivered at the annual meeting of the
Canadian Political Science Association in Quebec City on June 8, 1963.

[1]L. F. L. Oppenheim, *International Law*, ed. by H. Lauterpacht, 8th ed.,
London: Longmans, Green and Co. (1955), vol. I, p. 546.

[2]A. S. Hershey, *The Essentials of International Public Law and Organization*,
rev. ed., New York: Macmillan Co. (1935), p. 285.

[3]F. A. F. von der Heydte, "Discovery, Symbolic Annexation and Virtual
Effectiveness in International Law," *The American Journal of International Law*,
vol. 29, no. 3 (July, 1935), pp. 448–71.

[4]*The American Journal of International Law, Supplement*, vol. 3, no. 1 (Jan.,
1909), pp. 7–25; also *British and Foreign State Papers 1884–1885*, vol. LXXVI,
pp. 4–20.

later legal settlements would seem to have modified the requirement, at least where such modification has been warranted by the circumstances. These observations provide an outline of the legal framework in which the history of the sovereignty problem may be discussed, in relation to Canada's Arctic territories.

Rights of sovereignty in any territory are likely to be based to a large extent upon the record of human activity therein. In the case of the Canadian Northland this record may be broadly divided into three phases, of which only two are of particular relevance here. Up to about A.D. 1500, the only peoples to enter the region were wandering Indians and Eskimos, and, to a lesser extent, Norsemen. During the middle period, from approximately 1500 to the third quarter of the nineteenth century, Indians and Eskimos were joined by white explorers, fur traders, whalers, and missionaries, and a number of territorial claims were made. With the transfers of 1870 and 1880, Canada assumed full responsibility for these territories, and in the period following undertook to bring them under her jurisdiction. For the purpose of this essay the first period may be disregarded. Although the Indians and Eskimos may have been monarchs of all they surveyed in ancient times, their "sovereignty" has had no consequences for the situation of today. Neither people had well-developed concepts of ownership of land, and in any case both were pushed aside by the white man upon his arrival. The Norsemen, whose wanderings in what is now Canada are still only vaguely known, established no permanent settlements,[5] and in modern times neither Norwegian nor Danish claims in the Canadian Arctic attempted to derive any benefit from their voyages.

With the Columbian discovery of America a new phase begins. The first post-Columbian explorer to land on the northeastern coast was evidently John Cabot, in 1497, and the first to land in the archipelago was Martin Frobisher, in 1576. During the three hundred years after Frobisher, the main geographical outlines in the North, both continental and insular, were gradually filled in, except for those of the more remote islands north of Lancaster Sound. For almost the whole period, exploration was concentrated mainly upon the goal of a northwest passage, and proceeded in a series of waves, each stopping before being succeeded by another. During the first years after the initial discoveries, in the time of the Cabots and their contemporaries, a vague familiarity with

[5]See Helge Ingstad, "Discovery of Vinland," *The Arctic Circular*, vol. XV, no. 1, Jan., 1963, pp. 2–6, where the author on the basis of impressive evidence locates the long-sought Vinland of the Norsemen at the northern tip of Newfoundland. The article also brings out the uncertainties that still persist regarding many aspects of the Norse voyages.

the coasts of Newfoundland, Labrador, and south Greenland was acquired. Frobisher and his immediate successors Davis, Hudson, Baffin, and others, collectively penetrated into Davis Strait, Baffin Bay, Hudson Strait, and Hudson Bay. After the founding of the Hudson's Bay Company in 1670, fur traders pushed on to the northwestern extremity of Hudson Bay by water and across the northwestern interior overland to the Arctic and Pacific Oceans. After a lapse following the great expeditions of Alexander Mackenzie, exploration began again in 1818, and during the next thirty years the Rosses, Parry, Franklin, Richardson, Back, Beechey, Simpson, and Rae practically finished tracing the Arctic coast and also became acquainted with the lands adjacent to some of the principal water passages. Later, the search for the lost Franklin expedition and repeated efforts to reach the rumoured open polar sea and the North Pole greatly extended knowledge of the region. By the time of the transfers the larger islands were all known, with the exception of those discovered afterwards by Sverdrup and Stefansson.

It was common practice for explorers to claim the lands they discovered on behalf of their monarchs. Thus, John Cabot was authorized by Henry VII of England to "conquer, occupy, and possess" lands unknown to other Christians,[6] and Martin Frobisher claimed "Meta Incognita" in Frobisher Bay for Queen Elizabeth at his first arrival, ordering his crew to bring him "whatsoever thing they could first finde, whether it were living or dead, stocke or stone, in token of Christian possession."[7] The pattern established by the early explorers was generally followed thereafter, even into the twentieth century, and thus claims to territory were numerous indeed. Attempts were often made to fortify rights of discovery by symbolic acts of appropriation, such as the raising of flags, the erection of crosses or cairns, the reading of proclamations, and the depositing of records. Whether symbolic acts of appropriation helped greatly in establishing title to land has often been questioned by authorities on international law, but the practice was universal. The authors of a detailed study on the subject have concluded that they were by no means without value, and in earlier times were considered to enhance mere rights of discovery.[8] Obviously discoveries and annexations

---

[6]H. P. Biggar, ed., *The Precursors of Jacques Cartier 1497–1534*, Ottawa: Government Printing Bureau (1911), pp. 8–10.

[7]Richard Hakluyt, *The Principal Navigations, Voyages, Traffiques, and Discoveries of the English Nation*, 12 vols., Glasgow: J. MacLehose and Sons (1903–5), vol. VII, p. 282.

[8]A. S. Keller, O. J. Lissitzyn, and F. J. Mann, *Creation of Rights of Sovereignty Through Symbolic Acts 1400–1800*, New York: Columbia University Press (1938), esp. pp. 148–51.

were not all of equal force; an official annexation of newly discovered land at the direction and on behalf of a monarch or government would carry more weight than the unauthorized and unsupported claim of a private explorer. Obviously, too, a state would be likely to magnify the value of its own claims and pay as little heed as possible to those of others.

It is conspicuous that in what is now the Canadian Arctic, practically all the expeditions, discoveries, and claims prior to about mid-nineteenth century were British. The most important exceptions were French voyages in Hudson Bay prior to the conquest, especially at the time of Pierre Le Moyne d'Iberville. There was also the expedition of the Dane Jens Munk to Hudson Bay in 1619, during which he claimed "New Denmark" for his monarch Christian IV.[9] However, nothing was done to follow up his claim. Some of the British claims were also ineffective, such as Frobisher's to south Greenland in 1578[10] and Cook's to the Alaskan territory around Cook Inlet in 1778.[11] Others were invalid, such as Simpson's at Point Barrow in 1837[12] and Moore's to small islands nearby in 1850.[13] These territories had been placed outside Britain's orbit by the British-Russian treaty of 1825, which established the 141st meridian as the common frontier.[14] After 1850 foreign explorers, mostly American, aided in the Franklin search and undertook independently to reach the supposed open polar sea and the North Pole. Their interests were generally non-political, however, and they made few outright claims to land. An exception, perhaps, was Hall's raising of the American flag in Frobisher Bay in 1861, which, judging from his narrative, may have been intended to show American possession.[15] On the whole the activities of the predominantly British explorers were of considerable importance, because they provided the main basis for the assumption by the British government in the 1870's that Britain had certain territorial rights in the archipelago which could be transferred to Canada.

The Hudson's Bay Company was the principal authority in the regions

[9]C. C. A. Gosch, ed., *Danish Arctic Expeditions 1605 to 1620*, 2 vols., London: Hakluyt Society (1897), vol. II, pp. 15, 19, 23, 83.

[10]Hakluyt, *op. cit.*, vol. VII, p. 326.

[11]W. Ellis, *An Authentic Narrative of a Voyage Performed by Captain Cook and Captain Clerke*, 2 vols., London: Robinson et al. (1783), vol. I, pp. 262–63.

[12]Thomas Simpson, *Narrative of the Discoveries on the North Coast of America . . . etc.*, London: R. Bentley (1843), pp. 8, 153.

[13]*Arctic Papers*, vol. II, no. 97 (March 7, 1851), p. 33.

[14]*Treaties and Conventions Between Great Britain and Foreign Powers*, vol. III, pp. 362–66.

[15]C. F. Hall, *Life with the Esquimaux*, 2 vols., London: S. Low, Son, and Marston (1864), vol. II, pp. 111, 118, 119.

north of Canada for two hundred years following the granting of its charter by Charles II in 1670. There is no doubt that the charter was intended to make the Governor and Company "true and absolute lords and proprietors" of Rupert's Land. It specified their authority over certain matters, such as land, trade, lawmaking, immigration, and settlement, and its wording indicates the Crown's intention that they should be sovereign in all respects whatsoever, excepting only the obligation of allegiance to the Crown itself. Unfortunately, although the charter attempted to define the territories it granted, the state of geographical knowledge at the time did not permit this to be done with precision. This circumstance, along with doubts as to the charter's validity, exposed the company to continual attack, from the French colony to the south until 1763, from other fur interests based on Montreal until 1821, and from the two Canadas, separate or united, until Confederation.

Rivalry with the French colony began with the founding of the company, and continued intermittently for almost a hundred years. During the Wars of the League of Augsburg and the Spanish Succession, the French dominated Hudson Bay and captured the company's posts, but these advantages were lost when France renounced all claims to the Hudson Bay region in the Treaty of Utrecht in 1713.[16] Troubles continued, however, partly because of the still unsettled boundary between Rupert's Land and the French colony, and also because of the French attempt, led by the Vérendryes, to move into the region southwest of Hudson Bay. The surrender of New France in 1763 ended for all time the French threat to Rupert's Land.[17] Almost immediately another challenge appeared, in the form of English-speaking interlopers from Scotland and New England, who established themselves in Montreal and employed experienced French-Canadian voyageurs in an energetic prosecution of the western fur trade. During the first two decades of the nineteenth century the Hudson's Bay Company waged a life-and-death struggle against the Montreal interests, now consolidated into the North-West Company, and triumphed when the strife was ended in 1821 by an amalgamation that really constituted a victory for the older company. A further triumph for the Hudson's Bay Company was the reaffirmation of its rights in Rupert's Land by a statute of the British Parliament in 1821.[18] From 1821 to 1870 the company was at the pinnacle of its power and prestige, but during the same period it came increasingly

---

[16]George Chalmers, ed., *A Collection of Treaties Between Great Britain and Other Powers* 2 vols., London (1790), vol. I, pp. 340–90. See esp. Art. 10.

[17]*Ibid.*, vol. I, pp. 467–94 (The Peace of Paris).

[18]*Statutes of Great Britain*, 1–2 Geo. IV, c. 66, July 2, 1821.

under attack from the Canadas. Understandably they resented the colossus that claimed dominion over most of the territories into which they might otherwise expect to expand, and they were determined to bring its charter monopoly to an end.

The company defended its position with considerable tenacity. For support it still relied principally upon the Imperial authority which had granted its charter, and it is true that during the long history of controversy over the charter this support was seldom denied. As an eminent Canadian historian has put it:

> Few documents have been challenged by such powerful interests or recognized at one time or another for two centuries, by such an array of official evidence—by order-in-council, by act of parliament, by royal commission, by the opinion of law officers of the crown, by treaty, and by select parliamentary committee.[19]

Finally, however, the Imperial authorities, even though still disposed to uphold the charter's validity, could hardly avoid coming to the conclusion that it was necessary for the company to surrender at least its control of the land. In coming to this decision they were influenced by pressure from Canada, by the evident need to promote settlement in the fertile parts of the Hudson's Bay Company territories, and by fears that American immigrants might turn these parts into another Oregon. In these circumstances the company's rule was brought to an end.

The claims of explorers, and the long proprietorship of the Hudson's Bay Company, provide the principal elements in any historical consideration of how Canada became heir to these northern territories. Other activities prior to the transfers, principally of whalers and missionaries, may be more briefly noted. The first whalers in the region appear to have been Dutchmen, who moved into Davis Strait from the waters east of Greenland in the early 1700's, after the Spitsbergen whaling industry had begun to decline. Later in the century they were joined by Englishmen and Scotsmen. They all appear to have gone no further than south Greenland coastal waters and Davis Strait until Ross and Parry showed the way into Baffin Bay and Lancaster Sound in 1818 and 1819. American whalers entered the scene towards mid-nineteenth century, concentrating their activities on the west side of Davis Strait south of Cumberland Gulf, and in Hudson Strait and the northern part of Hudson Bay. Later the English whalers retired from the area, and the Americans abandoned Davis Strait to the Scots, devoting their own attention to Hudson Bay. Unlike the Scots, the Americans adopted the habit of

[19]Chester Martin, "The Royal Charter," *The Beaver*, Outfit 276 (June, 1945), p. 26.

wintering in the whaling grounds, and so they provisioned their ships for two years. Later the Scots developed "land stations" on Baffin Island, operated by a few whites with native help. After the 1870's, whaling in both Davis Strait and Hudson Bay went into decline. In the meantime other American whalers were pushing through Bering Strait into the western Arctic, but they did not reach Canadian waters until 1889, when they first arrived at Herschel Island.[20]

Missionary activity in the North, of little importance here, was divided among Moravians on the northern Labrador coast and Anglicans and Roman Catholics elsewhere in the northern mainland; but prior to the 1870's none of these sects had any permanent missions in the archipelago.[21]

The Transfers of 1870 and 1880

The preceding section shows, as stated earlier, that the only white men to penetrate the region under consideration before the 1870's were explorers and fur traders, and to a lesser extent whalers and missionaries. Their activities were for the most part unofficial, and the only administration of any kind was that of the Hudson's Bay Company. It was in these circumstances that the two great transfers of 1870 and 1880 were arranged, which suddenly presented Canada with responsibility for half a continent. The territories of the Hudson's Bay Company, comprising Rupert's Land and the North Western Territory, were surrendered to Great Britain in 1869, and Canada accepted them from Great Britain in 1870. All other British territories or territorial rights in the Arctic, involving approximately or ostensibly the archipelago, were handed over in 1880. Whether these were genuine cessions in the international sense is doubtful, since in each case one form of British sovereignty was substituted for another. The transfers were certainly binding upon British subjects, but not necessarily upon foreign states, which conceivably

[20]There does not appear to be a comprehensive treatment of whaling in the North American Arctic. A. P. Low, *The Cruise of the Neptune 1903–04*, Ottawa: Government Printing Bureau (1906), pp. 248–82, gives a good deal of information about whaling in Hudson Bay and Davis Strait during the nineteenth century and up to 1904. See also B. Lubbock, *The Arctic Whalers*, Glasgow: Brown, Son, and Ferguson (1937 and 1955); and for an earlier classic, W. Scoresby, *An Account of The Arctic Regions and of the Whale-Fishery*, 2 vols., Edinburgh: Constable and Co. (1820).

[21]For the history of the Moravian misions see J. E. Hutton, *History of the Moravian Church* London: Moravian Publication Office (1922). T. C. B. Boon, *The Anglican Church from the Bay to the Rockies*, Toronto: Ryerson Press (1962) tells of early Anglican activity in the North; Rev. P. Duchaussois, *Mid Snow and Ice: The Apostles of the North-West*, London: Burns, Oates, and Washbourne (1923) tells of Roman Catholic.

could have raised some awkward questions about them. Fortunately for Canada, this did not happen at the time.

Pressure upon the Hudson's Bay Company to surrender its territories had been mounting, especially after a Select Committee of the British House of Commons in 1857 had recommended that it turn over at least the fertile areas.[22] The incorporation of the company's territories into the new Dominion of Canada was anticipated by the insertion of a clause (no. 146) for this purpose in the BNA Act of 1867, and by the passing of the Rupert's Land Act of 1868.[23] While the surrender was being arranged, the Canadian delegates showed extreme unwillingness to recognize the company's title, but the Imperial authorities insisted that since the company had been lord-proprietor for two hundred years it would have to be treated as such for the purpose of the transfer. Thus, whatever its validity may have been, the charter was upheld by Imperial authority until the end. Addresses from the Canadian Parliament having been passed on two occasions requesting the transfer,[24] the deed of surrender was signed in November, 1869,[25] and an Imperial order in council of June 23, 1870,[26] finally admitted the Hudson's Bay Company territories into the Dominion of Canada.

None of these documents attempted any further clarification of the limits of either Rupert's Land or the North Western Territory. The company itself had come to adopt the seemingly obvious implication in the charter that Rupert's Land comprised all territories draining into Hudson Bay and Strait, a view firmly stated by Governor Simpson before the Select Committee of the House of Commons in 1857.[27] The North Western or Indian Territory, which it held under license, was considered to include all remaining British continental territories west of Hudson Bay except British Columbia. Two of the most sensitive boundaries, which were also international, were well established. These were the southern and northwestern, along the 49th parallel and the 141st meridian respectively. Others, notably those between the territories and on their north, were left without precise definition.

[22]*Report from the Select Committee on the Hudson's Bay Company, with Proceedings, Minutes of Evidence, Appendix, and Index*, July–August, 1857, pp. iii–iv.

[23]*Statutes of Great Britain*, 31–32 Vict., c. 105, July 31, 1868.

[24]Addresses of Dec. 16–17, 1867, and May 29–31, 1869. See in *Statutes of Canada*, 35 Vict., 1872, pp. lxvii–lxxvii.

[25]*Ibid.*, pp. lxxvii–lxxxiii.

[26]*Ibid.*, pp. lxiii–lxvii.

[27]*Report from the Select Committee on the Hudson's Bay Company* . . . etc., p. 46 (*supra*).

The circumstances of the transfer of 1880 were quite different.[28] The islands in question were even less inhabited than the remoter parts of Rupert's Land, having no permanent white population and only a scattering of wandering Eskimos. The transfer was initiated by two requests for whaling and mining bases in Cumberland Sound, Baffin Island, in 1874, by a British citizen and an American. Investigation revealed that the Hudson's Bay Company had not considered this territory their property before 1870, and that it was too remote to have been part of Canada before Confederation. It seemed that the activities of explorers, and to a lesser extent of whalers, provided the only basis upon which Britain could claim Baffin Island or, for that matter, any other island in the archipelago. The uncertainty of both British and Canadian officials as to the reliability of Britain's title is clearly revealed in contemporary Colonial Office correspondence, as is their inability to define precisely the limits of the territories to be transferred. The correspondence also shows that Britain was anxious nonetheless to hand over to Canada all her remaining territories or rights in the region, and that her primary motive for so doing was to forestall any attempt by the United States to establish herself there. A revealing memo by a Colonial Office official reads as follows: "The object in annexing these unexplored territories to Canada is, I apprehend, to prevent the United States from claiming them, and not from the likelihood of their proving of any value to Canada."[29] The assumption apparently was that the United States would object less to Canadian than to British proprietorship in the islands, and that they could be looked after more easily from Ottawa than from London.

Although the first step was taken in 1874 towards what would appear a relatively simple transaction, it took fully six years to bring the matter to a conclusion. The long delay was caused mainly by indecision as to how the boundaries of the territories to be transferred should be drawn, and whether the transfer should be brought about by an Act of the British Parliament or an Imperial order in council. In the end it was decided that an order in council would be adequate for the purpose, and all attempts at precise delimitation were abandoned. The order in council accomplishing the transfer defines the territories in this wonderfully vague and all-inclusive fashion: "all British territories and possessions

---

[28]Gordon W. Smith, "The Transfer of Arctic Territories from Great Britain to Canada in 1880, and Some Related Matters, as Seen in Official Correspondence," *Arctic*, vol. 14, no. 1 (March, 1961), 53–73.

[29]*Colonial Office Papers*, Series No. 42, vol. 759, p. 19 (Jan. 29, 1879).

in North America, not already included within the Dominion of Canada, and all islands adjacent to any of such territories or possessions . . . with the exception of the Colony of Newfoundland and its dependencies. . . ."[30] Taking the passage quite literally, one would be justified in concluding that it referred to British Honduras, Bermuda, and the British West Indies as much as to the islands of the Arctic archipelago.

The most that can be said for the deal is that it was a voluntary gift to Canada of whatever Arctic rights Britain possessed. As Judge Huber remarked in his celebrated decision regarding the ownership of Palmas Island, however, a state attempting to transfer territory to another state could hardly give more than she herself possessed.[31] What Britain's rights were at the time of the transfer no one really knew, either then or afterwards.

Canada's Efforts to Establish Her Sovereignty in the Northern Territories

Thus, within a period of ten years, the young Dominion of Canada found itself responsible for virtually the northern half of the continent and adjacent islands, except Newfoundland, Alaska, and Greenland. Steps were speedily taken to develop the more habitable, southerly parts of the West and bring them under control, and progress there was rapid. But in the remoter northerly parts, especially the islands, little or nothing was done for fifteen years after 1880. The Dominion government attempted to discover from the Hudson's Bay Company what action might be required in these territories, but could get little information, and so decided, in effect, to do nothing. An order in council dated September 23, 1882, recommended "that no steps be taken with the view of legislating for the good government of the country until some influx of population or other circumstance shall occur to make such provision more imperative than it would at present seem to be."[32] Coincidentally, it was at this very time that the conference on Africa in Berlin was imposing the requirement of effective possession as a condition for full rights of sovereignty in the newly appropriated parts of Africa. If a foreign state had deliberately undertaken to establish a claim in the archipelago at this time, Canada's legal position would have been, to say the least, vulnerable.

[30]*Imperial Order in Council*, July 31, 1880.
[31]"The Island of Palmas Award," *The American Journal of International Law*, vol. 22, no. 4 (Oct., 1928), 879.
[32]*Dominion Order in Council*, P.C. no. 1839, Sept. 23, 1882.

The first real attempt to legislate for the northernmost territories was made in 1895. In that year a Dominion order in council was passed creating the four provisional districts of Ungava, Yukon, Mackenzie, and Franklin, the last-named of "indefinite extent," but including the archipelago.[33] Other measures soon followed, their obvious purpose being to demonstrate that the regions marked out by the order in council were under the control of the Canadian government. The reason or reasons for the change in policy are not entirely clear, but it is apparent that involvements with other countries and their nationals in the North, during roughly the two decades preceding World War I, provide much of the answer.

These years saw the development of the Alaska boundary dispute, the outcome of which, in 1903, did little to relieve Canadian anxiety over territorial problems with the United States.[34] The rush to the Klondike, beginning in 1896, immediately dumped in the lap of the Canadian government the immense problem of maintaining law and order among the hordes of mostly foreign gold hunters.[35] The American explorer Robert Peary was making repeated attempts to reach the North Pole, and in 1909, using Ellesmere Island as his base, he finally succeeded in planting the American flag at or near the pole and claiming "the entire region and adjacent" for the United States.[36] Another explorer, the Norwegian Otto Sverdrup, discovered the so-called Sverdrup Islands (Axel Heiberg and the Ringnes Islands) during his expedition of 1898–1902, and claimed them for Norway.[37] His countryman Roald Amundsen took a ship through the Northwest Passage for the first time in 1903–6, and explored some unknown coast in Victoria Island on the way.[38] And the uninhibited and sometimes lawless

---

[33]*Dominion Order in Council*, P.C. no. 2640, Oct. 2, 1895. See also the later order in council, P.C. no. 3388, Dec. 18, 1897, which was designed to include certain islands off the Arctic coast which seemed to have been left out by the 1895 order. The two orders, and other relevant matters, are discussed in considerable detail in W. F. King, *Report upon the Title of Canada to the Islands North of the Mainland of Canada*, Ottawa: Government Printing Bureau (1905).

[34]*Alaska Boundary Tribunal: Protocols, Arguments, Award, etc.*, London (1903).

[35]Pierre Berton, *Klondike: The Life and Death of the Last Great Gold Rush*, Toronto: McClelland and Stewart Ltd. (1958), recounts in vivid style the disorders of gold rush days.

[36]Robert E. Peary, *The North Pole*, New York: F. A. Stokes Co. (1910), p. 297.

[37]Otto Sverdrup, *New Land: Four Years in the Arctic Regions*, 2 vols., London: Longmans, Green, and Co. (1904), vol. II, pp. 449–50.

[38]Roald Amundsen, *The North West Passage*, 2 vols., London: A. Constable and Co., Ltd. (1908).

behaviour of American whalers in both Hudson Bay and the Beaufort Sea was a continuing source of concern to the Canadian government, especially because they were suspected of debauching and misusing the Eskimos in both areas.[39] On the whole, then, the Canadian authorities had some reason to fret over the situation in the territories where they had recently assumed responsibility.

As stated, the order in council of 1895 was the first of a number of measures between that date and World War I designed to bring the northern territories under effective control. A series of federal statutes separated the Yukon from the rest of the territories,[40] created the provinces of Alberta and Saskatchewan,[41] and enlarged Manitoba, Ontario, and Quebec,[42] thus leaving the Northwest Territories by 1912 in approximately the form familiar to us in recent years. The North-West Mounted Police were sent to the Yukon, the Beaufort Sea region, and Hudson Bay, with salutary results in each case. Government expeditions commanded by William Wakeham in 1897,[43] A. P. Low in 1903-4,[44] Major Moodie of the Mounted Police in 1904-5,[45] and Joseph E. Bernier in 1906-7,[46] 1908-9,[47] and 1910-11[48] were dispatched to patrol the waters of Hudson Bay and the eastern Arctic islands and to assert Canadian sovereignty there. Under government instructions they took note of all activities at the places visited, imposed licenses upon Scottish and American whalers, collected customs duties upon goods brought into the region, and generally impressed upon both Eskimos and whites that henceforth they would be expected to obey the laws of Canada.

[39]See, e.g., Report of NWMP Commissioner for 1903, in *Sessional Papers*, vol. XXXVIII, no. 11, Paper no. 28.

[40]*Statutes of Canada*, 61 Vict., c. 6, June 13, 1898; 1 Edw. VII, c. 41, May 23, 1901.

[41]*Ibid.*, 4-5 Edw. VII, cc. 3 and 42, July 20, 1905.

[42]*Ibid.*, 2 Geo. V, cc. 32, 40, 45, April 1, 1912. Each of the three provinces had already been extended northwards, Manitoba to approximately the middle of Lake Winnipeg by Canadian statute (44 Vict., c. 14, March 21, 1881), Ontario to the Albany River by British statute (52-53 Vict., c. 28, Aug. 12, 1889), confirming an 1884 award of the Judicial Committee of the Privy Council, and Quebec to the Eastmain by Canadian statute (61 Vict., c. 3, June 13, 1898).

[43]William Wakeham, *Report of the Expedition to Hudson Bay and Cumberland Gulf in the Steamship "Diana,"* Ottawa: Queen's Printer (1898).

[44]A. P. Low, *The Cruise of the "Neptune" 1903-4 (supra)*.

[45]*Report of the Royal North-West Mounted Police 1905*, part IV.

[46]Joseph E. Bernier, *Cruise of the "Arctic" 1906-7*, Ottawa: King's Printer (1909).

[47]Bernier, *Cruise of the "Arctic" 1908-9*, Ottawa: Government Printing Bureau (1910).

[48]W. W. Stumbles, et. al., *The Arctic Expedition 1910*, Ottawa: Department of Marine and Fisheries (n.d.).

Scientists representing various disciplines were regularly taken on the voyages, in the hope that their researches would increase knowledge of the region. Ceremonies of taking possession were performed by Wakeham, Low, and Bernier at a number of places, with government authorization or approval, culminating with Bernier's sweeping claim on Melville Island, July 1, 1909, to the entire archipelago—"all islands and territory within the degrees 141 and 60 west longitude."[49] This proclamation was in line with the sector principle enunciated by Senator Poirier in 1907,[50] which, although not adopted at the time, later became official in virtually every respect except that it was not incorporated in a statute. An amendment to the Fisheries Act in 1906 declared that Hudson Bay "is wholly territorial water of Canada."[51] Little outright resistance to these measures was encountered, and during the decade or so before World War I it could fairly be said that the Far North, or at least the part of it frequented by white men, was being brought under Canadian jurisdiction.

During the war and immediately afterwards there was a general lapse of activity in the North, no doubt attributable to the exigencies of the war effort. A conspicuous exception was the Canadian Arctic Expedition under Vilhjalmur Stefansson, which operated in the western Arctic from 1913 to 1918.[52] Stefansson took possession of several islands he discovered for Canada, as he was directed to do,[53] but it does not appear that he used his authority to investigate whaling and collect customs.

Not long after the war was over, government activity in the North was resumed on a larger scale than before, and since that time it has been continuous and expanding, especially since the war of 1939–45. The immediate reason for the resumption of activity was the flat denial of Canadian sovereignty in Ellesmere Island by the Danish explorer Knud Rasmussen, and the endorsement of his denial by the Danish government. When the Canadian government requested that Danish authorities restrain the killing of musk oxen by Greenland Eskimos on Ellesmere Island, Rasmussen wrote that the only authority on the island was that which he exercised from his station at Thule, and that he needed no assistance whatever from the Canadian government. The official reply of the Danish government was that they thought they could

[49]Bernier, *Cruise of the "Arctic" 1908–9*, p. 192 (*supra*).
[50]Canada, *Senate Debates*, Feb. 20, 1907, pp. 266–73.
[51]*Statutes of Canada*, 6 Edw. VII, c. 13, July 13, 1906.
[52]Vilhjalmur Stefansson, *The Friendly Arctic*, rev. ed., New York: Macmillan Co. (1943).
[53]*Dominion Order in Council*, P.C. no. 406, Feb. 22, 1913.

"subscribe to what Mr. Rasmussen says."[54] It seems probable that the course of action adopted was at least partly the result of Stefansson's urging that if Canada did not occupy the northern islands she might lose them. Stefansson, who was full of projects at this stage, wanted to organize an expedition in 1919 for the purpose of occupying the islands, but according to his own account the Canadian cabinet split on the issue of whether he or Shackleton should lead it, and the expedition did not materialize.[55] Stefansson also undertook to appropriate Wrangel Island, north of Siberia, largely to dramatize the unreliability of the sector principle,[56] but the Canadian government, at first willing to accept the gain although not the expense, backed off with red faces after one expedition had come to disaster and a second had been forcibly removed by the Russians. Prime Minister King's statement to the Commons in 1922—"The Government certainly maintains the position that Wrangel Island is part of the property of this country"[57]—had by 1925 been replaced by Minister of the Interior Stewart's protest to the same body: "We have no interest in Wrangel Island."[58]

Canada replied to the Danish challenge in Ellesmere Island with a strong protest that the entire island was Canadian territory.[59] In 1922 the ship patrol of the eastern Arctic was reconstituted in the Low-Bernier tradition, but now on an annual, permanent basis, under the Department of the Interior.[60] Again the Mounted Police accompanied the patrol, and now a number of permanent and semi-permanent police posts were established in the islands, starting in 1922 with Craig Harbour in Ellesmere Island and Pond Inlet in Baffin Island.[61] A number of post offices were opened, although in some cases the Mounties, who doubled as postmasters, were the only ones present to send or receive mail. A North-West Territories Council, provided for in 1905,[62] was finally appointed

[54]"Report of Advisory Technical Board," in folder *Arctic Islands Sovereignty*, Public Archives, Ottawa.

[55]Stefansson, *The Friendly Arctic*, pp. 688–92 (*supra*).

[56]V. Stefansson, *The Adventure of Wrangel Island*, London: J. Cape (1926). See also D. M. Le Bourdais, *Northward on the New Frontier*, Ottawa: Graphic Publishers (1931).

[57]Canada, *House of Commons Debates*, May 12, 1922, vol. III, p. 1751.

[58]*Ibid.*, June 1, 1925, vol. IV, p. 3773.

[59]"Report of Advisory Technical Board," in folder *Arctic Islands Sovereignty* (*supra*).

[60]*Canada's Arctic Islands: Canadian Expeditions 1922–23–24–25–26*, Ottawa: Department of the Interior (1927).

[61]*Ibid.*; also H. P. Lee, *Policing the Top of the World*, London: John Lane, The Bodley Head Ltd. (1928).

[62]*Statutes of Canada*, 4–5 Edw. VII, c. 27, July 20, 1905.

in 1921,[63] and functioned continuously thereafter. Its ordinances, along with federal statutes and orders in council, left little activity in the Territories outside regulation. Some of the more important were those licensing scientists and explorers,[64] requiring the registration of births, marriages, and deaths,[65] regulating exportation of furs,[66] and protecting Eskimo archaeological ruins.[67] A federal order in council of 1925 created the Northern Advisory Board, whose particular concern was the matter of sovereignty.[68] Very little publicity was given to its proceedings. Another order in council created the Arctic Islands Game Preserve in 1926, with boundaries following the lines of Canada's sector claim right up to the North Pole.[69] Still another, in 1928, prohibited walrus hunting in Canadian waters south of 74° N, except by natives.[70] There were numerous other measures relating to the Territories, but the above examples serve to illustrate the scope and purpose of what was being done.

While the Canadian government was thus endeavouring to solidify its northern claims, other countries were losing interest. Denmark evidently let the issue of Ellesmere Island drop, and, at least tacitly, accepted Canadian sovereignty there. Russia made no attempt to retaliate for Canada's bad manners in the Wrangel Island affair, and stayed on her own side of the North Pole, as indeed she was logically bound to do after she had promulgated her own sector decree in 1926.[71] Norway formally recognized Canadian sovereignty over the Sverdrup Islands in 1930, at the same time, however, stressing that this recognition was in no way based upon sanction of the sector principle.[72] Later in the same year the Canadian government paid Sverdrup the sum of $67,000 for all his original maps, notes, diaries, and other documents relating to his expedition.[73] And in the United States, where newspapermen and international lawyers had for years been asking embarrassing questions about various aspects of Canada's sovereignty in the North, there was evidently

[63]*Dominion Orders in Council*, P.C. no. 1328, April 20, 1921, and P.C. no. 2033, June 16, 1921.

[64]*Ordinance of the Northwest Territories Council*, June 23, 1926.

[65]*Ibid.*, June 23, 1926.

[66]*Ibid.*, May 7, 1929.

[67]*Ibid.*, Feb. 5, 1930.

[68]*Dominion Order in Council*, P.C. no. 603, April 23, 1925.

[69]*Ibid.*, P.C. no. 1146, July 19, 1926; also P.C. no. 807, May 15, 1929.

[70]*Ibid.*, P.C. no. 1036, June 20, 1928.

[71]*British and Foreign State Papers 1926*, vol. CXXIV, no. 1064–65; T. A. Taracouzio, *Soviets in the Arctic*, New York: Macmillan Co. (1938), p. 381.

[72]Dominion of Canada, *Treaty Series 1–18* (1930), no. 17.

[73]Canadian Press Dispatch, Nov. 11, 1930.

little official disposition to contest Canadian claims, at least to land territory.[74] When the American explorer MacMillan omitted getting the requisite permits before entering the archipelago in 1925, the Canadian authorities insisted that their requirements be fulfilled,[75] and MacMillan complied for his expeditions of 1926, 1927, and 1928.[76]

Writing in *The Canadian Historical Review* in March, 1933, V. Kenneth Johnston argued that by this time foreign claims in the archipelago had disappeared, and that Canada's own claim had been established.[77] The first statement is undoubtedly true, but what about the second? As the foregoing pages have shown, Canada's responsibility for these northern territories dates only from the transfers of 1870 and 1880; prior to that time whatever authority existed had been exerted by the Hudson's Bay Company and the British government. Canada's title may well have been deficient for a considerable number of years after she assumed responsibility, for several reasons: the dubious nature of the transfer of 1880, her inactivity until 1895, her withdrawal from the North during and just after World War I, and the existence of foreign claims. However, with her renewed activity on a more comprehensive scale in the 1920's, and with the disappearance of foreign claims by 1930, the question becomes primarily one of whether her own jurisdiction was sufficiently positive, comprehensive, and permanent to merit international respect.

It would appear that if any doubts remained at the time when the above-mentioned article was published, they were removed by an event of decisive importance soon afterwards. This was the decision of the Permanent Court of International Justice in the dispute between Norway and Denmark over the ownership of East Greenland.[78] Already, in fact, a trend in international law had appeared modifying the requirements

[74]One should perhaps say land territory under adequate occupation and administration, since in an oft-quoted statement of April 2, 1924, to Norwegian Minister Bryn, in connection with proposed Arctic claims by Amundsen, American Secretary of State Charles E. Hughes had made it clear that the United States would not recognize modern claims based only upon discovery and formal taking of possession. See Green H. Hackworth, *Digest of International Law*, 8 vols., Washington: Government Printing Office (1940), vol. I, pp. 399–400.

[75]Canada, *House of Commons Debates*, June 1, 1925, vol. IV, p. 3773; June 10, 1925, vol. IV, p. 4069. See also Richard Finnie, "First Short-Wave in the Arctic— 11," *The Beaver*, Outfit 281 (March, 1951), p. 23.

[76]A. E. Millward, *Southern Baffin Island*, Ottawa: Department of the Interior (1930), pp. 100–101.

[77]V. Kenneth Johnston, "Canada's Title to the Arctic Islands," *The Canadian Historical Review*, vol. XIV, no. 1 (March, 1933), pp. 24–41.

[78]Permanent Court of International Justice, *Judgments, Orders, and Advisory Opinions*, Series A/B, Fascicule No. 53, "Legal Status of Eastern Greenland," (April 5, 1933).

for sovereignty over remote or inaccessible or thinly settled or even
uninhabited territories—a trend clearly evident in the cases of Bouvet
Island in 1928,[79] Palmas Island in 1928,[80] and Clipperton Island in
1931.[81] The *East Greenland Case*, decided in 1933, reinforced the trend,
since the court recognized Denmark's title not merely to east Greenland
but to all Greenland, even though it is more than nine-tenths uninhabited.
The analogy between Denmark's and Canada's Arctic territories in this
connection is by no means perfect, but it is strong, and in some respects,
for example the capacity to maintain supervisory contact with all outlying portions, might even be favourable to Canada. The main difference
is that Greenland is essentially a single huge island, whereas Canada's
most northerly territories take the form of an archipelago of many
islands, large and small. Thus the former involves to some extent the
doctrine of continuity, the latter what is commonly known as contiguity.[82] Even allowing for this distinction, and considering all other
circumstances, it is difficult to see how any adjudication after 1933
could have denied to Canadian claims the recognition that had been
extended to Danish.[83] If at any time subsequent to 1933 Canada's title
to the archipelago had been formally challenged in law, the precedent
of the *East Greenland Case* would in all probability have been sufficient
to decide the case in her favour.

The Recent and Current Situation

There is no reason to fear that Canada's legal position has deteriorated
since the 1930's. On the contrary, it has probably improved. No new
foreign claims have been made. Canada's own programme of governmental and other activity has steadily expanded since the end of World War II.
The moderating trend in the legal requirements for territorial sovereignty,

[79]Hackworth, *op. cit.*, vol. I, pp. 468–70.
[80]"The Island of Palmas Award," (*supra*).
[81]*British and Foreign State Papers 1931*, vol. CXXXIV, pp. 842–46.
[82]Some authorities (e.g., von der Heydte, *op. cit.*, p. 468), reject the distinction
between continuity and contiguity. The status of either, or both, in international
law is uncertain. Much has been made of Judge Huber's categorical rejection of
contiguity in the *Palmas Island* award, but elsewhere in the same case Huber
alleged that ownership of the principal island in a group might determine the fate
of the others (*op. cit.*, pp. 910, 894). Sounder, it seems to me, is the viewpoint
of von der Heydte, who accepted contiguity within limitations, and, criticizing
the abuse of it in regions such as the polar regions, remarked that "such unjusti-
fiable reliance on this principle in certain cases cannot serve as proof against the
existence of the principle itself" (*op. cit.*, pp. 463, 470–71).
[83]Or Norwegian, one might add, in reference to the Allied recognition by
treaty of Norway's sovereignty over Spitsbergen on Feb. 9, 1920. See *British and
Foreign State Papers 1920*, vol. CXIII, pp. 789–97.

as highlighted by the *East Greenland Case*, does not appear to have been reversed, if one may judge from the award of the International Court of Justice in the Minquiers and Ecrehos Islands dispute between Great Britain and France.[84] In this case, perhaps the outstanding recent example of its kind, the court proceeded on the assumption that these insignificant islets would be awarded either to Great Britain or to France, even though, as one of the judges remarked,[85] they are practically uninhabited and mostly uninhabitable. The United States has for over twenty years participated with Canada and generally had the leading role in joint northern projects, but successive Canadian administrations have been careful to insist upon maintenance of Canada's sovereign rights, and the United States has apparently shown no unwillingness to meet Canadian wishes. This attitude has applied consistently to wartime projects such as the Alaska Highway[86] and the Canol Pipeline,[87] and to postwar and cold war projects such as the joint weather stations[88] and the DEW Line.[89] In these circumstances it may be asserted with confidence that Canada's legal title to her northern territories, and particularly to the archipelago, is secure today and has been at least since the 1930's.

Nevertheless one still sees occasional comments, in the press or in Hansard, revealing doubts about the status of our Arctic regions, and perhaps also implying that additional measures should be taken to safe-

[84]The *Minquiers and Ecrehos Case* (*United Kingdom* v. *France*), Judgment of Nov. 17, 1953, *International Court of Justice Reports 1953*, pp. 47–109.

[85]*Ibid.*, Individual Opinion of Judge Basdevant, p. 78.

[86]See Canada, *House of Commons Debates* (March 6, 1942), vol. II, p. 1091; *ibid.* (March 18, 1942), vol. II, p. 1410; *ibid.* (Feb. 1, 1943), vol. I, pp. 20–21 (statements by P.M. Mackenzie King); also exchanges of notes between Canada and the US in *Canada Treaty Series 1942*, no. 13 (March 17–18, 1942); *ibid. 1943*, no. 2 (Jan. 27, 1943).

[87]Canada, *House of Commons Debates* (July 9, 1943), vol. V, pp. 4604–5; *ibid.* (May 5, 1944), vol. III, pp. 2648–52; also exchanges of notes in *Canada Treaty Series 1942*, nos. 23, 24 (June 27–29, 1942; Aug. 14–15, 1942). See later exchanges of notes, e.g., *Canada Treaty Series 1943*, nos. 18, 19.

[88]Canada, *House of Commons Debates* (March 4, 1947), vol. II, pp. 989–90; *ibid.* (June 11, 1947), vol. V, p. 4013. In his announcement of March 4, Mr. Howe said that the weather stations would "of course be under the control of the Canadian government." See also *The Polar Record*, 5, nos. 33, 34 (Jan.–July, published Dec., 1947), 95–97; also later exchange of notes, *Canada Treaty Series 1952*, no. 36 (Oct. 9, Dec. 12, 1951, Feb. 7, 1952).

[89]See exchange of notes in *Canada Treaty Series 1955*, no. 8 (May 5, 1955). Important clauses in the agreement, in this context, were those providing for Canadian retention of title to land used, application of Canadian law, and reservation of Canada's right, on reasonable notice, to take over operation and manning of the stations. (Annex, Secs. 1, 6, 7a.)

guard our sovereignty there. Is there any longer need for such concern about these territories? Canada could still lose them, of course, through either dereliction on her own part or the application of force by a stronger power; but in the first case the loss would result from indifference or deliberate abandonment, and in the second the issue would obviously be decided by might rather than right. There is little likelihood of dereliction, and any resolution by force would presumably be in a situation where the fate of the northern territories would be bound up with our entire national existence. There has been a military threat for over twenty years, first from the Axis during the Second World War, when Japan and Germany established themselves in the Aleutians and eastern Greenland respectively, and then from Russia after the onset of the cold war, but this has little to do with the legal status of the territories.

There has been another possible danger, less tangible, less likely to result from deliberate policy or lack of it, and hence, perhaps, of greater concern in the long run. It has resulted directly from the recent situation in the Arctic, which caused Canada and the United States to pool their efforts in the interests of continental security and defence, with the United States providing by far the greater proportion of men, money, and materials and assuming the major responsibility. In the circumstances this joint effort has been necessary and could become necessary again. The danger is that even with completely satisfactory arrangements to preserve Canada's rights, and with unqualified agreement and the best of intentions on both sides, a massive and quasi-permanent American presence in the Canadian North such as we have seen during and since World War II could in due course lead, gradually and almost imperceptibly, to such an erosion or disintegration of Canadian sovereignty that the real authority in the region, in fact if not in law, would be American. This is the remaining non-military threat to Canadian sovereignty in her northern territories, if one exists, and it is for this reason that Canada's concern about the matter, although at times amounting almost to hypersensitivity, has a measure of justification. It is necessary to add that at this point the issue becomes part and parcel of the entire picture of Canadian-American relations, and Canada's uneasiness in this matter is only one aspect of her concern over the benevolent but all-embracing American influence upon Canadian affairs generally. Of course, the situation in the North has changed greatly in recent days as the threat from the other side of the Pole has receded.

The Sector Principle

The sector principle or theory has been advocated as a simple, convenient, and logical means of apportioning territory in the polar regions.
As such it ranks as one of the most interesting geographical or geo-
political concepts of the twentieth century, and has had some striking
applications. It has special significance for Canada, because there is
a greater area of island territory north of the Canadian mainland than
there is north of the mainland of any other nation bordering on the
Arctic Ocean. If the sector principle won formal acceptance in international law, Canada's sovereignty over almost all the Arctic territories
she has claimed would automatically be validated,[90] and all the effort
she has lavished upon cementing her title to them by other means would
have been unnecessary.

The principle itself, as put forward by Canadian Senator Pascal
Poirier in a Senate speech in 1907,[91] is simple and straightforward. It
asserts that each state with a continental Arctic coastline automatically
falls heir to all the islands lying between this coastline and the North
Pole, which are enclosed by longitudinal lines drawn from the eastern
and western extremities of the same coastline to the Pole. Thus geographical sectors are similar in shape to geometric sectors, or, to use the
common illustration, to pieces of pie. Arctic sectors are not drawn with
geometric precision, however, owing to the irregularity of the southern
boundaries and also the need to take account of other irregularities, as,
for example, the curving water passage between Canadian and Danish
Arctic territories. In the Antarctic the theoretical justification for sectors
is missing, since there are no adjacent continental coastlines from which
sectors might be drawn, the only coastline being that of the Antarctic
continent itself. Sectors in Antarctica, which are usually based upon
lines of latitude in the open sea, have been drawn to mark out coveted
parts of the southern continent, rather than in consequence of the
principle as conceived for the polar islands in the northern hemisphere.

The sector principle, while generally attributed to Senator Poirier,
clearly did not originate with his speech. Poirier himself remarked that

[90]A possible exception might be northeastern Ellesmere Island, which lies
immediately north of, not the Canadian mainland, but Greenland.
[91]Canada, *Senate Debates*, Feb. 20, 1907, pp. 266–73.

it was "not a novel affair," and mentioned a meeting of the Arctic Club in New York the year before, attended by Captain Bernier, where a sector division had been proposed as a means of settling territorial questions in Arctic regions. There are a number of much older precedents, at least for the notion of marking out territories by drawing meridian lines to one of the Poles, and in some cases even from Pole to Pole. The Russian-American treaty of 1867, which brought about the sale of Alaska, stated that the dividing line between Russian and American territories should proceed "due north, without limitation, into the same Frozen Ocean."[92] Pope Alexander VI's bull of 1493, and the Spanish-Portuguese Treaty of Tordesillas which altered it one year later, both divided Spanish and Portuguese colonial territories by means of lines running from North Pole to South Pole.[93] The Canadian order in council of December 18, 1897, delimiting provisional districts, had included within Franklin District all lands and islands between the 141st meridian and Davis Strait;[94] and a map published by the Department of the Interior in 1904 had shown sector lines running along the 141st and 60th meridians to the North Pole.[95] These and other examples notwithstanding, Poirier's speech is not unjustly regarded as the first deliberate enunciation of the sector principle.

Poirier assigned sectors to "Norway and Sweden," Russia, the United States, and Canada, but for some reason not to Denmark. He did not make it clear whether in his view the sovereignty of an Arctic state should extend to water and ice as well as land within its sector, but the wording of his speech would indicate that he was primarily concerned with land. On the other hand he left no doubt that he considered the state entitled to all lands within its sector which might be discovered in the future, as well as those known at the time.

Poirier's proposal was not accepted when he made it,[96] but nevertheless Canada afterwards proceeded, by a series of semi-official and official actions and pronouncements, to stake out a sector claim. It was only about two and a half years later that Captain Bernier left his tablet on

---

[92]W. M. Malloy, ed., *Treaties, Conventions, International Acts, Protocols, and Agreements between the United States of America and Other Powers*, vol. II, pp. 1776–1909, Washington (1910), p. 1522.

[93]S. E. Dawson, "The Line of Demarcation of Pope Alexander VI in A.D. 1493 and that of the Treaty of Tordesillas in A.D. 1494 . . .," *Proceedings and Transactions of the Royal Society of Canada*, 2nd Series, vol. V (May 26, 1899), pp. 467–546.

[94]*Dominion Order in Council*, P.C. no. 3388, Dec. 18, 1897.

[95]This map accompanies some, but not all, of the copies of W. F. King, *op. cit.*

[96]See remarks of Sir Richard Cartwright immediately afterwards, *op. cit.*, pp. 273–74. Cartwright was Minister of Trade and Commerce.

Melville Island claiming the entire sector for Canada, and with Minister of the Interior Stewart's statements in the House of Commons in 1925 that Canada claimed "all the territory lying between meridians 60 and 141" and extending "right up to the North Pole," the Canadian claim could be considered official in every respect, except that it had not been incorporated in a statute.[97]

Since Poirier's speech in 1907 a number of other states have made use of the sector idea, in both Arctic and Antarctic. By Letters Patent of July 21, 1908,[98] amended by further Letters Patent of March 28, 1917,[99] Great Britain claimed all islands and Antarctic territories between 20° and 50° west longitude, south of 50° south latitude, and between 50° and 80° west longitude, south of 58° south latitude. These were entitled the Falkland Islands Dependencies, and were placed under the administration of the Governor of the Falkland Islands. By Order in Council of July 30, 1923, Britain carved out the Ross Dependency on the other side of Antarctica, comprising all islands and territories south of 60° S and between 160° E and 150° W, and placed it under the administration of the Governor General of New Zealand.[100] Ten years later, on February 7, 1933, another British order in council placed a huge sector of Antarctica under the jurisdiction of Australia,[101] and Australia formally accepted it by Act of Parliament on June 13, 1933.[102] It included all islands and continental territories south of 60° S and between 45° E and 160° E, except the little coastal enclave Adélie Land, which had been claimed by France in 1924. Adélie Land, extending from 136° E to 142° E and from 66° S to 67° S, had been attached to Madagascar by France in that year,[103] and in 1938 another French decree enlarged the territory so as to include all islands and land within the above-mentioned eastern and western limits from 60° S to the South

[97]Canada, *House of Commons Debates*, June 10, 1925, vol. IV, pp. 4069, 4084; June 1, 1925, vol. IV, p. 3773.

[98]*British and Foreign State Papers 1907–1908*, vol. CI, pp. 76–77. Published in *The Falkland Islands Gazette*, vol. XVIII, no. 9 (Sept. 1, 1908).

[99]*British and Foreign State Papers 1917–1918*, vol. CXI, pp. 16–17. Published in *The Falkland Islands Gazette*, July 2, 1917.

[100]*British and Foreign State Papers 1923*, vol. CXVII, pp. 91–92. Published in *The London Gazette*, July 31, 1923; and in *The New Zealand Gazette*, Aug. 16, 1923.

[101]*British and Foreign State Papers 1934*, vol. CXXXVII, pp. 754–55. Published in *The London Gazette*, Feb. 14, 1933.

[102]*Statutes of Australia*, no. 8 (1933). *Australian Antarctic Territory Acceptance Act.*

[103]Minister of Colonies Report and Presidential Decree, Nov. 21, 1924. Published in *Journal Officiel*, Nov. 27, 1924. See also *Journal Officiel* March 29, 1924, which publishes a decree of March 27, 1924, claiming Adélie Land and several southern islands.

Pole.[104] Argentina and Chile, who allege historic rights in the continent but who did not assert them strongly until quite recently, both consider themselves sovereign over Antarctic sectors, Argentina over all lands south of 60° S and between 25° W and 74° W,[105] Chile over all between 53° W and 90° W.[106] Obviously their claims conflict with the British claim to the Falkland Islands Dependencies and with each other (Map 1). In the Arctic, Russia has been the only state other than Canada to make a sector claim. After public notification in 1916 and again in 1924 that she considered the islands north of her coast to be Russian property, she issued a sweeping decree on April 15, 1926, formally claiming "all lands and islands already discovered, as well as those which are to be discovered in the future" between her coast and the North Pole, from 32° 4′ 35″ E to 168° 49′ 30″ W.[107] (See Map 2.)

The above are the important sector claims that have been made in the two polar regions. Norway claimed the Antarctic coast between 20° W and 45° E and "the land situated inside this shore" in 1939, but her decree did not make clear whether she claimed the entire sector down to the South Pole or not.[108] If her Antarctic policy was consistent with the Arctic policy she expressed to Canada in 1930 when recognizing Canadian sovereignty over the Sverdrup Islands, she did not.[109] Germany, Japan, Belgium, Sweden, and the Union of South Africa have all at one time or another indicated interest in Antarctica, but none has ever made a sector claim or any other specific territorial claim.

[104]Presidential Decree, April 1, 1938. Published in *Journal Officiel*, April 6, 1938.

[105]See Argentine decrees of July 15, 1939, and April 30, 1940, published in *The Polar Record*, vol. 4, no. 32 (July, 1946, published April, 1947), pp. 412–15. See also E. W. Hunter Christie, *The Antarctic Problem*, London: Allen and Unwin (1951), pp. 309–13, for letter of Jan. 28, 1948, from Argentine Foreign Minister Bramuglia to British Ambassador Leeper, stressing Argentina's rights and disputing Britain's. Because of her assertion of a historic right, Argentina evidently took the view that it was unnecessary for her to make a formal declaration of her claim.

[106]Presidential Decree no. 1747 (Nov. 6, 1940), in *Boletín Oficial*, Nov. 6, 1940. See also *The Polar Record*, vol. 4, no. 32 (July, 1946, published April, 1947), pp. 416–17; and Oscar Pinochet de la Barra, *Chilean Sovereignty in Antarctica*, Santiago: Editorial del Pacifico (1955), esp. pp. 53–54.

[107]W. Lakhtine, "Rights over the Arctic," *The American Journal of International Law*, vol. 24 (1930), pp. 703–17. The decree of 1926 may be seen in *British and Foreign State Papers 1926*, vol. CXXIV, pp. 1064–65 (translation from Izvestia).

[108]*Norwegian Order in Council*, Jan. 14, 1939. See in Hans Bogen, *Main Events in the History of Antarctic Exploration*, reprint from *The Norwegian Whaling Gazette*, Sandefjord (1957), pp. 91–92; and in *The American Journal of International Law*, vol. 34 (1940), Supplement, pp. 83–85.

[109]*Supra*, at fn. 72.

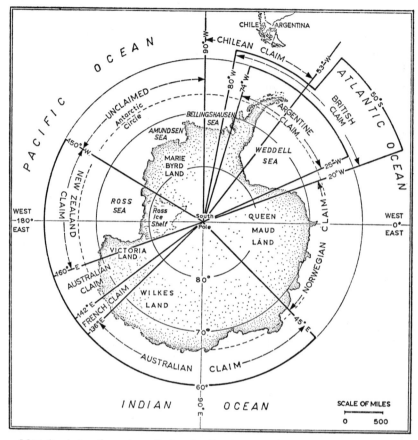

MAP 1. Antarctic sectors. Scale of miles is approximately accurate only near the Pole.

The German Antarctic Expedition of 1938–39 made obvious gestures towards establishing a German title in the region claimed shortly afterwards by Norway,[110] but the events of World War II removed Germany from competition. Japan made a reservation to Chile's 1940 claim, but in the peace treaty of 1951 specifically renounced all claim to any right or title in Antarctica.[111] The United States has consistently refused to recognize the various claims in Antarctica, while reserving all rights

[110]Walter Sullivan, *Quest for a Continent*, New York: McGraw-Hill (1957), pp. 124–27. See also Capt. Alfred Ritscher, *Deutsche Antarktische Expedition, 1938–39*, Leipzig (1942).

[111]*The Polar Record*, vol. 6, no. 44 (July, 1952), pp. 548–49. For full text see *British and Foreign State Papers 1951*, vol. 158, pp. 536–52.

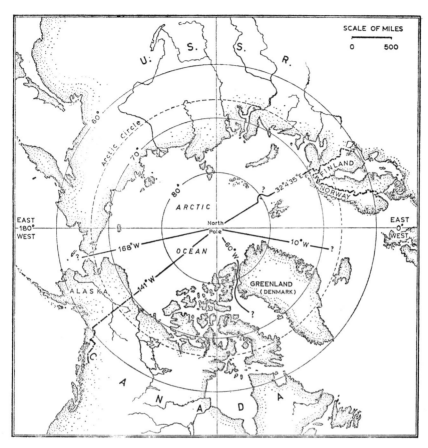

MAP 2. Arctic sectors. The line along 10° W shows Danish and Norwegian-Finnish sectors as proposed in 1927 by L. Breitfuss, who also assigned an Alaskan sector to the United States. Scale of miles is approximately accurate only near the Pole.

she herself may have. Her obvious disinclination to claim formally either the Alaskan sector[112] or the unappropriated Antarctic sector between those claimed by New Zealand and Chile[113] shows clearly her rejection

[112]See, e.g., Secretary of the Navy Adams to Secretary of State Stimson (Sept. 23, 1929), quoted in Hackworth, *op. cit.*, vol. I, pp. 463–64.

[113]See statements of American position by Under Secretary of State Dean Acheson in 1946, in *16 Dept. State Bull. 30* (1947), cited in P. C. Jessup and H. J. Taubenfeld, *Controls for Outer Space*, New York: Columbia University Press (1959), p. 156. And see John Hanessian Jr., "Antarctica: Current National Interests and Legal Realities," *Proceedings of the American Society of International Law*, 52nd meeting, Washington (1958), pp. 145–64, esp. pp. 158–63.

of the sector principle. Soviet Russia has made no sector or other specific claim in Antarctica, but in recent years, at least since 1950, has insisted that she will not be left out of any final settlement there.[114] The ratification of the Antarctic Treaty[115] in 1961, of course, had the effect of immobilizing any and all territorial claims of the twelve signatories for the duration of the treaty, as well as any claims by other states which might accede to it later on.[116]

Various attempts have been made to justify or validate sector claims. As seen above, Senator Poirier's proposal for Arctic sectors embodied the concept of automatic ownership; each state fronting upon the Arctic Ocean was entitled to the islands between its Arctic coastline and the North Pole. The American jurist David Hunter Miller saw Canada's claim as based upon the debatable notion of contiguity or territorial propinquity, and perhaps vaguely related to the old hinterland doctrine.[117] In the view of the Russian authority Lakhtine, the USSR, like other Arctic states, was entitled to the adjacent northern islands on grounds that they were located in what he called her "region of attraction."[118] In the Antarctic, where no independent state lies within five or six hundred miles of the continent, other means of validating titles have had to be sought. Argentina and Chile, the closest, attempt to invoke contiguity, although even their territory is separated from Antarctica by several hundred miles. They also base their claims upon inheritance from Spain, the contention that Graham Land (O'Higgins Land) is

[114]Soviet Memorandum on the Antarctic, June 7, 1950, in *USSR Information Bulletin*, vol. 10, no. 12 (June 23, 1950), p. 380. Also in *The Polar Record*, 6, no. 41 (Jan., 1951), 120–121. See also P. A. Toma, "Soviet Attitude Towards the Acquisition of Territorial Sovereignty in the Antarctic," *The American Journal of International Law*, vol. 50, no. 3 (July, 1956), pp. 611–26.

[115]The text of the treaty may be seen in *United States Treaties and Other International Agreements*, vol. 12, part 1 (1961), pp. 794–829. See also *The Conference on Antarctica*, Department of State Publication 7060, Washington (1960), pp. 61–67.

[116]A most useful summary of territorial claims and statements of interest in Antarctica is given as an appendix in L. M. Gould, *The Polar Regions in Their Relation to Human Affairs*, Series Four of *Bowman Memorial Lectures*, New York: The American Geographical Society (1958), pp. 36–54. See also J. F. da Costa, *Souveraineté sur l'Antarctique*, Paris: Expéditions Polaires Françaises; missions Paul-Emile Victor (1958); D. W. Heron, "Antarctic Claims," *Foreign Affairs*, vol. 32, no. 4 (July, 1954), pp. 661–67; R. D. Hayton, "The Antarctic Settlement of 1959," *The American Journal of International Law*, vol. 54, no. 2 April, 1960), pp. 349–71; and the several articles by John Hanessian, Jr., in *Polar Area Series*, published by American Universities Field Staff.

[117]David Hunter Miller, "Political Rights in the Polar Regions," in *Problems of Polar Research*, ed. by W. L. G. Joerg, New York: American Geographical Society (1928), p. 244.

[118]Lakhtine, *op. cit.*, pp. 705, 707.

geographically and geologically an extension of the South American continent, the concept of an American quadrant, security requirements, and rights of occupation and administration. It is apparent that neither state limits its claim to the meridians of its own eastern and western extremities. If either did, its sector would obviously be much smaller. The other claimant nations, more remote geographically, rely variously upon discovery, exploration, formal acts of possession, scientific and administrative activities, and occupation. Looking at both polar regions, it is evident that theoretical justification for sector claims varies greatly.

The sector principle has aroused a mixed reaction among legal and other authorities. In general it may be said that while some have endorsed it, a large majority either have been doubtful or have firmly refused to concede that it has any force in law. Among those who have approved it, in more or less extreme form, are a group of Russians including L. Breitfuss, W. Lakhtine, E. A. Korovin, and S. V. Sigrist,[119] and, at least by implication, the Canadian V. K. Johnston.[120] Its validity has been denied by many including Gustav Smedal,[121] T. A. Taracouzio,[122] John C. Cooper,[123] Elmer Plischke,[124] C. H. M. Waldock,[125] John J. Teal Jr.,[126] and Oscar Svarlien,[127] although some of these, including Taracouzio[128] and Svarlien,[129] have expressed the view that it might have limited applicability if used simply as a means of marking out land territory. Others who have expressed qualified approval of it in this

---

[119]T. A. Taracouzio, *Soviets in the Arctic*, New York: Macmillan Co. (1938), pp. 320–66, gives in translation a selection of the relevant writing of all four, with a detailed commentary. See also L. Breitfuss, "Territorial Division of the Arctic," *The Dalhousie Review*, vol. VIII (1929), pp. 456–70 (translation by M. B. A. and R. M. Anderson); also Lakhtine, *op. cit.*

[120]V. Kenneth Johnston, "Canada's Title to Hudson Bay and Hudson Strait," *The British Year Book of International Law*, vol. XV (1934), pp. 1–20.

[121]Gustav Smedal, *Acquisition of Sovereignty over Polar Areas*, Oslo (1931), p. 64.

[122]Taracouzio, *op. cit.*, pp. 345–46.

[123]John C. Cooper, "Airspace Rights over the Arctic," *Air Affairs*, vol. 3, no. 3 (Dec., 1950), p. 539. Article originally written for *Encyclopedia Arctica*, under US Office of Naval Research Contract NR 162–218 with Stefansson Library.

[124]Elmer Plischke, *Jurisdiction in the Polar Regions*, unpublished doctoral dissertation written at Clark University, Worcester (1943), pp. 596–600.

[125]C. H. M. Waldock, "Disputed Sovereignty in the Falkland Islands Dependencies," *The British Year Book of International Law*, vol. XXV (1948), pp. 311, 341–42, 345.

[126]John J. Teal Jr., "Europe's Northernmost Frontier," *Foreign Affairs*, vol. 29, no. 2 (Jan., 1951), p. 273.

[127]Oscar Svarlien, "The Sector Principle in Law and Practice," *The Polar Record*, vol. 10, no. 66 (Sept., 1960), pp. 256, 260.

[128]Taracouzio, *op. cit.*, pp. 363, 366.

[129]Svarlien, *op. cit.*, p. 261.

or a similarly limited sense are René Waultrin,[130] Paul Fauchille,[131] David Hunter Miller,[132] W. L. G. Joerg,[133] and M. F. Lindley.[134] There have been innumerable other opinions, of course, but the above examples suffice to show that the variety of views among qualified authorities is at least as great as are the variations in state doctrine and practice.

The Canadian attitude towards the sector principle, official or quasi-official, appears to have undergone some interesting fluctuations since 1907, if one can judge from periodic statements by responsible figures in the government. As seen, the principle was at first rejected, then applied in Captain Bernier's sweeping claim in 1909,[135] temporarily abandoned when the government belatedly endorsed Stefansson's attempt to take Wrangel Island, and reasserted when claim to Wrangel Island was given up and Minister of the Interior Stewart announced that Canadian sovereignty extended throughout her sector and up to the North Pole. The Stewart statement seems to have set the pattern for official policy during the following years. In 1938, Minister of Mines and Resources T. A. Crerar declared in the House of Commons that according to his advice Canada had never claimed Wrangel Island; the sector principle was "very generally recognized"; and "on the basis of that principle as well our sovereignty extends right to the pole within the limits of the sector."[136] In 1946 Mr. Lester Pearson, then Canada's ambassador to the United States, defined the Canadian Arctic as "not only Canada's northern mainland, but the islands and the frozen sea north of the mainland between the meridians of its east and west boundaries, extended to the North Pole."[137] In 1949 Dr. H. L. Keenleyside, at the time Deputy Minister of Mines and Resources, spoke of Canada's Arctic and sub-Arctic regions as "the Yukon Territory, the North-West Territories including the Arctic Islands and their waters, the northern

[130]René Waultrin, "La Question de la Souveraineté des Terres arctiques," Revue générale de Droit international public, vol. XV (July–Aug., 1908), p. 417.

[131]Paul Fauchille, Traité de droit international public, 8e ed., Paris: Rousseau (1925), vol. I, 2e partie, p. 659.

[132]Miller, op. cit., pp. 243, 247.

[133]W. L. G. Joerg, Brief History of Polar Exploration since the Introduction of Flying, 2nd ed., rev., New York: American Geographical Society (1930), pp. 61, 63.

[134]M. F. Lindley, The Acquisition and Government of Backward Territory in International Law, London: Longmans, Green, and Co. (1926), pp. 5–6, 235.

[135]The official status of Bernier's pronouncement is perhaps doubtful. He was certainly the authorized representative of the Canadian government in Arctic waters, under orders to protect Canadian sovereignty there. Whether he was also instructed to make his pronouncement, in the terms used, is another question.

[136]Canada, House of Commons Debates, May 20, 1938, vol. III, p. 3081.

[137]L. B. Pearson, "Canada Looks 'Down North,'" Foreign Affairs, vol. 24, no. 4 (July, 1946), pp. 638–39.

half of Quebec and Labrador, and that segment of the ice-capped polar sea that is caught within the Canadian sector."[138] And on December 8, 1953, when moving the second reading of the bill creating the Department of Northern Affairs and National Resources, Prime Minister St. Laurent remarked in the Commons that "we must leave no doubt about our active occupation and exercise of our sovereignty in these northern lands right up to the pole."[139]

All these statements indicate endorsement of the sector principle, and to some extent application of it to regions of ice and water as well as land. However, on August 3, 1956, Minister of Northern Affairs and National Resources Jean Lesage addressed the Commons as follows: "We have never subscribed to the sector theory in application to the ice. We are content that our sovereignty exists over all the Arctic islands. . . . We have never upheld a general sector theory. To our mind the sea, be it frozen or in its natural liquid state, is the sea; and our sovereignty exists over the lands and over our territorial waters."[140] Several months after the change of government in 1957 Mr. Lesage, possibly with tongue in cheek, asked his successor the Honourable Alvin Hamilton if the waters in the so-called Canadian sector, up to the North Pole, were Canadian waters, eliciting the following rather doubtful reply:

Mr. Speaker, the answer is that all the islands north of the mainland of Canada which comprise the Canadian Arctic archipelago are of course part of Canada. North of the limits of the archipelago, however, the position is complicated by unusual physical features. . . . Consequently the ordinary rules of international law may or may not have application.

Before making any decision regarding the status which Canada might wish to contend for this area, the government will consider every aspect of the question with due regard to the best interests of Canada and to international law.[141]

Returning to the same theme several months later Mr. Hamilton seemed to imply rejection of the sector principle: "This great northland of ours is not ours because it is coloured red on a map. It will only be ours by effective occupation"[142] and a few weeks afterwards: ". . . you can hold a territory by right of discovery or by claiming it under some sector theory but where you have great powers holding different points of view the only way to hold that territory, with all its great potential

[138]H. L. Keenleyside, "Recent Developments in the Canadian North," *Canadian Geographical Journal*, vol. XXXIX, no. 4 (Oct., 1949), p. 163.
[139]Canada, *House of Commons Debates*, Dec. 8, 1953, vol. I, p. 700. This statement was reprinted in *External Affairs*, vol. 6, no. 1 (Jan., 1954), p. 16.
[140]Canada, *House of Commons Debates*, Aug. 3, 1956, vol. VII, p. 6955.
[141]*Ibid.*, Nov. 27, 1957, vol. II, p. 1559.
[142]*Ibid.*, July 7, 1958, vol. II, p. 1989.

wealth, is by effective occupation."[143] Nevertheless his chief appeared to retain a measure of approval for the sector concept: witness Mr. Diefenbaker's assertion of his desire that "everything that could possibly be done should be done to assure that our sovereignty to the North Pole be asserted, and continually asserted, by Canada."[144] Continuing uncertainty is discernible in the following exchange, which took place in the House of Commons on March 29, 1960:

MR. HELLYER: Can the minister tell us whether the Canadian government still subscribes to the sector theory of sovereignty?

MR. FLEMING (Eglinton): We subscribe to the Canadian theory of sovereignty.

MR. HELLYER: This was a Canadian theory. I just wondered whether the government still holds to it.[145]

There seems to have been no reply, at least in the House of Commons.

Perhaps too much emphasis should not be placed upon such statements, which may be made hastily or in the stress of debate. Nevertheless, one might judge from their general tenor that there is rather less inclination in government circles to rely upon the sector principle than there was some thirty or forty years ago. In some respects, however, it is still applied without apparent modification. The Arctic Islands Game Preserve, created in 1926, still follows sector lines to the North Pole, according to the latest official reissue of the game laws of the North-West Territories, dated January 1, 1963.[146] Government maps still show a Canadian sector, although there is a lack of consistency in how the sector is drawn. The line along the 141st meridian to the North Pole is shown without apparent variation, as is the line along the 60th meridian from the Pole to the northern end of the channel separating Ellesmere Island and Greenland. Here consistency ends, and the line is variously shown terminating at this point, at some point in the water passage separating Canadian territory from Greenland, and even as far south as Cape Chidley, at the northern extremity of Labrador. Trevor Lloyd, among others, has noted the absence of any arrangement between Canada and Denmark for a dividing line in this water passage.[147] Uncertainty about the eastern boundary of the sector and its southern terminus may partly explain why no Canadian government has ever

[143]*Ibid.*, Aug. 14, 1958, vol. IV, p. 3540.
[144]*Ibid.*, Aug. 16, 1958, vol. IV, p. 3652.
[145]*Ibid.*, March 29, 1960, vol. III, p. 2577.
[146]Canada, *Game Laws Northwest Territories*, issued under the authority of the Commissioner of the Northwest Territories, Ottawa (Jan. 1, 1963), pp. 49–51.
[147]Trevor Lloyd, "The Political Geography of the Arctic," in *The Changing World*, ed. by W. G. East and A. E. Moodie, London: Harrap and Co. (1956), p. 969.

undertaken to establish a Canadian sector by Act of Parliament. But it is apparent that other states, even if miraculously willing to overlook all other doubtful legal points about the sector principle, can hardly be expected to respect a Canadian sector if Canadian authorities cannot make up their own minds as to how they think it should be drawn. As Isaiah Bowman once remarked, a boundary line "has to be here, not hereabouts."[148]

So far as the status of the sector principle in international law is concerned, the most favourable thing that can be said is that it remains unsettled. It has never been subjected to a definitive test or judgment, since it has never been brought before an authoritative international tribunal. The few legal and diplomatic cases involving the polar regions that have resulted in clear-cut settlements, such as the question of Norwegian sovereignty over Spitsbergen, the *East Greenland Case*, and the *Anglo-Norwegian Fisheries Case*, made little or no reference to it.[149] Neither, apparently, did the American-Russian dispute over the RB-47 incident in 1960.[150] Some pronouncement about it might have emerged if the Anglo-Chilean-Argentine dispute over Antarctic claims had gone to the International Court of Justice but this did not happen because the two Latin American countries consistently refused Britain's offer of judicial settlement.[151] The Antarctic Treaty has eased tensions in the matter but, contrary to popular impression, it does nothing specifically either to establish or to destroy sector claims, and it makes no pronouncement about the validity of the principle itself. All sector and other claims are simply shelved for the duration of the treaty, during which time no signatory state can either improve its own claim or diminish any other. However, the mere fact that the claimant nations have agreed to the treaty might constitute a certain derogation of the sector concept.

If an international tribunal were to pass judgment upon the validity of the sector principle, its verdict would almost certainly be negative.

---

[148]Quoted in John J. Teal Jr., *op. cit.*, p. 273. Cf. Separate Opinion of Judge Hsu Mo in *The Fisheries Case* (*United Kingdom* v. *Norway*), Judgment of Dec. 18, 1951, *International Court of Justice Reports 1951*, p. 157: "Precision is vital to any prescriptive claim to areas of water which might otherwise be high seas."

[149]*Supra*, at fns. 83, 78, and 148. Norway denied it, of course, when recognizing Canadian sovereignty over the Sverdrup Islands in 1930.

[150]See O. J. Lissitzyn, "Some Legal Implications of the V-2 and RB-47 Incidents," *The American Journal of International Law*, vol. 56, no. 1 (Jan., 1962), pp. 135–42, and documents cited therein, esp. at fns. 24–28.

[151]For background information, see I.C.J. Reports 1956, pp. 12, 15; Walter Sullivan, *op. cit.*, p. 269; *The Polar Record*, vol. 7, no. 48 (July, 1954), pp. 213–15; *The Polar Record*, vol. 5, nos. 37, 38 (Jan.–July, published Sept., 1949), p. 361; *ibid.*, vol. 5, no. 40 (July, 1950), pp. 635–36; vol. 6, no. 42 (July, 1951), pp. 277–78; vol. 6, no. 44 (July, 1952), p. 549; vol. 6, no. 46 (July, 1953), p. 838; vol. 7, no. 48 (July, 1954), p. 226; vol. 7, no. 50 (May, 1955), p. 425; etc.

As indicated, a heavy preponderance of legal opinion has been against it. The question has been muddled, however, by uncertainty as to whether the sector idea is to be understood as applying to land only, or to water, floating ice, and airspace as well. Some comments on this subject will be made later on, but for the moment one may at least say that in the latter sense it would be even less acceptable than in the former.

In these circumstances it is difficult to understand why Canadian authorities have continued to trifle with the sector principle, and it is even more difficult to understand why attempts have been made, as indicated by various official decrees, pronouncements, and maps, to try to apply it to regions other than land. In earlier years it may have served a purpose, at least from a narrow view of national self-interest, in helping to keep other nations out of the so-called Canadian sector while we were busy establishing our title to the Arctic islands. With this claim, a reasonable one, validated, no useful or reasonable purpose is served by clinging to it any longer, if indeed there ever was one. In any event, Canada's record of uncertain and fluctuating adherence to what most legal authorities have labelled a weird perversion of international law has hardly been in harmony with what we like to consider the traditional Canadian image of responsibility in international affairs; and in this instance we have undoubtedly set a poor example, no better than the several Latin American states who have made extravagant claims to jurisdiction over adjacent waters up to two hundred miles from their coasts.

In sum, the sector principle has not been recognized in international law, and it lacks any genuine legal foundation. In the Arctic the only two states that have resorted to it have in reality established their sovereignty over claimed lands by other means, and in the Antarctic the "principle" does not exist. As a practical means simply of delimiting or dividing land territory, however, the sector idea may be unobjectionable, if other elements in the situation are satisfactory.

The Law of the Sea in Relation to Canadian Arctic Waters

General remarks

In general it has been more difficult, at the international level, to formulate laws for the earth's water than for its land.[152] Almost all

---

[152]There is a vast literature on this subject. Following are a few of the outstanding works: H. A. Smith, *The Law and Custom of the Sea*, 2nd ed., London: Stevens and Sons Ltd. (1950); T. W. Fulton, *The Sovereignty of the Sea*, Edinburgh: Blackwood and Sons (1911); C. J. Colombos, *The International Law of the Sea*, 4th rev. ed., London: Longmans (1961); Gilbert Gidel, *Le droit international public de la mer*, 3 vols, Paris (1932–1934).

land is the property of some particular state, and is thus subject to its laws. In the case of regions of water it is necessary first to determine whether they fall under the jurisdiction of individual states or whether they belong to the community of states, and then, if the latter, to reach common agreement as to rules. The waters of the Arctic and Antarctic present additional complications, because of their unusual physical characteristics and the resultant question of whether they should be subject to special regulation.[153]

In ancient and mediaeval times assertions of sovereignty over portions of the sea were common, and were often maintained by force. By the early stages of the great voyages of discovery there was hardly any known part of the seas that was not claimed by some state. In the modern age, starting perhaps with the wide-ranging voyages of the Elizabethan seadogs, such claims were gradually replaced by the developing concept of freedom of the high seas. The new trend was reinforced by the writings of legal authorities, by judicial decisions, and, after about mid-nineteenth century, by progress in the codification of the international law of the sea. Recently, however, there has been a tendency to subvert the now traditional principle of the freedom of the seas, or more accurately perhaps, to attempt to place areas formerly considered part of the high seas under some form of national jurisdiction.

In modern times the surface waters of the world have commonly been divided into three categories—internal waters, the territorial or marginal sea, and the high seas.[154] Internal waters comprise all those which lie within the base or inner line of the territorial sea, essentially

[153]Background information in Report of Second Committee, Art. 1 (Observations), in *The American Journal of International Law, Supplement*, vol. 24 (1930), p. 240; also Jens Evensen, "Certain Legal Aspects Concerning the Delimitation of the Territorial Waters of Archipelagos," U.N. Doc. A/CONF. 13/18, Prep. Doc. no. 15 for United Nations Conference on the Law of the Sea, Geneva (1958), p. 289. "Territorial waters" is applied to internal waters and the territorial sea together. "Marginal sea" and "maritime belt" are commonly used as equivalents for "territorial sea." See also articles by J. S. Reeves, R. W. Hale, M. O. Hudson, S. W. Boggs, and D. H. Miller in *The American Journal of International Law*, vol. 24 (1930), and documents in *Supplement* (*supra*).

[154]The terminology has varied to some extent. I have adopted what seems to be current usage, notably "territorial sea" instead of the older "territorial waters," a change recommended at the Conference for the Codification of International Law at the Hague in 1930. See Report of Second Committee, Art. 1 (Observations), in *The American Journal of International Law, Supplement*, 24 (1930), 240; also Jens Evensen, "Certain Legal Aspects Concerning the Delimitation of the Territorial Waters of Archipelagos," U.N. Doc. A/CONF. 13/18, Prep. Doc. no. 15 for United Nations Conference on the Law of the Sea (Geneva, 1958), p. 289. The term "territorial waters" is applied to internal waters and the territorial sea together. "Marginal sea" and "maritime belt" are commonly used as equivalents for "territorial sea."

all fresh water and a certain amount of salt water that may include bays, ports, and the waters surrounding coastal islands. The territorial or marginal sea comprises a belt extending from the outer limit of internal waters to the inner limit of the high seas. The high seas comprise all the rest, including the vast oceans of the world. Regarding jurisdiction, each state exerts as complete control over its internal waters as it does over its land territory. A state also has control over its territorial sea, but with accepted limitations, principally certain rights of innocent passage for foreign vessels. The high seas are free for the use of all. Perhaps the greatest problem has been to establish generally acceptable dividing lines between internal waters and the territorial sea, and also between the territorial sea and the high seas. The recent trends, highly controversial, have been to move both lines outwards and to widen the territorial sea. Another trend has been towards the establishment of a contiguous zone of limited jurisdiction, adjacent to and beyond the territorial sea.

Repeated efforts have been made to solve these problems. An international conference at the Hague in 1930[155] attempted to achieve, as one of three unrelated goals, a codification of laws for the territorial sea, but broke up in disagreement, largely over the issue of its breadth. A conference at Geneva in 1958 dealt solely but comprehensively with the law of the sea, and had better luck, reaching substantial agreement on all issues except those of the territorial sea and the contiguous zone. Another conference was held at Geneva only two years later, specifically to deal with these troublesome remaining questions, but again agreement could not be found.

The problems summarized above are of obvious importance in the polar regions. The Arctic Ocean has not as yet figured largely in world commerce, but it lies between some of the largest and most important states, and with the advent of submarine traffic beneath its icy surface it may become more important. The Canadian Arctic, like the Russian, is a labyrinth of islands and sea passages, and it is possible that problems such as those relating to territorial waters and the contiguous zone will appear here in their most complicated form. Apart from considerable academic discussion, international law has not as yet taken particular note of the circumstances peculiar to polar waters, and there do not appear to be any special international conventions or agreements to cover them. On the other hand, certain unilateral measures have been taken, some of which may be of doubtful validity.

[155]See articles by J. S. Reeves, R. W. Hale, M. O. Hudson, S. W. Boggs, and D. H. Miller in *The American Journal of International Law*, 24 (1930), and documents in *Supplement* (*supra*).

The chief complicating circumstance in the polar seas is, of course, the presence of vast quantities of ice. The ice that is above land causes no difficulty; it is subject to the sovereignty of the state that owns the land. But the status of ice that rests upon the surface of polar waters is less easy to determine. Sea ice in the Arctic is of three principal kinds, fast ice, pack ice, and the Arctic pack, the first two forming concentric belts around the third.[156] Fast ice is immobile young ice attached to the shore, which usually disappears in the summer; the Arctic pack is the mass of older, more or less permanent ice which occupies the central and largest part of the Arctic Ocean; and the pack ice is the less stable, drifting ice between the other two. It is impossible to determine conclusively their quantities and proportions at any given time, since these are variable, fluctuating from place to place, from season to season, and from year to year. Neither can the proportions of water and ice at the ocean surface ever be definitively ascertained. Furthermore the ice, except fast ice, is continually in motion, being propelled by Arctic winds and water currents. In consequence, the surface of the Arctic Ocean is never in a state of permanence or stability.

So far as questions of sovereignty are concerned, they depend mainly upon whether the sea ice of the polar regions is to be related to water or land. Obviously it bears certain resemblances to both, but is not identical in all respects with either. Chemically it is the same as water, although in a frozen state; while physically it is more comparable to land, since it is a solid. Those who stress the former characteristic maintain that, like the high seas, it is not subject to sovereignty;[157] while those who stress the latter maintain that since, like land, it can to some extent be occupied and controlled, it similarly lends itself to ownership.[158] In the first case the factors of non-permanence and movement mentioned in the preceding paragraph are of little importance, but in the second new complications are added.

Neither municipal nor international law has had much to say about the problem of sovereignty over regions of floating ice. The various sector

---

[156]N. A. Transehe, "The Ice Cover of the Arctic Sea, with a Genetic Classification of Sea Ice," in W. L. G. Joerg, ed., *Problems of Polar Research*, pp. 91–123 (*supra*).

[157]E.g., Taracouzio, *op. cit.*, p. 359; Cooper, *op. cit.*, p. 538; Plischke, *op. cit.*, p. 545; Colombos, *op. cit.*, p. 111.

[158]Cf. the interesting comment in C. C. Hyde, *International Law*, 2nd rev. ed., Boston: Little, Brown and Co. (1945), vol. I, p. 348:

"It is not apparent why the character of the substance which constitutes the habitual surface . . . should necessarily be decisive of the susceptibility to a claim of sovereignty of the area concerned. This should be obvious in situations where the particular area is possessed of a surface sufficiently solid to enable man to pursue his occupations thereon. . . ."

decrees mentioned above are generally vague, and seem to avoid claiming ice, being applied specifically only to lands and islands. The existence of a precise claim to a marginal belt, for example Russia's twelve-mile claim, would appear to indicate renunciation of any claim to water and ice beyond this limit, in the absence of some statement to the contrary. It is commonly held that ice within the territorial sea is under the sovereignty of the littoral state. But what if such ice, even if occupied, floats out? Or if other ice floats in? It is also commonly held that shelf ice should be considered subject to the sovereignty of the littoral state. But huge chunks of shelf ice may break off and float away. Does their status change, and if so, how? The number of such questions, hypothetical or actual, than can be raised is virtually unlimited, as Taracouzio demonstrated some twenty-five years ago,[159] and answers to them are as conspicuous by their absence now as then. Neither have there been many cases to provide practical tests. One that is frequently cited involved the establishment of a gambling house upon ice just beyond Alaskan territorial limits, near Nome, but on this occasion the American authorities ignored the technicality and asserted jurisdiction anyway.[160] It is possible that the ice islands, referred to later, might bring some of these questions to a head.

It is sometimes asserted that international law has made no distinction between water and ice,[161] and therefore the rules applying to water must apply to ice. This is hardly reasonable, and it could be asserted with at least equal logic that if international law does not say that from its point of view water and ice are different, neither does it say they are the same, and therefore there is no obligation to apply the rules for water to ice. The truth is that international law has not as yet resolved the question, and it must be acknowledged that while ice and water are alike in some respects, they are different in others. These differences should be taken into consideration. What consequences there might be, if any, is uncertain, but the problem cannot be dismissed simply by assuming that the absence of a particular law is in itself proof that another law exists. Clearly there is here a gap in international law, of concern to all states with interests in the polar regions.

The territorial sea and the contiguous zone

One of the most controversial problems of sea law is that of the

[159]Taracouzio, *op. cit.*, pp. 355 ff.

[160]Louis Rolland, "Alaska, Maison de Jeu établie sur les Glaces au delà de la Limite des Eaux territoriales," *Revue générale de Droit international public*, vol. XI, Paris (1904), pp. 340–45.

[161]E.g., Taracouzio, *op. cit.*, p. 359

territorial sea or maritime belt.[162] It is presently important in polar waters, and potentially more so, and it remains unsettled. For several hundred years the existence of the maritime belt as such has been recognized in international law, but the line of commencement, breadth, method of delineation, and jurisdictional rights of the littoral state have all been matters of dispute. In recent years some clarification of these doubtful points has emerged.

At the beginning of the eighteenth century the Dutch legal authority Cornelius van Bynkershoek put forward his classic suggestion that the dominion of a coastal state should extend seaward to the limit of a shorebased cannon.[163] Afterwards the breadth of the marginal belt tended to become standardized at three nautical miles. However, and contrary to popular impression, the cannon-shot rule did not originate with Bynkershoek, although it is familiarly associated with his name;[164] and others were responsible for the adoption of the three-mile rule, which evidently resulted from a Scandinavian concept of a marginal sea of consistent breath and a French suggestion that it be standardized at three nautical miles.[165] During the nineteenth century and the present one, most states, especially maritime states, have retained three nautical miles as their standard. In spite of an impressive amount of support and confirmation in national and international legislation and practice, however, the three-mile limit cannot be said to have ever had universal acceptance, except possibly as a minimum,[166] and in recent years, particularly, there has developed a considerable movement in favour of extending it.

[162]Among the leading general references are P. C. Jessup, *The Law of Territorial Waters and Maritime Jurisdiction*, New York: Jennings Co. (1927); W. E. Masterson, *Jurisdiction in Marginal Seas*, New York: Macmillan Co. (1929); H. G. Crocker, *The Extent of the Marginal Sea*, Washington: Government Printing Office (1919); Bustamante y Sirven, *La Mer territoriale*, translated from Spanish by P. Goulé, Paris: Recueil Sirey (1930). Canada's case has been dealt with in considerable detail in J. Y. Morin, "Les Eaux territoriales du Canada au regard du Droit international," *Canadian Yearbook of International Law*, March, 1963, pp. 82–148.

[163]Cornelius van Bynkershoek, *De Dominio Maris Dissertatio*, Magoffin translation ed. by James Brown Scott (New York: Oxford, 1923), pp. 43–45.

[164]Wyndham L. Walker, "Territorial Waters: The Cannon-Shot Rule," *The British Year Book of International Law*, XXII (1945), 210–231, refutes strongly the common ideas that Bynkershoek himself invented the cannon-shot rule and was responsible for the three-mile rule. See also Fulton, *op. cit.*, pp. 537–75.

[165]H. S. K. Kent, "The Historical Origins of the Three-Mile Limit," *The American Journal of International Law*, 48, no. 4 (Oct., 1954), 537–53.

[166]A number of classifications have been made of theory and state practice respecting the breadth of the territorial sea. E.g., see Jessup, *op. cit.*, pp. 62–66; Fulton, *op. cit.*, pp. 650–92; H. A. Smith, *op. cit.*, pp. 15–17; G. G. Wilson, *Handbook of International Law* (3rd. ed., St. Paul: West Publishing Co., 1939),

The problem of the territorial sea[167] is often complicated by the presence of bays and adjacent islands. In principle, bays have been generally accepted as territorial waters if their entrance is narrower than double the width of the maritime belt (six miles if the three-mile limit is assumed), and the waters between coastal islands and the mainland have also been recognized as territorial if the shores are separated by less than the same distance.[168] However, there have been many historic exceptions to these rules, generally of benefit to the littoral state, through agreement, or judicial decision, or tacit acceptance. Thus, Delaware[169] and Chesapeake Bays[170] in the United States and Conception Bay[171] in Newfoundland, all with entrances of more than ten miles, have been claimed and evidently established as territorial waters. On the other hand an adjudication in 1853 rejected the British claim to the Bay

---

pp. 100–101; A. E. Moodie, "Maritime Boundaries," in East and Moodie, *op. cit.,* pp. 953–54; S. Whittemore Boggs, "National Claims in Adjacent Seas," *The Geographical Review,* XLI, no. 2 (April, 1951), pp. 185–209, esp. 192–203. The most conspicuous feature of these and other such classifications is their demonstration that although in modern times there has always been much support for the three-mile limit, this support has never been unanimous.

[167]Cornelius van Bynkershoek, *De Dominio Maris Dissertatio,* Magoffin translation ed. by James Brown Scott, New York: Oxford University Press (1923), pp. 43–45. Wyndham L. Walker, "Territorial Waters: The Cannon Shot Rule," *The British Year Book of International Law,* vol. XXII (1945), pp. 210–31, refutes strongly the common ideas that Bynkershoek himself invented the cannon shot rule and was responsible for the three-mile rule. See also Fulton, *op. cit.,* pp. 537–75. H. S. K. Kent, "The Historical Origins of the Three-Mile Limit," *The American Journal of International Law,* vol. 48, no. 4 (Oct., 1954), pp. 537–53. A number of classifications have been made of theory and state practice respecting the breadth of the territorial sea. See, e.g., Jessup, *op. cit.,* pp. 62–66; Fulton, *op. cit.,* pp. 650–92; H. A. Smith, *op. cit.,* pp. 15–17; G. G. Wilson, *Handbook of International Law,* 3rd ed., St. Paul: West Publishing Co. (1939), pp. 100–101; A. E. Moodie, "Maritime Boundaries," in East and Moodie, *op. cit.,* pp. 953–54; S. Whittemore Boggs, "National Claims in Adjacent Seas," *The Geographical Review,* vol. XLI, no. 2 (April, 1951), pp. 185–209, esp. 192–203. The most conspicuous feature of these and other such classifications is their demonstration that, although in modern times there has always been much support for the three-mile limit, this support has never been unanimous.

[168]E.g., H. A. Smith, *op. cit.,* p. 10; Oppenheim, *op. cit.,* p. 505; Colombos, *op. cit.,* pp. 103, 152; Jessup, *op. cit.,* pp. 66, 358; T. E. Lawrence, *The Principles of International Law,* 7th ed., rev. by P. H. Winfield, London: Macmillan and Co. (1927), pp. 140–41.

[169]John Bassett Moore, *A Digest of International Law* (8 vols., Washington: Government Printing Office, 1906), I, 735–39.

[170]J. B. Moore, *History and Digest of the International Arbitrations to Which the United States has been a Party* (6 vols., Washington: Government Printing Office, 1898), IV, 4332–41.

[171]*Direct US Cable Co.* v. *Anglo-American Telegraph Co.* (1877) *L.R. 2 App. Cas.* 394.

of Fundy, the entrance of which was considered to be sixty-five miles wide.[172] The ten-mile rule for bays has received a considerable measure of approval, notably in the British-French Fisheries Convention of 1839,[173] the North Sea Fisheries Convention of 1882,[174] and the North Atlantic Fisheries Arbitration between Great Britain and the United States in 1910,[175] but it was not accepted as an established rule of international law in the Anglo-Norwegian *Fisheries Case* in 1951.[176]

The wide and irreconcilable differences on the subject of the territorial sea were brought into sharp relief at the Hague Conference in 1930, where according to one computation twenty states wanted to establish the three-mile limit, twelve favoured six miles, three favoured four, one (Russia) opposed any definite limit but advocated maximum freedom of navigation, and one (Czechoslovakia) abstained because it had no coastline.[177] Similarly insurmountable was the disagreement over the proposed contiguous zone for control of certain matters such as customs, sanitation, and fishing, although a number of states favoured it in principle. On these issues this phase of the conference foundered.

This decision persisted at the Geneva Conference on the Law of the Sea in 1958,[178] which again failed to standardize either the territorial sea or the contiguous zone, but reached a large measure of agreement on almost everything else. It succeeded in drafting four conventions: on the territorial sea and the contiguous zone, on the high seas, on fishing and conservation of the living resources of the high seas, and on the continental shelf; and it adopted a protocol on the settlement of disputes.

[172]J. B. Moore, *International Arbitrations*, IV, 4342–44.

[173]*British and Foreign State Papers 1838–1839*, XXVII, 983–90.

[174]*Ibid. 1881–1882*, LXXIII, 39–48.

[175]*Ibid. 1909–1910*, CIII, 86–132. Sir Cecil Hurst, "The Territoriality of Bays," *The British Year Book of International Law*, III (1922–1923), 42–54, approved the ten-mile rule.

[176]*The Fisheries Case (United Kingdom v. Norway)*, Judgment of Dec. 18, 1951, *International Court of Justice Reports* 1951, p. 131.

[177]J. S. Reeves, "The Codification of the Law of Territorial Waters," *The American Journal of International Law*, 24, no. 3 (July, 1930), p. 492. Soviet Russia had already passed decrees in 1921 and 1927 establishing a 12-mile territorial sea; thus her stand at the conference appears inconsistent with her practice. See T. A. Taracouzio, *The Soviet Union and International Law* (New York: Macmillan Co., 1935), p. 63, and decrees cited.

[178]*Final Act of the United Nations Conference on the Law of the Sea*, A/CONF. 13/L. 58 (Geneva, April 30, 1958). The proceedings and documents in full are published as *United Nations Conference on the Law of the Sea: Official Records*, A/CONF. 13/37–43, 7 vols. (Geneva, Feb. 24–Apr. 27, 1958). For a brief but comprehensive account of the conference, setting forth in particular the American viewpoint, see A. H. Dean, "The Geneva Conference on the Law of the Sea: What was Accomplished," *The American Journal of International Law*, vol. 52, no. 4 (Oct., 1958), pp. 607–28.

The first convention[179] endorsed in principle both the territorial sea and the contiguous zone, even though it could decide the breadth of neither; in the case of the contiguous zone, however, it was agreed that the maximum breadth should be no more than twelve miles from the territorial sea baseline. Normally this baseline would be the low water line (Art. 3), but nevertheless the convention also endorsed, in certain circumstances, the system of straight baselines from headland to headland to determine the line of commencement of the territorial sea (Art. 4). It thus confirmed the decision of the International Court of Justice in the important *Anglo-Norwegian Fisheries Case* of 1951, where the court rejected Britain's contention that Norway's use of this method was illegal.[180] This decision has been criticized, however, on grounds that it will not be workable without some further elaboration to limit the length of the straight baselines and their maximum distance from other parts of the coast.[181] The convention also accepted a twenty-four-mile closing line for bays (Art. 7). During the conference, in the hope of finding some common meeting-ground among the varied points of view, Canada put forward a compromise proposal for a six-mile territorial sea with a further six-mile contiguous zone for the regulation of fishing. The proposal attracted considerable interest and support, but it failed to win the two-thirds majority necessary in plenary session, as did other proposals which were advanced.[182]

At the 1960 Geneva Conference,[183] which dealt only with the territorial sea and the contiguous zone, Canada and the United States got together on a compromise proposal, which almost won acceptance, to allow a six-mile territorial sea plus an adjacent six-mile fishing zone, with an interim ten-year period of fishery rights in the outer zone for any state or states that could show use of these waters for fishing during a preceding five-year period. Although the proposal was adopted in the

[179]*Convention on the Territorial Sea and the Contiguous Zone*, A/CONF. 13/L. 52 (April 28, 1958).

[180]*Op. cit.*, p. 143.

[181]E.g., Lauterpacht in Oppenheim, *op. cit.*, pp. 489–90 (text and fn. 5); also C. H. M. Waldock, "The Anglo-Norwegian Fisheries Case," *The British Year Book of International Law*, vol. XXVIII. (1952), pp. 114–171; J. E. Brierly, *The Law of Nations*, 5th ed., Oxford: Clarendon Press (1955), pp. 174–76. See also the dissenting opinions of Judges McNair and Read in the case.

[182]*International Conference on The Law of the Sea*, reprinted from *External Affairs*, vol. 10, nos. 1, 4–5 (1958), p. 8.

[183]*Second United Nations Conference on the Law of the Sea: Official Records*, A/CONF. 19/8–9, 2 vols. (Geneva, Mar. 17–Apr. 26, 1960). See also A. H. Dean, "The Second Geneva Conference on the Law of the Sea: The Fight for Freedom of the Seas," *The American Journal of International Law*, vol. 54, no. 4 (Oct., 1960), pp. 751–89; D. W. Bowett, "The Second United Nations Conference on the Law of the Sea," *The International and Comparative Law Quarterly*, vol. 9, pt. 3 (July, 1960), pp. 415–35.

Committee of the Whole, where only a simple majority was needed, it fell one vote short of the required two-thirds majority in plenary session. No other proposition came as close, and so once again the questions of the territorial sea and the contiguous zone were left unsettled.

In the absence of agreement on these questions, there has been a natural tendency for each state to revert to its former position and continue propagandizing for its own point of view. For example, A. H. Dean, who led the American delegation at both conferences, wrote that the United States would 'continue to adhere to the long-established and currently recognized territorial sea of three miles."[184] However, the efforts of 1958 and 1960 were not entirely barren of results, demonstrating, as they did, progress to the point that one more positive vote would have brought a decision. Certain other consequences, direct or indirect, are also evident. Among these are a British-Norwegian fisheries agreement closely following the Canadian-American joint proposal for a twelve-mile zone with a ten-year phasing-out period,[185] Britain's abandonment of claims to fishing rights in Iceland's twelve-mile zone,[186] American recognition of the twenty-four-mile rule for bays in a fishery taxation case in Bristol Bay, Alaska,[187] and a British announcement indicating intention to establish a contiguous fishing zone.[188]

The problems of the territorial sea and the contiguous zone are of the greatest importance to Canada, since she possesses probably the world's longest coastline and huge fishing interests in the Atlantic, Pacific, and Arctic oceans. The complexity of her problem is heightened by the extremely irregular conformation of much of her coastline, and the presence of numerous bays and offshore islands, both large and small. Further complications peculiar to the Arctic regions are added by the archipelago with its intricate and usually ice-laden water passages, the alleged "historic" character of the waters of Hudson Bay and Strait, and the uncertain status of the waters of Baffin Bay, Davis Strait, the Beaufort Sea, and the high Arctic within the so-called Canadian sector.

[184]A. H. Dean, op. cit., (1960), p. 788.
[185]ibid., p. 789; also P. C. Jessup, "The Law of the Sea Around Us," The American Journal of International Law, vol. 55, no. 1 (Jan., 1961), p. 108, citing London Times (Sept. 29–30, 1960).
[186]New York Times (Feb. 28, 1961).
[187]Arctic Maid Fisheries, Inc., et al. v. State of Alaska, Supreme Court of Alaska, No. 316 (April, 1963), in International Legal Materials, pub. by The American Society of International Law, vol. II, no. 3 (May, 1963), pp. 524–29. See especially letter from Secretary of State Rusk to Attorney General Kennedy (Jan. 15, 1963).
[188]The Economist, May 4, 1963, p. 442. In the article, entitled "Fishery Limits: Herring-do," the author (anonymous) spoke disparagingly and facetiously of what he labelled "this unmannerly dogfish-in-the-manger attitude" and "this new and fishy form of imperialism."

Under a strict interpretation of even the three-mile rule, much of the archipelago waters lie within Canada's territorial sea, because of the multiplicity of islands, each one having, according to recognized international law, its own marginal belt.[189] So do a number of narrow straits such as Simpson, Bellot, and Fury and Hecla, the first two of which have been used as possible routes for a Northwest Passage. Under a six-mile rule or (for the limited purposes intended) a twelve-mile rule, the proportion of Canadian waters is correspondingly increased, especially if the system of straight baselines is adopted, and the amount of the archipelago waters remaining as international is lessened. This is a trite observation, but it is about all that can be said in general terms, other than that the practical task of delimiting the waters and ice of the archipelago under any such system, and distinguishing between internal waters, territorial sea, and contiguous zone, would be enough to defy the ingenuity of man.

After the failure of her six-plus-six proposals in 1958 and 1960, Canada in practice continued to endorse the more traditional three-mile marginal belt without a contiguous zone. However, not long after his election victory in April, 1963, Prime Minister Pearson announced his government's intention of establishing a twelve-mile exclusive fisheries zone along the whole of Canada's coastline by May, 1964, and also of applying the headland-to-headland system to determine the baseline from which both the territorial sea and the fisheries zone will be measured.[190] The announcement received qualified support from the three opposition parties and was greeted enthusiastically by Canadian fishing interests; but it also drew criticism, notably from Maxwell Cohen, one of Canada's few well-known voices in the realm of international law, in an article in the *Montreal Gazette*.[191] The decision was apparently based upon practical and economic considerations involving protection of the Canadian fishing industry, upon the wide support the concept of the twelve-mile fishing zone attracted at the conferences of 1958 and 1960, and also upon the fact that numerous other states, over fifty according to Mr.

[189]This proposition has received the general endorsement of authorities, e.g., Jessup, *op. cit.*, p. 66; H. A. Smith, *op. cit.*, p. 10; Brierly, *op. cit.*, p. 174; Colombos, *op. cit.*, p. 103. It was put forward at the Hague Conference in 1930, and incorporated in the Convention on the Territorial Sea and the Contiguous Zone at the Geneva Conference in 1958.

[190]Canada, *House of Commons Debates*, June 4, 1963, vol. I, p. 621–23; also *Montreal Gazette*, June 5, 1963; *Ottawa Journal*, June 5, 7, 1963.

[191]*Montreal Gazette*, June 12, 1963. Professor Cohen's chief objection seemed to be that Canada was "going it alone," and that "such a unilateral policy would not square with the Canadian tradition of having a decent regard for international law."

Pearson, had already extended their fisheries limits beyond three miles. The Prime Minister's announcement also stressed that in establishing her new system Canada would take full account of the treaty and historic rights of other nations such as the United States and France.[192]

There have been other recent indications that Canadian policy is following the current widespread tendency among states to extend national waters to the maximum limit recognized by law. On November 15, 1962, Prime Minister Diefenbaker announced in the House of Commons that some Russian fishing vessels in the Bay of Fundy would be asked to leave, remarking at the same time that these waters had been considered territorial "since the earliest days" by successive British and Canadian governments.[193] The statement appears to indicate disregard for the arbitral decision of 1853; it should be added, however, that under the recently approved twenty-four-mile rule, and by counting several islets at its mouth, the argument can be made that the bay does become territorial.[194] A statement on March 4, 1963, attributed to a Canadian fisheries official, to the effect that his department considered the Gulf of St. Lawrence to be territorial waters, would be harder to justify since although the Strait of Belle Isle is much less than twenty-four miles wide, Cabot Strait is much more. An American source is reported to have replied that so far as the United States is concerned, the Gulf of St. Lawrence is part of the high seas.[195] In the North, Canada has of course claimed Hudson Bay and Hudson Strait as historic waters for many years, basing her claim upon the charter rights and exclusive proprietorship of the Hudson's Bay Company until 1870, and thereafter upon her own administrative acts including the order in council of 1897, the amendment to the Fisheries Act in 1906,[196] and an order in council of 1937 directing that the bay and strait be enclosed by a baseline from Button Island to Resolution Island.[197] Apart from the historic aspect, Canada can point to the facts that the bay and strait are almost completely enclosed by Canadian territory, and that they provide no possible route to other than Canadian ports. The main objections are the huge

[192]American rights arise from the treaties of 1783 and 1818 and subsequent modifications (J. B. Moore, *A Digest of International Law*, vol. I, p. 767 ff.; *British and Foreign State Papers 1909–1910*, vol. CIII, pp. 86–132); French from the treaty of 1904 (*British and Foreign State Papers 1903–1904*, vol. XCVII, pp. 31–36).

[193]Canada, *House of Commons Debates*, Nov. 15, 1962, vol. II, p. 1650; also *Montreal Gazette*, Nov. 16, 1962.

[194]J. Y. Morin, *op. cit.*, pp. 104–6.

[195]*Ottawa Journal*, March 6, 1963.

[196]*Supra*, at fns. 19, 33, and 51.

[197]*Canadian Order in Council*, P.C. no. 3139, Dec. 18, 1937.

size of the bay and the approximately forty-mile entrance to the strait. The Canadian claim has been debated pro[198] and con[199] for years, and still lacks formal recognition, notably from the United States. It was strengthened recently, no doubt, by a study prepared by the UN Secretariat, which conceded in principle the legitimacy of historic waters including bays, saying that each case should be judged on its own merits.[200] All things considered, it is most unlikely, especially in view of recent trends, that Canada's claim to Hudson Bay and Hudson Strait is in danger of meeting with international rejection.

In connection with recent Canadian and other propositions for a contiguous fishing zone, there appears to be a technicality which has perhaps escaped notice. The Convention on the High Seas, adopted in 1958, stresses the freedom of the high seas, saying that "no State may validly purport to subject any part of them to its sovereignty," and it specifically names fishing as one of these freedoms.[201] The Convention on the Territorial Sea and the Contiguous Zone identifies the contiguous zone as part of the high seas, and in enumerating the controls that may be exercised therein, says nothing about fishing (Art. 24). And yet the contiguous zone was considered at the conferences of 1958 and 1960 and afterwards largely in relation to fishing. At the Hague Conference of 1930, on the other hand, the contiguous zone was contemplated mainly in connection with other matters, including customs. Unless the fishing zone is to be considered different from the contiguous zone legitimized in principle in 1958, some change in wording of the conventions would appear desirable. In any case, it is evident that the trend of state practice indicates growing approval of the fishing zone.

In connection with the application of laws respecting the territorial sea and contiguous zone to the Arctic regions, it is well to reiterate that their applicability or suitability may be affected by the different climatic conditions. A passage that looks broad and open on a map may be partially or totally blocked by ice during part or all of any given year, and even when usable may be limited to a narrow, hazardous channel among floating or stationary masses of ice. This may be true of even such a broad passage as Lancaster Sound or, in a more limited way, Hudson Strait. Whether this should affect the delineation of the

[198]E.g., V. Kenneth Johnston, "Canada's Title to Hudson Bay and Hudson Strait," *The British Year Book of International Law*, vol. XV (1934), pp. 1–20.

[199]E.g., T. W. Balch, "Is Hudson Bay a Closed or an Open Sea?" *The American Journal of International Law*, vol. 6, pt. 1 (1912), 409–59; "The Hudsonian Sea is a Great Open Sea," *ibid.*, vol. 7, no. 3 (July, 1913), 546–65.

[200]*Juridical Regime of Historic Waters, Including Historic Bays*, United Nations Secretariat, A/CN. 4/143 (March 9, 1962), p. 72.

[201]A/CONF. 13/L. 53 (April 29, 1958), Art. 2.

territorial sea or contiguous zone is a question, but the point merits consideration. An extreme application of the sector principle would of course solve such problems, but it is difficult to see how any consideration of the territorial sea and contiguous zone in the above terms could be reconciled with any concept of the sector principle as applied to regions other than land.

The continental shelf

Among maritime legal problems the continental shelf is one of the most recent to assume practical importance, and it is also one that has apparently been settled in fairly comprehensive fashion.[202] The settlement was one of the major accomplishments of the Geneva Conference in 1958, where a convention was adopted covering most of the points at issue.[203] Claims to parts of the seabed and its resources beyond territorial waters have been fairly common in both the remote and the recent past, but they appear to have provoked little interest or controversy until after World War II. A few of the more familiar examples are the successive Portuguese, Dutch, and British claims to the pearl fisheries off the coast of Ceylon, the British Sea Fisheries Act of 1868[204] similarly claiming oyster beds off the coast of Ireland; the claim by the Bey of Tunis to sponges on a bank beyond territorial limits; and the treaty between Great Britain and Venezuela in 1942[205] for the division of the seabed and subsoil of the Gulf of Paria between Trinidad and Venezuela.[206] With President Truman's proclamation of September 28,

---

[202]This subject has aroused much discussion, especially in recent years. See, e.g., Sir Cecil J. B. Hurst, "Whose is the Bed of the Sea?" *The British Year Book of International Law*, vol. IV (1923–1924), pp. 34–43; F. A. Vallat, "The Continental Shelf," *ibid.*, vol. XXIII (1946), pp. 333–38; H. Lauterpacht, "Sovereignty over Submarine Areas," *ibid.*, vol. XXVII (1950), pp. 376–433; E. Bouchard, "Resources of the Continental Shelf," *The American Journal of International Law*, vol. 40, no. 1 (Jan., 1946), pp. 53–70; R. Young, "Recent Developments with Respect to the Continental Shelf," *ibid.*, vol. 42, no. 4 (Oct., 1948), pp. 849–57; R. Young, "The Legal Status of Submarine Areas beneath the High Seas," *ibid.*, vol. 45, no. 2 (Apr., 1951), pp. 225–239; A. E. Moodie, "Maritime Boundaries," in East and Moodie, *op. cit.*, pp. 942–59, esp. 945–52. Perhaps the most comprehensive work on the subject is M. W. Mouton, *The Continental Shelf*, The Hague: M. Nijhoff (1952). See also C. H. M. Waldock, "The Legal Basis of Claims to the Continental Shelf," *The Grotius Society: Transactions for the Year 1950*, vol. 36 (1951), pp. 115–48.

[203]U.N. Doc. A/CONF. 13/L. 55.

[204]*Statutes of Great Britain*, 31–32 Vict., July 13, 1868, c. 45, s. 67.

[205]Great Britain, *Treaty Series*, no. 10 (1942), Cmd. 6400. Britain followed up the treaty with an order annexing her part of the sea bed and subsoil to Trinidad and Tobago. *Statutory Rules and Orders*, vol. I (1942), p. 919.

[206]These and other such claims are discussed in Hurst, *op. cit.*; Young, *op. cit.*; and Fulton, *op. cit.*, pp. 696–98.

1945,[207] to the effect that the natural resources of the subsoil and seabed of the adjacent continental shelf appertain to the United States, the continental shelf and its riches became a matter of general interest and concern, a principal reason being the possibilities offered for the exploitation of oil resources. The example of the United States was quickly followed by many other nations, including most of the coastal Latin American states and many of the Middle Eastern states and sheikdoms.[208] Some, for example Chile and Argentina, claimed sovereignty not only over the continental shelf but also over the waters above, and Chile specified that her jurisdiction was to extend to a line 200 miles distant from her coast.

The continental shelf, along with other maritime problems, was studied by the International Law Commission of the United Nations during its meetings from 1949 to 1956;[209] and the final report of the Commission, presented to the General Assembly in 1956,[210] formed the basis of the convention that was accepted at the Geneva conference in 1958. Essentially the convention asserted the sovereign right, for exploration and exploitation of natural resources, of the coastal state over the continental shelf; and for its purpose the continental shelf was defined as

(a) the seabed and subsoil of the submarine areas adjacent to the coast but outside the area of the territorial sea, to a depth of 200 metres or, beyond that limit, to where the depth of the superjacent waters admits of the exploitation of the natural resources of the said areas

(b) the seabed and subsoil of similar submarine areas adjacent to the coasts of islands.

The convention asserted further that the right of the coastal state excluded activity by other states without its permission, and did not depend upon any form of occupation or proclamation. On the other hand, the status of the superjacent waters was to be unaffected, as was

[207]Proclamation No. 2667, 10 Federal Register 12303. See text also in The American Journal of International Law, Supplement, vol. 40 (1946), pp. 45–46.

[208]Young, as cited; also "Saudi Arabian Offshore Legislation," ibid., vol. 43, no. 3 (July, 1949), pp. 530–32; "Further Claims to Areas Beneath the High Seas," ibid., vol. 43, no. 4 (Oct., 1949), pp. 790–92.

[209]See H. W. Briggs, "Jurisdiction over the Sea Bed and Subsoil Beyond Territorial Waters," The American Journal of International Law, vol. 45, no. 2 (Apr., 1951), pp. 338–42, for an approving comment on the work of the commission during its early stages.

[210]International Law Commission, Report of 8th Session, U.N. Doc. A/3159 (1956), pp. 40–45. The text of the report, with commentary, may be seen in The American Journal of International Law, vol. 51, no. 1 (Jan., 1957), pp. 242–253.

that of the airspace, and they were to remain as high seas and open airspace respectively.[211]

The importance of the convention for the Canadian Arctic is obvious. There is a continental shelf of considerable size here, the resources of which now fall under the exclusive jurisdiction of Canada. Under the provisions of Article I (b), quoted above, Canada's right to jurisdiction over the resources of the shelf adjacent to the Arctic archipelago is also assured. It is to the northwest of the Queen Elizabeth Islands, in fact, where the shelf is broadest. Although the jurisdiction of the littoral state is technically incomplete, being limited to exploration and use of natural resources, in a practical sense it may be close to absolute, since there will probably be little reason or opportunity for other forms of activity. In any case it is more complete than it was before, because according to traditional views of the continental shelf it was either *res communis* (open for use by all states but owned by none) or *res nullius* (unclaimed but presumably open to acquisition by any state).[212] The concession of a limited but generally recognized form of sovereignty is a distinct asset in a case such as this, where for reasons of climate and geography it might be difficult otherwise to maintain control. Under the convention, and assuming ratification, as long as Canada retains her sovereignty over the archipelago her legal position in the adjacent continental shelf is secure.

The very comprehensive Canadian Polar Continental Shelf Project was organized in 1958 by the Department of Mines and Technical Surveys to carry on a long-term programme of scientific research on the Arctic section of Canada's continental shelf, and it has functioned during the warmer months of each year since that time. The project was brought into being as the result of a memorandum to the Cabinet from the Minister of Northern Affairs and National Resources on April 5, 1958,[213] while the Geneva conference was in session and about three weeks before the convention was signed. It was approved in principle

[211]U.N. Doc. A/CONF. 13/L. 55, Articles 1–3. See also J. A. C. Gutteridge, "The 1958 Geneva Convention on the Continental Shelf," *The British Year Book of International Law*, vol. XXXV (1959), pp. 102–23; Marjorie M. Whiteman, "Conference on the Law of the Sea: Convention on the Continental Shelf," *The American Journal of International Law*, vol. 52, no. 4 (Oct., 1958), pp. 629–659. Miss Gutteridge was a member of the British delegation, Miss Whiteman of the American. See also the trenchant criticism of the convention in R. Young, "The Geneva Convention on the Continental Shelf: A First Impression," *The American Journal of International Law*, vol. 52, no. 4 (Oct., 1958), pp. 733–38.

[212]See comment in A. E. Moodie, *op. cit.*, p. 945.

[213]Memorandum to the Cabinet (Apr. 3, 1958), entitled *Canadian Activities in the Polar Basin*. It was concurred in by the Minister of Mines and Technical Surveys.

by the Cabinet about six weeks later, on May 22. Statements have been made to the effect that the main purpose of the project was to maintain Canada's rights in the Arctic;[214] if this was so, it would appear to have been unnecessary, at least so far as the continental shelf itself is concerned, in view of the outcome of the conference. On the other hand, it is evident that the Russians, as a result of numerous expeditions in the area, knew far more about the oceanography of the regions off the Queen Elizabeth Islands than Canadians did.[215] Understandably it was felt that this was primarily an area of Canadian responsibility, for research purposes as well as others. So far as can be judged from published reports, the basic aims of the project are at least as much scientific as political, and a great deal is being accomplished in a variety of scientific fields.[216]

The waters of an archipelago

Another problem spotlighted by recent developments is the status of the waters of an archipelago. There have been both claims and denials as to territoriality; but oddly enough, although Canada's Arctic archipelago is one of the most interesting in this connection, as well as one of the largest, it seems to have received little discussion at the international level.

It is obvious, of course, that where sovereignty over an archipelago itself is in doubt, this uncertainty will automatically extend to its waters. Quite another matter is the juridical status of such waters when sovereignty over the archipelago is accepted as fact. As has already been noted, it is generally recognized that an island has its own territorial waters; thus a state with an archipelago is entitled, as a minimum, to the internal waters, marginal sea, and contiguous zone of the islands taken separately, in accordance with currently prevailing norms of international law. It would also be entitled to any additional historic or other rights it could establish. There remains, however, the question of whether the waters of an archipelago may be considered a single, indivisible unit, so that they all become territorial. And if this possibility is conceded, the further question arises as to whether such waters are to be classified as internal waters or marginal sea.

[214]E.g., articles by Irwin Shulman in *Montreal Star*, June 17, 1958, and by Tom Fairley in *Ottawa Citizen*, July 30, 1960.

[215]See *The Polar Times*, no. 52, June, 1961, p. 9 (article reprinted from *The Christian Science Monitor*); also *Edmonton Journal*, July 2, 1957; *New York Times*, Jan. 13 and 26, 1960; *Montreal Star*, Mar. 16, 1961.

[216]E.g., E. F. Roots, "The Polar Continental Shelf Project, 1959," *The Arctic Circular*, vol. XII, no. 3 (Feb., 1960), pp. 32–38; E. F. Roots, "Canadian Polar Continental Shelf Project, 1959–62," *The Polar Record*, vol. 11, no. 72 (Sept., 1962), pp. 270–76.

These questions have not been conclusively answered, but there are some interesting straws in the wind. A number of writers, among them Jessup,[217] Hyde,[218] and Colombos,[219] agree that the waters of an archipelago, like the islands, may form a unit. H. A. Smith would only allow this where a perimeter may be drawn from island to island of straight lines no more than six miles long.[220] A. H. Dean objects on grounds that the waters would probably be classed as internal and there would be no right of innocent passage.[221] A number of states, either having the conformation of archipelagos themselves or possessing archipelagos, have declared that their waters are territorial—notably the Philippines,[222] Indonesia,[223] and Equador in connection with the Galapagos or Colon Archipelago.[224] These declarations have been protested, notably by the United States. As if to underline the point, the United States sent the submarine "Triton" submerged through Philippine and Indonesian waters during its circumnavigation of the globe in 1960.[225] Great Britain in the 1951 *Fisheries Case* took pains to point out that she had not claimed the waters of the Fiji Islands or the islands off British Honduras as territorial, and maintained that the rules governing single islands should apply to the islands of an archipelago.[226] A draft submitted by Professor Alvarez to the International Law Association in 1924 proposed to grant limited recognition to archipelago waters as territorial,[227] as did the American Institute of International Law in 1926[228] and L'Institut de Droit international in 1928.[229] L'Institut would have imposed the same limitation as H. A. Smith (above). The conferences of 1930 and 1958, while agreeing that a single island has its own territorial sea, were both unable to formulate a rule for archipelagos, and the judgment in the

[217]Jessup, *op. cit.*, p. 457.

[218]Hyde, *op. cit.*, vol. I, p. 487.

[219]Colombos, *op. cit.*, pp. 103–4.

[220]H. A. Smith, *op. cit.*, p. 10.

[221]A. H. Dean, *op. cit.* (1958), p. 612; (1960), pp. 753, 765 ff.

[222]Note from Philippine Ministry of Foreign Affairs to United Nations Secretariat (Dec. 12, 1955), in *Laws and Regulations on the Regime of the Territorial Sea*, U.N. Doc. ST/LEG/SER. B/6 (1956), pp. 39–40.

[223]Act no. 4 (Feb. 18, 1960), in Addendum to Supp. to *Laws and Regulations on the Regime of the Territorial Sea*, U.N. Doc. A/CONF. 19/5/Add. 1 (1960), pp. 3–4. Cited in A. H. Dean, *op. cit.* (1960), p. 753, fn. 4.

[224]Evensen, *op. cit.*, p. 298.

[225]A. H. Dean, *op. cit.* (1960), p. 753.

[226]*The Fisheries Case (United Kingdom v. Norway)*, Judgment of Dec. 18, 1951, *International Court of Justice Pleadings, Oral Arguments, Documents*, 4 vols., vol. II, pp. 524–25; vol. I, pp. 79, 83.

[227]Evensen, *op. cit.*, p. 291.

[228]*The American Journal of International Law, Special Supplement*, vol. 20 (1926), p. 319 (Project. no. 10, Art. 7).

[229]L'Institut de Droit international, *Tableau général des Résolutions 1873–1956*, ed. by H. Wehberg, Bâle (1957), p. 124.

1951 *Fisheries Case* took note of the fact that none existed.[230] It thus remains a controversial and undecided question, but evidently with a growing movement on the part of interested states to establish at least their own claims.

It is necessary to draw attention to the distinction between coastal archipelagos and outlying or high-seas archipelagos, and to observe that the above remarks refer primarily to the latter. In principle, the question concerning the former has been decided in favour of the littoral state, by the 1951 *Fisheries Case* and by the 1958 Convention on the Territorial Sea and the Contiguous Zone (Sec. II, Art. 4), as well as by recent state practice. Evensen, in taking note of this distinction, favours in principle the territoriality of the waters of an outlying archipelago, where this is reasonable, saying that geographical features will largely determine each case. On the question of whether such waters may be considered internal, he would treat each case on its individual merits.[231]

There are some interesting examples of both types of archipelagos in the polar regions besides Canada's own. The Spitsbergen treaty of 1920 gave Norway sovereignty over all islands in the archipelago, but made no attempt to define their territorial waters. Evensen, who as a Norwegian supreme court advocate is in a position to know, says that Norway has not yet (1957) laid down limits, but will probably consider the archipelago a unit and use straight perimeter baselines. Iceland, which Evensen regards as a mid-ocean archipelago, has used this method, including all islands except a few far out at sea. On the other hand, the United States makes no such claims for the various archipelagos off the coast of Alaska.[232]

There appears to be no well-defined or consistent Canadian attitude over the past sixty years regarding the waters of our Arctic archipelago, no doubt largely because of vagaries of policy concerning the sector principle. As suggested, the Canadian archipelago seems to have been overlooked in international discussions; Evensen, for example, in considering a large number of cases in his work on this subject does not even mention it.[233] There have been, of course, a number of official or semi-official statements to the effect that Canada regards these waters as territorial, notably one by Prime Minister St. Laurent in the House of Commons in 1957.[234] There appears to be no statute or order in council

[230]*Op. cit.*, p. 131.
[231]Evensen, *op. cit.*, pp. 301–2.
[232]*Ibid.*, pp. 297–98.
[233]*Ibid.*, pp. 295–99.
[234]Canada, *House of Commons Debates* (April 6, 1957), vol. III, p. 3186: "Oh, yes, the Canadian government considers that these are Canadian territorial waters."

dealing specifically with the subject, however; and the important order in council of December 18, 1937, dealing with territorial waters, deliberately excluded Arctic waters from its recommendations.[235]

In the last few years it has become increasingly likely that Canada's case will be determined by, or at least greatly affected by, events elsewhere. To some extent this may have happened already. States such as Indonesia and the Philippines doubtless feel a greater urgency than Canada to have their cases settled, and a decisive pronouncement for any of them would have considerable bearing upon others, including Canada. If Canada should proceed to claim the archipelago waters in definitive fashion, it would evidently be at the expense of whatever is left of her sector claim as applied to regions other than land, unless she felt that she could simultaneously claim archipelago waters under one principle and sector waters under another.

A number of other questions may be suggested which are easier to pose than to answer. For example, is the Canadian archipelago coastal or outlying, or part one and part the other? If the last, where is the dividing line and how is it established? In this connection the distinction between islands such as King William and Ellesmere is very apparent. Again, supposing Canada should establish her right to the archipelago waters, would their status be as internal waters, or marginal sea, or some of both? Would there be any aspect of historic rights? Would there be a clearly established right of innocent passage for foreign states, especially through the several possible routes for a northwest passage? Would these routes be reserved as international straits, on grounds that they provide necessary passages between two large bodies of water which are clearly international, namely the Atlantic and the Pacific? On these last points a recent Canadian commentator has expressed the view that there should be the right of innocent passage,[236] which would presumably mean that the northwest passage or passages, at least, would not be classed as internal waters. It is apparent that a claim to territoriality of the archipelago waters may raise as many problems as it solves.

Submarine passages

Vilhjalmur Stefansson's vision of submarine traffic under the ice of the Arctic Ocean,[237] which Sir G. H. Wilkins tried unsuccessfully to

[235]*Canadian Order in Council*, P.C. no. 3139, Dec. 18, 1937.

[236]J. Y. Morin, *op. cit.*, p. 145.

[237]V. Stefansson, *The Northward Course of Empire*, New York: Harcourt, Brace, and Co. (1922), pp. 189–99. Stefansson (p. 194) refers to comments on his submarine plans by Admiral Peary on Jan. 10, 1919, as evidence of earlier

initiate in 1931,[238] became a reality a quarter of a century later. The American nuclear submarine "Nautilus," under Commander W. R. Anderson, got to within 180 miles of the North Pole in August 1957; and then, one year later, succeeded in completing the first under-ice crossing of the Arctic Ocean, travelling from Bering Strait to the Greenland Sea.[239] A few days afterwards another American nuclear sub, the "Skate," under Commander J. F. Calvert, reached the Pole from the Atlantic side, but returned in the direction from which it had come.[240] Other voyages followed—a mid-winter cruise by the "Skate" from Atlantic to North Pole and back in 1959,[241] another mid-winter cruise by the "Sargo" from Bering Strait to the Pole and back in 1960,[242] and then, in August 1960, the first negotiation of the Northwest Passage through Canada's archipelago waters, by the "Seadragon" under Commander G. P. Steele.[243] On July 31, 1962, the "Skate" and the "Seadragon" met at the North Pole, returning afterwards to their home bases in Atlantic and Pacific respectively.[244] In the spring of 1961 the British carried out experiments in Arctic waters with the two conventional-type submarines "Finwhale" and "Amphion,"[245] but so far as is known they have attempted no Arctic crossings. What the Russians may have done is anybody's guess. One of Stefansson's last public statements was a reiteration of his earlier oft-expressed belief that in time the Arctic Ocean would provide usable routes for subsurface ships, especially large oil tankers which would fill up, voyage, and unload beneath the surface without coming to the top.[246] Plans are already visualized for nuclear-powered cargo submarines of this type, but dampers have also been cast on the idea, for example by Hanson W. Baldwin of the New York Times and Commander Calvert of the "Skate," the former holding that the shallow waters in and north of Bering Strait will limit or prevent

---

interest. See *The National Geographic Magazine*, vol. XXXVII, no. 4 (Apr., 1920), p. 339.

[238]Sir G. H. Wilkins, *Under the North Pole*, New York: Brewer, Warren, and Putnam (1931).

[239]Commander W. R. Anderson, *Nautilus—90—North*, Cleveland: World Publishing Co. (1959); also *New York Times*, Aug. 9, 1958.

[240]*New York Times*, Aug. 15, 1958; *The Polar Times*, no. 47, Dec., 1958.

[241]*New York Times*, Mar. 28, 1959; *The Polar Times*, no. 48, June, 1959.

[242]*New York Times*, Feb. 11, 1960; *The Polar Times*, no. 50, June, 1960.

[243]Commander G. P. Steele, *Seadragon: Northwest Under the Ice*, New York: E. P. Dutton and Co. (1962).

[244]*The Polar Times*, No. 55, Dec., 1962.

[245]*The Polar Record*, 11, No. 70, Jan., 1962, 89.

[246]CBC-TV programme, Feb. 13, 1963, recorded shortly before Stefansson's death on Aug. 26, 1962.

emergence of submarines into the Pacific,[247] the latter that costs will be prohibitive.[248]

The importance of this new development from the military point of view is obvious. Published reports indicate that since early 1959 Canada has been investigating the problem of submarine detection in Arctic waters, with the long-range objective of setting up a detection system. There are also some interesting legal implications. The old sector problem appears again, though in rather different form. Questions involving rights to undersurface navigation, sovereignty over floating ice and the waters beneath, the territoriality of archipelago waters, and international straits, are also raised. If the Arctic Ocean is high seas, and if archipelago waters are not territorial, then submarines are at liberty to navigate in them without let or hindrance. If not, then their right is limited. To illustrate the practical importance of such questions, would Russia have just legal grounds for complaint if an American submarine navigated unseen to within fifteen miles of her Arctic coast somewhere between Bering Strait and the White Sea, as could now easily be done? The problem does not appear entirely academic when put in these terms.

The judgment in the *Corfu Channel Case* in 1949 strongly affirmed, or reaffirmed, the right of states to send warships through international straits in peacetime, with the proviso that the passage be "innocent."[249] The Convention on the Territorial Sea and the Contiguous Zone in 1958 confirmed this right for all ships (Art. 16, Sec. 4), as well as the same right for all ships to pass through the territorial sea (Art. 14, Sec. 1). On the other hand, no such right is granted in internal waters. These points being clear, the problem becomes, in Canadian Arctic waters as elsewhere, one of distinguishing among internal waters, territorial sea, and high seas, and the distinctions would presumably affect submarines as well as other vessels. A further rule reiterated by the 1958 convention and applicable specifically to submarines is that during innocent passage they must navigate on the surface and show their flag (Art. 14, Sec. 6). This requirement incidentally exposes the weakness of the argument that no legal distinctions can be permitted between ice and water, since in ice-covered waters surface navigation at a given place or time might be difficult or impossible.

Maxwell Cohen in his above-mentioned article apparently assumed that the "Nautilus" and "Skate" had travelled considerable distances in

[247]*New York Times*, Aug. 15, 1958.
[248]*Ottawa Journal*, Aug. 21, 1961. Article by J. English, referring to First International Symposium on Arctic Geology in Edmonton (Jan., 1960).
[249]Corfu Channel Case, Judgment of April 9, 1949: *International Court of Justice Reports 1949*, pp. 28, 29, 30.

the Canadian sector in 1958 without obtaining Canadian permission. However, maps and accounts of their voyages indicate that they barely entered the Canadian sector, if at all. The "Seadragon" sailed right through archipelago waters in 1960, of course, but the presence aboard of a Canadian representative in the person of Commodore O. C. S. Robertson indicates Canadian co-operation and implicit or explicit approval. American accounts of their polar voyages stress repeatedly that they remained in international waters, but what concept of international waters is applied is not made clear.[250] Professor Cohen's final suggestion that Canada should assert, presumably unilaterally, "some kind of authority" over her sector icecap and the waters beneath indicates the concern that unrestricted voyages of this type might arouse in states with an Arctic frontier, and also the need to achieve a satisfactory accommodation between demands for security on the one side and freedom of navigation on the other. The prospects of obtaining any form of recognition for such a claim would doubtless be slim, however, and there is probably no readier legal solution here than in the case of submarines cruising below the surface outside the territorial limits of the Atlantic or Pacific coasts. Whether Canada could limit submarine traffic in her sector is thus a question, and it is equally doubtful whether she could deny submarines the right to innocent passage through the channels leading from Atlantic to Pacific. If such traffic ever becomes large-scale, any remaining uncertainties of a legal nature will press increasingly for solution.

Ice islands

The question of jurisdiction over floating ice has been given a new emphasis and also a new twist in recent years by the quasi-permanent or at least long-term occupation of ice islands in the Arctic Ocean.[251] These ice islands, composed of extremely durable and evidently aged ice, are believed to have broken off from the Ellesmere Island ice shelf, and have only been identified in recent years. They vary greatly in area, some being as large as 300 square miles, and are gradually reduced by breaking-off and melting. They drift slowly around the Arctic Ocean in a generally clockwise direction at a variable rate of one or two miles per day, their circumpolar wanderings sometimes being interrupted or ended by their running aground or getting lost in the channels of the Canadian

---

[250]E.g., *New York Times*, Aug. 9, 1958; Feb. 11, 1960; *The Polar Times*, no. 55, Dec., 1962, pp. 18–19.

[251]L. S. Koenig, K. R. Greenaway, Moira Dunbar, and G. Hattersley-Smith, "Arctic Ice Islands," *Arctic*, vol. 5, no. 2 (July, 1952), pp. 67–103, and subsequent articles in the same journal. Much information about ice islands may be found in *The Polar Record* and *The Polar Times*.

archipelago or the waters northeast of Greenland. Starting with the landing on Fletcher's Island (T-3) by an American party in March, 1952, both Americans and Russians have kept a number under occupation for as long as several years without interruption, changing the occupying parties frequently and supplying them by airplane or, when possible, by ship. T-3 had originally been sighted by a Canadian Air Force plane in April, 1947; but T-1, the first to be seen, was sighted by a USAF plane in August, 1946.

The establishment of such bases has removed from the area of discussion the question of whether the floating ice of the Arctic Ocean can in any way be subjected to genuine physical occupation. It is now being occupied, and that is decisive.[252] Whether an ice island may also be subjected to any legal form of sovereignty, and if so, under what conditions or limitations, is not so easy to determine. An application of the sector principle to ice islands, even if acceptable in other respects, would not answer the problem, since they eventually drift out of the sector. On the other hand a more than temporary sovereignty of the occupying state is of doubtful propriety, as an ice island may ultimately drift into the territorial sea or internal waters of another state. Here it is perhaps more logical to think of an ice island not as analogous to land (which it certainly is in that it can be made into a well-equipped base with buildings and even airstrips), but rather as analogous to a huge ship or aircraft carrier. Under this analogy an ice island which has been occupied by one state but which has drifted into the territorial waters of another would remain the property of the former but would be subject to a measure of regulation by the latter. The analogy is doubtless far-fetched, however, and soon breaks down because the movements of an ice island, up till the present time at least, cannot be controlled as those of a ship can be. Even so, it seems better than the alternatives, and thus, if an ice island is subject to any form of sovereignty, it evidently must be possessed more or less as a ship is possessed.

The advent of occupied ice islands must weaken sector claims to regions of floating ice, and especially the claims of extremists to the substance itself. A sector claim, if applied to such a region, must evidently claim what might be termed icespace rather than the ice itself, in the same manner as a state claims the airspace above its soil rather than the air.

It does not appear that outright claims to proprietorship over ice

---

[252]Cf. C. C. Hyde's remark of some years ago respecting sovereignty over polar areas in general (*op. cit.*, vol. I, p. 347): "Whether the polar areas as such may be subjected to rights of sovereignty appears no longer to be a moot question. States are in fact asserting that they may be; and that is decisive."

islands have been made, nor have there been disputes as to ownership or rights of occupation. It is noticeable, however, that on at least one occasion an American party abandoned an ice island (or ice floe) as it approached the Siberian shore,[253] and similarly the Russians have abandoned others as they drifted into the vicinity of northeastern Greenland.[254] On the other hand neither the United States nor Russia has restricted its occupation to its own sector, and both have entered the Canadian. So far as is known there are no formal agreements of any kind to cover the situation. The absence of both disputes and agreements, however, should not obscure the fact that there is plenty of room for friction and even provocative incidents, as for example if an American party insisted upon continuing occupation of an ice island as it drifted along the Siberian coast, or if a Russian party attempted to set up a base on an ice island already occupied by Americans. An arrangement like that in Antarctica would leave the Arctic seas, including the ice islands, open for scientific investigation by all but ownership by none. This might be a reasonable way out. If, on the other hand, the ice islands are considered subject to sovereignty as well as occupation, then the problems indicated above may have to be solved, and this might prove complicated and troublesome. The ultimate solution no doubt lies, as it so often does, in common sense, restraint, and co-operation more than in fine points of law.

Jurisdiction over Polar Airspace

The establishment of a comprehensive system of law to govern air traffic and rights over airspace is a development of the modern age.[255] Until this was accomplished two ancient principles were in conflict—one holding that the air, like the sea, should be free to all mankind, the other that the lord of the soil was also lord of the heavens. What had been

[253]The Polar Times, no. 52, June, 1961, p. 6; no. 53, Dec., 1961, p. 5.

[254]Ibid., no. 40, June, 1955, p. 28; no. 50, June, 1960, p. 9. It should be added that both Americans and Russians apparently abandoned their bases because they were grounding or breaking up; reports nevertheless indicate that there was doubt as to the wisdom of continuing to occupy them in waters adjacent to foreign shores.

[255]The literature on this subject is voluminous. Some of the principal works are K. W. Colegrove, International Control of Aviation, Boston: World Peace Foundation (1930); O. J. Lissitzyn, International Air Transport and National Policy, New York: Council on Foreign Relations (1942); John C. Cooper, The Right to Fly, New York: Henry Holt and Co. (1947); C. N. Shawcross, K. M. Beaumont, and P. R. E. Browne, Air Law, 2nd ed., London: Butterworth and Co. (1951); Sir A. D. McNair, The Law of the Air, 2nd ed., London: Stevens and Sons (1953).

largely a matter of doctrinal discussion acquired immense practical importance after flight by powered heavier-than-air machine was inaugurated by the Wright brothers in 1903. Up to World War I the view that the air should be free may be said to have predominated in international discussions, although state legislation, insofar as it dealt with the subject, favoured the concept of national sovereignty over superjacent airspace. World War I decisively ended any real hope that the first principle might prevail, and afterwards the second was formally accepted in the Convention for the Regulation of Aerial Navigation, which was drawn up at the Peace Conference in 1919.[256] It was not seriously challenged thereafter, and was repeatedly reaffirmed in international agreements, notably the Pan American Convention on Commercial Aviation at Havana in 1928,[257] and in municipal legislation. With its incorporation in the definitive Chicago Convention of 1944[258] its acceptance as part of the international order, at least by the overwhelming majority of independent states, was no longer in doubt. The United States, although not a party to the 1919 convention, joined the Chicago Convention; Russia, although party to neither, made clear by state decrees that she demanded sovereignty over her superjacent airspace.[259]

The basic rules of international air law, this one included, may be said to have been fairly well established since the convention of 1919. They have been well stated by O. J. Lissitzyn in what he terms "three simple, yet fundamental principles" as follows:

1. Each state has sovereignty and jurisdiction over the air space directly above its territory (including territorial waters).
2. Each state has complete discretion as to the admission or non-admission of any aircraft to the air space under its sovereignty.
3. Air space over the high seas, and over other parts of the earth's surface not subject to any state's jurisdiction, is free to the aircraft of all states.[260]

The same authority adds "Although of recent origin, these principles are now among the least disputed in international law." The essence of them is that the status of airspace depends upon the status of the region directly below, and if the latter is established, the former follows as a

[256]For text, see *The American Journal of International Law Supplement*, vol. 17, no. 4 (Oct., 1923), pp. 195–215. See esp. Art. I.
[257]*Ibid.*, vol. 22, no. 3 (July, 1928), pp. 124–33.
[258]For text, see *Canada Treaty Series 1944*, no. 36 (Dec. 7, 1944). Art. I reads as follows: "The contracting States recognize that every State has complete and exclusive sovereignty over the airspace above its territory."
[259]E.g., Soviet Air Code of 1932, given in translation in Taracouzio, *The Soviet Union and International Law*, Appendix XII, p. 401 (*supra*).
[260]O. J. Lissitzyn, *International Air Transport and National Policy*, p. 365 (*supra*).

consequence. The major exception to this rule is that the right of innocent passage for ships in the territorial sea does not extend to airplanes
in the airspace above it.

In spite of the apparent simplicity of the foregoing, there are possible
areas of uncertainty and confusion. To begin with, any uncertainty
respecting the status of land, or water, communicates itself to the airspace above. To some extent the same consequence results from the
lack of international agreement about the breadth of the territorial sea,
and about the status of certain waters claimed on historic or other
grounds. The acceptance in principle of the contiguous zone of limited
jurisdiction in sea law raises the question of whether the airspace directly
above it should also be a zone of limited jurisdiction. There is also the
question of a much broader contiguous air zone for customs or defence
purposes. During the Korean War, the United States and Canada unilaterally established Air Defence Identification Zones for the control of
aircraft outside national boundaries (ADIZ and CADIZ respectively),
which were somewhat comparable to the contiguous sea zone but much
wider.[261] A theoretical justification for the great breadth of such zones
(up to about 300 nautical miles in the case of the American defence
zone) was that the one hour's flying time it approximated was comparable with the one hour's sailing time of the contiguous sea zone.[262] This
concept is less appropriate today in view of the fantastic increases in
airplane speeds even within the past dozen years. Such measures have
been defended as necessary for security purposes, but nevertheless they
lack international sanction and raise new problems in air law.

The brief survey in the preceding paragraphs is applicable to the
Arctic regions as elsewhere, and it would appear that problems peculiar
to these regions, if there are such, involve the sector principle and the
question of jurisdiction over airspace above masses of floating ice.
Extreme exponents of the sector principle, notably the Russians
Lakhtine,[263] Breitfuss,[264] and Korovin,[265] have argued that airspace
above a sector should be under the control of the sector state. Most

[261]For a detailed discussion, and an attempted justification, see J. T. Murchison,
The Contiguous Air Space Zone in International Law, Ottawa: Department of
National Defence (1956). See also J. A. Martial, "State Control of the Air Space
Over the Territorial Sea and the Contiguous Zone," *The Canadian Bar Review*,
vol. XXX (1952), pp. 245–63.

[262]Martial, *op. cit.*, p. 256.

[263]*Op. cit.*, pp. 714–15.

[264]*Op. cit.*, p. 467. Breitfuss, less extreme than the others, actually recommended that sovereignty should be exercised "in a certain measure, still to be
determined internationally."

[265]Cited in Taracouzio, *Soviets in the Arctic*, pp. 361–62 (*supra*).

others disagree, especially those who refuse to accept either the sector principle or the concept of sovereignty over ice-covered waters.[266] Maxwell Cohen's suggestion that Canada "assert some kind of authority over its sector of the ice cap"[267] raises the question as to whether she should assert a similar authority over the airspace above. Another interesting suggestion, hinted at in a recent work, is that Canada might reverse the normal order of things and use the air to establish control of the surface, in this case ice.[268] The consequences would be interesting, because if sovereignty over the ice could be legally established in this manner, sovereignty over the airspace above would automatically follow. Thus would be presented, in novel form, the time-honoured problem of the chicken and the egg.

Up till the present time there does not seem to have been any particular effort to resolve these matters, even though use of Arctic and trans-Arctic air routes has increased greatly in recent years. Arctic flying was pioneered in the 1920's by men like Richard Byrd and Sir George Hubert Wilkins and by Canadian bush pilots, and the use of Arctic and sub-Arctic routes for military purposes became common in World War II.[269] After trial flights from Los Angeles to Copenhagen and Los Angeles to Oslo in 1952 and from Oslo to Tokyo in 1953, Scandinavian Airlines System inaugurated regular trans-Arctic commercial service between Copenhagen and Los Angeles in November, 1954. Other companies followed—Canadian Pacific Airlines in June, 1955, Pan American World Airways and Trans World Airlines in 1957, Air France and KLM in 1958, and Japanese Airlines in 1961.[270] The companies have naturally used different routes, but in general have avoided the high Arctic, probably to take advantage of well-equipped stopping places such as Anchorage and Frobisher Bay. No particular legal

[266]E.g., Taracouzio, op. cit., pp. 364–66; Plischke, op. cit., pp. 566–72; also "Trans-Polar Aviation and Jurisdiction over Arctic Airspace," The American Political Science Review, vol. XXXVII, no. 6 (Dec., 1943), pp. 1012–13; Cooper, "Airspace Rights over the Arctic," op. cit., pp. 537, 540.

[267]Cohen, "Polar Ice and Arctic Sovereignty," op. cit., p. 36.

[268]Ivan L. Head, Canadian Claims to Territorial Sovereignty in the Arctic Regions (Harvard Ll.M. Thesis, 1960). pp. 131–32.

[269]An excellent summary of early Arctic flying is given in Trevor Lloyd, "Aviation in Arctic North America and Greenland," The Polar Record, vol. 5, nos. 35, 36 (Jan.–July, published Dec., 1948), pp. 163–71.

[270]See brief accounts of the inauguration of these flights and services in The Polar Record, vol. 7, no. 48 (July, 1954), pp. 207–209; vol. 7, no. 50 (May, 1955), pp. 418–19; vol. 8, no. 52 (Jan., 1956), p. 42; vol. 8, no. 54 (Sept., 1956), p. 253; vol. 8, no. 57 (Sept., 1957), pp. 520–22; vol. 9, no. 58 (Jan., 1958), p. 49; vol. 9, no. 60 (Sept., 1958), p. 266; vol. 9, no. 62 (May, 1959), pp. 471–72; vol. 11, no. 72 (Sept., 1962), pp. 261–64.

arrangements appear to have been made regarding flights over the Arctic icecap, if and when these should occur, and the only conclusion that can be drawn is that problems have not arisen or have been put aside. It is noticeable, however, that flights betwen European countries and Japan have not gone over the Russian sector, although this would be a shorter route. Lack of available bases might be the explanation; if so, flights over the Soviet sector may be anticipated as planes develop ranges long enough to make them independent of such bases. On this subject it is evident that the utility Stefansson and others foresaw for Arctic islands as transpolar bases is already being outstripped by events. Regarding the legal status of the airspace above the Canadian Arctic archipelago, it can only be said that under a narrow interpretation of territorial waters it would be a confusing puzzle, and this may be a further justification for a view that the archipelago waters should be considered a unit.

CONCLUSION

The conclusions emerging from this study may be stated briefly, some with confidence, others more doubtfully or tentatively.

Canada's legal right to her northern territories, in particular the islands, has been well established at least since the early 1930's. If she lost part or all of them now, it would only be through abandoning them, having them taken from her, or, less tangibly, passively accepting American control of them.

The sector principle, although asserted unilaterally by some states, has been denounced by others, and since it lacks international sanction, is of dubious validity. As a device simply for marking out land territories where sovereignty has been established or is to be established by other means, it may be unobjectionable; but as a justification in itself for claims to land, and even more to waters beyond territorial limits or airspace above, it could only be judged invalid. Canada would do well to abandon all semblance of a sector claim as such, even the sector lines of the Arctic Islands Game Preserve, and to make it clear beyond doubt that there is no longer any pretense of such a claim. By doing otherwise she really has little to gain but international disrespect, and on this issue invites, ultimately, some form of rebuff or humiliation.

The rules of international law respecting territorial waters, contiguous zones, bays, straits, islands, continental shelves, submarine passages, and airspace apply in the polar regions generally, and in the Canadian North particularly, subject to whatever modifications may result from the exceptional circumstances there. These circumstances involve mainly floating ice, temporarily or permanently blocked water passages, the complex archipelago form of the land territories, the possibility of historic rights, and (for what it is worth) the sector principle. Some of the resultant legal problems remain unresolved. They may be unimportant; on the other hand they may acquire an importance not presently apparent.

Canada's case for the territoriality of sector waters, ice, and airspace would doubtless be very weak from a legal point of view. On the other hand she probably would have a much stronger and more reasonable case for the territoriality of water, ice, and airspace within archipelago limits.

In the event of her establishing the territoriality of archipelago waters, the question would remain as to international use of the several northwest passages. Since they link the Atlantic and Pacific Oceans, it might be difficult and unwise for her to attempt to restrict use of them. Here again the problem is small today, but it could become more important.

In resolving these problems it is far more desirable to maintain a decent respect for international law than to attempt to bend or stretch it to serve national ends. Two basic principles, freedom of the high seas and freedom of airspace above international waters, have been under severe attack in recent years. Canada, in common with other nations, has far more to gain in the long run by upholding these principles than by subverting them. This is particularly true in the Arctic, where what there is to be gained is small compared with what there is to be lost in other parts of the world.

The Strategic Significance
of the Canadian Arctic

◀ R. J. SUTHERLAND* ▶

PRIOR TO THE SECOND WORLD WAR, Canada's northern regions represented, not a military frontier, but a vast and impenetrable strategic barrier. There were, to be sure, vague recollections of piratical expeditions into Hudson's Bay during the seventeenth and eighteenth centuries; but these took place in the days of sailing ships, fur traders, and an almost unpopulated continent. In 1940, Professor C. P. Stacey (soon to become Colonel C. P. Stacey, the distinguished historian of the Canadian Army) wrote:

On the Dominion's northern territories those two famous servants of the Czar, Generals January and February mount guard for the Canadian people all year round. It is not impossible that the continuing development of aircraft will lend these Arctic and Sub-Arctic Regions an increased military significance in the future; but for the moment, though they cannot be entirely forgotten they are clearly not particularly important, and this fact greatly narrows, for practical purposes, Canada's actual areas of defence.[1]

A senior officer described the situation even more succinctly; in Canada's northern regions there is, from a military point of view, nowhere to go, and nothing to do when you get there.

This is not, however, the whole story. Canadian military men, in common with other Canadians, have seen in Canada's northern regions a national challenge and a national destiny. During the twenties and thirties the armed forces made an important contribution to northern

*Operational Research Establishment, Defence Research Board, Ottawa. Acknowledgment is made of the assistance of Mr. H. L. Robertson. Opinions expressed are those of the author and do not purport to represent the views of the Department of National Defence.

[1]C. P. Stacey, *The Military Problems of Canada* (Toronto, Ryerson, 1940), p. 5.

development, the army in the field of radio communications, and the RCAF in the development of northern flying. In 1922, a few years after a British Vickers Vimy bomber had managed to stagger across the Atlantic, Vilhjalmur Stefansson, the famous Arctic explorer and publicist wrote:

A glance at the map of the northern hemisphere shows that the Arctic Ocean is in effect a huge Mediterranean. It lies between its surrounding continents somewhat as the Mediterranean lies between Europe and Africa. It has, in the past, been looked upon as an impassable Mediterranean. In the near future, it will not only become passable but will become a favourite route . . . much shorter than any other air route that lies over the oceans that separate the present day centres of population.[2]

These words were much quoted by military essayists, and always with approval.

The analogy between the Arctic and the Mediterranean, which Stefansson expounded with so much eloquence over a period of forty years, has captured the imagination of many Canadians including Canadian military men. The explanation, it seems evident, is that the development of the North represents a fundamental Canadian aspiration, an important element in the national consciousness. This has been increasingly the case as the Canadian North has become the only major frontier remaining on the North American continent. To this extent, Stefansson's Arctic Mediterranean thesis was prophetic. But it has also proved, at least to the present, a very bad prediction. Today, when the number of intercontinental commercial flights each month has risen into the thousands, the number passing over the Canadian Arctic amounts to a mere handful. The stimulus to the development of the North which occurred during the past quarter century must be ascribed mainly to an increase in the military significance of Canada's northern areas. Economics took second place to strategy; commercial aviation was the very junior partner of strategic airpower.

It is of some interest that no Canadian military man, however keenly interested in the development of the North, foresaw that Canada's Arctic regions would soon become an important military frontier. The cautious words used by Professor Stacey are about as visionary as any Canadian strategist permitted himself to be. This is scarcely surprising; the great

[2]Vilhjalmur Stefansson, *The Northward Course of Empire* (New York, 1922), p. 168. A criticism of the "Arctic Mediterranean" thesis, which has been borne out by events, can be found in an article written in 1944 by the then Assistant Secretary of Commerce of the United States, William A. Burden, "American Air Transport Faces North" in *Compass of the World*, eds. H. W. Wergert and V. Stefansson (New York, 1944), p. 137.

accretion to the strategic significance of the Canadian Arctic was the result of a series of developments in military technology, in political circumstances, and in strategic doctrine and concepts which could scarcely have been foreseen. In the field of technology these developments included radar, nuclear weapons, and the long range jet bomber. Changes in political circumstances were perhaps even more dramatic: the Second World War, abandonment of American isolationism, Soviet imperialism, a North American military guarantee to western Europe, the East-West conflict and the Cold War. Scarcely less significant were the changes in the strategic concepts by which military power was related to the demands of policy.

No one could possibly have foreseen the totality of these developments. And even if some inspired prophet had foreseen each one, it is a near certainty that he could not have predicted the interaction between them. What is equally to the point, he could not have foreseen the precipitate pace of change which was itself a product of circumstances— the conflict between the policies of major governments, the great expansion of military research and development, and the changing climate of national and international opinion. For it is the pace of change, quite as much as the extent of change, which has presented difficult problems in the adjustment of policies and ideas.

There is a lesson here which deserves to be noted. The great alteration which has taken place in the strategic significance of Canada's northern regions has been a matter of dynamic adjustment to rapidly changing circumstances. We are now confronted with new developments which may have equally important consequences. These include the ICBM, nuclear-powered submarines armed with ballistic missiles, possible defences against ballistic missiles, and earth-orbiting satellites. One should not, especially over a period of time, ignore the possibility that there may be equally important changes in political circumstances and in strategic policies. The significance of Canada's northern regions in the present international military and political balance can be understood only in terms of a series of important developments which have taken place during the past quarter century. One must understand that change continues and that the recent past is not necessarily in all respects a reliable guide to the future.

THE SECOND WORLD WAR

In 1939, no responsible authority in Canada believed that there was a serious threat to the security of Canada's northern regions. All available evidence suggests that American military planners were similarly unconcerned. The alteration in this view was the result of a number of cataclysmic events of which the first was the German victory in France in 1940. Almost overnight the United States and Canada were compelled to contemplate the possibility that Britain might be defeated and that the resources of Europe might be organized to threaten the security of North America.

A direct result of the German victory in France was the Ogdensburg Agreement of August 1940 and the establishment of the Permanent Joint Board on Defence. In effect, the Ogdensburg Agreement converted into an explicit alliance the quiet understanding which had grown up between Canada and the United States over the previous twenty years. The authors of the Ogdensburg Agreement, President Roosevelt for the United States and Prime Minister King for Canada, regarded it as possessing validity for the indefinite future and not merely for the duration of the Second World War. Interestingly enough, this alliance, the oldest and certainly the most durable of contemporary American alliances, was achieved by no more formal method than an exchange of diplomatic notes, and was entered into at a time when Canada was at war and the United States was not.

The German victory in France did not lead to any particular apprehension with regard to the security of Canada's northern regions. It did lead to the British military occupation of Iceland and to the dispatch of Canadian and subsequently of American troops. It also led to what might be called the American military discovery of Greenland.[3] The American interest in Greenland led in the post-war period to the great American base at Thule. The existence of this base has had a significant effect upon the military importance of the Canadian Arctic and upon Canadian–American relations. If Thule had not been available to the United States the question of a major US base in the Canadian Arctic Archipelago would certainly have arisen.

Pearl Harbor and the Japanese victories in the southwestern Pacific administered an even more severe shock to North American military planners. For a time early in 1942 it appeared that the United States might lose control of the eastern Pacific and that Alaska might be vulnerable to attack. Three major projects were undertaken in order to create secure communications to Alaska and to develop the area as a potential theatre of operations: establishment of the North-West Staging

[3]References to a contemplated Canadian military expedition to Greenland are contained in: S. W. Dziuban, *US Army in World War II, Special Studies— Military Relations Between the United States and Canada, 1939–45*, Office of the Chief of Military History, Department of the Army (Washington, 1959), pp. 149–55; Maurice A. Pope, *Soldiers and Politicians* (Toronto, 1962), pp. 144–45 and *The Memoirs of Cordell Hull* (New York, 1948), pp. 755–76.

Route; construction of the Alcan Highway; and, the Canol project. There were also a number of more minor projects undertaken in the Canadian North. Quite apart from their military significance these projects resulted in a major improvement in communications, especially in the eastern sub-Arctic. Not less important was the considerable impetus given to research and development and the acquisition of experience in such matters as construction of buildings, roads and airfields and the operation of aircraft and vehicles.

The North-West Staging Route, on which some work had already been undertaken by Canada, comprised a series of airfields in Alberta, northern British Columbia, and the Yukon. These were constructed in 1942 and early 1943. The purpose of the route was to establish a secure and rapid air line of communications to Alaska. However, the most important use of the North-West Staging Route during the Second World War was in ferrying short ranged tactical aircraft from the United States to Russia via Alaska and Siberia.

A military highway linking the United States and Alaska was considered by the United States War Department during the thirties. Following the attack on Pearl Harbor the decision to embark upon construction of the Alcan Highway was made with considerable haste. On February 11, 1942, President Roosevelt approved construction. The project was recommended by the Permanent Joint Board on Defence on February 24, 1942, and the final arrangements were set forth in an exchange of notes between Canada and the United States of March 17 and 18, 1942. This agreement provided that the cost of construction would be borne by the United States but that at the end of the war the road would be turned over to Canada.[4]

The purpose of the Canol project was to develop a source of petroleum products closer to the Alaskan theatre than the continental United States. Extensive exploration was carried out at Norman Wells; new wells were drilled and a refinery and a number of pipelines were constructed. Unlike the Alcan Highway and the North-West Staging Route, the Canol project made little contribution to the development of the Canadian North. Local demand was found insufficient to support economical production and transport costs to more distant markets proved to be excessively high. Operations were closed down in mid-1945.[5]

By the summer of 1942, the battles of the Coral Sea and Midway had shifted the balance of seapower in the western Pacific in favour of the United States. Thereafter American strategic planning in the Pacific

[4]Dziuban, pp. 217–21.
[5]Dziuban, p. 235.

theatre was concerned mainly with the penetration of the Japanese defensive perimeter and the development of military operations against the Japanese homeland. Alaska was, however, a point of some sensitivity until the Japanese were finally expelled from the Aleutians in 1944. One school of thought, which found an ardent spokesman in Stefansson, held that the most appropriate base from which to strike at Japan was Alaska. Stefansson pointed out that Alaska is actually closer to the Japanese home islands than Hawaii and that the Aleutians and the Kuriles present a natural line of approach towards Japan. He also argued that an indigenous source of petroleum products could be developed at Norman Wells. The failure to follow this strategy Stefansson ascribed to the general Western disposition to think of the world as cylindrical.[6] Actually Stefansson's argument was a tribute to his hardihood as an explorer rather than to his proficiency as a military strategist. In the circumstances of the Second World War, the dense fogs and atrocious weather of the Aleutians represented a more formidable strategic obstacle than the greater distances of the Central and South Pacific or even such island fortresses as Kwajalein, Eniwetok, Saipan, and Iwo Jima.

In retrospect, it seems clear that the United States' fears for Alaska were somewhat exaggerated. A significant factor was, very probably, a desire to achieve a secure line of communications to Alaska as a long term requirement of United States defence. Perhaps even more important was the need to initiate some vigorous action at a time when American military power was still in the process of mobilization. Well before the end of the war American interest in this area had diminished. In 1944 it was proposed that Canada take over responsibility for the Alcan Highway although this did not take place until 1946.

The Second World War left a legacy to the future in the form of the alliance between Canada and the United States in North America, including the principal agency of the alliance, the Permanent Joint Board on Defence. This North America alliance has been the cornerstone of post-war Canadian defence policy—something which was clearly foreseen by the Canadian Prime Minister in 1940. However, there was a second inheritance which was more negative. This was Canadian aversion to the presence of American forces in Canada and extreme sensitivity to the potential derogation of Canadian sovereignty.

In accordance with the war-time arrangements United States facilities

[6]Stefannson, "The North American Arctic," in *Compass of the World*, pp. 231–40. See Col. C. P. Stacey, *Six Years of War*, pp. 492–98. Also Dziuban, pp. 252–59; Samuel Eliot Morison, *History of Naval Operations in World War II, Aleutians, Gilberts and Marshalls* (vol. VII) pp. 1–66; W. F. Craven and A. L. Cote, eds. *The Army Air Forces in World War II*, vol. IV pp. 354–401.

in Canada were turned over to Canada. Certain financial arrangements presented minor difficulties but were settled promptly and, on the whole, amicably. There remained, however, a feeling that United States military commanders in Canada had been rather insensitive to the niceties of Canadian sovereignty and in a few cases had come close to regarding Canada as occupied territory. Whatever the justification for this feeling —and it is true that the number of incidents was not very large—it has had a significant bearing upon Canadian policy and attitudes.[7]

THE IMMEDIATE POST-WAR PERIOD

In Canada's post-war defence policy the potential importance of Canada's northern regions figured more prominently and more explicitly than was the case in 1939. As a result of the war and the larger international responsibilities which had been assumed, Canada's defence budget and programmes were substantially increased over their pre-war levels. Prior to 1939, Canada's peace-time defence budget was barely enough to maintain the rudiments of a mobilization base. In the post-war reorganization, provision was made for small forces in being as well as a modest programme of research and development. As a result it was possible for the Department of National Defence to adopt a more vigorous policy with respect to the Canadian North.

In the immediate post-war period, defence policy, in so far as it related to the defence of Canada's northern regions, was concerned with a potential threat rather than with an actual one. This potential threat took two forms. The most important threat concerned long ranged bombers carrying nuclear weapons and directed against the great cities of North America or important military and industrial installations. In the period of 1945–50 it was expected that such aircraft would carry kiloton rather than megaton bombs. The second potential threat involved an invasion by airborne troops transported over the polar regions. In 1945, the former threat did not exist although it was foreseen that it might develop with considerable rapidity. The latter threat was also somewhat nebulous. Although the military capability existed or might exist, its strategic utility to a potential enemy was considerably less than obvious. However, in the immediate post-war period the possibility that air bases in the Canadian North might be seized by airborne

[7]See, for example, Rt. Hon. Vincent Massey, *What's Past is Prologue* (Toronto, 1963), p. 371.

assault was rather more plausible than it has since become, partly because in the era of short-ranged aircraft and few nuclear weapons the potential value of such bases was substantial.

Canadian policy with respect to the potential threat of invasion by airborne troops rested on four major points: (*a*) the alliance with the United States in North America; (*b*) acquisition of the ability to carry out northern operations by the Canadian Army and the RCAF; (*c*) cold weather operations provided a desirable area of specialization for the Canadian armed services and for Canadian research and development; and, (*d*) military activities in the North including research and development could contribute to the development and exploitation of Canada's northern regions. In accordance with this general policy, a number of programmes were initiated. The army assumed responsibility for the North-West Highway System and the RCAF for the airfields of the North-West Staging Route. An Arctic test and development station was established at Fort Churchill. The army and the RCAF embarked upon a programme of northern training including joint exercises. A number of research and development projects were initiated involving vehicles, clothing, and ancillary equipment for northern operations. At a later date, the Royal Canadian Navy constructed the large icebreaker, HMCS "Labrador."

Although the alliance with the United States remained the cornerstone of Canadian policy, it was not in the immediate post-war period especially active. The Permanent Joint Board on Defence continued to operate, and a number of joint projects were agreed upon, of which the most important was the establishment of joint weather stations at Resolute, Eureka Sound, Mould Bay, Isachsen, and Alert. This agreement was reached in March 1947. In February 1947, a Canada-US agreement was signed which facilitated co-operation between military staffs but this agreement stopped well short of any commitment to a joint command or integrated planning. In accordance with this agreement the USA assisted in the development of the test station at Fort Churchill and shared in the use of its facilities. The United States established a continental Air Defence Command in March 1946, but it was not until December 1, 1948 that Air Defence Command, RCAF, was established. The discussions which led to the Pinetree radar system began in 1949 and the exchange of notes which provided for the construction of the system took place in August 1951. There are, however, some indications that the United States advanced informally a number of proposals which Canada considered to be excessive and inopportune.

The essence of the Canadian policy was summed up in a statement made by the Prime Minister in the House of Commons on February 12, 1947.

I should like to comment briefly on the problems of northern defence . . . some quite unfounded suggestions have been put forward. There is a persistent rumour, for example, that the United States government has asked for bases in the Canadian North. This is a rumour I should like to deny emphatically. There has been talk of Maginot lines, of large scale defence projects, all of which is unwarranted and much of it fantastic. It is apparent to anyone who has reflected on the technological advances of recent years that new geographic factors have been brought into play. The polar regions assume new importance as the shortest routes between North America and the principal centres of population of the world. Our defence forces must, of course, have experience in the conditions of these regions, but it is clear that most of the things that should be done are required apart altogether from considerations of defence . . . our primary objective should be to expand our knowledge of the North, and of the conditions necessary for work and life there, with the object of developing its resources.[8]

The general approach towards defence of the North was to co-operate with terrain and climate rather than to attempt to defy them. It was recognized that major installations in the Canadian North, and especially airfields, might give rise to a need for local defence. The simplest solution to this problem was not to build the installations in the first place. This was not a dogma since it was recognized that both military and non-military considerations would eventually create the need for such installations. There was, however, a conviction that no good purpose could be served by getting ahead of the demand. This general concept was described expressively by Mr. Pearson as that of "scorched ice."[9]

CONSTRUCTION OF THE AIR DEFENCE WARNING SYSTEMS

In the years 1945–50 the defence of the Canadian North involved a potential threat rather than an actual one. A series of developments, political as well as technological, tended to render this threat more tangible from the military point of view and more pressing from the political point of view. The trend of political events was dramatized by the signature of the North Atlantic Treaty in April 1949. The growing imminence of a military threat was demonstrated by the appearance of the first Tu-4 (a Russian copy of the B-29) in the May Day fly-past of

[8]Hansard, 1947, vol. I, pp. 345–47, "A Statement on the Security Relations between Canada and the United States in North America."
[9]L. B. Pearson, "Canada's Northern Horizons," *Foreign Affairs*, vol. 31, no. 4 (July, 1953), p. 583.

1948 and was confirmed by the explosion of the first Soviet nuclear device in August 1949.

It is extremely difficult to describe in a few words the process by which the North American air defence system, including the Arctic warning lines, was conceived and implemented. One reason is the sheer magnitude of the endeavour. Between 1951 and 1961 the United States and Canada invested more than $50,000,000,000 in continental air defence. Another reason is the very great number of points of view and influences which played some role in the planning of the air defence system. But the most fundamental reason is the very rapid pace of events. During the fifties there was not one but a series of genuinely revolutionary changes in military technology and in strategic concepts. A crucial factor was the more than four-fold increase in North American defence budgets which occurred after the outbreak of the Korean War in June, 1950.

Changes in the technology of strategic offensive weapons are well known: thermonuclear weapons, longer-ranged and higher performance aircraft, aerial refuelling and, at the end of the decade, the long-ranged missile. Changes in the technology of air defence were perhaps even more dramatic: supercession of anti-aircraft guns by missiles, radical improvements in fighter armament and performance, higher performance radars, and the automation of the ground environment. This revolution in weaponry was not accidental. It was a response to a series of challenges, and was possible only because very large resources were devoted to it. The creation of the technology was a vital part of the total activity.

Quite as important as the changes in weaponry were the changes in strategic concepts by which this weaponry was related to the requirements of policy. To illustrate this point, in 1948 the United States War Plans provided for a relatively leisurely deployment to overseas bases, and for a World War II type campaign using a strictly limited number of kiloton weapons.[10] By 1961 the United States Strategic Air Command possessed a virtually unlimited number of megaton weapons and was prepared to launch 50 per cent of its first-line strength on the basis of fifteen minutes' warning. In 1951, almost no one, except perhaps General Le May, believed that such a condition of super-alert could be sustained for any period of time.

In 1951 there was an important school of thought which opposed any large expenditure upon air defence on the grounds that "offence is the

[10]See, for example, Herman Kahn, *On Thermonuclear War* (Princeton, 1960), pp. 420–24.

best defence." Recognition of the vital distinction between first-strike and second-strike capabilities was a response to this very crude doctrinal argument. It is a fact that the difference between first and second strike was understood only as the result of prolonged study and debate over a period of several years. As late as 1951 it is probably fair to say that almost no one understood this distinction or its essential implications. During the early fifties, it came to be recognized that although continental air defence could contribute little to first-strike capabilities it was essential to the maintenance of second-strike capabilities and that an assured second-strike capability was the price of a responsible and rational policy. An insecure and vulnerable retaliatory force would, in a period of severe crisis, constitute an invitation to pre-emptive attack on the part of the opponent. From one's own point of view it would tend to present the choice between pre-emptive attack and a Munich-style surrender.

It was probably not until the middle fifties that the relationship between the air defence of North America and the defence of Europe was perceived with any clarity even by North Americans. It should be said very clearly that the primary purpose of the enormous nuclear striking power which was acquired by the United States was not the direct defence of North America. The critical requirement against which this power was measured was and remains that of giving miliary validity to the American guarantee to NATO. The same comment applies to continental air defence and most particularly to the distant warning lines. In a very real sense these were the front lines of NATO. The policy of immediate use of tactical nuclear weapons for the defence of Europe which was adopted in 1954, tended to confirm this situation. This policy, in the circumstances of the time and in view of the weapons systems available, came very close to a policy of automatic nuclear escalation. The result was that in any severe crisis the USSR would be tempted, almost invited, to attempt to destroy the United States Strategic Air Command. The policy of nuclear response in Europe therefore tended to transfer the burden of European defence to the North American continent. The purpose of the North American air defence system was to ensure that this burden could be borne even in a period of acute crisis by ensuring that the US nuclear guarantee to NATO would remain credible.

There is a point here which bears very directly upon the strategic significance of Canada's northern regions and the effect of these regions upon Canada's role in world affairs. Domestic North American concerns were sufficient to bring about the Canada–United States alliance, but they did not call forth the great expansion in United States nuclear striking power, the build-up in continental air defences or the construction of the Arctic warning systems. These were an investment in security. The beneficiaries of the investment included Canada and the United States owing to their fundamental interest in the security of western Europe. But the most immediate beneficiaries were the nations and peoples of western Europe. This is something which few North Americans and even fewer Europeans have understood with any clarity.

The construction of the Arctic warning system involved a series of technical investigations, military studies, and negotiations of considerable complexity. These are much too numerous and complicated to attempt to discuss in detail, but the essentials of the matter can be described fairly briefly. One should bear in mind that at all stages in the planning there were very large elements of uncertainty—technological, strategic, operational, and financial. An important source of uncertainty was the cost, and even the gross economic feasibility, of carrying on major military activities in the Far North.

From a military point of view Canada's northern regions offered potentially three things. The first was additional warning against Soviet bombers approaching targets in the central portions of North America along the shortest and most direct routes. The second was defence in depth. By extending the air defence system northwards such bombers could be engaged before reaching their intended targets. Almost equally important, by extending the area of radar coverage the risk of saturation of the defences could be reduced. Finally, by locating strike aircraft or refuelling aircraft on northern bases, the range and speed of response of the strike forces could be improved.

In each case there were a substantial number of alternatives. With respect to warning, the options included large radars capable of providing height and track information, simpler equipment which would provide less information, and airborne radars carried in large aircraft. There were two major alternatives for "defence in depth." The first was to extend northwards the system of radars and airfields: the second was to construct a long-ranged aircraft possessing integral radar which could operate beyond the area of contiguous radar cover. In the case of the strike forces, the options were even more complex and included many combinations of aircraft, bases, and operating policies.

The planning of the North American air defence system involved, to a large extent, an attempt to define and to compare these various alternatives. It also involved an attempt to dispel the major sources of uncertainty by technological investigations, military staff appreciations, and war games. Underlying these technical and military considerations was a larger problem: the essential requirements of North American and Western security and the priority which should be given to continental air defence within the total spectrum of potential defence requirements.

In the event, it was only in the field of warning that the potentialities of Canada's northern geography were fully exploited. The active defence system was extended northwards but well short of the northern-most limits. Arrangements were made for the use of certain existing airfields as refuelling bases for strike aircraft but there was no attempt to construct a major base complex for strategic striking forces in the Canadian Arctic or sub-Arctic. Many technically feasible options were declined mainly because of the additional cost of conducting major defence activities in the Far North. Cost was not the only consideration but it is fair to say that it was the principal consideration. This was the underlying theme of nearly all the relevant appreciations; technology has rendered all parts of the Canadian North accessible but the costs remain very high.

The first serious consideration by Canadian defence planners of the construction of an Arctic warning line occurred in 1947. The conclusion reached was that such a system would cost more than it was worth.[11] In the circumstances of the time this was an entirely reasonable conclusion. The construction of the Arctic warning systems depended upon two later developments: the increase in the severity of the threat, and the large increase in North American defence budgets which occurred after the outbreak of the Korean War. If the latter had not taken place, the Arctic warning systems would almost certainly have remained beyond the realm of financial and military feasibility. A practical consequence of the 1947 appreciation was the initiation of certain development projects which produced the equipment ultimately employed in the Mid-Canada Line.

The sequence of events which led to the construction of the Arctic warning systems began, for all practical purposes, in 1951 with Project Charles. This was a major air defence study organized by the United States but with unofficial Canadian participation. Project Charles did not recommend construction of the Arctic warning systems but it did call attention to the very great value of additional warning. Similar conclusions were reached by an independent study carried out in Canada upon the initiative of the then Chairman of the Defence Research Board, Dr. O. M. Solandt. The next major event was the Lincoln Summer

[11]Statement of the Honourable H. B. Claxton, Minister of National Defence, Hansard, 1953–54, vol. I, p. 362.

Study of 1952. Again this was an American enterprise but it included a number of Canadian participants, military and scientific. The Lincoln Group recommended a Distant Early Warning system consisting of two lines of radars separated by about four hundred miles and extending across the northern limits of North America. The continental warning system was to be supplemented by a set of "seawings"—airborne and shipborne radars extending from Alaska to Midway in the Pacific and from Labrador to the United Kingdom in the Atlantic.

The recommendation of the Lincoln Group was not immediately accepted. The proposal was vigorously criticized on several grounds and in particular by those who saw in North American air defence a budgetary threat to the continued build-up of United States nuclear striking power.[12] Nevertheless, early in 1952, and in anticipation of the recommendations of the Lincoln Group, the United States Air Force contracted with the Western Electric Company to carry out a major engineering and systems study of the problems involved in constructing, operating and maintaining a distant early warning system. This project included the construction of a pilot station at Barter Island off the north coast of Alaska. By 1954 Western Electric had demonstrated that an early warning system could be constructed, and could provide a "ball-park" estimate of costs. The apparent urgency of the matter was confirmed by the first Soviet thermonuclear test in August 1953, and by the display of the first Badgers, comparable to the American B-47, in the May Day fly-past of 1954.

Meanwhile a number of staff discussions and joint studies were carried out between Canada and the United States. For this purpose a Canada-US Military Study Group was established under the general aegis of the Permanent Joint Board on Defence. The Military Study Group, in turn, was served by a subordinate body, the Canada-US Scientific Advisory Team, which conducted joint systems studies and evaluations. In November 1953, Canada agreed to permit the initiation of siting surveys. In June 1954, the Military Study Group recommended through the appropriate authorities in the two countries that the two governments should agree in principle upon the need for the DEW Line and that further action should be taken with a view to determining the military characteristics and construction programme. There then followed an intensive series of technical discussions and diplomatic negotiations. The conclusion of the basic agreements between the two countries for the construction of the DEW Line was announced to the Canadian

[12]See, for example, Samuel P. Huntington, *The Common Defence: Strategic Programs in National Politics* (New York, 1961), pp. 326, 341.

Parliament in November 1954. Construction was initiated during the summer of 1955. The DEW line became fully operational during the late summer of 1957.[13]

The construction of the DEW Line marks an important step in the northwards extension of Canada's economic frontier. As a direct result of the construction of the DEW Line Canadian firms gained greatly in experience of northern operations in such fields as aerial survey, construction and, above all, air transportation. This represented a major accretion to the national capacity to carry out large-scale operations in the Canadian North. No single figure has ever been given officially for the cost of constructing the DEW Line. This is easily understandable since many of the costs were rather thoroughly intertwined with the costs of other major programmes. However, a figure of half a billion dollars for construction has been rather generally accepted with about one-tenth of this sum for annual operating costs. With minor exceptions, construction was paid for by the United States.

Simultaneously with the negotiation of Dew Line agreements, Canada undertook to construct the Mid-Canada Line. This consisted of an alerting "fence" using equipment developed in Canada and was located well south of the DEW Line. The Mid-Canada Line represented Canada's contribution to the construction of the northern warning systems. The division of responsibility between the two countries was based, in part, upon administrative considerations; joint control of construction and joint financing would have introduced a great many complications. There was also some difference of opinion between the two countries with respect to the relative value of the two systems.

The construction of two Arctic warning systems, rather than a single system calls for some explanation. The key point was that no single line of radars could be sufficiently invulnerable to countermeasures and deception, a fact recognized by the Lincoln Study, which recommended two lines rather than one. The Mid-Canada Line represented an additional opportunity for detection. Moreover, since it employed essentially different equipment, it presented an additional set of problems to the attacker from the point of view of countermeasures and deception. A further consideration was that the Mid-Canada Line, although it did not provide maximum warning, provided information of greater potential value in the planning and control of the air battle.

The construction of the Arctic warning systems had a number of consequences which are worth noticing. In the first place, as a result of

[13]For further details see James Eayrs, *Canada in World Affairs, 1955–57* (Canadian Institute of International Affairs, 1959), pp. 141–52.

the DEW Line Agreements, Canada secured what the United States had up to that time assiduously endeavoured to avoid, namely, an explicit recognition of Canadian claims to the exercise of sovereignty in the Far North. A second consequence was to diminish, although it did not entirely eliminate, the possibility of hostile encroachments into the Canadian Arctic. As it was made clear that this region constituted part of the security zone of North America and NATO, it was also made clear that minor encroachments would involve entirely disproportionate hazards.

One further consequence is worth noting. As a result of the joint studies of the problems of North American air defence, Canadian military planners and some officials of civil departments gained a deep insight into the problems of continental air defence and the more basic problems of nuclear deterrence. It has been said by a senior member of the Rand Corporation that it was a Canadian rather than an American who first drew attention to the vital distinction between first-strike and second-strike capabilities, and to the corollary, that the key targets of a Soviet first-strike would be the bases of the United States Strategic Air Command rather than North American cities.

THE ICBM ERA

In 1957 the launching of the first Sputnik dramatized the arrival of a new era in military technology. It has been claimed that air defence planners failed to anticipate the introduction of the ICBM, but this is far from being the case. In 1952 certain members of the Rand Corporation criticized the DEW Line proposal because, among other reasons, the manned bomber would be superseded by a more advanced threat during the period 1957–60. This more advanced threat might consist either of ballistic missiles or of pilotless aircraft. This question was thoroughly debated in 1952. It was generally accepted that a fully operational Soviet ICBM would not exist until approximately 1960. It was believed unlikely that the ballistic missile would become the predominant threat before the middle sixties. It was also agreed that, even in the ICBM era, the bomber would have an important supplementary role owing to its ability to carry a large bombload and to deliver it with great accuracy. This would be particularly true if the air defence system were to be either non-existent or seriously defective. A period of serious risk was anticipated in the late fifties and early sixties, if, as seemed possible, the

USSR continued to build up its bomber force at the maximum feasible rate and if there were no compensating improvements in continental air defences. The latter contingency did not occur, but in the circumstances of the years 1952–54 it was a possibility which could not be overlooked. Furthermore, we do not know all the facts. It may be the case that it was the build-up in continental air defences and the associated build-up in the United States Strategic Air Command which convinced the Soviet government that an all-out competition with respect to strategic bombing forces would not produce a useable instrument of Soviet policy.

The prevailing view during the middle fifties was that the first operational Soviet ICBMs would appear about 1960, and that it would be 1965 before the ICBM would replace the manned bomber as the major threat to North America. This was an underestimate by about one year. The view that the bomber would continue to be an important weapons system, warranting continued attention to continental air defence, has been vindicated by the continued existence of a significant Soviet bomber force.

It is nevertheless true that the world has entered a new era in military technology and that the general effect is to decrease the strategic priority attaching to defences against the manned bomber. This was reflected in the cancellation of the Canadian Arrow project and in a general cutting back in continental air defences. If this trend continues a question will undoubtedly arise with respect to the continued need for Canada's Arctic warning systems.

The effect of the ICBM upon the strategic policies and doctrines of the major powers, and upon the significance of Canada's northern regions, is far from simple. The immediate effect is undoubtedly to diminish the strategic significance not only of Canadian geography but of most other geography. Strategic nuclear striking power can be exerted from home territories. Overseas bases may, as in the case of Cuba, offer improved accuracy and the means of outflanking a warning system. However, these considerations are likely to be of steadily diminishing importance owing to the increased number of relatively invulnerable missiles. There is for the present no serious prospect of any type of anti-missile defence other than a terminal system, that is, one which is located in the immediate vicinity of the target. United States Ballistic Missile Early Warning radars have been located in Alaska, northern Greenland and Britain. On military grounds a case can be made for the siting of additional warning radars in northern Canada, but it seems clear that these would not be worth the cost.

It could easily be argued that the value of Canada's Arctic warning systems is bound to diminish to a point at which it will no longer be worthwhile to maintain them. This is, however, an over-simplification. The ICBM has not merely replaced the bomber; it has led to a very important change in strategic concepts and policies. It is an important characteristic of ballistic missiles that they cannot be launched upon warning; the possibility of a false alarm or accident is entirely unacceptable. Even more important, missiles need not be launched upon warning provided the launchers and their associated communications are adequately protected by "hardening," mobility or increase in the number of aiming points.

These characteristics of a missile force have made possible a fundamental change in strategic concepts which is summed up in the phrases "flexible response" and "controlled general war." It is now the policy of the United States that if strategic nuclear weapons were to be used their use would not be all-out. The United States would seek to employ as little force as was compatible with the achievement of the essential aims of United States policy. The greater part of the United States nuclear striking forces would quite probably be held in reserve in order to deter attack on Western cities and to force the USSR to make peace on terms acceptable to the United States. The USSR has not, up to the present, formulated a similar policy, and, indeed, it has been highly critical of the US policy. However, Soviet actions indicate rather strongly that Soviet use of military power is not likely to be irrational or unrelated to the aims of Soviet policy.

An important consequence of this new emphasis upon restraint is to increase the number of possible contingencies which must be considered. In the bomber era there were essentially two plausible contingencies: a retaliatory strike following a first strike by the USSR, and a first strike by the United States following major aggression by the USSR in Europe. The American policy of "flexible response" and "a wider range of options" tends to offer these same choices to the USSR. Consequently, many plausible contingencies must receive at least some consideration. These include such possibilities as an attack on the United States command and control system or upon missile control centres. To many, such a possibility may well appear bizarre—the creation of a perverse and over-ingenious imagination. However, in a severe international crisis in which the fate of governments and nations would be at stake the situation might appear very differently.

It is in this context that the future of continental air defence, including Canada's Arctic warning systems must be considered. As long as the USSR continues to maintain a significant long-range bomber force, there will be a strong case for the maintenance of at least one of the northern warning systems. This will be more particularly the case as long as the United States depends to a significant extent upon a manned bomber force. One should bear in mind that although the BMEWS radars can provide warning against ICBM's they provide no warning against bombers.

There are other possible developments which might increase the military significance of Canada's northern regions. These include the development and deployment of an effective defence against missiles; the need for improved defences against missile-launching submarines operating in Canada's Arctic waters or Hudson Bay; or the need for improved defences against conventionally-armed submarines moving into the North Atlantic via the Davis Strait. All of these are contingent; they involve not one but several very large "if's."

If an effective defence against ballistic missiles were to be developed and deployed, the result might be to restore to the manned bomber its former pre-eminence as the principal nuclear delivery system. One might then see another generation of manned bombers as well as another generation of anti-bomber defences. If Western anti-submarine defences were to be improved to the extent that Soviet missile-launching submarines could not survive in the Atlantic or the Pacific, it is possible that the USSR might choose to deploy such submarines in Canada's northern waters. It might then be necessary and advisable to deploy major anti-submarine forces in these areas. In the same way, if Soviet conventionally-armed submarines were denied access to the North Atlantic by any other route, it might be desirable to deny such access via Canadian waters.

The common denominator of these possible developments is that all would involve very large increases in defence budgets, and a major increase in the proportion of gross national product devoted to defence. It is worth noticing that even if a general increase in defence budgets were to occur, programmes in the Canadian North would not appear at the top of the military shopping list. An effective defence against ballistic missiles might lead to renewed interest in defence against bombers, but first there would have to be a large investment in ballistic missile defences. In the same way, before there could be any strong case for the deployment of major anti-submarine forces in the Canadian North, there would have to be a large improvement in capabilities in the Atlantic.

It is evident therefore that the future strategic significance of Canada's northern regions depends in the first instance upon the general state of international tensions and the total size of defence budgets. Technology is an important consideration. However, there is no foreseeable development in technology which is likely to render any of the relevant military capabilities other than extremely expensive. Consequently, an increase in the strategic importance of Canada's northern regions is likely to depend, for the foreseeable future, upon a general increase in defence programmes rather than upon any specific development. For the present, such an increase in the general level of defence budgets appears improbable.

Coincident with the arrival of the ICBM era there has been a general withdrawal by the Department of National Defence from several northern activities and programmes. The icebreaker, HMCS "Labrador," was transferred to the Department of Transport. The army has turned over the North-West Highway System and the remaining stations of the North-West Territories and Yukon Radio System to civilian agencies. Responsibility for the northern test station at Fort Churchill has also passed to other government departments. This is not a matter of the abandonment of responsibilities by the Department of National Defence, but rather of their assumption by other departments and authorities. From the very outset of these activities it was recognized that responsibility should, at some point, be assumed by civilian agencies. The transference of these activities from the Defence Department is, in part, a reflection of diminished military importance and political development of the Canadian North which has occurred during the past decade.

THE ROLE OF THE CANADIAN ARCTIC IN ARMS CONTROL

Consideration of the strategic significance of the Canadian Arctic would be incomplete without some attention to its role, or potential role, in arms control and disarmament. This issue first arose in connection with President Eisenhower's "open skies" proposal in 1955. In 1957 the United States, after consultation with Canada, advanced a more specific proposal for agreed zones of mutual inspection. At this time and subsequently the Canadian government made clear its willingness to grant inspection rights over the Canadian Arctic in return for any equivalent concession by the USSR.[14] A number of suggestions have been advanced informally by individual Canadians. One such proposal is that the USSR should be allowed access to the information from the

[14]See James Eayrs, *Canada in World Affairs, 1955–57*, pp. 236–42. Statement by the Prime Minister, Hansard, 1958, vol. I, p. 37 (May 13, 1958).

Arctic warning systems in the same fashion as the United States.[15] In this way, it is argued, Canada's Arctic warning systems could serve to alleviate Soviet fears of surprise attack as well as those of Canada and the USA.

So far as is known, the USSR has never at any time shown interest in the inspection of the Canadian Arctic although in 1958 the USSR registered an objection in the Security Council to flights by the Strategic Air Command across the Arctic.[16] The explanation for this lack of interest may be the fact that the USSR is badly placed to bargain about Arctic inspection schemes. Major population centres are found much further north in the USSR than is the case in Canada. The same is true of major military bases and installations. One suspects, however, that there is a more fundamental reason—that the USSR attaches very little importance to what can be achieved through inspection of the Canadian Arctic. If so, the Soviet position is entirely understandable. At most, such inspection could provide only a few additional hours of warning against a bomber attack. If the USSR were to place any particular confidence in this warning, very expensive programmes and facilities would be required. It is relatively easy to "edit" the input to a radar scope. If the USSR were to rely on information received from radar installations in the Canadian Arctic, it would need to control the entire station including the associated communications.

Although it is not widely realized, technology, geography, and policy have combined to produce in the Canadian Arctic an area of arms limitation somewhat similar to those which have been proposed under various disarmament plans. There are no missile bases in the area, largely for reasons of policy, but also because the additional costs of Arctic construction and operation outweigh any potential gain in military capability. The only major military activities conducted in the area relate to surveillance and local defence. Installations on certain major airfields to permit their use as refuelling bases in an emergency are in the process of being dismantled, essentially for reasons of cost.

One is tempted to see in the Canadian Arctic a precedent and a prototype for schemes of arms control to be applied in other parts of the world. To argue in this way is, however, to miss the essential point. The Canadian Arctic has developed as an informal zone of arms limitation precisely because it has, in itself, little intrinsic strategic importance. It

[15]W. H. Pope, "Let the Russians Use the DEW-Line too?" *Maclean's Magazine*, 72: 10, 60–61, (Dec. 5, 1959).

[16]See Trevor Lloyd, "Open Skies in the Arctic?" *International Journal*, vol. XIV, no. 1 (winter, 1958–59), p. 42–43.

is not the focus of a major conflict of policies and interests. The barriers of climate, distance, and costs operate in many portions of the world, but it is probable that only at the two ends of the world, the Arctic and the Antarctic, that they combine so effectively. The Antarctic is, of course, already the subject of an explicit arms control agreement.[17]

CONCLUSIONS

During the past quarter century the strategic importance of Canada's northern regions has increased very markedly. This took place discontinuously and in two major increments: the war-time expansion of facilities especially in the eastern sub-Arctic, and the construction of the Arctic warning lines. An important effect of these developments was a major acceleration of northern development, most obviously in terms of facilities, but not less importantly in terms of national competence and commitment.

It is tempting to say that Canada's northern regions were of great importance to Canadian policy and to Canada's role in world affairs. This, however, is open to doubt. The growing threat from the North was undoubtedly a factor in making Canadians more rather than less conscious of Canada's international responsibilities. Nevertheless, the alliance with the United States in North America preceded the consciousness of such a threat. It is also true that the commitment to NATO was made before there was any particular awareness of a strong military threat to North America. But having said this, one must also say that Canada's northern regions have had an important bearing upon Canada's place within the general structure of Western security and in the complex relationship between the defence of Europe and the defence of North America.

What of the future? It seems evident that this will depend upon two sets of influences, political and technological. One is tempted to emphasize the role of technology, and it is true that modern technology has triumphed over geography to the extent that even the formidable terrain and climate of the Canadian Arctic no longer constitute a secure strategic barrier. But one should observe that over long periods of time technology is shaped by politics as well as the reverse. The great revolution in military technology which has altered so drastically the effective military geography of the entire world is not the result of accident. It was the product of political circumstances and of a very major commitment of

[17]See *United States Treaties and Other International Agreements*, vol. 12, part 1, 1961.

intelligence and resources. Looking towards the future, to the extent that any rational prediction is possible, it is likely that the key lies in political and economic circumstances and to a much lesser extent in technology.

For the foreseeable future, it is improbable that Canada's northern regions will ever become a great centre of industrial and political power. This means that, in the future as in the past, the strategic importance of these regions will depend upon developments outside of the region itself. The military importance of Canada's northern areas will depend upon the general pattern of international relationships.

It is possible that over the next one or two decades the strategic importance of Canada's northern regions will increase. This depends mainly upon relations between the two great military alliance systems, and, in particular, upon the military policies and defence budgets of the two super-powers. Some developments in military policy and in technology could place great emphasis upon the defence of the Canadian North. The common denominator of these developments is that they would require large increases in defence budgets. Notwithstanding the real opposition of policies and interests between the two major alliance systems, such increases appear in present circumstances to be improbable.

During the past several years there has been a downwards tendency in defence budgets of the major powers as a fraction of gross national product and trend towards limited measures of arms control. Should these trends continue it can be predicted that the strategic significance of Canada's northern regions will diminish. The effect of geography, climate and distance as a natural defence will tend to increase. The Canadian Arctic will continue to be of potential strategic significance but emphasis will be transferred to the word *potential*. We can never again revert to the complacency of 1939 but we may be less immediately conscious of a threat from the North. Should this occur, the corollary is that military programmes will be less important as a stimulus to general economic development. One can anticipate an alteration in the pattern of development. The primary stimulus to economic development will be the natural resources of the area. The primary determinant of the strategic importance of the area will tend to become the importance of these resources to the nations which depend upon them. But whatever the future may hold, one can be certain that the existence of Canada's northern regions will exercise a powerful influence upon our national character and destiny, and this will be true in the field of military policy as in other important domains of our national life.

International Scientific Relations
in the Arctic

◄ G. W. ROWLEY* ►

THE POPULATION of the North-West Territories settlement of Baker Lake in 1946 consisted of a Royal Canadian Mounted Police sergeant born in Ireland, his wife from the United States and their Canadian-born daughter, a Scottish trader from Dundee, an Anglican missionary from Wales, two Roman Catholic missionaries, one from France, the other from Belgium, and a number of Eskimos who hunted and trapped in the vicinity. There was nothing unusual about this, for no part of Canada is more international in composition. The vast expanses of the North, exaggerated on many maps owing to the common use of Mercator's projection, attract people from all lands and, although these far fields could never be described as looking green, distance certainly lends enchantment. Scientists are as susceptible as other people to the pull of the North, and for them there is the additional incentive of scientific discovery.

While the shortcomings of Mercator's projection have often been blamed for popular misconceptions of the North, it is not so generally recognized that, until this century, Mercator's projection gave a very satisfactory presentation of the polar regions. In general, travel became more difficult the higher the latitude, and for practical purposes therefore distances were longer, with the unattainable poles at infinity. It was only as man became able to travel in the far North, and particularly to fly over it, that the Arctic contracted to a finite area, and Mercator's projection became obsolete. The polar projections that have replaced

*Advisory Committee on Northern Development, Department of Northern Affairs and National Resources, Ottawa.

Mercator show how the nations are drawn together in the North and, though they are still separated by an ocean, it is small and covered for the most part by ice, ice that drifts across national boundaries and those meridians of longitude that converge at the pole, and delineate what are, to some undefined extent, sectors of influence. The Arctic Ocean has often been described as a northern Mediterranean, a picturesque term that used to be rather unrealistic but is now achieving more than just a geographical significance following the development of submarines capable of operating under the Arctic ice. The Arctic regions have in fact a degree of homogeneity and contiguity not found in zones at lower latitudes. This uniformity dwarfs the wide differences of terrain and climate that are of course found in such a large area. Many scientific problems are accordingly circumpolar in nature, require study on a circumpolar basis, and hence demand international scientific co-operation.

Geophysical research, concerned with the whole world, and with the world as a whole, is obviously a field in which all nations have an interest that cannot be restricted by national boundaries. The Arctic and Antarctic are of particular significance in geophysics owing to the presence of the magnetic, geophysical, and geographical poles. The extent of this is becoming increasingly recognized as knowledge of geophysics expands. It was in fact only as a result of the International Geophysical Year programme that the Van Allen radiation belts were discovered with their zones of minimum intensity centred on the geophysical poles. Another recent development in geophysics is the study of ionospheric phenomena at geomagnetically conjugate points in the Arctic and the Antarctic. The charged particles that follow the lines of force of the earth's magnetic field cause simultaneous aurora, absorption layers, magnetic fluctuations, and other effects that require co-ordinated observations in both polar regions. In research carried out from satellites the rotation of the earth about the geographical axis is of great importance since satellites with polar orbits would pass over the geographical poles on each circuit. Stations at high latitudes would therefore be in a very favourable position to communicate with and control them.

The scientific importance of the polar regions is by no means confined to geophysics. The extreme climate, the unequal distribution of daylight and darkness in summer and winter, and the low angle of the sun's rays have important biological effects and hence are of great interest in animal and plant physiology. Several species of fauna and flora are circumpolar in distribution and should be studied on a circumpolar basis. Some species, including most birds, migrate to the South each fall and cannot be fully studied in the Arctic alone, or the South. Conservation methods can be frustrated if in the one case they apply to one part of the Arctic alone, or in the other even if they cover the whole Arctic. Another field in which the Arctic plays a most important part is the expanding science of oceanography. The study of water masses requires a knowledge of the great ocean currents flowing into and out of the polar regions. The heat budget of the earth cannot be fully worked out from one area alone or be complete if information from one area is missing. The polar regions illustrate the conditions that existed over a much wider area during the ice ages, and form a vast natural laboratory for pleistocene research. As science develops, it is becoming more international in character. No nation can work in isolation and hope to keep in the main stream of scientific progress. It is a truism to say that science knows no frontiers. The frontiers are however there, and are certainly recognized by the politicians.

Although comparatively recent developments have emphasized the need for international scientific co-operation in the Arctic, it is not a new concept; it has a history that goes back to the time when the North was largely an unknown geographical area. Around the middle of the last century, Commander M. F. Maury of the United States Navy suggested an international approach to the scientific investigation of the unknown parts of the earth. Several years later an Austrian polar explorer and naval officer, Lt. Karl Weyprecht, drew attention to the fact that expeditions to the Arctic were bringing back little in the way of scientific results. He considered this was owing to the efforts of expeditions being concentrated on geographical discovery with no arrangements for co-ordinated and simultaneous scientific observations, and he suggested that the nations should co-operate in sending a number of expeditions to the polar regions in order to make co-ordinated meteorological and magnetic observations over a period of a year. In 1879 his proposals were discussed in Hamburg at an international conference and the delegates formed an International Polar Commission to draw up more detailed plans. The Commission met again at the Second International Polar Conference at Berne in 1880, and the third at St. Petersburg in 1881. Weyprecht died in 1881 and Professor Neumayer, Director of Deutsche Seewarte, took the leading part in making arrangements for the International Polar Year, which lasted from August 1882 to August 1883. Eleven countries[1] established twelve stations[2] in the Arctic and two in the Antarctic. Weather observations were carried out according to a common plan and magnetic and aurora data were also recorded. At

[1]Austria, Denmark, Finland, France, Germany, Great Britain, Holland, Norway, Russia, Sweden, and the USA.

[2]Three of these stations were in Canada; one was established by the United States of America at Fort Conger, Ellesmere Island; one by the United Kingdom at Fort Rae; and the third by Germany in Cumberland Sound, Baffin Island.

the Fourth and Fifth International Polar Conferences, in Vienna in 1884 and Munich in 1891, arrangements were made for publication of the twenty-seven volumes of scientific results, and the International Polar Commission was dissolved.

The idea of international co-operation in polar work was revived in 1905. In that year a number of polar explorers at a conference on world economic expansion at Mons decided to establish an International Association for the Study of Polar Regions, and on the initiative of the Belgian government an International Congress for the Study of Polar Regions met at Brussels in 1906 to consider the organization of the association in more detail. Fifteen countries[3] were officially represented at the Congress and representatives of learned societies from four others[4] also attended. An International Polar Commission was again established and its main objects were defined as establishing closer scientific relations between polar explorers, co-ordinating scientific observations and techniques, discussing the results of expeditions, and assisting polar work, particularly by indicating scientific problems. The commission was not however to carry out or patronize any expeditions, or to have any financial dealings.

In 1907 an International Polar Institute, supported entirely by Belgian government funds and concerned mainly with bibliography, was established in Brussels. The second meeting of the International Polar Commission was held in 1908, again in Brussels, and twelve countries[5] were officially represented. The commission next met in Rome in 1913. Representatives from twelve countries[6] were again present but the proceedings were very brief and interest was limited. The next meeting, planned for St. Petersburg in 1916, did not take place owing to the First World War and the commission was not revived. The International Polar Institute at Brussels also ceased to function during the war.

The years following the First World War saw the gradual recognition of the important role that aircraft would play in the polar regions and an international scientific society for the exploration of the Arctic by aircraft, *Aeroarktik*, was founded in Berlin in 1924 by Walter Bruns and Leonid Breitfuss. Two general meetings were held, one in Berlin in 1926 and the other in Leningrad in 1928, and the journal *Arktis* was

---

[3]Argentina, Belgium, Chile, Congo, Denmark, France, Germany, Italy, the Netherlands, Portugal, Rumania, Russia, Spain, Sweden, and the USA.

[4]Australia, Great Britain, Greece, and Mexico.

[5]Argentina, Australia, Belgium, Denmark, Hungary, Italy, the Netherlands, New Zealand, Rumania, Russia, Sweden, and the United States.

[6]Austria, Belgium, Chile, Denmark, Great Britain (unofficially represented by the Royal Scottish Geographical Society), Hungary, Italy, the Netherlands, Rumania, Russia, Sweden, and the United States.

published from 1928 to 1931. The society organized the Graf Zeppelin flights over parts of the Soviet Arctic in 1930, and in 1931 its membership totalled about four hundred from twenty-two countries. In the years before the Second World War *Aeroarktik* became inactive and in 1937 it ceased operations.

In 1928 Admiral H. Dominik, the Director of Deutsche Seewarte, proposed that a second International Polar Year should be held fifty years after the first. The International Meteorological Congress, which met in Copenhagen in 1929, supported the proposal and the General Assembly of the International Union of Geodesy and Geophysics held in Stockholm in 1930 also endorsed it. An International Commission for the Polar Year 1932–33 was established, Dr. D. la Cour, Director of Dansk Meteorologisk Institut, was appointed its president, and comprehensive plans were drawn up. Many of these plans, especially those for work in the Antarctic, had to be curtailed owing to the world economic crisis, but forty-four governments made appropriations, support was received from the Rockefeller Foundation, and fifteen countries[7] organized special expeditions. Altogether twenty-two expeditions were in the field during the period August 1932 to August 1933, and observations were made at many other locations so that over one hundred stations, almost all in the north, took part in the programme. As in the First International Polar Year the main emphasis was on meteorology, and magnetic and auroral data were also recorded, but the programme was broadened to include certain ionospheric studies.

In Canada the United Kingdom again despatched an expedition to Fort Rae, but the United States' plans to reoccupy Fort Conger did not materialize. The Meteorological Service of the Canadian government sent special expeditions to Chesterfield Inlet and Coppermine in the North-West Territories, extended their programme for the year at Cape Hopes Advance in northern Quebec and Meanook in northern Alberta, and made supplementary observations at a number of other meteorological stations in northern Canada.

The International Commission met after the International Polar Year had been completed and a start was made on publishing the scientific results. This work was interrupted by the Second World War, following which a Temporary Commission on the Liquidation of the Second Polar Year was appointed and a central bureau in Copenhagen set up to arrange for the completion and publication of all scientific work by the end of 1950.

The only other step taken between the two World Wars towards

[7]Austria, Canada, Denmark, Finland, France, Germany, Great Britain, Iceland, the Netherlands, Norway, Poland, Sweden, Switzerland, USSR, and the USA.

international scientific co-operation in the polar regions was by the Norwegian government. In 1938 Norway announced plans for an international exhibition of polar exploration to be held in Bergen in 1940. It was to present a general survey of polar exploration and of the physical features, natural resources, and conditions of life in the Arctic and Antarctic. The plans for the exhibition, and for a conference on polar exploration to be held in conjunction with it, were cancelled owing to the outbreak of the Second World War.

In 1950 it was proposed that a Third International Polar Year should be held, twenty-five years after the second. It became evident however that something much more comprehensive was needed and as a result the International Geophysical Year (IGY) was organized by the Comité spéciale de l'année géophysique internationale (CSAGI) under the auspices of the International Council of Scientific Unions (ICSU). This covered a wide range of geophysical interests[8] and was extended to a period of eighteen months, from July 1, 1957 to December 31, 1958.[9] It was not restricted to the polar regions, though the Arctic and especially the Antarctic were to receive special attention. The period coincided with a time of maximum sun spot activity making many of the data particularly useful. The International Geophysical Year became the most outstanding example of international co-operation in the history of science with sixty-seven nations[10] from both sides of the Iron Curtain working together in harmony.

Up to the time of the International Geophysical Year any attempt to organize polar research internationally had been short-lived. On the other hand the organization of international science according to scientific disciplines had been making rapid progress. The International Union of Geodesy and Geophysics, the World Meteorological Organization, and the International Union of Biological Sciences are typical of these agencies which now cover virtually every field of science. Polar organizations on the other hand either were for some specific objective and hence self-liquidating, or else failed for lack of interest or authority. During the present century a number of polar institutes have been established in several countries but they have been predominantly national in

[8]Meteorology, magnetism, aurora and air glow, ionosphere, solar activity, cosmic rays, latitude and longitude, glaciology, oceanography, seismology, and gravity.

[9]A modified programme was continued into 1959 and known as International Geophysical Co-operation, 1959. The International Years of the Quiet Sun cover the period January 1, 1964 to December 31, 1965 and are intended to obtain comparative data for a period of minimum sun spot activity.

[10]The only countries that were either large or of particular geophysical interest and did not take part were China, Turkey, Sudan, Libya, Iceland, Afghanistan, Iraq, and Saudi Arabia.

character. The Scott Polar Research Institute in England keeps in touch with polar work throughout the world and publishes in the Polar Record brief accounts of expeditions, other polar information of wide interest, and a selected bibliography of recent polar literature in all languages, but it does not take any other steps towards organizing polar research on an international basis. The Arctic and Antarctic Institute in Leningrad, the Arktisk Institut in Copenhagen, and the Norsk Polarinstitutt of Oslo are examples of purely national bodies. In the United States and Canada small polar institutes have been formed in a number of universities and the Arctic Institute of North America is constituted as a bi-national body with the aim of furthering the scientific study and exploration of the Arctic. Its publications include the Arctic Bibliography which provides a systematic retrospective record of significant works, again in any language, which have resulted from the exploration and scientific investigation of northern regions. The institutes correspond with one another and occasionally hold meetings, sometimes general in nature, sometimes dealing with particular topics, in which nations of other countries may be invited to participate. In northern Scandinavia, Greenland, northern Canada, and Alaska, scientists from other Western countries are welcomed and frequently assisted in carrying out their work. This is usually arranged however separately for each individual or party on a bilateral basis and no institute has any recognized responsibility for co-ordinating polar research on an international scale.

The evolution of the International Polar Years into the International Geophysical Year fell into this general pattern of organizing international science by scientific field rather than by geographical areas. It appeared in fact to herald the end of the concept of an international scientific organization exclusively polar in nature. In this case however the phoenix arose from its ashes.

In December 1956 the United States National Committee for the International Geophysical Year proposed to CSAGI that the IGY Antarctic programme should be continued for an additional year in order to realize the full scientific benefit from the large investment in stations and equipment made by the twelve nations[11] participating in the programme. The proposal was approved at the fourth CSAGI Conference in June 1957 and a recommendation was submitted to the ICSU Executive Board that a committee should be set up to examine the merits of further general scientific investigations in Antarctica. The ICSU Board approved the creation of an *ad hoc* committee which met in Stockholm

[11]Argentina, Australia, Belgium, Chile, France, Japan, New Zealand, Norway, South Africa, United Kingdom, USA, and the USSR.

in 1957. This committee resolved that there was a need for further international organization of scientific activity in Antarctica and recommended that ICSU should establish a Special Committee on Antarctic Research[12] (SCAR) to undertake this task. It also resolved that the continuation of scientific activity in Antarctic research should be regarded as being inspired by the interest roused by the activities of the IGY but in no way as an extension of the IGY.

The Antarctic was not a promising area for any sort of international co-operation. Several nations claimed sectors of the continent and some of these claims overlapped. Other nations with an active interest in Antarctica made no territorial claims on their own account, but did not recognize any of the claims made by others. At the time of the IGY the only international agreement covering the area was a tripartite naval declaration between the UK, Argentina, and Chile, renewed annually, that they could foresee no need to send warships south of 60° S, apart from customary movements in support of scientific expeditions. This in itself was a convincing illustration of the difficulty of the political situation there.

The Special Committee on Antarctic Research was organized early in 1958 and was constituted as a special committee of ICSU, charged with furthering co-ordination of scientific activities in Antarctica with a view to framing a scientific programme of circumpolar scope and significance. Membership was limited to delegates from each country actively engaged in Antarctic research,[13] representatives of those international scientific unions federated in ICSU which had indicated their interest in Antarctic research, and observers who might be invited from other international organizations and special committees of ICSU. The first meeting of SCAR was at The Hague in February 1958 and the second in Moscow in August of the same year. Since then meetings have been held every year; in Canberra, March 1959, Cambridge, August 1960, Wellington, October 1961, Boulder, October 1962, and Cape Town, September 1963.

The position of SCAR was greatly strengthened as a result of the signing on December 1, 1959 of the Antarctic Treaty. The signatories to this treaty were the twelve nations represented on SCAR and the preamble acknowledges "the substantial contributions to scientific knowledge resulting from international co-operation in scientific investigations in Antarctica," and expresses conviction "that the establishment of a firm foundation for the continuation and development of such co-opera-

---

[12]The name was changed in 1961 to Scientific Committee on Antarctic Research (the initials remaining the same).

[13]These were the same twelve countries who had had IGY programmes there.

tion on the basis of freedom of scientific investigation in Antarctica as applied during the International Geophysical Year accords with the interests of science and the progress of all mankind." Article II of the treaty assures the continuation of freedom of scientific investigation in Antarctica:

Freedom of scientific investigation in Antarctica and co-operation toward that end, as applied during the International Geophysical Year, shall continue, subject to the provisions of the present Treaty.

Article III deals with the exchange of information on scientific plans, scientific personnel, and scientific observations and results:

1. In order to promote international co-operation in scientific investigation in Antarctica, as provided for in Article II of the present Treaty, the Contracting Parties agree that, to the greatest extent feasible and practicable:

(a) information regarding plans for scientific programmes in Antarctica shall be exchanged to permit maximum economy and efficiency of operations;

(b) scientific personnel shall be exchanged in Antarctica between expeditions and stations;

(c) scientific observations and results from Antarctica shall be exchanged and made freely available.

2. In implementing this Article, every encouragement shall be given to the establishment of co-operative working relations with those Specialized Agencies of the United Nations and other international organizations having a scientific or technical interest in Antarctica.

Article IX makes arrangements for consultation:

1. Representatives of the Contracting Parties named in the preamble to the present Treaty shall meet at the City of Canberra within two months after the date of entry into force of the Treaty, and thereafter at suitable intervals and places, for the purpose of exchanging information, consulting together on matters of common interest pertaining to Antarctica, and formulating and considering, and recommending to their Governments, measures in furtherance of the principles and objectives of the Treaty, including measures regarding:

(a) use of Antarctica for peaceful purposes only;

(b) facilitation of scientific research in Antarctica;

(c) facilitation of international scientific co-operation in Antarctica;

(d) facilitation of the exercise of the rights of inspection provided for in Article VII of the Treaty;

(e) questions relating to the exercise of jurisdiction in Antarctica;

(f) preservation and conservation of living resources in Antarctica.

2. Each Contracting Party which has become a party to the present Treaty by accession under Article XIII shall be entitled to appoint representatives to participate in the meetings referred to in paragraph 1 of the present Article, during such time as that Contracting Party demonstrates its interest in Antarctica by conducting substantial scientific research activity there, such as the establishment of a scientific station or the despatch of a scientific expedition.

3. Reports from the observers referred to in Article VII of the present Treaty shall be transmitted to the representatives of the Contracting Parties participating in the meetings referred to in paragraph 1 of the present Article.

4. The measures referred to in paragraph 1 of this Article shall become effective when approved by all the Contracting Parties whose representatives were entitled to participate in the meetings held to consider those measures.

5. Any or all of the rights established in the present Treaty may be exercised as from the date of entry into force of the Treaty whether or not any measures facilitating the exercise of such rights have been proposed, considered or approved as provided in this Article.

Other articles allow the use of military personnel or equipment for scientific research and define the area to which the treaty applies as the area south of 60° S, including all ice shelves but excluding any rights on the high seas. Provision is also made for other countries to accede to the treaty, with the consent of all contracting parties whose representatives are entitled to attend the meetings provided for under Article IX. At the first Antarctic Treaty Consultative Meeting, held in Canberra in July 1961, it was agreed that

the representatives recommend to their governments that they should facilitate the continuation of the exchange of information regarding plans for scientific programmes as now carried on through the Special Committee on Antarctic Research (SCAR) (now the Scientific Committee on Antarctic Research) and through other member unions and committees of the International Council of Scientific Unions (ICSU) and by such other means as may ensure the availability of this information

and that

the representatives recommend to their governments that they should promote the continuation of the exchange, on a basis of bilateral arrangements, of scientific personnel amongst their expeditions, and should make available such of their facilities as may be helpful to this purpose.

During its first six years SCAR has made very great progress. Relations have been established with other scientific bodies interested in Antarctic research, and permanent working groups have been set up covering various subjects.[14] A comprehensive plan for the scientific exploration of Antarctica has been prepared and kept revised, the plans and accomplishments of national expeditions have been reported to the committee, and regular bulletins have been published. Symposia on a number of subjects of Antarctic interest have been organized, either by SCAR alone or jointly with other scientific bodies. Several measures to

[14]These are biology, communications, geodesy and cartography, geology, geomagnetism, glaciology, logistics, meteorology, oceanography, solid earth geophysics, and upper atmosphere physics.

standardize observations and procedures, such as the adoption of common symbols on maps, have been agreed. A particularly encouraging development is co-operation in the scientific work itself. There is a regular exchange of scientists between different Antarctic countries and a close working relationship in certain projects, an example being the data recorded at the Russian station of Vostok as part of a United States investigation of ionospheric conditions. Implementation of the recommendations of SCAR is effected through the national Antarctic committees which have now been established by each of the twelve Antarctic powers.

To an increasing extent SCAR and its working groups are providing a means for most of the world's polar scientists to meet and exchange their views. One result of the success of SCAR is that it is becoming in effect an important agency for the discussion and informal co-ordination, not only of Antarctic research, but also to some extent of polar research in general. This can become a matter of real concern to Canada, which has a vital interest in polar research but is not eligible for representation on SCAR. Receiving the results of Antarctic research cannot compensate for being excluded from the meetings where the plans, techniques, and observations are discussed, especially as these may affect the North as well as the South.

The constitution of SCAR provides for membership by any country actively engaged in Antarctic research but it does not define the meaning of "actively engaged." A few years ago Poland was planning to send an expedition to the Antarctic, and SCAR agreed at that time to admit Poland to membership as from the date of disembarkation of their wintering party on the Antarctic continent. In the Netherlands a National Committee for Antarctic Research has been established and four Dutch scientists are participating in a Belgian expedition, but it is not clear whether this will be considered by SCAR to be a sufficient qualification for membership. Canada could become eligible by sending an expedition to the Antarctic but this is a stiff entrance fee for a country whose scientists are, and should be, more concerned with the Arctic. It would however confer the right to attend the Antarctic Treaty Consultative Meetings provided Canada also acceded to the Antarctic Treaty.

A serious problem is, in fact, developing owing to the exclusiveness of SCAR. Canada is most affected, but it must be of concern to other countries who are not members of SCAR, especially Iceland, Denmark, Sweden, and Finland which all have a particular interest in Arctic research. One possible course would be the establishment of a scientific committee on Arctic research, parallel to that on Antarctic research and limited either to countries with Arctic territory or to those actively engaged in northern research. It might be argued that a special committee on Arctic research is unnecessary and that the Arctic, unlike the Antarctic, has reached the stage of development where no special measures are necessary and scientific co-operation should be left to existing international scientific organizations. It is difficult to sustain this argument when the present close scientific co-operation in the Antarctic is contrasted with the situation in the Arctic. For nearly thirty years, the Soviet Arctic has been a closed book, and no scientists from the West have visited any part other than the Murmansk area. Until recently no detailed information has been published on the progress of Soviet science in the North. Only two Soviet scientists have been in the Canadian North; Professor B. A. Tikhomirov of the Botanical Institute of the Academy of Sciences, who was a member of a group that visited Great Whale River, Knob Lake, Frobisher Bay, Resolute, Cambridge Bay, and Coral Harbour in August 1959 following the Ninth International Botanical Congress in Montreal; and Professor P. A. Shumskiy of the Committee for Antarctic Research of the Academy of Sciences who, at the invitation of the Canadian government, spent a few days with the Polar Continental Shelf Project in the Queen Elizabeth Islands in September 1963. Scientists in both the East and West frankly admit their ignorance of what is going on in the other half of the Arctic, and regret that they are not able to learn from one another.[15]

The situation, both geographically and politically, is of course very different in the Arctic from that in the Antarctic. One is a central ocean almost surrounded by land, and the other a central continent surrounded by ocean. In one there are no current problems of sovereignty over the land areas, in the other there are conflicting claims. One lies between the main world powers, the other is far from their borders and vital interests. The political difficulties facing scientific co-operation in the North spring from much the same factors that make scientific co-operation there so desirable. Because the nations are drawn together geographically in the north they are apprehensive of one another. Since the

[15]More recently a closer relationship has been developed between Canada and the Soviet Union in northern matters. In May and June, 1965, the Canadian Minister of Northern Affairs and National Resources led a small delegation, in which the writer was very fortunate to be included, to the USSR, where visits were made to Irkutsk, Bratsk, Yakutsk, Khandyga, Dzhebariki Khaya, and Norilsk in Siberia, and to Syktyvkar in the European North. Later in the year a return delegation headed by a member of the Council of Ministers of the Soviet Union, and including Professor P. I. Melnikov, Director of the Permafrost Institute at Yakutsk, and other scientists, came to Canada. They visited Schefferville, Churchill, Fort Smith, Pine Point, Hay River, Yellowknife, Inuvik, Whitehorse, and Elsa, as well as places farther south. It appeared that both countries considered these visits would open the way for closer co-operation in Arctic research, including exchanges of northern scientists and specialists.

North is a comparatively unknown area, the nations seek to keep secret any knowledge they gain that might be useful to defence, and especially to conceal any military measures they have taken. Defence activities are more obvious in the North than elsewhere for there is little to hide them. At the same time means of transportation are few and easily controlled and it is comparatively simple to protect security by denying access. In cases of doubt, security authorities the world over hold the view that it is better to be safe than sorry. Even where there is nothing to hide, security remains a problem because of the intelligence value of negative information—"Ye are spies; to see the nakedness of the land, ye are come." (Genesis 42 : 9). Nevertheless, the political situation is improving and suggestions for co-operation in Arctic research have a much better chance of being accepted and implemented now than they had a few years ago. It would be over-optimistic to expect the political difficulties that face international scientific relationships in the North to melt away completely in the general thaw of East-West relations. A scientific committee on Arctic research would however be in a far better position to develop principles for scientific co-operation in the North than a number of international scientific organizations concerned with different scientific fields and acting independently. The representatives on such a committee would also be able to recommend to their own governments general policies on scientific co-operation based on these principles.

The pattern of co-operation in the Arctic would necessarily be different from that in the Antarctic. With no unresolved questions on sovereignty except possibly in the Polar Basin there would be no immediate problems of jurisdiction. Scientific expeditions in the north would continue to require the consent of the "host" country. Owing to the comparative accessibility of the Arctic there would be no need for the establishment of major bases or for the large scale use of military resources to support scientific work. In any event the political sensitivity of the area would argue against the employment of significant military resources on scientific work especially outside their own country. Co-operation would lie rather in the co-ordination of scientific programmes and observations, the exchange of scientists to work in scientific laboratories or with expeditions, the joint development of special techniques and equipment, and the sharing of the results of research. One question that arises is the extent to which a scientific committee on Arctic research could be effective without the support of an Arctic treaty. The Scientific Committee on Antarctic Research however antedated the Antarctic Treaty and provides a precedent for international scientific co-operation being established in the absence of a political agreement.

Another possible development would be to broaden the terms of reference of SCAR and to amend its constitution to cover the Arctic as well as the Antarctic. It could become in effect the scientific committee on polar research. So many of the scientific problems of the two areas are parallel or related, so many of the techniques are similar, and so often are the same scientists involved, that this proposal has much to recommend it. There are of course a number of matters pertaining to Antarctic scientific research that are of concern only to the nations actively engaged there; these lie mainly in the fields of administration, communications, and logistics. In the same way there are other matters of interest only to those working in the Arctic. These could be handled by special working groups, one for the Arctic and one for the Antarctic, but both within the framework of the scientific committee on polar research. Some countries already follow much the same pattern in their internal organization, committing both Arctic and Antarctic matters to a single body. A Scientific Committee on Polar Research under the auspices of the ICSU, would both resolve the difficulties arising from the limited membership of SCAR and also provide machinery for the close co-ordination of Arctic and Antarctic research.

Canada has a large area of Arctic territory and a comparatively small population to explore and exploit it. It is therefore very much in her interest to encourage international scientific co-operation in the north. There is at present no Canadian government committee on Arctic research with terms of reference comparable to those of the Antarctic committees of the Antarctic Treaty powers. The Advisory Committee on Northern Development, however, is responsible for advising the Canadian government on questions of policy relating to northern Canada and providing for the effective co-ordination of all government activities there. The Scientific Research Sub-Committee of the Advisory Committee has representatives of the government departments concerned with northern research and indeed performs many, if not all, the functions that would be carried out by a national committee on Arctic research.

At the present time the improved political relations, the example of the Antarctic, and the rapid pace of scientific development all argue strongly for devising machinery to ensure close and continuing co-operation in northern research. Science must learn a lesson from geography where the terms east and west lose their normal significance at the North Pole. It remains for some country to take the initiative in putting forward definite proposals, and there is no country better placed to play this role than Canada.

The International Implications
of Arctic Exploitation

◄ GEORGE W. ROGERS* ►

ANYTHING written on the Arctic comes out as a strange mixture of
realism and fantasy, be it the memoirs of explorers or the objective
observations of scientific investigations. The element of fantasy may be
introduced consciously to express the writer's emotional experience or
vision, but more often it is indicative of the limits of fact and the uncertainties of the writer faced with his imperfectly understood environment.
If we are to make anything of our handful of Arctic knowledge we must
fill in the empty space with our imaginations.

When we project our fragmentary knowledge of the Arctic into the
future, as must be done in this essay, the element of fantasy becomes
almost overwhelming. This is unavoidable but it need not lead to silly
speculation if our exercise of imagination is rooted in reality. When
Nansen made his 1913 trip through Siberia the feasibility of regular sea
traffic in the Kara Sea appeared to depend upon the fantasy of flying
machines capable of guiding surface navigation by scouting ice-condi-
tions ahead, and Stefansson's more ambitious projection of the Arctic
Basin as the Mediterranean of the future was based upon the Jules
Verne fantasy of undersea craft as well as of aircraft capable of non-
stop trips between the continents that ring the Basin. Such devices were
four or five decades in the future at the time, but their ancestors existed
in the fabric and wood aeroplanes and submergible U-boats of World
War I and technological progress in time transformed these former
fantasies into realism.

*College of Business, Economics and Government, University of Alaska,
Juneau.

The last word in the title of this chapter is intended to indicate the direction I believe our imaginations must take when making a contemporary appraisal of the future of the Arctic. The choice of the word "exploitation," with its sometimes unpleasant associations, rather than the more pleasing conceit of "development," was deliberate. "Development" connotes population growth and stability, combined with balanced and optimum use of all natural resources. The use of this term in connection with the Arctic, however, has led to some bad fantasies.

Immediately after World War II we were regaled with stories about Soviet colonization of the Arctic, of small settlements growing into cities of thousands and tens of thousands in the space of a decade. There was confusion or carelessness in the use of the term "Arctic," though this passed unnoticed. Soviet agriculture was pictured as pushing out to the northern limits of land. As evidence of this former United States Secretary of Agriculture Henry Wallace brought some new "Arctic" cereals and grains to the University of Alaska upon his return from a goodwill visit to Russia.

This challenge did not go unheeded in North America. One official United States response was a 1952 report of the US Bureau of Reclamation on the development potential of Alaska. Noting what was allegedly being done in the Old World, the report replied: "However, it does not necessarily follow that American methods and ingenuity will be less effective in subjugating Arctic lands to agricultural use than those of other countries. The United States takes a second place to none in the effective economic use of land on the 'dry' margin of land development. There is no reason why it should be less effective on the 'cold' margin."[1] With the aid of a hopeful if unrealistic and confused analogy between population densities in Norway, Finland, and Sweden, and land area in Alaska, it was concluded that in place of the 1950 population of 128,643 persons "it is not unlikely that Alaska ultimately will have 10 million inhabitants." How much of this population would be located in the Arctic is not indicated, but the "subjugating [of] Arctic lands to agricultural use" implies something in proportion to land area. The pace of such development was suggested in a statement that "present population will increase tenfold within a decade" with the development of potential hydroelectric power.[2]

Though we still hear echoes of this early belief that anything is pos-

---

[1]U.S. Department of the Interior, *Alaska: A Reconnaissance Report on the Potential Development of Water Resources in the Territory of Alaska*, House Document 197, 82nd Congress, First Session, January, 1952, p. 109.
[2]*Ibid.*, p. 85.

sible in the Arctic, including settlement and balanced development, some of the "true believers" have become skeptics and the official tone is generally more cautious and qualified. The necessities of military and air transport have forced us to intensify our efforts to get acquainted with the Arctic, continuously pushing realism derived from new knowledge into areas we formerly filled with fantasy. And there appears to be a change in the Soviet tone too, a lessening of the note of urgency of the 1930's and 1940's to get into the Arctic and get out what it had to provide on a forced basis. There may be a correlation here with recent Soviet willingness to turn to normal world trade channels in meeting material requirements. A recent appraisal by Soviet geographers and regional planners on the type of industrial development they consider possible in their northern regions suggests a more sober current assessment.

Northern Industry. The complexes of this type are located in the forest and even tundra zones of the northern regions. The population here as a rule, is sparse owing to the difficult climatic conditions. Under the conditions governing the conquest of territory, only the selective method of developing lands by separate oases and areas is possible, as a rule. It is often necessary to rely not only on permanent cadres of local population, but also on the periodic importation (for definite terms) of labor force from other, more southerly regions of the country. The principal aim of creating a complex is the working of especially valuable mineral resources, forests, and the wealth of fish and other sea animals. Modern technology and economics permit the development of this northern wealth through especially high mechanization of the processes and the shifting of the processes to such forms of energy as water and oil power, which make it possible to reduce sharply the expenditure of live labor. . . .[3]

This is not a down-grading of the potential importance of northern resources in the total economy of the USSR. It is a clear statement of what now must be considered to be the best way of realizing this potential. That way is exploitation, not development. Exploitation will cause population changes, but this will be minimized through use of seasonal and/or transient labour forces and labour-saving devices. The exploitation will be selective, taking only the "especially valuable" resources available. Totally absent is any notion that these activities will cause or should cause any large migration into the sparsely settled northern lands. The basic purpose is to meet raw materials requirements

[3]N. N. Kolosovskiy, "The Territorial-Production Combination (Complex) in Soviet Geography," *Journal of Regional Science*, vol. 3, no. 1 (summer, 1961) (Philadelphia), p. 24. This article was translated and edited to conform to journal space limitations from *Principles of Economic Regionalization* (*Osnovy Ekonomicheskogo Rayonirovaniya*) (Moscow, 1958).

that cannot be met more readily from other sources, not to foster settlement for the sake of filling up empty spaces or proving that it can be done. Abstracting military activities and settlement from the whole Arctic, the quoted statement is an excellent generalization of what has been going on or is going on wherever man has gone into the Arctic. Coming as it does from the nation with the longest and most intensive interest in the Arctic, it provides a key guide to our speculations on the future.

The nature and timing of resource exploitation in the Arctic will be determined by knowledge of resource availability and the ability of these resources to enter world markets in competition with resources from other sources of supply—in short, knowledge and effective economic demand. Exploitation to meet local (Arctic) requirements has been and will continue to be minor. Exploitation will therefore be for export from the Arctic to markets elsewhere in the world. This process will have important international implications. How important and what kind? Perspective can be acquired here by considering the major causes of past international interest in the Arctic.[4]

Prehistoric population movements around the Arctic Basin or between continents which touched it extended over vast periods of time in response to population pressures and climate changes which such a time-scale permitted. Beyond this we can make only the wildest guesses as to why early man entered these regions. Whatever the reasons, the spherical shape of the earth and the location and form of its main land masses resulted in these northern routes being reasonably sure means for primitive man, moving by foot on land or in small open craft on the sea, to hop from continent to continent.

The Arctic and sub-Arctic remain among the least densely inhabited regions of the earth. There is very little to recommend them to the majority of mankind as desirable places to live. Any northward direction of historic man's attentions must be sought not in things within the Arctic, but in the outside economic, political, and social conditions of particular times and places.

One such period was the Renaissance, that age of discovery and adventure when mediaeval man was transformed and became a transformer, seeking to break out of the enclosed universe which held him within well-defined limits. Possessed of the concept of the world as a

[4]An excellent treatment of polar exploration in its full historical and social context which attempts to analyze and appraise the economic, strategic, personal and political motives and impulses which gave rise to man's interest in the polar regions is given in L. P. Kirwan, *A History of Polar Exploration* (Penguin Books, 1962; originally published as *The White Road*, 1959).

globe, and anxious to expand and improve commerce with "fabled Cathay" on the other side of the world, he logically looked north in his search for the shortest way to the Far East.

In 1496 John Cabot received a commission from Henry VII to search out the North-West Passage to Cathay and India across the top of the North American continent, and this set in motion a search which has continued down to our own period. The search for the North-East Passage was launched in 1553 by Sir Hugh Willoughby, Captain Richard Chancellor, and Cornelius Durfourth. Their initial attempt did not succeed, but two years later the Muscovy Company was chartered "for the discovery of regions, dominions, islands, and places unknown" and, more importantly, for the establishment of a flourishing trade between England and the Great Muscovite Empire. Similarly, the first period of search for the North-West Passage culminated in 1670 with the chartering of the "Governor and Company of Adventurers of England Trading into Hudson's Bay" and the grant to it of extraordinarily sweeping privileges and powers.

Voyages of discovery continued, but the original dream of feasible northern routes for broad and thriving commerce between Western Europe and the Far East dropped from the popular mind. The practical men of commerce who had initially sparked the search turned to the more round-about east–west routes for the conduct of their trade, having to content themselves with the half-loaf of the great circle routes of the North Pacific and Atlantic. Realization of the original dream was thwarted by the hard facts of land-form, sea ice, and climate, and the limitations of a transport technology based upon wooden ships and sail.

Although commercial motivations for continued probes around or across the top of the world were to decline, exploration for its own sake went on. The men who lead and supported these expeditions were the products of other eras in Western civilization, as were the aims and motivations of their efforts. The earlier age of discovery had only revealed the outlines of scattered fragments of the earth's surface, and men of the seventeenth and eighteenth centuries wished for more than quaint renderings of mermaids and land monsters to fill in the blank spaces on their maps. There was much to know, not only about the configuration of land and sea masses, but about their nature as well.

This urge to know however was not limited to a desire for knowledge for its own sake. These were times of intense national rivalries for territories and trade, and the race to lay claim to new empire or to establish clear boundaries and "prove up" on existing claims provided strong military and economic motivations. There appeared on the scene of polar exploration the pioneer naturalists, botanists, oceanographers, cartographers, and other scientific investigators, generally as members of or supported by naval units. The Great Northern Expedition to Arctic Russia (1725–42), broadly co-ordinated under the Admiralty College, determined the extent of Russia's Siberian empire, traced the general outlines of its Arctic coastline, discovered the Aleutian Island and the Alaska mainland, and laid claim to the northwest corner of the North American continent. Captain James Cook charted the coast of Alaska from Icy Cape southward and positively concluded that Bering Strait separated North America and Asia (1778). On the North American side of the Arctic, the explorations of Samuel Hearne (1770–72) and Alexander MacKenzie (1789) filled in blank spaces on the map and added to knowledge.

The strategic importance of the Arctic and sub-Arctic lands around the Polar Basin had been recognized for many years. This partly explained British and United States naval interest in renewed exploration during the nineteenth century. It also prompted President Andrew Johnson's Secretary of State, Seward, to engineer the purchase of Alaska from Russia in 1867. (It was a negative defence consideration—recognition of inability to hold its North American possessions—which caused Russia to encourage the sale.) Seward's broad plans for national security (frustrated by lack of popular understanding) included the purchase of Iceland and Greenland from Denmark. Although his defence plans took the Arctic into consideration, his concepts of geography and strategy were essentially oceanic rather than polar, and they aimed at giving the United States dominance over the Atlantic and Pacific. The physical aspects of the Arctic ocean in relation to the then technology of warfare necessarily limited the reach of his strategic planning in relation to the whole Arctic area.

Man now overcomes the physical barriers of the earth's surface by using aircraft, and the aeroplane very early in its career (immediately following World War I) was pressed into service in Arctic exploration. The first successful non-stop flights from eastern Europe to the United States by Soviet fliers in 1937 foretold what is now common-place, namely, the regular trans-polar commercial flights of giant jets between Europe and the Orient and North America. As regards passenger travel and the transport of high value freight, the long-sought shortest route between East and West via the North is now an economic as well as physical reality. But far overshadowing the commercial significance of these advances have been military considerations, which have given the Arctic much of its recent international significance. With long-range jet bombers, land-based ICBM's or submarine-launched Polaris missiles as the weapons of modern warfare, and the geographic array of the world's principal military powers around the Arctic Basin, frantic activities have been going on throughout the Arctic and sub-Arctic over the past two decades.

Quests for shorter trade routes, increased knowledge of the earth, and national security will continue to be part of international interest in the Arctic. The earth is, after all, as spherical as it was in the days of Cabot and, to our knowledge, the land forms have not significantly shifted their locations, sizes, or shapes, although climate has changed. Over the intervening centuries man has developed new patterns of use and occupancy of the earth's surface. Nine-tenths of the earth's population today is to be found in the northern hemisphere and, with the exception of China and India, the capitals of all major military and industrially developed nations are closer to the Arctic Circle than they are to the Equator.

Natural resource exploitation has also played a role in the international significance of the Arctic, as the formation of the great trading companies of the past testifies. Hard on the heels of Hudson's explorations came the whalers; and for generations the northern seas served as major sources of whale oil and by-products, until the resource was exhausted by ruthless and unregulated exploitation, aided in its final stages by improved technology. Hunters and trappers moved across the Arctic and sub-Arctic and private fortunes were built upon the rich harvest of furs. From the beginning and continuing to this day, northern waters have been a major source of fisheries production. Of the nonrenewable resources of the land, gold was an early attraction and until recently it served as one of the main props in the northern economies of Siberia, Canada, and Alaska. Until recently, however, this process of exploitation has been sporadic, narrowly specialized, and often ruthless. Although part of the total interest in the Arctic, natural resources never comprised more than a small part of the region's broad importance to the rest of the world. Man's present patterns of population concentration and his economic progress alone should have affected the international importance of the Arctic. But it has been modern technology that has made possible the old dream of sailing from east to west and from west to east around the brim of the Arctic Basin as well as the added dividend of flying across or travelling under the ice from one side to the other. Transportation technology and world population changes, moreover, have caused Arctic natural resource potentials to take on new international significance. The passage of time alone has been or will be a factor causing the richer or more accessible resources of the world to be worked out. It has increased the pressure for the development of more and more of these northern resources. But if the resources themselves have become more accessible through new modes of transportation and new trade routes, the rate of increase in their real economic value has been speeded up correspondingly. Today mankind is entering a new and different age which could modify the international significance of the Arctic through greater emphasis upon its natural resource potentials.

We must now construct a context in which to view the Arctic and its international role in the future. The elements present in past eras will continue to be present in varying proportions in the years ahead. World population growth will go on, accompanied by continuing international competition and conflict short of total war. We have no certainty for this last assumption, but it must be made. If competition and conflict are not kept within reasonable bounds there will be no future worth mentioning. Looking at the world and mankind as a whole (after brushing aside the surface chaos of national rivalries) we find that we are today and will be increasingly in the future engaged in a race between world population growth and natural resource development, and that, at the same time, we must attempt to reverse trends widening the gap between living standards in the poor and rich nations. On the outcome rests the future of civilized life on this planet.

There have been many constructions of the future. Avoiding the wilder fantasies, and limiting consideration to projections of past statistical trends, there is an area of agreement or near agreement in most of these studies. This starts with the fact that world population has increased progressively in recent centuries, and it adopts the assumption that the increase will probably continue at a declining rate in the future. Beginning with an estimated population of a quarter of a billion at the beginning of the Christian era, it took 1,650 years to double this number to one-half billion. The doubling periods then occurred with startling rapidity: two hundred years to double to one billion; eighty years from one to two billion; and it probably will take only forty-five years to increase to four billion by 1975. A levelling off of the growth rate is expected to take place about and after the year 1980, on the assumption that some population control methods and practices will have found more general acceptance. Even so, world population is expected to reach somewhere between five and seven billion by the year 2000.[5]

[5]President's Committee on Natural Resources, *Natural Resources, A Summary Report*, Publication No. 1000; and *Social and Economic Aspects of Natural Resources*, Publication No. 1000-G, National Academy of Sciences-National Research Council (Washington, 1962). The year 2000 projections are the United Nations' high and low estimates in *Future Growth of World Population* (1958).

World-wide natural resource demand will continue to grow not only as a result of this unprecedented population growth but also as a result of increasing per capita demand. The aspirations of the low income nations of Asia, Africa, and South America, whose people will comprise an estimated three-quarters of the world's population by the year 2000, and their need for rapid industrialization and for more and better food, housing, and clothing will accelerate this already growing demand.

The translation of these expectations into specifics has been attempted in a number of studies. One recently published by Resources for the Future, Inc., avoids the equally unlikely extremes of the neo-Malthusian's dismal prophesies and the technologist's future Golden Age. On the basis of population and economic trends during the past decade— especially where reliable statistics are available—and assuming a population of nearly seven billion by 2000 and per capita resource demands at levels now found in the more developed places, the following very tentative views were advanced as representing the general magnitude of increases which will be required to meet world-wide demands for resources: (i) a tripling of aggregate food output just to provide adequate calories, and considerably more to provide adequate proteins and vitamins; (ii) a fivefold increase in energy output; (iii) perhaps a fivefold increase in output of iron ore and ferro alloys, and somewhat less in copper, but a much larger increase in bauxite-aluminum, (iv) a possible quadrupling of lumber output.[6]

In this context of rising resource demand curves, it can be expected that all known Arctic natural resources will be given greater consideration and possibly achieve greater eventual development than in the past. It is also reasonable to assume that new and possibly more favourable discoveries will be made under the stimulus of these population-induced resource pressures. But the future development of the Arctic will still be an extension of its past development, which was influenced by the physical limitations of the resource base and the limited extent to which its products could be made competitive in world markets. Of the four general categories of resources summarized, the Arctic could at most contribute to world needs in only two. By definition these regions would not contribute to the lumber output; and, by their physical nature, they are hard put to it today to make any significant contribution toward meeting their own food requirements. The North American Arctic, even at its present low level of settlement, probably imports 90 per cent or

[6]Joseph L. Fisher and Neal Potter, *World Prospects for Natural Resources: Some Projections of Demand and Indicators of Supply to the Year 2000* (Baltimore, 1964), p. 51.

more of its food. Food production undoubtedly could be increased if we accept the views of the more ardent advocates of the "friendly Arctic" and some of the more enthusiastic reports from the Soviet Arctic. Despite greater efforts to improve the output of reindeer herding and to extend cereal and vegetable cultivation ever northward, the Arctic regions of the USSR probably still import more than three-quarters of their food requirements. It should therefore be anticipated that the increased development of the Arctic regions will act as a drain on food supplies, rather than contributing food for consumption elsewhere.

The Arctic's contribution to the world's mineral and energy needs will be determined by the extent to which the more accessible sources of world supply become depleted and the extent to which products based upon Arctic resources can be made competitive in world markets. Looking first at the minerals identified in the year 2000 projections, the largest world-wide demand increase appears to be for iron ore. Northern Norway is already making a contribution to meeting Western Europe's iron requirements. There is ample evidence of the existence of other potentially large deposits of iron of varying grades throughout the Arctic and the sub-Arctic. Within the State of Alaska, for example, high hopes for the development of pig iron and steel output in the next twenty to thirty years have been based upon the rather fragmentary present knowledge of iron deposits and occurrences.[7] Although made by reputable private consulting firms, these projections ignore or minimize economic factors of high labour costs, remoteness from markets and relative inaccessibility of some of the ore occurrences, and the generally low grade of known deposits, as well as their troublesome titanium content. Although it is technically feasible to up-grade the titaniferous magnitite from these deposits sufficiently to permit processing in electric furnaces, to do so imposes a further competitive handicap. There are better sources to be found in Alaska and elsewhere throughout the Arctic but, once again, their competitive position will be narrowed by costs and by extensive world reserves of much higher grade direct-shipping ore.[8] Resources for the Future, Inc., estimates that world reserves of high grade ore will be twice the projected world demand for the year

[7]Battelle Memorial Institute, *Integrated Transport System to Encourage Economic Development of Northwest North America*, U.S. House Document No. 176, 87th Congress, 1st Session (May 25, 1961); Development and Resources Corporation, *The Market for Rampart Power*, Committee Print, U.S. Senate, 87th Congress, 2d Session (April 23, 1962)

[8]Similar prospects that exploitation will not take place in the "foreseeable future" are reported in regard to "rich deposits of iron ore" in the Siberian north, Samuel V. Slavin, "Economic Development of the Siberian North", *Arctic*, June 1964, pp. 104–108.

2000, not considering the rate at which new deposits in areas previously classified as inaccessible are being opened up. This study characterizes the future as "one of abundance" as regards iron ore "without even speculating on ore that needs beneficiation."[9]

Sometime well beyond the year 2000 there will be need to go into lower grade ores on a large scale and into less accessible reserves. In the next century further and major development of the iron ore reserves in the Arctic, therefore, can be reasonably anticipated. But with the flexibility provided by use of scrap and substitution of other metals in meeting demands, there are no foreseeable world shortages which would give any major Arctic exploitation critical international implications. This flexibility in meeting supply together with the existence of huge reserves elsewhere will cause such Arctic development to be merely another phase in a long-range process extending over centuries of time. An earlier appraisal of adequacy of world iron reserves, for example, concluded that with present technology and production at the 1956 world rates, the then estimated exploitable reserves would last for another 250 years.[10] Since 1956 estimates of world reserves of "shipping grade iron ore" have been increased substantially, but this would be off-set, of course, by the projected five-fold increase in the rate of production by the year 2000.

The future supply of ferro-alloys cannot be appraised in relation to the projected five-fold increase in demands in any satisfactory manner, due to the difference of materials involved and the complexity of their inter-relations and substitutability, the important and unpredictable role of technological innovation, to say nothing of the present lack of reasonably complete and reliable estimates of reserves. Resources for the Future anticipate that the world-wide "manganese situation should take care of itself" until the end of the century, while uncertain or inadequate reserves in chromium, nickel, tungsten, molybdenum, cobalt, and vanadium will require exploitation of low-grade ores, greatly stepped up exploration and large-scale substitution of other metals during the next few decades.[11] This would include the Arctic in meeting ferro-alloy demands before A.D. 2000.

Referring again to the 1956 study of world mineral reserves, at the 1956 rate of production it was estimated that the remaining exploitable

[9]Hans H. Landsberg, Leonard L. Fischman, Joseph L. Fisher, *Resources in America's Future: Patterns of Requirements and Availabilities, 1960–2000*, (Baltimore, 1963), p. 434.
[10]Ferdinand Friedensburg, "The Future Supply of Metals," *Zeitschrift für Erzbergbau und Metallhüttenwesen*, December, 1957, pp. 573–76.
[11]Landsberg *et al.*, pp. 438, 442, 446, 449–451.

reserves of copper would last until 1985, zinc until 1980, lead until 1970 and tin until 1990.[12] We need not give too much weight to these dates. They are enough to tell us that the future of most key non-ferrous metals are to be measured not in centuries, as in the case of iron ore, but only in decades. Even with what appear now as adverse cost factors, any deposits of these metals found in the Arctic will be given consideration for production within the immediate future. The international implications of these developments, however, will be lost in the gradual process of taking over the function of supply from reserves depleted elsewhere.

Greenland is making a minor contribution to world aluminum production by mining cryolite, but beyond this there appears to be no great prospect that the Arctic will make significant future minerals contributions to this industry. On the other hand, the north-flowing rivers of Canada and the USSR, and the Yukon River in Alaska, afford a number of large potential hydroelectric power projects which if developed could provide energy required to increase world primary aluminum production significantly. There are the usual limitations to this possibility, namely, the remoteness of these projects from major world sources of bauxite and aluminum markets. Long-distance transmission of power is technically feasible but it reduces the competitive advantages of low-cost power at the generation site by progressively increasing transmission costs. Technological change, of course, will alter the future aluminum supply and market picture. Development of direct reduction and other processes now in an advanced experimental stage may greatly reduce the power requirement in aluminum production or expand the raw material base beyond bauxite to clays available in quantity in the Arctic.

In considering aluminum production in relation to the Arctic, however, we must go beyond these elementary matters of resource availability and competitiveness in world markets. The future has been described as an age which will be dominated by a race between population growth and natural resource demands. There will also be a critical need to raise the general level of human life. Not only will the raising of world-wide living standards require more resources, but it will also require a shift of the pattern of distribution in industrial production between developed and under-developed nations. The production of aluminum provides an obvious means of accomplishing this purpose in a number of regions outside the Arctic. The under-developed nations contain most of the world's large hydro-electric potentials and are the source of more than two-thirds of the world's bauxite, but they produce less than 2 per cent of its aluminum. The chief barrier to redressing this

[12]Friedensburg, pp. 573–76.

imbalance, other than political unrest, is the absence of enough capital to provide alumina and aluminum plants together with the necessary power. It can be expected that ultimately the developing nations will secure the capital and technical assistance necessary to achieve a higher degree of industrialization.

Abundant low-cost energy and economic progress have gone hand in hand, and with them have come higher standards of living. Recognition of this partnership has caused us to focus on continuing supplies of energy in all forms. Fossil fuels supply about 90 per cent of present energy requirements. The President's Committee on Natural Resources concluded in 1962 that so long as the world depends on fossil fuels for its principal source of energy "there appears to be little ground for the humanitarian hope of significantly improving the standard of living by industrialization of the underdeveloped areas of the world." Of the alternatives to the exhaustible reserves of fossil fuels, solar power cannot be practicably concentrated, and water power, though large, is inadequate. "This leaves us ultimately with only nuclear energy as a source which is both adaptable to large-scale power generation and of sufficient magnitude to meet the world's potential requirements." Although resources for fission and fusion energy are also exhaustible, their total reserves are so huge in relation to energy output that "for all present purposes, nuclear energy may be regarded as being essentially inexhaustible in terms of human usage." Man's salvation, in short, would appear to lie in the development of these new energy sources.[13]

The Arctic contains huge proven and estimated reserves of fossil fuels and it is on these energy sources and the shorter run future—to the year A.D. 2000 and immediately beyond—that we must focus our attention. Reducing the estimates made in the President's Committee on Natural Resources to a common denominator of kilowatt-hours, the ultimate world reserves are represented by 71.6 per cent coal, 17.3 per cent petroleum and natural gas, and 11.1 per cent tar sands and oil shale. Of the estimated remaining recoverable coal reserves (2,330 billion metric tons) 25.8 per cent are estimated as being within the USSR, 34.4 per cent in North America and 21.8 per cent in China. Of the other principal industrial regions of the world, Europe has altogether only 13.0 per cent of the world coal reserves and Japan 0.2 per cent. The world reserves of crude oil (1,250 billion bbls.) and natural gas and natural gas liquids (1,500 billion bbls.) are estimated as being

[13]President's Committee on Natural Resources, *Energy Resources*, Publication No. 1000-D, National Academy of Sciences-National Research Council, (Washington: 1962), pp. 132–139.

24.0 per cent in the Middle East and North Africa, 16.0 per cent in the USSR, 14.0 per cent in the United States (including its offshore areas), 3.6 per cent in South America, 4.3 per cent in Asia (mostly Indonesia), 1.1 per cent in Europe, and 30.4 per cent offshore excluding the United States. Much less is known, or even guessed, concerning oil shales and tar sands.[14]

In estimating the "life span" of these fossil fuel reserves, the significant time span is that during which cumulative production increases from 10 per cent to 90 per cent of the ultimate reserves. The energy content of the fossil fuels consumed by the end of 1961 amounted to about 4.7 per cent of the ultimate reserves of the world (4.1 per cent for coal, 10 per cent for petroleum and natural gas, and zero for tar sands and oil shales). The significant remaining life of world coal reserves is projected as 350 years with the peak occurring about A.D. 2150, when it will have achieved a production rate of three times the present rate. If the whole world were to be industrialized to the same level as is the United States, however, the peak would have to be five times the present world rate of production, and on this basis the life span of world coal reserves would be reduced from 350 years to less than a century. For world petroleum and natural gas reserves, with 10 per cent already consumed it is projected that an additional 40 per cent will be produced between 1960 and 2000 when the production peak will achieve twice the present rate, and another 40 per cent between 2000 and 2040. On the assumption that the world is to be industrialized to the present level of the United States, 80 per cent of the world's supply of crude oil and natural gas would be consumed by 1975 or 1980. Something within the time span of these two sets of projections would appear most likely, which leads to the conclusion that before the end of the present century "a transition must be begun from crude oil and natural gas to the more abundant reserves of oil shale and tar sand, and ultimately to coal, for our supplies of liquid and gaseous fuels."[15]

In this context of diminishing world fossil fuel reserves, it can be assumed that exploration, development, and production for and of these resources will become increasingly active in the Arctic in the decades and even the years immediately ahead. Turning back to the discussion of non-fuel minerals, a similar situation applies to ferro-alloys, copper,

---

[14]*Ibid.*, pp. 37, 74, 96–91. The method used in estimating reserves takes into account presently proven reserves plus cumulative future discoveries. These are reserves assumed to be recoverable by present technology.

[15]*Ibid.*, pp. 88–91, 132.

lead, zinc, and tin as a minimum list. These generalizations are made in relation to total world requirements without regard to differences in national needs and resource endowments. This is merely a statement of the conclusion that the Arctic will increase in importance as a source of world minerals. The element of nationalism introduces further modifications and will indicate the broad outlines of the international implications of such Arctic exploitation.

Under the dual influences of international and national forces, the Soviet government very early embarked upon a programme of accelerating Arctic resource exploitation. But beyond official praise for the success of these enterprises, some statistics on population increases, etc., the average interested but technically uninformed Westerner (among whom I include myself) has no way of assessing or guessing the significance of all of this. The motivations for this early entry into the Arctic on the part of the USSR can be readily surmised: Arctic lands and resources comprise an important part of the Soviet Union's total territory and resources; there was an early unwillingness or inability to obtain raw materials from abroad; there were the challenge and the rewards in national pride to be found in attempting the difficult or impossible.

Future major developments in the Soviet sector of the Arctic will probably continue to be internally integrated, and it would be tempting to say that this exploitation would have no significant international implications if it were not for gold. The Soviet Union is today the second largest exporter of gold after South Africa. It is anticipated that more than a half billion dollars worth of Soviet gold will be bought up this year (1964) by the US Federal Reserve and European central banks through the London gold pool.

According to *Time* magazine, this influx of gold has been a boon to the West. "The new supply of Soviet gold has eased the West's acute gold shortage and helped stabilize the free market price of gold at very near the official US price of $35 per ounce. The Soviet gold has not only eased the pressure on the dollar but has also alleviated much of the drain on US gold reserves, since European bankers are now able to bolster their holdings with Soviet gold. Chiefly because of the Russian sales, the US partially replenished its own reserves by buying $300M in gold from the London pool last year."[16] For its part, the Soviet Union benefited from the sale of its gold in covering its huge purchases of Australian, Canadian, and US wheat and its increasing trade with non-Communist nations. The decisions made during the 1930's to build up

[16]"That Russian Gold," *Time*, May 15, 1964.

Russia's northern gold-mining industries not only have made possible trade with the non-Communist world, but have also resulted in the further irony of bolstering the capitalists' banking systems.

The international implications of exploitation in the Soviet Arctic could be as bizarre and as far-reaching as we have seen in the case of gold, if we are looking at the short-run. They may be indirect, affecting the development of domestic resource reserves and industrial output in the USSR, or they may be direct, operating, as with gold, through expansion of foreign trade. Whatever they are, they will be the result of international political forces.

The United States' share of the Arctic and sub-Arctic has assumed a more direct international position. Alaska's most promising world market is in the area of the North Pacific Great Circle Route with Japan at its western end. Japan is supported primarily by a manufacturing economy, only about 10 per cent of its basic raw materials coming from domestic sources. Like the United Kingdom, Japan has in the past depended upon overseas colonial sources for the remaining materials needed to feed its huge industrial complex. Today it must compete with other industrial nations for sources of raw materials. To meet its natural resource needs, Japan has already been attracted to Alaska, which is accessible at water transportation costs as low or lower than from many alternative sources for imports.

Although some distance from the Arctic proper, Japan has already invested substantially in pulp and lumber facilities and operations in southeast Alaska. In the sub-Arctic, a second industrial group is considering the possibility of large-scale exploitation of the interior forests of the Kuskokwim and Yukon river basins. There is strong Japanese interest in exploiting almost any available Alaskan mineral resource, an interest which has been stalled somewhat by the very limited knowledge of what we really have. The prospects for establishing iron and steel production, referred to above, were related to Japanese interest immediately after World War II. Although this interest was lessened by the more recent prospect of availability to Japan of pig iron from the extensive deposits of high-grade iron ore in Western Australia, it is far from dead. Alaska's huge coal reserves, including those in the Arctic, are being considered as possible sources for meeting the fossil fuel requirements of Japanese industry, and plans are underway for construction of special tankers for the transport of liquified natural gas from Alaska to Japan.

The plan to relate Alaska's resources to Japan's raw materials requirements is of vital interest to the United States. To the State of Alaska it means that its resources will probably come under exploitation decades earlier than could be anticipated if they were oriented only to domestic United States markets. This is a matter of the greatest importance to the fiscal survival of the State of Alaska, currently facing the almost equally unpleasant alternatives of continued Federal subsidy or bankruptcy.

At the national level, United States foreign economic policy includes a belief that Japan's economic health is of vital concern to the free world and in particular to the United States itself. Greater trade with Japan is considered to have important priority, even over certain segments of the United States' economy, and making Alaskan resources available fits into this general pattern. In the words of a congressional report, "If Japan should shift to a Neutralist or pro-Communist policy, there would result a profound shift in the power balance in Asia, with grave results for the US position in that part of the world."[17]

Within the State of Alaska, petroleum and natural gas exploration and development by private interests has been the most exciting and promising natural resource activity of the past decade. Recently this activity has shifted into the Arctic proper, in the section of the state north of the Brooks Range, where the federal government has already done much of the basic exploration under Navy auspices. Although our present supply situation seems satisfactory, these activities are prompted by the future petroleum and natural gas supply situation faced by the United States. Because the United States has been the world's largest producer of crude for nearly a century, it is also the farthest advanced toward ultimate depletion of its major domestic oil-producing areas. According to the President's Committee on Natural Resources, the United States is expected to reach its peak production and depletion of fifty per cent of its reserves by 1970 and 90 per cent of ultimate reserves by 2005. Included in these estimates are reserves, for the most part as yet unproven, which we hope will be found in Alaska. If we do not discover and develop them shortly, the outlook will be even more critical.

When considered in relation to the United States' ultimate domestic reserves, the present oil exploration activity in the Canadian Arctic islands does not appear too far fetched nor too far ahead of its time. At stake is the prize estimated by some geologists at as much as 10 billion barrels of recoverable oil within the Canadian Arctic mainland and an additional 21 billion barrels in the Arctic islands. This would

[17]A full statement is contained in "Japan in United States Foreign Economic Policy," Subcommittee on Foreign Economic Policy of the Joint Economic Committee, US Congress, 87 Congress, 1st Session (Washington, 1961), p. 3.

go a long way toward easing the United States' approaching critical reserve situation and providing a hedge in bargaining for imports from South America and the Middle East.

The current popular Canadian expectation appears to be that Arctic oil will go into Western European markets by submarine tankers, and that the costing of such an enterprise demonstrates a market price competitive with oil imported from the Middle East.[18] This certainly is a more adventurous prospect than shipping the oil to the United States. But the possible relation with European markets could never be more than a minor one. Despite current political unrest and strife in Africa and the Middle East, Western Europe will undoubtedly continue its longstanding economic relations with these areas, and the arrival of oil by submarine from the Canadian Arctic would at most provide a transition period supply, if the more traditional sources are temporarily cut off.

The international implications of Arctic resource exploitation will not be conditioned by increasing world resource shortages alone, but also by the concurrent need to raise world-wide standards of living. This will have the initial effect of off-setting or minimizing somewhat the *world-wide* importance of Arctic resources. Three-quarters of mankind will be in under-developed nations by the year 2000 and will be seeking natural resource developments within their own borders without regard to the honoured economic principles of comparative advantage. They will be motivated by nationalistic considerations more than economic considerations. The underlying goal of raising per capita income will require a change from their former agricultural-subsistence and colonial-raw material economies as income growth has been associated with growth in manufacturing and services. Availability of energy will be one of the key determinants of the feasibility of such development. The under-developed regions of the world are generally short of reserves of fossil fuels, but, as has been indicated in relation to aluminum, they are rich in potential hydroelectric sources and in the future they could make up energy deficiencies by utilization of nuclear energy.

The developed industrial nations will be actively seeking new sources of natural resources in the more remote regions of the earth, in order to replace disappearing domestic sources and resources previously obtained from their former colonial areas. Because the Arctic is already in the hands of these nations, or accessible to those who do not exercise sovereignty there, exploitation of its resources will be primarily for the

[18]T. C. Fairley, "Oil-Chasers of the Far North," reprinted in *North*, November-December 1961, pp. 34–39.

purpose of maintaining the continued growth of the developed portion of the world. The world-wide importance of this exploitation, therefore, probably will be indirect via the release of pressures from the resources elsewhere which would be accessible to the underdeveloped world.

We view the Arctic's future through a glass darkly now, not only because our knowledge of Arctic resources is limited but also because we tend to confine our thinking about markets to those accessible by traditional transport technology. Our international thinking is also, in the nature of things, more or less limited to the present. Any or all of these elements—which will determine the future—will hold surprises. Whatever the course of the future it will be concerned increasingly with growing population pressures upon natural resources. In this context the exploitation of Arctic resources will take on greater international significance. But the nature of this significance will be to provide a hedge of reserves for the developed nations, with actual exploitation taking place against the background of inevitable national rivalries and eventual resource depletion. Arctic resources will be pawns rather than determining forces in the future.